BRAVE HEARTED

BRAVE HEARTED

THE WOMEN
of the
AMERICAN WEST
1836–1880

KATIE HICKMAN

Spiegel and Grau

S&G

Spiegel & Grau, New York
www.spiegelandgrau.com

Jacket design by Strick & Williams; Jacket photograph of Nellie Brown,
African American cowgirl, ca. 1880s, courtesy of Alamy Stock Photo
Interior design by Meighan Cavanaugh

Library of Congress Cataloging-in-Publication Data Available Upon Request

ISBN 978-1-954118-17-1 (hardcover)
ISBN 978-1-954118-18-8 (eBook)

Printed in the United States of America

First Edition
10 9 8 7 6 5 4 3 2 1

For my granddaughter, Eva,

brave and beloved

CONTENTS

CONTENTS

LIST OF MAPS

A NOTE ON NATIVE AMERICAN NAMES

The word *Sioux* has been used as a blanket term for seven related and allied people, known as the Oceti Sakowin, meaning the Seven Council Fires. Only one of these people, the Lakota, come into this book.

Also known as the Tetonwan, or Teton people, the Lakota were made up of seven different Tribes, or bands, which were in turn divided into many smaller groups, also referred to as bands. The seven principal Lakota bands sometimes had more than one name; for clarity I have put the secondary French or English name in brackets.

They are the Hunkpapa (Josephine Waggoner's mother's band), Minneconjou, Oglala, Sans Arc, Sicangu (meaning "burned thighs" and therefore sometimes referred to as Brulé—Susan Bordeaux's mother's band), Sihasapa (Blackfeet), and Oohenumpa (meaning "two boilings" and therefore also known as Two Kettles). In the nineteenth century, any or all these bands were often referred to interchangeably by whites under the blanket name of Sioux.

Lakota should not be confused with Dakota, which is a blanket term for the four eastern people of the Oceti Sakowin.

INTRODUCTION

I t has been said that all American heroes are western heroes, and in the past, of course, almost all these heroes have been men.

For all the considerable work done by historians over the last fifty years to correct that imbalance, in popular imagination the "Wild West" is still a man's world. Served up to us as entertainment, high on thrills if short on historical accuracy, to this day our masculine images of the West—of trappers and huntsmen, of gunslingers, outlaws, and train robbers, of cowboys and gold seekers—are an indelible part of America's foundation myth. Immortalized in a thousand ballads, novels, movies, and television shows, the names of men like Buffalo Bill, Wyatt Earp, and Butch Cassidy and the Sundance Kid still spring easily to our lips. But for all their enduring appeal, not one of them was more than a walk-on part in an epic story that transcends them all.

Women's experiences are the very core of any true understanding of the reality of the American West, which is not so much a story about gunslingers and cowboys, although they play their part, but a story about one of the largest and most tumultuous mass migrations in history.

When this great migration began, in 1840, the United States of America consisted of just twenty-six states, covering a landmass that was only a fraction of the size it is now. In those days, the "frontier" was more of a vaguely defined idea than an actual place, and one that was in a continual state of flux. Some Americans might have seen it as anywhere west of the Mississippi River, particularly the furthermost borders of the newly created states of Missouri and Arkansas, and what (until July 1836) was then still known as Michigan Territory.* But for many others it lay, for all practical purposes, along a particular stretch of the Missouri River, the great tributary of the Mississippi, where it flows along the western periphery of present-day Iowa and Missouri.

Beyond this, as the crow flies, lay two thousand miles of prairie, mountain, and desert, much of it designated on contemporary maps as either "Indian Territory" or, simply, "Unorganized Territory."† California, Nevada, Utah, Arizona, New Mexico, parts of Colorado and Wyoming, and the whole of Texas were at that time still Mexican sovereign territory. Present-day Oregon and Washington States, and large parts of Idaho and Montana, were lands disputed between the US and Britain but as yet belonged to neither. The British-owned Hudson's Bay Company had a small but vigorous settlement, Fort Vancouver, on the Columbia River in the

---

*After July 1836, the western portion of Michigan Territory was renamed Wisconsin Territory, in preparation for the eastern portion of the territory being admitted to the Union as Michigan State.

†After the Louisiana Purchase of 1803, the US had a notional claim to all the land from its original borders, as far west as the Rocky Mountains. In a global geopolitical chess game then playing itself out an entire continent away, Napoleon Bonaparte, anxious that it should not fall into British hands, had "sold" this vast area—530 million acres—to the American government for $15 million, just three cents an acre. What this meant was that the US had bought the "preemptive" right to obtain all these lands for itself, either by conquest or by treaty with the Native inhabitants, to the exclusion of all other colonial powers. It goes without saying that the Indigenous people who lived there were not consulted, and, as some historians have pointed out, the purchase was, at this point, largely "an imperial fiction," since in reality Native Americans controlled almost all of it, "the largest portion belonging to the Sioux." See Pekka Hämäläinen, *Lakota America*.

Pacific Northwest, but, with the exception of small numbers of traders and trappers and the odd missionary, the rest of this vast continental landmass was almost entirely untouched by whites: a wilderness of almost unimaginable size and beauty.

The westward migrations started slowly. In 1836, two Presbyterian missionaries, Narcissa Whitman and Eliza Spalding, became the first white women ever to attempt what was then "an unheard-of journey for females": a 2,200-mile overland trek, from the Missouri "frontier," across the Great Plains and over the Rocky Mountains to Oregon country. Encouraged by their success, two years later in 1838 four more missionaries, together with their husbands, joined them in the Pacific Northwest.

The news of these groundbreaking journeys spread fast. If missionaries could endure them, then why not other women settlers too?

Women on horseback

While small numbers of American men had gone west before this time, their presence had for the most part been either transitory or seasonal, usually in line with the hunting and trapping year. It was clear that long-term settlement of these lands could not be achieved by men alone. It was only when women could be persuaded to go west alongside their men that the business of putting down permanent roots could begin.* Homesteads and farms would then be built, the land would be plowed and crops sown, animals bred and husbanded. Most importantly, future generations would be born to carry on the work their parents had begun. The presence of white women would change everything.

Beginning in 1840, at least one settler family—Mary and Joel Walker and their four children—was emboldened to follow in the missionaries' footsteps, making the overland journey to Oregon in search of free land and new lives.† In 1841, a hundred settlers made the journey. In 1842, it was two hundred. In 1843, a thousand. The year after that the numbers doubled again. Soon, stories about Oregon country began to percolate back East, each one taller than the next, and then so magnified that Oregon became known as an almost mythic paradise—the first of many utopias white Americans would look for in the West. Oregon country, it was said, was a land of milk and honey where vegetables grew to prodigious size and the rain only ever fell as gentle dew. With each passing year, the numbers of hopefuls setting out West from the Missouri borderlands grew.

They knew they were making history. These early westward migrations, as well as those that came after them, are uniquely well documented, by women as well as men. But whose version of history do they tell? The millions of square miles of "empty" wilderness (or so it seemed to them) that

---

*While many trappers and mountain men married Native American women, the majority of these liaisons, important though they were, were themselves often regarded as transitory arrangements. Many of these men also had white wives and families waiting for them back home.

†I have used both *settler* and *emigrant* to describe these overlanders. Given that neither Oregon nor California were part of the US at this point, the word *emigrant*—which describes a person who leaves their own country to settle permanently in another land—is technically correct, and this is how they described themselves. The mass movement of these people is thus "an emigration," and the routes they traversed are known as "emigrant trails." However, from the Native American perspective, they would more accurately be described as settler-colonists, since the US government, in later years in particular, was actively seeking to replace the Indigenous population with a new society of white settlers. I have used both terms throughout, slightly favoring the word *settler*.

these early emigrant families traversed were not, in fact, empty. Nor was the "free" land on which they had set their sights in any truthful sense free.

For thousands of years before the arrival of Europeans, as many as five million people inhabited these lands. By the mid-nineteenth century, their numbers significantly depleted by warfare and diseases brought to them by whites, contemporary estimates indicated that only 250,000 to 300,000 Native Americans remained living in the trans-Mississippi west.* Organized into many hundreds of different nations, and speaking languages from as many as seven different linguistic families, these were politically and culturally complex societies. Webs of ancient trading trails stretched in every direction, and covered every corner of the land. While some of these nations led relatively simple hunter-gatherer lives, others, such as the seven closely interconnected bands of the Lakota people of the northern plains, were masters of an empire that, in terms of power politics, was every bit as sophisticated and cosmopolitan as that of their mid-nineteenth-century white neighbors. The land they oversaw was not only a source of power and wealth for these Native Americans, but "a dream landscape, full of sacred realities."[1]

For centuries, Native people lingered in the recesses of the American imagination as a kind of "dark matter" of history, in the memorable phrase of the historian Pekka Hämäläinen. "Scholars have tended to look right through them into peoples and things that seemed to matter more." Native Americans, he writes, were "a hazy frontier backdrop, the necessary 'other' whose menacing presence heightened the colonial drama of forging a new people in a new world."[2]

In the last few decades, particularly in scholarly circles, this perspective has undergone a much-needed and long-overdue shift. Native Americans have reclaimed their place in history as powerful protagonists. The legacies of great leaders such as Sitting Bull, Red Cloud, and Crazy Horse are now as well known as those of Custer, Sheridan, and Sherman.

---

*These figures are from Helen Hunt Jackson, *A Century of Dishonour.*

The experiences of women, however, are still far less easy to come by. What did these tumultuous events feel like to them? After all, within just four decades, Native women would see their entire world changed beyond all recognition.

The testimonies of the Native American women included here, while relatively few in number, are thus, I believe, the most important in this book. At once mirroring and refracting the settler experience, their accounts are essential to our understanding of the mid-nineteenth-century west. The missionary women Narcissa Whitman and Eliza Spalding traveled to Oregon in 1836 because the Cayuse and the Nez Percé, however much they may have later regretted it, wanted them there, and even vied for their services. The combined bands of the Lakota, having initially tolerated the emigrants for the trading opportunities they brought with them, later not only fought back, but for many years bested the US Army, forcing the government in Washington to agree to their own terms.

For the remarkable Josephine Waggoner, a woman of mixed Hunkpapa and Irish ancestry, it was the work of many years to gather together the testimonies of her people, lest the white version of their history be the only one to prevail (although her magisterial work, *Witness: A Hunkpapa Historian's Strong-Heart Song of the Lakotas*, was not published until 2013, more than seventy years after her death). To her we owe an exquisite description of a summer spent as a child in Powder River country, the Lakota heartland—the very last moment when her people were free to roam in the time-honored way, living in vast tented villages as many as ten thousand tipis strong. Susan Bordeaux Bettelyoun, Waggoner's friend and literary collaborator, meanwhile gives us a glimpse of the extraordinarily vibrant, hybrid world of the northern plains, in which relatives from her mother Red Cormorant Woman's Brulé Tribe lived side by side with French American fur trappers such as her father. Through her testimony we see a vision of what life in the West once was, and might even perhaps have remained, if the currents of history had not dictated otherwise.

But it was not to be. Within a decade of Narcissa Whitman and Eliza Spalding's arrival in Oregon, the journey that had once been considered impossible for women to undertake had now become almost a commonplace. "The past winter there has been a strange fever raging here," wrote Keturah Penton Belknap in the spring of 1847. "It is the 'Oregon fever.' It seems to be contagious and it is raging terribly. Nothing seems to stop it but to tear up and take a six months trip across the plains with ox teams to the Pacific Ocean.... There was nothing done or talked of but what had Oregon in it and the loom was banging and the wheels buzzing and trades being made from daylight until bedtime."[3]

While most of these early settlers headed for Oregon country, some chose to go to California, though the route was more challenging and even less well known. In 1849, however, after gold was discovered at Sutter's Mill, an estimated thirty thousand people made the journey west. "Gold Fever" replaced "Oregon Fever" in the American imagination (after the Mexican-American War, California was now conveniently part of the US). While the very earliest overlanders had no maps, no guides, and so little information about the route that they were forced, as one put it, to "smell their way west," by the 1850s wagon trains were traveling as many as twelve abreast and were many hundreds of miles long.

For three decades, from 1840 to the late 1860s, it is estimated that around half a million settlers like Keturah Belknap and her family poured across the Missouri River and headed west on foot, making it one of the largest peacetime mass migrations in history.* In the twenty years or so that followed the completion of the transcontinental railway in 1869, many millions more would follow these original settlers, filling up the lands in between. Within a period of just forty years, the "frontier" was no more.

I have beside me as I write a classic photograph taken on what had become known as the "Oregon Trail." It shows a woman in a sunbonnet

---

*Figures are from Merrill J. Mattes, *Platte River Road Narratives*.

standing next to her covered wagon. Bending slightly forward, her face almost obscured by shadow, she is engrossed in laying out lunch for her husband in the shade of the wagon: a loaf of bread and a tin mug full of coffee, some beans and a slice of bacon, all carefully arranged on a neat white cloth. Toward the front of the wagon, the white canvas covering—perhaps stitched, and possibly even woven, by her own hands—has been hitched up, revealing the contents inside: stores of food and clothing, perhaps (we might guess) a treasured heirloom like china plates or a family Bible, her sewing basket, her husband's work tools. Whatever was inside, it was likely to be everything she had in the world. Their horses, grazing to one side on the open prairie, still look sleek and well fed, and the cloth on the makeshift table is pristine, so the photograph is likely to have been taken early on in their journey.

This peaceful, pastoral scene belies the very real dangers settlers faced on their 2,200-mile journey west.

I first came across this image quite by chance. On a visit to the famous Parisian bookstore Shakespeare & Co., I picked up a well-thumbed second-hand copy of Cathy Luchetti's *Women of the West*, a collection of sublimely beautiful black-and-white photographs of women during the westward migrations. It has been on my shelves for more than ten years now, and I often take it down to ponder these all but forgotten lives.

Had the woman in my photograph, like so many of her fellow women travelers, just recently bid farewell to parents, siblings, and every friend she ever had, with the almost-certain knowledge that she would never see them again? Who knows how many more months' traveling were still ahead of her. Who knows how many of her few remaining poor possessions had to be jettisoned along the way to lighten the load for their, by now, half-starved and exhausted animals. Who knows if their supplies even held out. Did she, like so many of the early settlers, all but starve to death along the road? Or did some other catastrophe lie in store: cholera or "camp fever," or a pregnancy gone wrong, or perhaps attack or even capture by those she had been raised to know as "savages."

Or did she, quite simply, just get lost?

This photograph is a classic, some might say a cliché, of western emigration. The woman in it appears like a figure sprung directly from the pages of Laura Ingalls Wilder's *Little House on the Prairie*. Wilder was, of course, herself the child of restless pioneers, and the extraordinary power of her stories lies in her ability to extract exactly the same kind of details from her own lived experience—the warp and weft of everyday life—as can also be found in so many of the diaries and journals included in this book. Despite being altogether quieter tales and despite their relative scarcity, Wilder's stories, so passionately beloved by millions not only in America but throughout the world, have proven at least as influential as any "cowboy" movie in shaping our vision of the West, sealing (in the words of Wilder's biographer Caroline Fraser) complex and ambiguous reactions to western emigration inside the "unassailably innocent vessel" of a children's story.[4]

While some of the women in this book are white women with myriad similarities to the figure in my photograph, there are large numbers who do not fit that picture at all. They instead encompass an extraordinarily diverse range of humanity, of every class, every background, and of numerous different ethnicities, many of them rarely represented in histories of the West. From the very earliest days of the emigration, many free-born African Americans found themselves in the grip of "Oregon Fever." Although their experience would prove profoundly different from that of whites, they too made their way west, urgently motivated by their state of "unfreedom" in the hostile East. In the later years of the emigration, these white and Black Americans were joined along the rapidly proliferating trails by hundreds of thousands of Europeans, immigrants from as far away as Scandinavia, Germany, Russia, Ireland, and Great Britain, all eager to claim land and start new lives. Others, such as Ah Toy, one of many thousands of Chinese sex slaves trafficked against their will and sold openly on the docks of San Francisco, or the Mississippi slave Biddy Mason, had no choice in the matter.

Most of the women in this book, however, chose to go west. For many it was the prospect of free or very cheap farmland that drew them, and the chance to escape from the economic depression that throughout the 1830s had ruined many farmers in the East. For those who went to California, it was the lure of gold. For others, such as Catherine Haun, it was little more than a honeymoon jaunt and (incredibly) a health cure. Others would have more complex reasons. Miriam Davis Colt dreamed of starting a utopian vegetarian community on the plains of Kansas. For Priscilla Evans, a Welsh convert to Mormonism, it was religious freedom and the prospect of helping found a City of the Saints in Utah's desert salt flats. In 1856, Evans and her husband, having sailed from Liverpool to Boston, were among nearly three thousand "handcart pioneers"—fellow converts from Germany, Wales, Scotland, Sweden, and Denmark—who completed the punishing five-month overland journey from Iowa to Salt Lake City on foot. Too poor to afford the ox-drawn wagons used by most settlers, they trudged for up to fifteen miles a day, pulling all their possessions behind them in handcarts.

Others had experiences so extreme that their stories gripped the public imagination even in their own lifetimes: thirteen-year-old Virginia Reed, whose company, the Donner-Reed party, was reduced to cannibalism when they became trapped in the winter snows of the Sierra Nevada, or Olive Oatman with her mysterious facial tattoos, adopted by the Mohave, with whom she lived for several years in Arizona after her family had been massacred by a neighboring Tribe. The account Oatman would later write about her experiences became an instant bestseller. *Life Among the Indians* remains one of the most famous "captivity narratives" of all time, transforming Olive Oatman herself, in all her otherworldly Gothic beauty, into one of America's first media stars.

Still others seemed barely to know why they were going at all, other than feeling a vague restlessness that even they found hard to justify. Sarah Herndon, a young woman who made the journey west in 1865 in the immediate aftermath of the Civil War, pondered exactly that. At the end of a glorious day in May—"the sky most beautifully blue, the atmosphere delightfully pure, the birds twittering joyously, [when] the earth seems filled with joy and gladness"—she sat down in the shade of her prairie schooner, a blank book in her hands, pen poised ready to record the events of their first day on the road. "Why are we here?" she wrote, on the very first page of her journal. "Why have we left home, friends, relatives, associates, and loved ones, who have made so large a part of our lives and added so much to our happiness?

"Are we not taking great risks, in venturing into the wilderness?" she wondered. "When people who are comfortably and pleasantly situated pull up stakes and leave all, or nearly all, that makes life worth the living, start on a long, tedious, and perhaps dangerous journey, to seek a home in a strange land among strangers, with no other motive other than bettering their circumstances, by gaining wealth, and heaping together riches ... it does seem strange that so many people do it."[5]

The motives did not seem to justify the many inconveniences and perils of the road. "Yet how would the great West be peopled were it not so?" she wrote. Although Herndon does not say so in so many words, vast numbers of Euro-Americans had come to believe, as she did, that it was their "manifest destiny" to move west.* "God knows best," she concluded. "It is, without doubt, this spirit of restlessness, and unsatisfied longing, or ambition—if you please—which is implanted in our nature by an all-wise Creator that has peopled the whole earth."

This claim, outrageous as it might sound to us today, was one that would have been shared by all her fellow overlanders. The fact that "the great West" was already richly peopled caused them not even the smallest moral hesitation in setting forth. It is hardly surprising then that within a year of Sarah Herndon's journey, the once-peaceful emigrant trails had erupted into violence and bloodshed.

The experiences of the women in this book, and the part each played in the transformation of the West, are so diverse that they defy any easy categorization. They have only one thing in common: whoever they were, and wherever they came from, their decision to uproot themselves from everything they held dear and make the journey west was the defining moment of their lives. More than eight hundred diaries and journals written by women and describing their experiences are known to exist, both published and in manuscript form.† More unusual still, they range from the literary musings of well-to-do, highly educated middle-class women to the poignant streams of consciousness of the barely literate. For those who either did not or could not write—enslaved African Americans, for example, were forbidden by law from even attempting to do so—a wide range of other documentary evidence exists: not only in oral records, but in census and law reports, US Army records, and many thousands of newspaper and magazine articles.

They do what women's records always do: they tell us what day-to-day life was really *like*. They vividly describe the practical realities of a particular

---

*The term *manifest destiny* and the idea that God had a special plan for Americans in the West was first posited by a New York journalist, John O'Sullivan.

†A total of 2,637 personal narratives of overland travel, deposited in more than thirty libraries and archives, of which perhaps a third are by women, are listed in Will Bagley's *Across the Plains, Mountains, and Deserts*.

time and place, sometimes in excoriating but often in marvelous detail too. One explains how the women on the trail would gather together in groups to relieve themselves, standing in a circle, each one holding up her skirts to give the others much-needed privacy. Another tells of the accouchement of a woman who gave birth to a child in the middle of a prairie thunderstorm, her female friends wading up to their knees in muddy water as they rallied round to help. Yet another gives us an extraordinary account of what it was like to feel the ground tremble at the approach of a 100,000-strong herd of buffalo—while viewing them, at a safe distance, through opera glasses. There is a freshness, and a drama, about their version of events, even quite ordinary ones, that is entirely undimmed by time.

The accounts by Native American women are more powerful still, although for the most part they make for somber reading. Who could ever forget the devastating testimony of Cokawiŋ, a Brulé elder left for dead after she had been shot by a US soldier at the Battle of the Blue Water, binding up her own wounds with strips of skunk skin? Or that of Sally Bell, from the Sinkyone Tribe in California, whose entire village, including almost all her family, was massacred by a vigilante militia during the Gold Rush years. Or that of Sarah Winnemucca, a Northern Paiute, whose most vivid childhood memory is of being buried alive by her mother, up to her neck in the ground, to hide her from a party of whites.

Time and again, these Native American women's accounts show how it was not only human but environmental destruction that followed inevitably in the settlers' wake. In her deceptively simple parable, Old Lady Horse, a Kiowa, gives us a piercing lament for the bison herds on which her people depended, some thirty million of which once roamed the prairies, but which she saw disappear entirely from the southern plains, hunted to extinction by whites.

This book covers the forty-five-year period from 1836, the year Narcissa Whitman and Eliza Spalding made their journey west, to 1880, the year when the US Census Bureau declared that the "frontier" was no longer. It is not intended to be a comprehensive history of that time. By confining myself mostly, but not exclusively, to the principal emigrant trails to California and Oregon, I am aware that there is much that I have necessarily left out (events in and around what is now Texas, for example, are beyond the scope of this book). But by telling the stories of just some of the women who lived through those times, I hope that the general arc of history will become clear.

This has not been an easy book to write, but of all the books I have written it is the one that means most to me. Even though there were many times when I felt overwhelmed by the sheer weight of material, both physically and emotionally, and even though the testimonies contained here have led me to write a story that has proved quite different from the one I thought I was going to write, I have come to feel a profound connection with these women. They were wives and daughters, mothers and grandmothers—just as I am, and just as are many of you reading this book. They were doing what women always do: they kept going, looking after their families as best they could, no matter what the circumstances. While many women lived to tell their tales about their part in the westward migrations, a great number of them did not. Included here are some of the most extreme stories I have ever come across, and I felt a particular responsibility to tell these truthfully. It is not a simple picture. For every moment of heroic resilience, I found its counterpart in savagery and betrayal. For every story of hope and new beginnings, I found another of suffering and death. But as I went along, I also came to realize that to make simple heroes or villains of either side is to make caricatures of both, to allow cardboard cutouts to take the places of their all-too-human complexities.

For better and for worse, women were at the beating heart of everything that happened.

This is their story.

BRAVE HEARTED

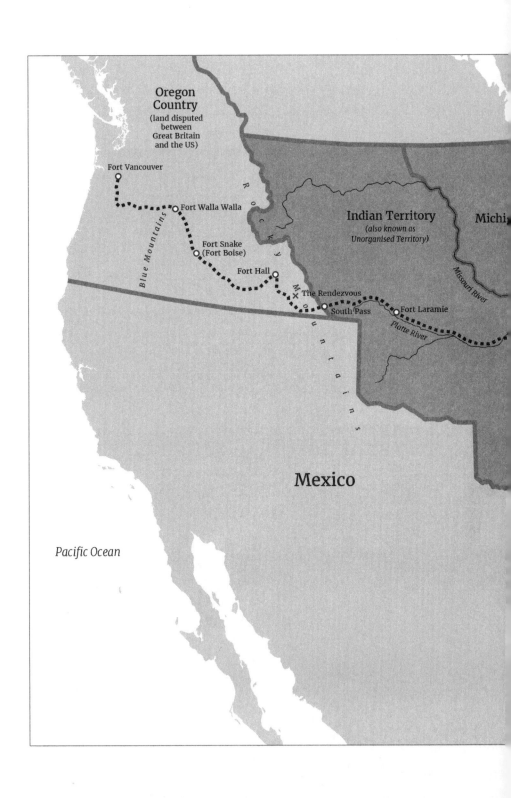

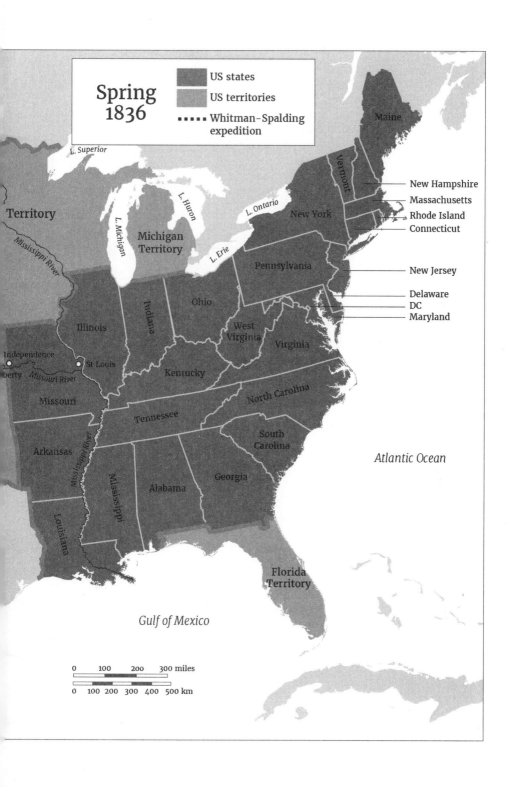

Spring
1836

US states
US territories
····· Whitman–Spalding
expedition

L. Superior

Territory

Mississippi River

L. Michigan

L. Huron

Michigan
Territory

L. Ontario

New York

L. Erie

Maine

Vermont

New Hampshire
Massachusetts
Rhode Island
Connecticut

Indiana

Ohio

Pennsylvania

New Jersey

Illinois

West
Virginia

Delaware
DC
Maryland

Independence
Liberty

St Louis

Missouri River

Virginia

Kentucky

Missouri

Tennessee

North Carolina

Mississippi River

South
Carolina

Arkansas

Mississippi

Alabama

Georgia

Atlantic Ocean

Louisiana

Florida
Territory

Gulf of Mexico

0   100   200   300 miles

0   100   200   300   400   500 km

1

"AN UNHEARD-OF JOURNEY FOR FEMALES"

When Narcissa Whitman prepared to go west in 1836, she took with her a pair of rubber boots, a passport from the US War Department, and a husband she barely knew. Shortly after her death, almost exactly ten years later, a friend who knew her well, the Reverend Henry Perkins, wrote a letter to her sister back East. It contained these truthful, if not perhaps particularly consoling, words. Narcissa "was not a *missionary*, but a *woman*," he wrote, "a highly-gifted, polished American lady" who was adapted to a very different destiny from the one she found among the Cayuse in Oregon Territory. "She loved company, society, excitement and ought always to have enjoyed it," he added. "The self-denial that took her away from it was suicidal."[6]

It had not always seemed that way. Narcissa Whitman was born Narcissa Prentiss in Prattsburgh, in the state of New York, on March 14, 1808. The daughter of a prosperous middle-class farmer and carpenter, she was well liked, vivacious, and widely admired for her beautiful singing voice. She was also unusually well-educated for a woman of her day, having attended not one but two local schools where she had received some training as a teacher.

Like the rest of her family, she was a devout member of the recently re-organized, and vigorously evangelizing, Presbyterian Church.*

The early nineteenth century was a time of intense religious revivalism in the northern United States, a period sometimes referred to as the Second Great Awakening, in which women played an unusually active role.† Narcissa grew up steeped in stories of heroic missionary activity among the "benighted heathen," disseminated not only from the pulpit, but also from a flourishing evangelical press. They told of women, sometimes very young ones, not so very different from Narcissa herself. These women led noble, self-sacrificing lives, often in excitingly "exotic" places—South America, India, Africa—lives that took them far away from the usual domestic constraints of provincial life. The fact that many of these role models died during their missions abroad only added to their aura of saintliness and heroism.

While the undertaking was acknowledged to be a formidable one, the optimistic tone of such articles suggested that it was not impossible. Nowhere were the vast cultural and geographical challenges of such enterprises dwelled upon. Instead, these mission reports seemed to suggest that female missionaries, unlike their male counterparts, needed no particular training to be successful. Piety, cheerful devotion to the cause, and perhaps a little teaching and hymn singing were all that seemed to be required.

Aged sixteen, Narcissa seems to have undergone some kind of religious experience, and from this time on her heart, too, was set on becoming a missionary. As an unmarried female, however, her chances of becoming one were vanishingly small, so when a proposal of marriage came to her,

---

*Under the Plan of Union of 1801, the General Assembly of the Presbyterian Church and the Connecticut General Association of Congregational Churches agreed to merge. Later, the plan would also be approved by congressional associations in Vermont, New Hampshire, and Massachusetts.
†Britain was experiencing a similar evangelical revival at this time. Maria Edgeworth's *The Child's Companion* contains this "arithmetical puzzle": "If there are six hundred millions of Heathens in the world, how many missionaries are needed to supply one to every twenty thousand?"

apparently out of the blue, it must have seemed as if it were the hand of Providence at work. Marcus Whitman was a thirty-two-year-old medical doctor who, like Narcissa, also dreamed of a life of Christian service in foreign parts. Although it is not known exactly when the couple first met, since they attended churches that were only six miles distant from each other it is possible that they had been acquainted, albeit distantly, for some time. Both had been inspired by a preacher, the Reverend Samuel Parker, who in December 1834 was traveling through the communities of New York, preaching and raising money for what he hoped would be an exciting new mission.

Parker's story was an electrifying one. It told of four Flatheads from a distant land somewhere "west of the Rocky Mountains" who, having become curious about Christianity, had traveled to Saint Louis in the autumn of 1831, seeking out missionaries who would be willing to travel to their communities and bring them the word of God.* Unbeknownst to each other, both Narcissa and Marcus had volunteered. While Reverend Parker had initially rejected Narcissa's offer of help, Marcus was quickly appointed by the American Board of Commissioners for Foreign Missions to accompany Parker on an exploratory expedition to Oregon country. During the application process the board had also made inquiries as to Marcus's marital status, with the suggestion that if, in the future, a permanent mission were to go ahead, a wife would be a desirable helpmate. Knowing of her missionary ambitions, it is highly likely that Narcissa Prentiss was suggested by Reverend Parker as a suitable partner.

On the eve of what would be his first journey to Oregon country, Dr. Whitman traveled to Narcissa's home to sound her out. There was nothing

---

*Parker had not encountered these men himself but had been inspired by an article in the Methodist newspaper *The Christian Advocate and Journal and Zion's Herald*, written by a Methodist named William Walker. While it is possible that a meeting never in fact took place, there was enough truth in the story of the Tribe's interest in Christianity to cause elation in evangelizing circles, and the article was widely reprinted. "Hear! Hear! Who will respond to the call from beyond the Rocky Mountains," wrote the *Advocate*. "All we want is men. Who will go? Who?" See *Converting the West* by Julie Roy Jeffrey.

romantic in either his proposal or his appearance. Marcus was neither a polished nor a particularly sophisticated man—he was said by those who knew him to have "easy, *don't care* habits" and to lack "a sense of etiquette"— but he gave the impression of both purpose and energy. If Narcissa were ever to fulfil her dream of becoming a missionary, this was her chance. Over a single weekend, February 22 and 23 of 1835, the couple came to what was, to all intents and purposes, not so much an engagement as a business agreement.

While today this might seem like not only a bizarre but even a reckless decision, it was not unusual in missionary circles of the time. That Dr. Whitman must have seemed not only suitable but also pleasing to Narcissa is evinced by the fact that his was not the first offer of marriage she had received. A few years previously a man named Henry Spalding, he too burning with missionary zeal and in search of a suitable wife to help him in his work, had also proposed to her, but Narcissa had refused him—a fact that, in a bizarre twist of fate, would soon come back to haunt her.

Even as Marcus Whitman's wife-to-be, Narcissa's future was still very far from certain. Not only did the mission on which she had set her sights not yet exist, but Oregon was not even Oregon. In the 1830s the Pacific Northwest was still a foreign country, as geographically and culturally distant as China or Africa. Like all Americans, the Whitmans would have to obtain passports in order to go there. The journey, which stretched from the Missouri River across two and a half thousand miles of wilderness, had only very rarely been attempted by any whites other than the hardiest mountain men.

Undeterred by any of these obstacles, in the spring of 1835 Marcus set off on his exploratory journey to the Rockies. At the time there was only one way for an easterner with no experience of traveling beyond the frontier to do this. Every year for the previous decade, the American Fur Company had sent a caravan of pack animals and supplies out West, from Saint Louis, Missouri, to an extraordinary trade fair, known as the Rendezvous, on the Green River in the heart of the Rocky Mountains. Marcus was able to attach himself to the caravan, and thus travel in relative safety (although at first the mountain men resented his presence so much they threw rotten eggs at him). In July he attended the annual Rendezvous, and there he was able to meet with a number of Flathead and Nez Percé chiefs, who assured him of their interest in having missionaries among them. Perhaps more importantly, from Narcissa's point of view, he also learned that the American Fur Company had succeeded in taking twenty heavily loaded wagons across the mountains. Wherever a wagon could go, he concluded, a woman could go too.

At this point, no one back East could possibly have known what Marcus's findings were going to be. When Narcissa wrote her own letter of application to the American Board of Commissioners for Foreign Missions, her supporting letters from local ministers contained enthusiastic but vague testimonials about her suitability "in instructing the heathen in the way to Heaven." No one made any mention of the journey she would have to undertake, let alone the conditions she might face when she got there. Only one man, David Greene, the secretary of the ABCFM, expressed a momentary doubt: "Have you carefully ascertained & weighed the difficulties in the way of conducting females to those remote & desolate regions and comfortably sustaining families there?"[7] His question remained unanswered. Religious conviction, and a burning desire to bring the word of God to the Native Tribes, was all that was required. The board accepted Narcissa's application.

In December, Marcus returned east and set about recruiting a mission party to accompany the couple back to Oregon country the following March. In the absurdly little time that remained to them, there was one major hurdle still to be surmounted. The board had agreed to let the Whitmans go, so long as another missionary, who was also an ordained minister (which Marcus Whitman was not), could be found to accompany them.* Of the various contenders who had expressed an interest in working among the western Tribes, only one emerged as even a remote possibility: Henry Spalding.

---

*They also specified that the party should include a teacher, a farmer, and a mechanic.

That Marcus should have even considered Henry Spalding—Narcissa's rejected suitor—for the position is a measure of his desperation. It was the worst possible choice. Three years previously, Henry had finally met and married another woman, Eliza Hart, and in February 1836 the couple were already headed for their own mission among the Osage in western Missouri. With the board's permission, Marcus rode after them to try to convince them to change their minds.

He finally met up with the Spaldings at the Howard Inn, New York. On February 14, Eliza recorded the meeting in her diary. "Today we met with Dr. Whitman who has been laboring for some time to obtain associates to accompany him west of the Rocky Mountains to establish a mission among the Nez Percés Indians," she wrote. "He had failed in every other attempt to obtain someone to go out with him in the capacity of a minister, and if he did not succeed in getting Mr. Spalding to engage in this expedition, he should relinquish the idea of going out this season."[8] Despite Henry's previous unhappy connection to Narcissa, the couple agreed.

On March 3, just two weeks later, when a newly married Narcissa Whitman finally bade farewell, for the last time, to all her family and friends before setting out on her journey, it would be not only with a husband she barely knew, but also with traveling companions who would have plenty of cause to resent her.

Eliza Spalding and Narcissa Whitman were, on the surface of things, very similar. Eliza had been born in 1807, in Connecticut, into a family of ancient pioneering stock. Her father has been described as "a plain, substantial farmer."[9] Like Narcissa, she was well educated and extremely devout, and, just as Narcissa had done, she had agreed to marry a man whom she knew only slightly in order to pursue her dream of becoming a missionary, and to "accompany a stranger, to a land of strangers."[10] But, despite all these outward appearances, the two women could not have been more different.

In his *A History of Oregon*, William Gray, who was to become a last-minute addition to the 1836 missionary expedition, gave this astute comparison of the two women. "Mrs. Whitman . . . was a lady of refined feelings and commanding appearance," he wrote. "She had very light hair, light, fresh complexion and light blue eyes. At the time she arrived in the country in the prime of life, she was considered a fine, noble-looking woman, affable and free to converse with all she met." Eliza Spalding, on the other hand, was "above the medium height, slender in form with coarse features, dark brown hair, blue eyes, rather dark complexion, coarse voice, of a serious turn of mind, and quick in understanding language. In fact, she was remarkable in acquiring the Nez Percé language . . . And had been taught, while young, all the useful branches of domestic life; could spin, weave, and sew, etc; could prepare an excellent meal at short notice, and was generally sociable, but not forward in conversation with or in attentions to gentlemen. In this particular she was the opposite of Mrs. Whitman. With the native women, Mrs. Spalding always appeared easy and cheerful. . . . She was considered by the Indian men as a brave, fearless woman, and was respected and esteemed by all."[11] It was clear to him (and perhaps, in her heart of hearts, to Narcissa too) that, while completely lacking in Narcissa's outward polish and charm, it was skinny, mousy, linguistically and spiritually gifted Eliza Spalding who was the better equipped in every way to succeed as a missionary.

The two women first met while still en route to the frontier, in Cincinnati, on March 17. While their relationship was always outwardly cordial, none of the camaraderie that should have sprung up between the women—and which would become so important a part of the experience of later women settlers—seems ever to have existed between them. Instead, an underlying tension, not to say rivalry, is hinted at from the very outset.

The mission party that finally assembled at Liberty, Missouri, from where their overland journey by horse and wagon would begin, was composed of ten people: the Whitmans, the Spaldings, William Gray,* two helpers,† and three Nez Percé: "Richard" Takahtooahtis and "John" Aits,

---

*William Gray, a carpenter and cabinetmaker by profession, had been appointed by the board at the last moment as a lay assistant and mechanic to the expedition.
†These were a nineteen-year-old called Miles Goodyear and another man who is referred to only as Dulin.

who had traveled back East with Marcus Whitman in 1835 in order to attend school and learn English, and a third man, Samuel Temoni. Between them they also purchased a heavy farm wagon, twelve horses, six mules, and seventeen head of cattle. They carried with them a single, communal, home-made tent that the women had somehow constructed between them out of bed ticking, some rubber cloths for use as ground sheets, and a supply of blankets. In Rushville, Narcissa had had a pair of gentleman's boots made for her, "in brother Augustus's shoe store," and all took India-rubber life preservers with them, "so that if we fall into the water we shall not drown." In addition, each of them had a plate, a knife and fork, and a tin cup. It was almost unbelievably rudimentary.

Despite the fact that during the first six weeks the party had to travel hard to catch up with the American Fur Company caravan (which they had just missed when it left Saint Louis on March 29), at first the journey had an almost holiday feel to it—for Narcissa at least. As it would be for all settlers, this was the easiest stage of the journey: almost a thousand miles of gently rolling, rippling prairie grassland, following the winding course of the Platte River. "I think I may say easier traveling here than on any turn-pike in the [States]," she wrote. Under these conditions, the fresh air and vigorous daily exercise—the women could be in their saddles for up to thirty miles a day—did her nothing but good. Narcissa thrived. Her health, she wrote ebulliently, had never been better. While all the others had been feeling the effects of drinking river water, "I am an exception however," she noted with pride.

Not only was Narcissa enjoying the freedom of the outdoor life; she was also getting to know her husband for the first time.* "I have such a good place to shelter, under my husband's wings. He is so excellent. I love to confide in his judgement and act under him," she wrote to her sister. "Jane, if you want to be happy, get a good husband as I have got and be a missionary."

---

*The couple had been married on February 18 and had left on the first leg of their journey, to Liberty, Missouri, the following day.

Perhaps because she was so absorbed in what was, to all intents and purposes, her honeymoon, it would be three whole weeks from their first meeting before Narcissa made any reference to Eliza at all. Immediately, she was making comparisons between them—not all of them flattering to Mrs. Spalding.

"I think I shall endure the journey well, perhaps better than any of the rest of us," she wrote to her family on April 7. "Mrs. Spalding does not look nor feel quite healthy enough for our enterprise. Riding affects her differently from what it does me. Everyone who sees me compliments me as being the best able to endure the journey over the mountains from my looks." Having established her superior credentials as a traveler, Narcissa could then afford to be a little more gracious. "Sister S[palding] is very resolute," she wrote, "no shrinking with her. She possesses good fortitude. I like her very much. She wears well upon acquaintance," she concluded, adding (perhaps just a touch condescendingly), "She is a very suitable person for Mr. Spalding, has the right temperament to match him. I think we shall get along very well together; we have so far."[12] Eliza Spalding, on the other hand, does not mention Narcissa at all.

Toward the end of May, the missionary party finally caught up with the American Fur Company caravan, with whom the missionaries would be traveling as far as the Rocky Mountain Rendezvous, just as Marcus had done the previous year. "The Fur Com[pany] is large this year," Narcissa wrote. "We are really a moving village—nearly four hundred animals with ours, mostly mules, and seventy men." Soon, their days settled into a familiar routine. For her family's benefit, Narcissa went on to describe a typical day. On June 3, she wrote: "In the morn as soon as the day breaks the first that we hear is the word—arise, arise. Then the mules set up such a noise as

---

*Among the animals taken by the missionaries were seventeen head of cattle, including four milch cows. This is thought to have been the first herd of cattle ever to be driven over the plains and across the Rocky Mountains to Oregon. Without the fresh milk to sustain her, it is very likely that Eliza Spalding would not have survived the journey. See Drury, *Where Wagons Could Go.*

you never heard which puts the whole camp in motion. We encamp in a large ring: baggage and men, tents and waggons on the outside and all the animals, except the cows [which] are fastened to pickets within the circle. . . . While the horses are feeding, we get our breakfast in a hurry and eat it. By this time the word 'Catch up, catch up' rings through the camp for moving. We are ready to start usually at six—travel till eleven, encamp, rest and feed, start again about two—travel until six . . . then encamp for the night."

It was also a surprisingly sociable time, and some interesting niceties were observed. In addition to the Fur Company employees, a number of independent gentlemen had attached themselves to the party, including the wealthy Scots aristocrat and sportsman William Drummond Stuart and the mountain man Moses "Black" Harris.* Invitations—sometimes to take tea, at other times to dine—were offered, and then politely returned, between the various camps.

Even though they were now many hundreds of miles away from "civilization," food was always in good supply. The Fur Company kept a man on permanent guard to hunt for the camp, and soon they were eating fresh buffalo meat every day. Initially, Narcissa enjoyed this diet very much. "I never saw anything like buffalo meat to satisfy hunger. We do not want anything else with it. . . . I relish it well, and it agrees with me, my health is excellent, so long as I have buffalo meat I do not wish anything else." Not so Eliza Spalding. "Sister S is affected by it considerably and has been quite sick," Narcissa added.

By June they had reached Fort Laramie, a fur trading post on the confluence of the North Platte and Laramie Rivers.† Here they rested up, and a week later began the ascent up into the Rocky Mountains, crossing the

---

*Black Harris, who may have been of African American descent, was known for his striking appearance. The artist Alfred Jacob Miller, who traveled with the American Fur Company caravan to the Rendezvous the following year when Black Harris was leading the caravan, described him as "wiry of frame, made up of bone and muscle, with a face composed of tan leather and whipcord finished up with a peculiar blue black tint, as if gun powder had been burnt into his face." See *The West of Alfred Jacob Miller*.
†Known until 1836 as Fort William.

Continental Divide at South Pass. On July 6, after three months and thirteen hundred miles of hard traveling, they rode into the Rendezvous at last.

From its beginning in 1825 all the way until its end in 1840, the Rendezvous was an extraordinary event, surely one of the largest and most fantastic spectacles in all the American West. For two weeks every year, as many as four hundred fur trappers, many of them with their Native American wives and children, came together at a pre-appointed spot on the banks of the Green River to await the arrival of the caravan.* For these mountain men, the Rendezvous was not only an opportunity to sell the animal furs they had been collecting all year—beaver, buffalo, marten and mink, otter, skunk, muskrat and badger—and exchange them for much-needed supplies from Saint Louis, it was also the great social occasion of the year: a wild, two-week-long fiesta in which men who throughout the whole of the preceding year had been living a bitterly hard, cold, and often solitary life in the wilderness could meet their friends and drink, carouse, gamble, and race horses to their hearts' content.

The mountain men were not the only ones present. Several thousand Native Americans—Shoshone, Bannock, Nez Percé, Flathead, and Cayuse—also congregated there. Men, women, and children, together with their dogs pulling heavily laden *travaux*, and as many as ten thousand of their horses and mules, poured every year into the remote mountain valley. Almost overnight, a vast tented city would spring up: hundreds upon hundreds of lodges stretching for as many as six miles on either side of the Green River, their white hides glinting in the sun. Woodsmoke from a thousand campfires filled the air and, from the camps of the mountain men, the sweet strains of their fiddles and violins.

The arrival of Narcissa Whitman and Eliza Spalding at the Rendezvous on July 6, 1836, caused a sensation. "The American Fur Company caravan, was accompanied by Doctor Marcus Whitman, and lady, Mr. H. H. Spalding and lady, and Mr. W. H. Gray . . . on their way to [Oregon] to establish

---

*In 1836, this was at Horse Creek on the Green River, the site of present-day Daniel, Wyoming.

a mission among the Indians in that quarter," recorded one of the mountain men who was present at the gathering that day. "The two ladies were gazed on with wonder and astonishment by the rude savages," he wrote, "they being the first white women ever seen by these Indians, and the first that had ever penetrated into these wild and rocky regions.'"[13]

Although neither of the two women left a wider description of the Rendezvous, both wrote accounts of their first moments in the tented city. Hundreds of mounted warriors "carrying their war weapons, bearing their war emblems and . . . implements of music . . . skins drawn over hoops with rattles and trinkets to make a noise"[14] circled around them. When this display came to a halt, the two women found themselves in the middle of a fascinated crowd of Nez Percé, Flatheads, and Cayuse.

The women and children, in particular, flocked to look at them. "The women were not satisfied short of saluting Mrs. W. and myself with a kiss," Eliza wrote. "All appear happy to see us. If permitted to reach their country and locate among them," she added, "may our labors be blest to their temporal and spiritual good."[15] Narcissa, too, was almost overwhelmed by the warmth of the welcome they received. The women's kisses, in particular, were "unexpected, and affected me very much," she wrote. "After we had been seated a while in the midst of the gazing throng, one of the Chiefs . . . came with his wife and very politely introduced us. They say they all like us and that we have come to live among them."

The missionary party remained at the Rendezvous for almost two weeks. During this time, each woman would do what came naturally to her. Eliza Spalding, although she was still "quite feeble" (she was suffering from digestive problems which she believed were due to an excess of buffalo meat in her diet) and was often confined to her bed, nonetheless spent as much of her time as she could among the women, with whom "she seemed to be a great favorite."[16] Narcissa, on the other hand, who had no such natural

---

* They were, in fact, one of only a small handful of non–Native American women ever to witness the Rocky Mountain Rendezvous. Within just four years, it had ceased.

affinity, spent much of her time giving out Bibles to the mountain men and being regaled with stories of their daring exploits. As William Gray would later record: "All the refined education and manners of the daughter of Judge Prentiss, of Prattsburgh . . . found abundant opportunity to exhibit the cardinal ornaments of a religious and civilized society."[17]

The Spaldings and the Whitmans finally left the Rendezvous at Horse Creek on July 18. Having come thus far under the protection of the American Fur Company, they now joined a delegation from the British-owned Hudson's Bay Company, under the command of John L. McLeod and Thomas McKay, who were traveling back to the company's headquarters at Fort Vancouver on the Columbia River. For the missionaries, more than six hundred miles of hard traveling still lay ahead of them before they reached their destination at Fort Walla Walla, on the Columbia. Although this would be the shortest leg of their marathon journey, it would take them across terrain that was more rugged and mountainous than any of them had yet experienced.

To their dismay, the relatively easy two marches they had been used to, broken by a two-hour break in the middle of the day to eat and rest, was now replaced by one long march which sometimes lasted for as much as eight hours at a stretch. For the two women—particularly Eliza, who remained wretchedly ill—it was a punishing regime. They were also now obliged to break one of their most dearly held religious practices, which was to observe the Sabbath day of rest.

The unalleviated diet of buffalo meat, which Narcissa had once thought so delicious, was starting to pall, and her usually excellent digestion was beginning to suffer. During the long days in the saddle, she dreamed "as a hungry child would" of her mother's bread and butter. "I fancy pork and potatoes would relish extremely well. Have been living on fresh meat for two months exclusively. Am cloyed with it," she wrote in her diary. "I do not know how I shall endure this part of the journey."

Their route became more demanding by the day. "Very mountainous," she wrote on July 25. "Paths winding on the sides of steep mountains. In some places the path is so narrow as scarcely to afford room for the animal to place his foot. One after another, we pass along with cautious steps."

It was now almost five months since Marcus and Narcissa had left home, and they had been traveling rough with the Spaldings for four of them. The heat, even in the mountains, was "oppressive." Tempers were becoming increasingly frayed.

There were tensions between Narcissa and Marcus too. The wagon that the doctor had insisted on bringing from the Rendezvous, against all advice to the contrary, was becoming more of an impediment by the day. "Husband has had a tedious time with the waggon today. Got set in the creek this morning while crossing, was obliged to wade considerably in getting it out. After that, in going between two mountains, on the side of one so steep that it was difficult for horses to pass, the waggon was upset twice. Did not wonder at this at all," she wrote with unaccustomed sharpness. "It was a great wonder that it was not turning a somersault continually."

With another six weeks of "steady journeying" ahead of them, there was nothing for it but to endure. "Long for rest, but must not murmur." Food was becoming something of an obsession. Occasionally, along the sides of creeks they came across patches of wild berries—gooseberries; serviceberries, a kind of soft fruit that is common to Idaho, "very sweet and something like the Pear in its flavor"; and hawthorn berries, "as large as a cherry & taste much like a mealy sweet apple"—and sometimes they were able to catch fish, but in the main their diet still consisted almost entirely of buffalo meat. Soon, this was reduced to buffalo jerky, so sour, moldy, and "full of all manner of filth" that the party agreed they would not even have fed it to a dog. "I can scarcely eat it, it appears so filthy," Narcissa wrote, "but it will keep us alive, and we ought to be thankful for it."

They were out of the mountains now, and for several days had been riding along the dreary desert flats in what is now southern Idaho. Here they found "rocks and sandy plains covered with a species of wormwood called sage, of a pale green, offensive both to the sight and smell." The heat here was even more oppressive than it had been in the mountains.

Just a few days later they were in sight of Fort Hall, on the south side of the Snake River.* As with the other trading posts that the missionaries would pass on their journey—Fort Laramie and, later, Fort Snake—there was nothing particularly fortress-like about Fort Hall: a simple stockade of cottonwood logs, sixty feet square, within which there were some rudimentary living quarters and a storage space for furs. Despite this, both women were overjoyed by the sight of it: "Anything like a house makes us glad." They were even more cheered by the commander Captain Thring's invitation to dine with him, "the cool retreat of an upper room," "stools to sit on," and even a garden to walk in, in the cool of the evening.

On August 13 they forded the Snake River. Two of the tallest horses were selected for the women, but even so they had to wade against the current for half a mile or more upstream, "which made it hard for the horses the water being up to their sides." But by this time Narcissa was almost blasé about it. "I once thought that crossing streams would be the most dreadful part of the journey. I can now cross the most difficult stream without the least fear."

The same could not be said for the wagon. "Both the cart and the mules were capsized in the water and the mules entangled in the harness. The mules would have drowned, but for a desperate struggle to get them ashore." It was only by putting two of the strongest horses in front of the cart, and having two men swim behind to steady it, that they eventually succeeded.

Marcus now decided to lighten it as much as possible, obliging Narcissa to leave one of her trunks behind. In what would soon become a common refrain among settlers traveling west, all four were regretting having brought so much luggage. "It would have been better for us not to have attempted to bring any luggage whatever, only what [was] necessary to use on the way. If I were to make this journey again, I would make quite different preparations,"

---

*Fort Hall had been built just two years earlier by an independent fur trader, Nathaniel Wyeth, as protection against the hostile Blackfeet Tribe, through whose terrain they were now traveling.

Narcissa wrote. "To pack & unpack so many times & cross so many streams, where the packs frequently get wet, requires no small amount of labor, besides the injury done to the articles. Our books, what few we have, have been wet several times. . . . The custom of the country is to possess nothing & then you will loose nothing, while traveling."

By August 19 they had arrived at Fort Snake, which had been built, and was still owned, by Mr. McKay, one of the commanders of the Hudson's Bay caravan.* Here, once again, they were able to rest up for a few days, and to wash their clothes. "This is the third time I have washed since I left the States, or home either," Narcissa wrote. On the twenty-second, they set off on the last leg of their journey, to the Hudson's Bay Company fort at Walla Walla. "As for the waggon it is left at the fort, & I have nothing to say about crossing it this time," Narcissa wrote wearily. "Our animals were failing & the route in crossing the Blue Mountains is said to be impassable for it. . . . We regret now to loose the use of it when we have been at so much labor in getting it this far," but it could no longer be helped.

As well as parting company with the wagon, the Whitmans would now part company, albeit temporarily, with the Spaldings. It was agreed that Eliza and Henry, guided by one of the Nez Percé chiefs, would travel on slowly with the mules and the luggage, leaving Marcus and Narcissa to travel on at a quicker pace through the mountains with Mr. McLeod. While this was presented as a practical arrangement, the truth was that the couples needed a break from one another. Although none of the four referred to it at the time, serious personality clashes, particularly between Henry and Narcissa, would later come to light.[18]

If Mrs. Whitman was experiencing any doubts about the wisdom of casting in her lot with the Spaldings, for the time being she kept them to herself. "I never wished to go back. Such a thought finds no place in my heart," she wrote on August 27. "'The Lord is better to us than our fears.' I always find it so."

---

*Later renamed Fort Boise.

It was, in any case, far too late for regrets. Both couples, although traveling apart, now faced the most physically challenging part of their journey. After crossing the Wallowa Mountains, the trail took them through the Grande Ronde Valley and then, finally, toward the end of August, they began their ascent of the Blue Mountains.

At first the thickly forested landscape they rode through appeared to Narcissa like nothing so much as "the hills in my native county . . . Indeed, I do not know as I was ever so much affected with any scenery in my life. The singing of the birds, the echo of the voices of my fellow travelers, as they were scattered through the woods, all had a strong resemblance to bygone days." But these nostalgic reveries did not last. "Before noon we began to descend one of the most terrible mountains for steepness & length I have yet seen. It was like winding stairs in its descent & in some places almost perpendicular. We were a long time descending it. The horses appeared to dread the hill as much as we did. They would turn and wind in a zigzag manner all the way down. The men usually walked but I could not get permission to, neither did I desire it much. We had no sooner gained the foot of the mountain when another more steep and dreadful was before us."

That same evening they reached "the highest elevation," and just as they began yet another descent they were rewarded with an extraordinary view. There before them lay the Columbia River Valley in its entirety—two hundred miles of eastern Oregon spread out before them like a map. "Beyond the valley we could see two distant Mountains, Mount Hood and Mount St. Helens. These lofty peaks were of a conical form & separate from each other by a considerable distance. Behind the former the Sun was hiding part of his rays which gave us a more distinct view of this gigantic cone. The beauty of this extensive valley contrasted well with the rolling mountains behind us & at this hour of twilight was enchanting & quite diverted my mind from the fatigue under which I was laboring." Narcissa was at that moment looking down upon the only place she would ever again call home.

By the end of August the Whitmans were within days of reaching their destination. It was an extraordinarily intense time. While during the previous few days Narcissa had felt "weak, restless and scarcely able to sit on my horse," now, suddenly, she experienced a surge of adrenaline-fueled energy. "This morn my feelings were a little peculiar," she wrote to her mother. "Felt remarkably well and strong, so much as to mention it, but could not see any reason why I should feel any more rested than on the previous morn. Then when I began to see what a day's ride was before me, I understood it. If I had no better health today than yesterday, I should have fainted under it."

But they were not quite there yet. The custom of the country was to send "heralds" to the fort, to announce the party's imminent arrival, and to give the officials there time to prepare a suitable reception. As they waited, Narcissa described the strange calm that descended on their camp. "Our employment this afternoon is various. Some are washing their shirts & some are cutting their [hair] others shaving, preparing to see Walla Walla, and some are asleep. For my part I endeavored to divert myself the best way I could, doing a little mending for Husband, & trying to write while he & Mr. Gray are stretched upon the ground enjoying the refreshment of a sound sleep."

On September 1, the great day had finally arrived. "You can better imagine our feelings this morning than I can describe them," Narcissa wrote. "I could not realize that the end of our long journey was so near. We arose as soon as it was light, took our cup of coffee and ate of the duck we had given us last night, then dressed for Walla W. We started while it was yet early, for all were in haste to reach the desired haven. If you could have seen us now you would have been surprised, for both man & beast galloped almost all the way to the Fort."

There was, at first, almost too much to take in. "The door yard was filled with hens, turkeys, pigeons & in another place we saw cows, hogs & goats in abundance & I think the fattest cattle & swine I ever saw." And after five months' hard traveling, during which they had subsisted almost entirely on buffalo meat, Narcissa can be forgiven for her almost obsessive recording of what they were given to eat. For breakfast, to which they sat down almost immediately upon arrival, they were given "fresh salmon, potatoes, tea, bread and butter," followed by a dinner at four o'clock of "pork, potatoes, beets, cabbage, turnips, tea, bread & butter, my favorite dinner, and much like the last dinner I ate with Mother Loomis [her mother-in-law]." In between they were also treated to "a feast of mellons," which were the very "finest I think I ever saw or tasted."

The room she was given at the Fort had portholes instead of windows and was filled with a small arsenal of firearms, as well as a large cannon which was kept always loaded, but she was by now quite hardened to this kind of thing. "I am so well pleased with the possession of a room to shelter us from the scorching sun, that I scarcely notice them."

There was one particular detail that she did notice, however. "While at breakfast . . . a young cock placed himself upon the sill of the door and crowed. Now whether it was the sight of the first white females or out of compliment to the company I know not . . . [but] I was pleased with his appearance. You may think me simple for speaking of such a small circumstance as this. No one knows the feelings occasioned by seeing objects once familiar after a long deprivation, especially when it is heightened by the expectation of not meeting with them."

Had she but known it, the sound of a cockerel crow, with its hint of betrayal and death, was a presage of things to come.

2

FORT VANCOUVER

When Narcissa Whitman and Eliza Spalding arrived at Fort Walla Walla on the Columbia River in present-day Washington State, neither woman seemed to have been aware of the wider significance of what they had achieved. It was enough that they had survived.

"Do you ask whether I regret coming by land?" an ebullient Narcissa would later write to a friend. "I answer NO! *by no means*. If I were at home now, I would choose to come this way in preference to a seven-month voyage [by sea]." In fact, she seemed to have been positively energized by her experiences. "I feel remarkably well and rested, do not need to lounge at all, & so it is with us all," she had written on her arrival at Walla Walla. "I can scarcely believe it possible of myself, but it is true. I feel as vigorous & as well able to engage in any domestic employment as I ever did in my life."[19]

William Gray thought so too.* "Mrs. Whitman has endured the Journey like a heroine," he wrote; and even Mrs. Spalding's health and strength was

---

*He was sufficiently convinced to take his own new bride, Mary Dix, over the same overland route just two years later.

now "improved beyond all expectation."[20] All believed that it was "through the mercy of a kind Providence" that they had been kept safe through all the hazards of the journey. Surely, this was a sign of the rightness of their mission. "What a cause for gratitude & praise to God," Narcissa wrote. "Surely my heart is ready to leap for joy, at the thought of being so near the long desired work of teaching the benighted ones a knowledge of a Saviour."[21]

But before their mission could begin, there were formidable practicalities to overcome. There were houses to be built, gardens to be planted, crops to be sown, but what with? The missionaries had arrived with not much more than the clothes on their backs. Within just days of arriving at Walla Walla, the party was obliged to set out, yet again, to find supplies.

SITUATED AT THE CONFLUENCE of the Columbia and Willamette Rivers, some three hundred miles downriver and six days' traveling by boat from Walla Walla, Fort Vancouver* was the headquarters of the British-run Hudson's Bay Company.† When Narcissa later described it as "the New York of the Pacific Ocean," she was hardly exaggerating. This was no rough-and-ready stockade, such as the ones the mission party had briefly encountered at Fort Snake and Fort Hall, but "the grand emporium" of the company's trade west of the Rocky Mountains. As the missionaries arrived, the first thing they saw were two enormous British men-of-war, the *Columbia* and the *Neriade*, anchored in the bay, "dressed in complete regalia from stem to stern," their flags and pennants raised in welcome.

As if the sight of two British ships were not enough, the women's first glimpse of Fort Vancouver itself must have been an almost-overwhelming experience. Until now, in five months' hard traveling through the wilderness, the missionaries had seen no sign of permanent human habitation bigger

---

*Fort Vancouver lay at the site of what is now Vancouver, Washington, and should not be confused with Vancouver, Canada.
†One of the oldest fur-trading companies in the world, the Hudson's Bay Company had been founded in 1670, during the reign of Charles II.

than a few straggling Pawnee villages on the Platte River. Now they were about to enter what would have seemed to them like a metropolis: a thriving colony of more than five hundred Hudson's Bay Company employees, their wives and families, an extraordinary multiethnic, multilingual community of Scots, Irish, English, and French Canadians, as well as Native Americans from as many as thirty different nations.

It was not just the numbers of people that were surprising. The fort itself was by far the largest and most impressive they had yet encountered. Spread out over four acres, it contained about forty frame and log buildings centered around two piazzas. This was the depot to which all the furs from the smaller Hudson's Bay Company trading posts were brought, graded, bundled, and shipped to Britain. Here were to be found not only the company's trade offices—some for buying, "others for selling, others again for keeping accounts and transacting business"[22]—but also a school for as many as fifty children, a chapel, and Governor John McLoughlin's residence.

As it was the only settlement of its size for thousands of miles in any direction, it is hard to imagine the culture shock the two women must have experienced as they passed through the gateway of the twenty-five-foot-high stockade. Immediately, they were assailed by the unaccustomed buzz of human activity. From early in the morning, when a bell was rung to announce the start of the working day, "the sound of hammers, clink of the anvils, the rumbling of carts, with tinkling of bells, render it difficult to sleep after this time."[23]

Everything at Fort Vancouver was run with military precision. At noon, when the bell was rung for the midday meal, and again in the evening, the factors sat down at long communal tables to dine, in strict order of seniority. As a later visitor would observe: "Everyone appears to have a relative rank, privilege & station assigned to him, and military etiquette prevails."

Here, "everything, and of every kind and description, could be had ... [including] an extensive apothecary shop, a bakery, blacksmiths' and coopers' shops" as well as, perhaps most exotically of all, "shops for retail, where English manufactured articles may be purchased at as low a price, if not cheaper, than in the United States."[24] These items included pots and pans, coffee and tea pots, candlesticks, earthenware crockery, ship chandlery, linen, and blankets (many of these items later bought up by Narcissa for her future home at Walla Walla).*

On entering the fort itself, they were welcomed by the chief factor, Dr. McLoughlin, and his deputy, Mr. Douglas. "Soon after we were introduced to Mrs. McLoughlin & Mrs. Douglas, both natives of the country (half-breed)," Narcissa wrote. After "chatting with them a little," Eliza and Narcissa were invited to take a turn in the garden. "What a delightful place this is," Narcissa wrote. "What a contrast this to the rough barren sand plains through which we had so recently passed." This was no cottage garden, but a landscaped area with fine walks on each side lined with strawberry vines, and a pretty summer house covered in grape vines. "Here we find fruit of every description. Apples, peaches, grapes. Pear plum and fig trees in abundance. Cucumbers melons beans peas beats cabbage taumatoes and every kind of vegitable too numerous to mention."[25]

After promenading in the grounds for a little while, the missionaries returned to the Governor's Residence, only to find that there was yet another surprise in store for them. Narcissa and Eliza may have been the first two white women to cross the Rocky Mountains, but they were not the first to reach Fort Vancouver. "We were met by Mrs. Capendale, a Lady from England, who arrived in the Ship *Columbia* last May."† After dinner, they were also introduced to a second Englishwoman, Jane Beaver, the wife of the Reverend Herbert Beaver, a Church of England clergyman, who had arrived only the week before on the *Neriade*. "This was more than we expected when we

---

*Narcissa Whitman wrote that while "every article for comfort and durability" could be found at Fort Vancouver, "fancy articles are not here." Less than a decade later the Fort Vancouver account book (1844) listed such luxury articles as "ladies short kid gloves, hooks, eyes, ribbons, 'best diamond pins,' ladies round platted Hats, and shawls." I have often wondered who bought the diamond pins. See John Hussey, "The Women of Fort Vancouver."

†The Capendales were a husband-and-wife team: he had been brought out from England to supervise the company's farm, while his wife was to take charge of the dairy and "to superintend an infant school." Like the Beavers, they had made the journey by sea, around Cape Horn.

left home, that we should be privileged with the acquaintance and society of two English Ladies. Indeed, we seem to be nearly allied to old England itself, for most of the gentlemen of the Company are from thence & Scotland."

Narcissa seems to have been rather overawed by her experiences at the fort. Not long after her arrival, she received an entertaining lesson in local manners. In a letter dated November 1 (her last opportunity for writing home until the following spring), she drew attention to the wax seal, stamped with the McLoughlin signet, with which her letter was affixed. "They are over nice in following the rules of etiquette here in some particulars," she explained. "It is considered impolite to seal a letter with a wafer for the reason that it is wet with spittle. Very impolite to send spittle to a friend. You will laugh at this I know," she added, "but so it is. We are both of us without a Seal & if I use wax I shall have to make a stamp of my thimble."[26]

The "native born" métis (mixed-race) Marguerite McLoughlin was probably the last person on earth from whom Narcissa would have expected such a lesson. As it turned out, it was not the only thing Mrs. McLoughlin would teach her.

Until now, neither Narcissa nor Eliza had had any dealings of any real significance with the Native American women among whom they had come to live. That mountain men, almost as a matter of course, married Native women was a fact that would have been well known to them—there would have been many such families at the Rendezvous—but the rest, in Narcissa's vague and as yet unfocused gaze, were simply "savages," clearly (in her view) in need of all the teaching and guidance that the all-knowing white missionaries could dispense. Even the Nez Percé women who had traveled with their party for many weeks, from the Rendezvous to Fort Snake, had inspired nothing but pity in Narcissa: to her untutored eye, they appeared as "mere slaves" to their menfolk. Their introduction to Marguerite McLoughlin and Amelia Douglas, women of high status at Fort Vancouver, graciously showing them around their landscaped grounds and strawberry beds, and gently dispensing lessons in local etiquette, must have come as something of a shock.

Mrs. McLoughlin, in particular, the "First Lady" of Fort Vancouver, lived in a grander house, and in a far grander style, than anything for which Narcissa's rural upbringing could have prepared her. When Marguerite invited her to dine at the Governor's Residence, it was on mahogany chairs, at a dining room table that could sit twelve people. Her silver was marked with the McLoughlin family crest, and "at every new dish . . . [there was] a clean plate."[27]

Born in 1775, Marguerite was the daughter of a Swiss Canadian father, Jean-Étienne Wadin,* one of the original partners of the North West Company,† and an unnamed Cree woman from the Ojibwe Tribe of eastern Upper Canada. When she was nineteen, Marguerite had made a "country marriage" to Alexander McKay, a Scots

The half-Cree Marguerite McLoughlin, the much loved "First Lady" of Fort Vancover

Canadian and one of Wadin's partners in the North West Company (and later a founding member of the Pacific Fur Company), by whom she had three daughters, Annie, Marie, and Catherine, and a son, Thomas—the same Thomas McKay who had been one of the commanders in charge of the caravan that had escorted the Whitman party from the Rendezvous at Green River to Walla Walla. After McKay's death, Marguerite quickly married again, this time to Dr. John McLoughlin. McLoughlin already had one child, a baby son called Joseph, also by a Native American mother, and the couple went on to have four more of their own: John (born in 1812), Elizabeth (1814), Eloise (1817), and David (1821).

---

* Their name is also given variously as Waden, Wadden, and Waddens.
† The North West Company was later merged with Hudson's Bay Company.

It would be easy to assume that for a newly widowed mother, left all alone with four small children to support, the gain would have been all on Marguerite's side when she married for the second time, but this was very far from being the case.

Native American women, including many métis such as Marguerite McLoughlin and Amelia Douglas, had always played a critical role in the success of the fur trade. As far back as the seventeenth century, *mariages à la façon du pays*, or country marriages, were made not only for the intimacy and companionship they afforded men who might be marooned in the wilderness, sometimes for years at a time, but also for practical and even strategic reasons. Women were not only useful to their husbands for their practical skills in the field, but also as interpreters and guides.* Perhaps most critically, however, a marriage to a Native woman brought with it all the advantages of an alliance with her Tribe. It would allow a fur trapper access to her Tribal lands without fear of attack and would often ensure that he had preferential treatment relative to any of his competitors who might be trying to make inroads into that territory. "Kinship allowed traders to pass from 'outside' status to 'insider' status almost instantaneously."[28]

As "ladies inside the palisade," women such as Marguerite McLoughlin and Amelia Douglas were insiders of a slightly different kind. As daughters of high-ranking fur-company officers and their American Indian wives, they were highly sought after by ambitious young traders of the day. Amelia Douglas was the daughter of James Douglas's former boss, William Connolly, who had been the company's chief factor at Fort William, almost a thousand miles to the north in present-day British Columbia. As Marguerite's had been, Amelia's mother, Suzanne Pas-de-Nom (Suzanne No-Name),

---

*Famously, Meriwether Lewis and William Clark were heavily reliant on a Shoshone woman, Sacagawea, to be their interpreter and guide on their 1804 expedition across North America, shortly after the Louisiana Purchase. Sacagawea is well remembered for her part in this venture, but there were hundreds of Native women, their names and achievements now long forgotten, who provided similar vital assistance to fur trappers. Sacagawea was married to a French Canadian mountain man, Toussaint Charbonneau.

was a Cree. Amelia, or "Little Snowbird," had been married to James Douglas when she was sixteen. Much later, when her husband was knighted and
became governor of Vancouver Island and British Columbia, she would pre-
side over the community there as Lady Douglas. One of Marguerite's daughters, Eloise, would also follow in both her mother's and her grandmother's
footsteps when her hand in marriage was sought by not one but two prominent fur traders. Her father refused the first suitor, on the grounds that at
twenty years Eloise's senior he was too old. She eventually married William
Rae, a Scotsman from the Orkney Islands* and a company employee.†

The Hudson's Bay Company actively encouraged such liaisons. It was
not just the domestic happiness of the factors that they were thinking of; it
was good for business too. In April 1825, just a year after Fort Vancouver
was founded, the Governor of the company's North American operations,
George Simpson, had written from London to Dr. McLoughlin with the
extraordinary suggestion that one of his junior employees, John Work,
should be encouraged to marry the daughter of a prominent Cayuse chieftain. There is no evidence that Work had any personal reasons for doing
this—he may not even have met the woman in question; it seems to have
been suggested merely because he was an as yet unattached man. "Simpson
proposed that Work would then make frequent visits to Cayuse territory
with his new wife, thus providing support to HBC brigades who were hoping to travel, safely and profitably, in Cayuse territory."[29] While the records
do not show whether John Work complied with the request, the company's
trade in Cayuse lands improved significantly after this exchange.

Not everyone approved. Since such attachments usually only involved
Tribal rituals, these *mariages à la façon du pays* were not, so far as many
whites were concerned, true marriages at all. The fur companies took a more
pragmatic view: for their employees, stationed hundreds, perhaps even

---

*A majority of Hudson's Bay Company employees were from the Orkney Islands.
†When Rae was appointed clerk-in-charge at Fort Stikine, a remote Hudson's Bay outpost
in Russian Alaska, Eloise and their tiny baby accompanied him—the first of several extraordinary journeys she would undertake as his wife.

thousands of miles away from "civilization," the usual formalities, both cler-ical and religious, were simply not available. Often these were temporary arrangements, frequently open to abuse. It was not uncommon for the men to have legitimate wives and families still living (Étienne Wadin, Marguerite's father, was one such), to whom they would probably one day return. Sometimes these "country wives" and their children were simply abandoned; others were "passed on."*

To counter these abuses, by 1821 the Hudson's Bay Company had intro-duced its own standardized marriage contract, for use by its employees, "representing a sort of compromise between the priggishness of London society and the practical demands of the Company's field operations."[30] The contract asserted that "country" marriages were lawful but made it quite clear that the company expected its operators to support their wives and families financially, and to "remarry" them in the event that clergy became available.[†]

For all the pragmatism that was involved, many of these country mar-riages resulted in genuinely loving partnerships—Marguerite and John Mc-Loughlin's was one.[‡]

---

*A situation that has remarkably close parallels with the "wives," or *bibis*, of British officials of the East India Company during the seventeenth and eighteenth centuries. See my *She-Merchants, Buccaneers and Gentlewomen: British Women in India 1600–1900*.

†Marguerite and John McLoughlin took part in just such a remarriage, on November 19, 1842. The church records state that they were "legitimate spouses . . . wishing to renew their consent to marriage." The ceremony was officiated by the archbishop of Quebec. See T. C. Elliott, "Marguerite Wadin McKay McLoughlin."

‡Francis Parkman, a young Bostonian who in 1846 undertook "a journey of curiosity and amusement" into American Indian territories west of the Missouri, was so struck by one instance of this that he recorded it in his journal. "The squaw of Henry Chatillon [the French Canadian fur trapper with whom he was traveling], a woman with whom he had been con-nected for years by the strongest ties which in that country exist between the sexes, was dangerously ill. She and her children were in the village of The Whirlwind, at the distance of a few days' journey. Henry was anxious to see the woman before she died, and provide for the safety and support of his children, of whom he was extremely fond. To have refused him this would have been gross inhumanity. We abandoned our plans of joining Smoke's village, and of proceeding with it to the rendezvous, and determined to meet the Whirlwind, and go in his company." See Francis Parkman, *The California and Oregon Trail*.

There are several photographs of the remarkable Marguerite McLough-lin still in existence. Taken in her later years, they show a rather severe-looking, comfortably fleshed woman, neatly dressed in sleek black bomba-zine. It is hard to believe that they do her much justice. Marguerite was a woman of many talents: not only did she speak French and Cree as well as English, but she had a fine ear for music and was a highly skilled seam-stress.* To Narcissa, she was "one of the kindest women in the world." In John McLoughlin, she would inspire a lifelong devotion.

At six feet four inches, with a shock of long white hair, the Scots Cana-dian John McLoughlin was a great bear of a man; famously hospitable, and possessed of "great energy of character," he was, according to one contem-porary, "extremely well suited for the station he occupies, which requires great talent and industry."[31] He was also an admirable family man: "in pub-lic and in private, he was as loyal to [his wife] as if she had been a daughter of Queen Victoria," wrote one pioneer woman. Even in her later years, when Marguerite was "coarse, bent, fat and flabby, he treated her as a princess. . . . His gallantry to her knew no bounds."[32]

Unfortunately, not everyone saw their marriage this way.

From everything that is known about the marvelously named Reverend Herbert Beaver, it is hard not to imagine that some obscure joke was at play back at the Hudson's Bay Company headquarters in London when he was appointed chaplain to Fort Vancouver. He and his wife Jane—described in withering terms by a contemporary as "rather fierce" and "masculine to such an extent as to be accused of wearing the breeches"[33]—were not an attractive couple. Herbert Beaver, in particular, was unsuited in almost every way to his new post.

Within a very short time of their arrival, he seems to have offended just about everybody. When Eliza and Narcissa volunteered to help out at the school, he wrote them a long, pompous letter of complaint, and Dr.

---

* Her exquisite black-and-gold Chinese lacquer sewing bureau is today one of the treasures of the Fort Vancouver National Historic Site.

McLoughlin had to demand an apology from him.* As if this were not enough, the reverend found much else to complain about. In his opinion, the many "country marriages" at the fort were not only irreligious but very possibly illegal, and he complained bitterly of their "evil effects" and of the "dreadfully demoralized state of civil society."[34] Soon he was busy writing yet more angry letters, this time back to the head office in London, complaining about the "immoral and disgraceful" state of affairs at his new posting. Kind, hospitable, blameless Marguerite came in for his special disapproval. She was, he wrote, "a female of notoriously loose character" who was "the kept mistress of the highest personage . . . at this station."

For Dr. McLoughlin, who had already had to smooth things out with the missionaries, this was too much. He accosted Beaver and asked him to explain himself. "Sir," Beaver replied, "if you wish to know why a cow's tail grows downward, I cannot tell you; I can only cite the fact."[35] The studied insolence of this reply was the final straw. McLoughlin, who was at the best of times of a "florid complexion," simply exploded. In a fit of rage, he grabbed Reverend Beaver's walking cane, and it was only the intervention of some bystanders that prevented him from giving the chaplain a thorough thrashing.

Although the factors at Fort Vancouver strenuously opposed Beaver's criticisms, and eventually succeeded in having him recalled to London, the fact was that the writing was on the wall for these pleasantly multicultural liaisons.

Change was coming—and it was not only the arrival of outsiders such as the Whitmans, the Spaldings, and the Beavers, with their widely different world views, who brought it. For the Native people, whose ancient trade routes had already come to be dominated by foreign competitors, their traditional way of life was already under threat. Now, too, the British and

---

*It was the fact that they taught the children to sing hymns to which he took a particular exception. "Sacred music should only be used on solemn occasions, but it is made here a common entertainment of an evening, without the slightest religious feeling or purpose" (quoted in Whitman and Spalding, *Where Wagons Could Go*).

American fur companies themselves moved under gathering clouds. A change in fashions in men's top hats, which now favored silk instead of the once-popular beaver skin, would soon all but destroy the trade, which was, in any case, in sharp decline. Intensive trapping played its part, and so too did the vicious competition between the various fur companies. The Hudson's Bay Company had gone so far as to practice a "fur-desert" policy, deliberately trapping all fur-bearing animals south of the Columbia River to the point of extinction, in order to make the area less attractive to their American competitors.

If they were to survive, they had to diversify. John McLoughlin, for one, was shrewd enough to realize this. For some time now he had been working to make the settlement at Fort Vancouver as self-sufficient as possible. At a little distance from the fort itself was "a substantial village" in which the company's laborers were housed, and beyond it, spread out for several miles, was a flourishing farm: several hundred acres of arable land, "fenced into beautiful corn-fields—vegetable fields—orchards—gardens—and pasture-fields . . . interspersed with dairy-houses, shepherds' and herdsmen's cottages."[36] Sturdy breeds of sheep and cattle had been imported from England with the hope that eventually the company would be able to export their own hides, tallow, and wool back to England in its returning men-of-war.* Even in 1836 the fort was able to supply Russian ports as far north as Alaska and as far south as Mexican Yerba Buena (San Francisco) with grain, butter, and cheese. A program of shipbuilding had started as early as 1827.

Narcissa was deeply impressed. "They estimate their wheat crops at 4,000 bushels† this year, peas the same," she wrote on September 14. "Oats & barley between them 15 and 1700 bushels each. The potatoes & turnip fields are large and fine. Their cattle are numerous, estimated at 1000 head in all their settlements, also sheep & goats. . . . We find also Hens, Turkeys, Pigeons, but no geese." They also visited the dairy, where between fifty and

---

*The furs themselves took up relatively little space in the ship's holds.
†A bushel was a measure of dry goods, equal to eight gallons.

sixty cows were milked daily. Now under the expert supervision of the Englishwoman Mrs. Capendale, they would find "butter and cheese in abundance."

Even more welcome was the news that the company had not one but several mills, including one that was only five days' ride from Walla Walla, near which they were expecting to set up their mission, "from whence we expect to obtain our supplies of flour, also potatoes and pork. They have three hundred hogs [there]," Narcissa wrote. It was all so very encouraging. "[Dr. McLoughlin] appears desireous to afford us every facility for living in his power. No person could have received a more hearty welcome or be treated with greater kindness than we have been since our arrival." She then added: "[He] promises to loan us enough to make a beginning, & all the return he asks is that we supply other settlers in the same way."

The extraordinarily, perhaps even suspiciously, friendly welcome that they had received at the hands of John McLoughlin was at least in part the reaction of a man who had sensed an remarkable business opportunity.[*]

Narcissa Whitman and Eliza Spalding may have been unaware of the significance of their journey, but a shrewd trader such as Dr. McLoughlin was not. If these two women had been able to make the overland journey, then it was only a matter of time before others would surely follow—not so much a crack as an entire foot in the door leading west.

---

*McLoughlin's policy of helping American emigrants was controversial at the time, and not everyone at the Hudson's Bay Company agreed with it, urging him instead to turn the emigrants away when they came to him for help. One of John McLoughlin's main concerns was that if he did not help them, the incoming Americans would seek to open up their own chain of supplies.

3

OREGON FEVER

J ohn McLoughlin, the chief factor at Fort Vancouver, was not the only person who saw these possibilities.

Even if it were only in their imaginations, many Americans had long looked west. The first person to urge settlement of Oregon country (then still jointly claimed by both the United States and Great Britain) was an eccentric Boston schoolteacher, Hall Jackson Kelly. As early as the 1820s, Kelly had begun to write and publish pamphlets extolling Oregon's rich potential. The fact that the disputed lands were on the far side of a landmass the size of an ocean, and that Kelly himself had, as yet, never actually been there, did not deter him in the slightest. According to Kelly, Oregon was nothing short of an earthly paradise.* "From the plenitude of its resources it will soon be able to sustain its own operations and will hasten on to its own majesty and to a proud rank on the earth,"[37] he wrote, even producing a plan for a proposed city on the peninsula between the Columbia and Willamette

---

*Both the explorer Nathaniel Wyeth and the Methodist missionary Jason Lee were to claim that their knowledge of Oregon first came from Kelly's descriptions.

Rivers. Although most people would find Kelly's almost messianic fervor for a place he had never visited "a little touched," the society he founded, the Oregon Colonization Society, soon had an enthusiastic membership.

From the 1830s, however, a steady stream of information about Oregon country from a variety of other sources began to filter east. Not all of it was utopian fantasy. First came the tales gleaned from the fur trappers and then, in the latter part of the decade, from the early missionaries—not only Presbyterians such as the Whitmans and the Spaldings, but also a handful of Methodists and Catholics (all male) who had already begun to lay out their wares in remote parts of the Pacific Northwest. In the early 1840s, after the first tiny handful of non-missionary settlers had begun to arrive, yet more stories would make their way back to the United States. As Kelly had done, these early settlers too extolled the virtues of this land of milk and honey. The rivers were everywhere navigable, the timber super abundant, and the tilled land "yielded more to the acre, spontaneously, than the cultivated fields of Belgium and Britain"; the Columbia River and its tributaries were "literally choked with salmon." There was much excitement, too, about the size of wheat and the abundance of the crops, and soil "rich beyond comparison." In Oregon, it was said, the fevers and agues which so plagued the valleys of the undrained swamps of the Mississippi plains were scarcely known. People were healthier. Even the weather was better. "Rain rarely falls, even in the winter season; but the dews are sufficiently heavy to compensate for its absence."[38] According to one account, there was no rain at all, only gentle dew. Even the humblest garden vegetables grew to prodigious size. There was a beet (spotted in Narcissa Whitman's garden) that measured almost three feet in circumference, and a gigantic turnip "that will exceed five feet before pulling time."[39]

Back East, these extravagant tales fell upon the ears of a population that was already restless and suffering from hard times. Beginning in 1837, a severe economic depression had swept the country, causing wages to plummet by as much as 50 percent, banks to default, and unemployed laborers in the tens of thousands to demonstrate in the cities. Worse still, for farmers, was the fall in the price of crops: wheat was only worth ten cents a bushel, while corn, it was said, "could not be given away." Others would cite ill health as a reason for going. Some, particularly in the western states of Missouri, Iowa, and Illinois, simply felt crowded out by their neighbors and yearned for pastures new.*

By 1839 at least ten more Oregon societies, its members pledged to make the journey west, had been added to Kelly's original. Free-born African Americans, too, were quick to respond to these siren songs. The territory had become "a sort of pioneers' paradise"—and Oregon Fever gripped the country.

Not everyone believed the hype. When the "Oregon question" was debated in Congress, one senator, George McDuffie, said that he would not give a "pinch of snuff" for the entire territory. "What do we want with that vast, worthless area, that region of savages and wild beasts, of deserts, of shifting sands and whirlwinds of dust, of cactus and prairie dogs?" proclaimed another senator, Daniel Webster. "To what use could we ever hope to put those great deserts, those endless mountain ranges, impenetrable and covered to their bases with eternal snow? What can we ever hope to do with the western coast of three-thousand miles, rock-bound, cheerless and uninviting, with not a harbor in it? What use have we for such a country? Mr. President, I will never vote one cent from the public treasury to place the Pacific coast one inch nearer Boston than it is today."[40]

Others disagreed. Edward D. Baker stood up in the House of Representatives and declared that the citizens of the United States would "go for it . . . because they have been told that the soil was our own; and moreover, they believed it was our manifest destiny to occupy and people it. What was destiny?" he asked. "Was it not the duty of every statesman to look, not only at what the country is, but to look forward and see what (by the blessing of God) it may become?" Oregon should be claimed by the US, he argued,

---

*"I heard an old pioneer assign as a reason why he must emigrate from western Illinois the fact that 'people were settling right under his nose'—and the farm of his neighbor was twelve miles distant, along section lines!" See Verne Bright, "The Folklore and History of the 'Oregon Fever.'"

"because it was contiguous to our own territory, and would be peopled by those kindred to us in blood, in language, and in everything else." In fact, the whole territory "rightfully [belongs] to us, as long as our country shall be true to its manifest and ultimate destiny."[41]

Others were not convinced and deplored the potential loss of so many valuable citizens.

For most people, far away from the wrangles of their government in Washington, the more informal oratory of the wayside soapbox was having an electrifying effect. One woman, already on her way out West, would recall how she had met "a man from Oregon" who jumped up on his wagon tongue to declaim: "'Friends, you are traveling to the garden of Eden, a land flowing with milk and honey. And just let me tell you, the clover grows wild all over Oregon, and when you wade through it, it reaches your chin.' We believed every word."[42]

Another early pioneer recalled being taken by their father one Saturday morning to hear the frontiersman Peter Burnett speak. "Mr. Burnett hauled a box out on to the sidewalk, took his stand upon it, and began to tell us about the land flowing with milk and honey on the shores of the Pacific. . . . He told of the great crops of wheat which it was possible to raise in Oregon, and pictured in glowing terms the richness of the soil and the attractions of the climate, and then with a little twinkle in his eye he said 'And they do say, gentlemen, they do say, that out in Oregon the pigs are running about under great acorn trees, round and fat, and already cooked, with knives and forks sticking in them so that you can cut off a slice whenever you are hungry.'" At this, of course, everybody in the audience had laughed; but his words had had a profound effect. "Father was so moved by what he heard . . . that he decided to join the company that was going west to Oregon" and became one of the first to sign his name.[43]

ENCOURAGED BY THE SUCCESS of Eliza Spalding and Narcissa Whitman, in 1838 four more missionary women had also made the journey west, but it was not until 1840 that the first non-missionary women would attempt to do so. In that year, at least one settler family accompanied the American Fur Company caravan on its annual (and final) journey to the Green River Rendezvous. These were Mary Walker (née Young), her husband Joel, and their four children, John, Joe, Newton, and Isabella. Mary, who was pregnant at the time, gave birth to her fifth child, Louisa, in Oregon the following January.* The year after, 1841, an estimated hundred settlers followed them; the year after that, the numbers doubled again. And 1843, the year when Peter Burnett had so enthralled audiences from his soapbox, would prove a quantum leap from the three previous years: in all, a thousand hopeful overlanders—men, women, and children—would make the journey west that year.

In these first few years of the emigration west, there were no maps, no guides, and almost no information about what to take or how to get there. Many of these early expeditions would rely on little more than the clues left by a previous wagon party, slips of paper hidden in the sagebrush or nailed to a post. It was a level of unpreparedness that today is hard to conceive. "One man told them he had seen a map showing a great lake with two rivers running out of it clear to the Pacific Ocean. All they needed to do was find the lake and follow the rivers to the sea. . . . No-one had a compass. They just turned their team west and followed the Platte River. . . . They had no guide and so little information that they were forced, as one of them put it, to 'smell' their way west."[44]

Their resulting trials were biblical in scale and horror. Many got lost in the wilderness and were never to reach their destination. A journey that could realistically last six months or more was popularly believed to take

---

*It has been suggested that Mary's sister, Martha Young, and her family were also part of this company, but I have not been able to confirm this. In his "Reminiscences," dictated toward the end of his life, Mary's husband, Joel, declared that as many as forty other settlers had agreed to make the journey that year, but that they were not ready in time. The Youngs had originally intended to go to California, but they changed their mind at Fort Hall and went to Oregon instead.

only three or four. Most either took too few provisions with them, and ran the risk of starving to death, or, as was more often the case, too many. Oxen, with their superior strength, were usually favored over horses and mules, but the many long months on the road hauling the overloaded wagons often proved too much.

Exhausted and half-starved from lack of good grazing, the animals became simply too weak to pull heavy loads, with the result that settlers had no choice but to jettison most, sometimes all, of their possessions. And when their oxen finally gave out, entire wagons, together with everything in them, were simply left by the wayside. Seventeen-year-old Nancy Kelsey, who made the journey west in 1841, described how when her family's last remaining wagon finally had to be abandoned, she was forced to walk barefoot "until my feet were blistered," cradling her one-year-old infant in her arms. At first they had carried their food with them, but soon even these supplies ran out, and she had subsisted for two weeks on nothing more than boiled acorns.[45]

Treasured family heirlooms, however small, were the first to go. One settler would recall a man named Smith standing with a wooden rolling pin

in his hands. "I shall never forget how that big man stood there with tears streaming down his face as he said, 'Do I have to throw this away? It was my mother's. I remember she always used it to roll out her biscuits, and they were awful good biscuits.'"[46]

The detritus left by the wagon trains was sometimes compared to that made by a defeated and retreating army. One pioneer found an assortment of clothes, boots, shoes, hats, lead, iron, tinware, trunks, meat, wheels, axles, wagon beds, and even mining tools beside the trail. "A few hundred yards from my camp I saw an object, which reaching proved

Nancy Kelsey

to be a very handsome and new Gothic bookcase! It was soon dismembered to boil our coffee kettles."[47]

Often, the only reason that settlers survived at all was by picking over the detritus of those who had gone before them—if they were lucky. Tabitha Brown, a widow in her midsixties, described how when her party was simply abandoned by the "rascally fellow" who had passed himself off as a guide, she had lost literally everything she possessed except her horse. After three days without food she came to a canyon "strewn with dead cattle, broken wagons, beds, clothing and everything but the provisions of which we were nearly destitute."[48]

Many relied on hunting buffalo to replenish their supplies of food, but even this was fraught with difficulties. These gigantic herds, often hundreds of thousands strong, were one of the wonders of the trail, but they could be dangerous too. Settlers described how sometimes the entire horizon, for as far as the eye could see, would become black with an advancing herd. "One day a herd came in our direction like a great black cloud," recalled one woman, "a threatening, moving mountain, advancing toward us very swiftly and with wild snorts, noses almost to the ground and tails flying in midair. I haven't any idea how many there were but they seemed to be innumerable and made a deafening terrible noise. As is their habit, when stampeding they did not turn out of their course for anything. Some of our wagons were within their line of advance and in consequence one was completely demolished and two were overturned. Several persons were hurt, one child's shoulder dislocated, but fortunately no one was killed."[49]

Even for those whose oxen and supplies held out, the strange fluctuations in the weather could prove perilous. In dry years, the heat and dust could be unbearable. "You in the States know nothing about dust," wrote one woman with feeling. "It will fly so that you can hardly see the horns of your tongue yoke [and] it often seems that the cattle must die for the want of breath and then in our waggons such a spectacle beds cloths vituals and children all completely covered."[50] At other times, it was the cold. There could be frost as late as May, while even in the middle of July, hailstones the size of rocks could rip through the wagon canvas and concuss a grown man. Ferocious spring storms were known to tear through a camp and destroy everything in it in a matter of minutes, turning the prairie for miles around into a quagmire. Howling winds blew across the plains, their gusts so violent they threatened to overturn fully loaded wagons; sheet lightning caused their cattle to stampede. "Our tents were blown down as were the covers off our prairie schooners," wrote one survivor of just such a storm, "and in less than five minutes we were wet as drowned rats. Unless you have been through it you can have no idea of the confusion resulting from a storm on the plains, with the oxen bellowing, the children crying and the men shouting, the thunder rolling like a constant salvo of artillery; with everything as light as day from the lightning flashes and the next second as black as the depths of the pit."[51]

Sarah Damron Owens, whose company of forty wagons became one of the very first to reach Oregon in the emigration of 1843, recalled how the damage caused by one of these spring storms nearly jeopardized their entire endeavor.

At first their journey seemed remarkably trouble free. "We never saw an Indian to annoy or molest us," Sarah would recall, and the only accident was a man shooting himself by mistake through the hand. When they came to sagebrush country on the prairies, their captain divided them up into platoons of four wagons each, each platoon taking it in turns to take the lead, and breaking the road ahead of them by cutting through the sagebrush, which in places grew "taller than a man's head."

In the evening, "while the men were attending the cattle and the horses, their wives and daughters would be carrying buffalo 'chips' in their aprons, making fires and preparing supper, which was eaten and relished with appetites that only out-of-door life can give." The men hunted antelope, and sometimes buffalo, to supplement their provisions, and Sarah learned how to cut the meat into fine strips and string them together on ropes. When hung behind the wagons, the meat would be cured within three days. As many settlers would do, Sarah described the feeling of almost holiday elation at the outset of their journey. Theirs "was a jolly train," she would recall, with much music, singing, and dancing round the campfires at night.

And then disaster struck. One night, about midnight, "a fearful windstorm blew down our tents, and the rain fell on us in torrents. The next morning we found that half our cornmeal was wet. Then my husband said to the company: 'At least half our meal is wet, and unless it is converted into bread it will be lost, and my advice is that we make fires and at once make it all into bread.' This advice was, unfortunately, followed only by myself and a few other women." As it was, within a few weeks, because of their wastefulness, "starvation began to stare them in the face" and they were only saved due to the fact that Dr. Whitman (who, for reasons that will later be explained, was traveling with them) was able to send them provisions—wheat, corn, and peas—from his mission near Walla Walla. "Then the parching of wheat and corn and the grinding of coffee mills made sweet music to our ears, bringing encouragement and happiness to us all."[52] Without Dr. Whitman's intervention, most of their company would have died of starvation.

As it was, untold thousands would perish along the emigrant trails. Some starved to death; many others fell prey to disease—typhoid, cholera, "mountain sickness" and "camp fever," and numerous other unidentifiable "agues." Pregnant women were doubly vulnerable, having to face the additional peril of childbirth on the road, and from complications in its aftermath.

Others simply went mad. One emigrant was witness to a particularly unsettling scene when a woman in her company simply refused to travel another step. Her husband spent the best part of three hours trying to coax his wife to move on, "but she would not stur."

"I told my husband the circumstance and [he and two other men] went and took each one a young one and cramed them in the wagon and her husband drove off and left her siting she got up and took the back track travld out of sight cut across overtook her husband meantime he sent his boy back to camp after a horse that he had left and when she came up her husband says did you meet John.

"Yes was the reply and I picked up a stone and nocked out his brains."[53]

When her husband went back to ascertain the truth of this appalling confession, "she set one of his waggons on fire which was loaded with store goods the cover burnt off and some valueable artickles . . . he saw the flame and came running out and . . . then mustered enough spung to give her a good floging."

It was perhaps no wonder then that from an outsider's point of view, the settlers could present a less than favorable aspect. A young Bostonian, Francis Parkman, was at Fort Laramie when a group of settlers arrived, and the fort "was fairly taken by storm."

"A crowd of broad-brimmed hats, thin visages, and staring eyes appeared suddenly at the gate. Tall awkward men, in brown homespun; women with cadaverous faces and long land figures came thronging in together, and, as if inspired by the very demon of curiosity, ransacked every nook and corner of the fort." Curiosity satisfied, they at once got down to business. "The men occupied themselves in procuring supplies for their onward journey; either buying them with money or giving in exchange superfluous articles of their own."

Parkman was sufficiently intrigued by the settlers to visit their camp and was immediately struck by what he saw as "the extraordinary perplexity and indecision that prevailed among [them] . . . They seemed like men totally out of their elements; bewildered and amazed, like a troop of schoolboys lost in the woods." While it was impossible for him not to admire "the high and bold spirit" that had brought them this far, he was also perplexed by their "perturbed state of mind." It could not be cowardice, he decided. "Yet, for the most part they were the rudest and most ignorant of the frontier population; they knew absolutely nothing of the country and its inhabitants; they had already experienced much misfortune, and apprehended more; they had seen nothing of mankind, and had never put their own resources to the test."

He was particularly struck by the violent antipathy felt by the settlers against the "French Indians," as they called the trappers and traders. "They thought, and with some justice, that these men bore them no good will.

Many of them were firmly persuaded that the French were instigating the Indians to attack and cut them off. But the forest is the home of the backwoodsman. On the remote prairie he is totally at a loss. He differs as much from the genuine 'mountain man,' the wild prairie hunter, as a Canadian voyager, paddling his canoe on the rapids of the Ottawa, differs from an American sailor among the storms of Cape Horn."

A full portion of the settlers' suspicion fell upon Parkman and his companions. "Being strangers," he wrote, "we were looked upon as enemies." One man agreed to sell them some lead (for bullets), and some other "necessary articles," and the price had been negotiated, but the man later changed his mind when another of the party persuaded him that they were going to cheat him. "'Well, stranger,' he would observe, as he saw us approach, 'I reckon I won't trade!'"[54]

No matter how bewildered they may have seemed to Francis Parkman, all had started with the same dream, and all had taken many months to prepare. While in later years there would be scores of guidebooks available to advise prospective settlers about every possible aspect of their journey, at the time that Parkman was writing (1846) there was only one. Lansford Warren Hastings's *The Emigrants' Guide to Oregon and California* was first published in 1845. Hastings had made the journey west three years earlier, and he too had come back with predictable reports about the land of milk and honey west of the Rocky Mountains. The tone of his book was "imposingly confident and self-assured," despite the fact that there was still considerable uncertainty over the exact route and that the first item on his list of what to take was a good gun.

In addition to a gun, with a suggested five pounds of powder and twenty pounds of lead, Hastings made many other helpful suggestions about what to take. Basic provisions included two hundred pounds of flour or meal, one hundred and fifty pounds of bacon, ten pounds of coffee, twenty pounds of sugar, and ten pounds of salt. In addition to these basics, such edibles as ham, chipped beef, rice, dried fruit, dried beans, tea, pickles, mustard, and molasses could be added. Butter and milk could be obtained from the settlers' own cows, while game—buffalo and antelope—could be hunted along the way, and sometimes fish. While on the road, children as well as adults, he pointed out, would require twice as much food as they would do at home.

Also on Hastings's list were a baking kettle, frying pan, tea kettle, tea pot and coffee pot, tin plates, tin cups, ordinary knives, forks and spoons, and a coffee mill. At night he suggested blankets, sheets, coverlets, and pillows, "which being spread upon a buffalo robe, an oiled cloth, or some other impervious substance, should constitute the beds." Feather beds, he warned, "are sometimes taken by families, but in many instances they find them not only burdensome and inconvenient, but entirely useless."[55]

Hastings's advice, while containing some helpful tips, gives almost no idea at all of the sheer scale of the preparations that most prospective settlers were now making, and in which women would play an essential role.

Keturah Penton Belknap was one of many women who, even if they had been able to acquire a copy of Hastings's guidebook, had their own very definite ideas about what to take (which, in Keturah's case, most definitely included her feather bed).

It is hard to imagine anyone less like the perplexed, bewildered backwoodsmen of Parkman's description than Keturah Belknap. The extraordinary journal that she kept, from the age of fifteen throughout her life, describes in exquisitely precise detail all the preparations that fell to her lot prior to her family's departure to Oregon in 1848. Her memorandum, as she called it, was part reminiscence, part diary, much of it giving the vivid impression that it was penned almost on the spot. The result is a beautifully detailed account of her daily life written exactly as she spoke, and from which emerges a formidably capable, practical, and benevolent woman.

While there is no such thing as a "typical" settler, Keturah's peripatetic life, in which she and her family would move not once but multiple times, each time pushing steadily westward, was a characteristic shared by many. She was born in 1820, into true pioneering stock. On her father's side she was English and Irish, on her mother's Dutch and Swedish. In 1818, her parents had emigrated from New Jersey, across the Allegheny Mountains in wagons, to Ohio, where they lived first on her father's claim and later on a rented farm. Keturah spent her childhood living in a simple log cabin built by her father. Like all her many siblings, she was expected to work. From the age of six, she would recall, "when not shaking with fever [malaria]—I was kept busy weeding onions or picking the bugs off the cumber and melon vines for that had to be done evry day till the vines began to run." The whole family would go out early in the morning "while the bugs was stupid and search evry hill and catch the bugs and pinch their heads off."[56] But in the evenings there always seemed to be more. If left all night "they would just riddle the leaves and almost spoil the vines," and so the whole procedure had to be repeated all over again.

When Keturah—or Kit as she was known to her family—was nineteen, she married a neighbor, George Belknap, who had appeared out of the blue to court her "one pleasant Sabbath morning . . . dressed up with a Stovepipe Hat." The Belknaps were planning to sell their place in Ohio "and go west to a Prairie country," so within two weeks of her marriage, Keturah was on the move yet again. "We set our faces westward," she wrote, ". . . traveled thru part of Ohio and across Indiana and Illinois and crossed the Mississippi at Fort Madison into Iowa—was four weeks on the way and saw prairie to our heart's content, and verily we thot the half had never been told."

The Belknaps spent seven backbreaking years in Iowa building up their new claim: breaking and fencing their land, planting crops and a vegetable garden, and building a house, all the timber painstakingly hewed by hand from their own oak trees. But no sooner had they at last moved into their newly built home—no humble log cabin this time but a fine-looking frame house, and "the only one in sight on this prairie"—when suddenly, without warning, the siren call to move came yet again.

"This past winter there has been a strange fever raging here," Keturah wrote in her memorandum. "It is the 'Oregon fever.' It seems to be contagious and it is raging terribly. Nothing seems to stop it but to tear up and take a six months trip across the plains with ox teams to the Pacific Ocean."

The first preparation she made, in the spring of 1847, was to return to Ohio to visit her parents. "I knew it would be the last visit I would make there whether I lived or not but I kept all these thots buried in my own breast and never told them that the folks at home were fixing to cross the plains." When the time came to say their farewells, "it was hard for me not to break down but they all thot in about two years we would come again."

The couple returned to Iowa to find an atmosphere even more fevered than before. Their beautiful new house had already been sold, and the Belknaps had to lodge with a neighbor. "Everything was out of place and all was excitement and commotion," Keturah remembered. "There was nothing done or talked of but what had Oregon in it and the loom was banging and the wheels buzzing and trades being made from daylight until bedtime."

To Francis Parkman, the scion of a wealthy East Coast family, the settlers he observed at Fort Laramie might have seemed like so many rude and ignorant backwoodsmen, but they were not poor. A typical outfit—wagons, oxen, provisions, and any other animals they planned to take with them— could cost anything between five hundred and one thousand dollars.* It could take families many years to save up enough funds.

Keturah would begin her preparations a full six months before they started on their journey. To keep the cost down, she was determined to make as many items as possible by hand. Even for someone of such remarkable resourcefulness and energy as Keturah Belknap, it was a formidable undertaking. "Now I will begin to work and plan to make everything with an eye to starting out on a six months trip," she wrote on November 15, 1847; "the first thing is to lay plans and then work up the program."

While the men busied themselves trading for oxen and making the ox yokes and bows for the wagon, Keturah set herself to make the covers for it. In order to do this, she had first not only to weave the cloth that she would need, but also to spin the thread from raw flax: "will spin mostly in the

*Figures are from Lillian Schlissel, *Women's Diaries of the Westward Journey.*

evenings while my husband reads to me. The little wheel in the corner don't make any noise. . . . I must work almost day and night to get the filling ready to keep the loom busy."

By February 1 the following year, she had woven enough fabric to make a start on the covers. These came in two parts: first a lining made from muslin, then a heavier outer cover made from linen. "They both have to be sewed real good and strong." In addition to the wagon covers, she also made "a new feather tick for my bed" and enough dip candles "to last all winter after we get to Oregon."

She also had to make enough clothes to last the year. As with the wagon covers, Keturah had begun early, by weaving the cloth herself, as she noted on November 15, 1847: "Have cut out four muslin shirts for George and two suits for the little boy (Jessie) with what he has that will last him (if he lives)* until he will want a different pattern." Later, she would cut out "two pair of pants for Geo. (home made jeans)" and a coat and vest. In order to make him a new suit, a tailor had been found to cut out the pieces, which were then stitched together at home with the help of her husband's aunt, Betsey.

"I try not to think of the parting time," she wrote, even as the months flew by.

"And now it is March [1848] and we have our team allready and in good condition—three good yoke of oxen and a good wagon. The company have arranged to start the 10th April. George is practicing with the oxen. I don't want to leave my kind friends here but they all think it best so I am anxious to get off."

"I think we are fixed up very comfortable for the trip," Keturah added. Their "company" would consist of Father Belknap and his wife (her parents-in-law), with one wagon pulled by four yoke of oxen; Keturah, George, and little Jessie would follow in a second wagon. In addition to their three yoke of oxen, they were also taking three horses and ten cows.

---

*Three of her other children had died, the latest, "my dear little girl Martha," having passed away just two weeks earlier, on October 30, leaving them with only "one puny boy."

By the beginning of April, their departure was imminent. With each day that passed, the tension mounted.

"This week I cook up something to last us a few days till we get used to camp fare," she wrote on April 6. "Bake bread, made a lot of crackers and fry doughnuts, cook a chicken, boil ham, and stew some dryed fruit. . . . Tomorrow is Sat. and next Tues. we start so will put in some things today. only one more Sunday here. . . . We have had our farewell [church] meeting so I won't go—don't think I could stand it."

Three days later, the wagon was ready to be loaded. "I am the first one up, breakfast is over [and] our wagon is backed up to the steps. we will load at the hind end and shove the things in front. The first thing is a big box that will just fit in the wagon bed that will have the bacon, salt, and various other things then it will be covered with a cover made of light boards nailed on two pieces of inch plank about 3 inches wide. this will serve us for a table. there is a hole in each corner and we have sticks sharpened at one end so they will stick in the ground then we put the box cover on, slip the legs in the holes and we have a nice table then when it is on the box George will sit on it and let his feet hang over and drive the team.

"Now we will put in the old chest that is packed with our clothes and things we will want to wear and use on the way. This till is the medicine chest. then there will be cleats fastened to the bottom of the wagon bed to keep things from slipping out of place. Now there is a vacant place clear across that will be large enough to sit a chair—will set it with the back against the side of the wagon bed there I will ride—on the other side will be a vacancy where little Jessie can play he has a few toys and some marbles and some sticks for whip stocks, some blocks for oxen and I tie a string on the stick and he uses my work box basket for a covered wagon and plays going to Oregon. He never seems to get tired or cross."

A second box was packed with a few dishes and "things we wont need till we get thru." Next came a number of huge sacks made of homemade linen, each of which held 125 pounds—four sacks of flour and one of corn-meal. After that, the groceries—a wall of smaller sacks of dried apples and peaches, beans, rice, sugar, and coffee, "the latter being in the green state. we will brown it in a skillet as we want to use it." Everything had to be stored in strong bags; "no paper wrappings for this trip." In one remaining empty corner went her washtub, in which her lunch basket would just fit. "I am going to start with good earthen dishes and if they get broken have tin ones to take their place." The pièce de résistance took the form of "4 nice little table cloths so I am going to live just like I was at home.

"The ironware that I will want to use every day will go in a box on the hind end of the wagon like a feed box now we are loaded all but the bed. then there is a side of sole leather that will go on first, then two comforts [quilts] and we have a good enough bed for any one to sleep on. At night I will turn my chair down to make the bed a little longer so now all we will have to do in the morning is put in the bed and make some coffee and roll out."

Finally, she was able to stand back and admire her handiwork. "The wagon looks so nice—the nice white cover drawn down tight to the side boards with a good ridge to keep from saging its high enough for me to stand straight under the roof with a curtain to put down in front and one at the back end . . . now all is done and I get out of the tumult."

Finally, the great day came—Tuesday, April 10, 1848.

"Daylight dawned with none awake but me I try to keep quiet so as not to wake up anyone but pretty soon Father Belknap's voice was heard with that well known sound: 'Wife, wife, rise and flutter' and there was no more quiet for anyone. breakfast is soon over—my dishes and food for lunch is packed away and put in its proper place. The iron things are packed in some old pieces of old thick rags. Now for the bed (feather) nicely folded and the pillows laid smoothly on, reserving one for the outside so if I or the little boy get sleepy we have a good place to lie."

Finally, after more than six months of preparation, they were ready to start. "I get in the wagon and in my chair busy with some unfinished work, Jessie is in his place with his whip starting for Oregon. George and the boys have one out in the field for the cattle. Dr. Walker calls at the wagon to see me and give me some good advice and give me the parting hand for neither of us could speak the word Farewell. He told me to keep up good courage and said 'don't fret, whatever happens don't fret and cry. courage will do more for you than anything else.' [Then] he took the little boy in his arms and presented to him a nice Bible with his blessing and was off.

"Now we roll out—Father B is in the lead on old Polly. Rant is driving the team. Cory is on our old Lize, driving the loose stock our wagon is number 2, G. W. Bethers number 3, J. W. Starr, 4, Uncle Brather two wagons, Chatman Hawley two wagons, and I think they all had one horse but Uncle John Starr he had two yoke of oxen to each wagon one wagon was a very shaky old thing they had their provisions in it and when they got it lightened up, they would put everything in one wagon and leave the old shack by the road side.

"Now we were fairly on the road, it is one o'clock we got started at 10, will stop for an hour and eat lunch and let the oxen chew their cuds. We have just got out of the neighborhood the friends that came a piece with us [have turned back] and we will travel on. Jessie and I have had a good nap and a good lunch and now we will ride some more. Evening we come to water and grass and plenty of wood—what hinders us from camping here? . . . Everyone seems hungry and we make fires and soon have supper fit for a king. I will make the first call and am the [only] one that has a table and—it has a clean white cloth on."

4

JUMPING OFF

K eturah Belknap and her family reached Saint Joseph, Missouri, on April 23, 1848.

By the mid-1840s, the emigration had become sufficiently well established for a pattern to have emerged. Every spring, prospective settlers such as the Belknaps would assemble en masse at one of several "jumping-off" border settlements on the Missouri River—Saint Joseph and Independence, Missouri, being the principal ones*—to make their final preparations for the journey. By now, most people were aware of the imperative to cross the Missouri and be heading toward the Platte River by the end of April at the latest. The timing was essential: any earlier, and there would not be enough grass for their livestock to graze on; any later, and they ran the risk of the trails through the mountains being cut off by snow.

The year the Belknaps arrived at Saint Joseph, four thousand other settlers and their wagons, carts, and teeming flocks of cattle, sheep, mules, horses, and oxen arrived with them, all within a few weeks of each other. "As

---

*Others included Westport (Kansas City), Liberty, and Council Bluffs (Kanesville).

far as the eye can reach, so great is the emigration, you see nothing but wagons," wrote one woman. "This town presents a striking appearance—a vast army on wheels—crowds of men, women and lots of children and last but not least the cattle and horses on which our lives depend."[57]

The Missouri River settlements were no longer the small trading posts they had been just a few years previously. Within those few years, Saint Joseph and Independence had become thriving, cosmopolitan boomtowns. It was here, in these noisy streets ringing with the sounds of human activity, that the settler crowds would be able to buy any last-minute supplies, complete any outfitting that needed to be done, and make any repairs to their wagons and carts. Here too could be found dozens of grocery shops, bakeries, general stores, and even hotels. The business owners of Independence took out an advertisement in the *Daily Missouri Republican* that read: "Provisions and Implements of every kind suited to the wants of emigrants." These included "several large Wagon and Carriage Manufactories, in which are between 40 and 50 forges. These have on hand a large number of Baggage and Spring Wagons and Carriages, made expressly for emigrants, which may be bought from $80 to $100 . . . three large Saddlery establishments, which have on hand large and superior stocks of Saddles, Harness, etc, suitable for the Plains; one very extensive Hat manufactory; 2 gunsmiths and two tinshops."[58]

For a woman such as Keturah Belknap, used to a quiet country life, the experience must have been overwhelming. She would have been amazed, too, at the sheer diversity of the people who thronged the streets. Independence, in particular, was not only a gateway to the West, but the terminus of the Santa Fe Trail, the principal trading route with Mexico. Even before the emigration had got underway, these Missouri River trading posts had been frequented by an astonishingly cosmopolitan mix of nationalities, from French fur trappers and Scottish sportsmen to the Mexican, American, Spanish, German, and Jewish traders plying their goods along the Santa Fe Trail.* Here,

---

*The Santa Fe Trail, the most important overland trade route between the United States and Mexico, predated the emigrant trails by several decades.

too, Native Americans could be found from many different Tribes, also eager to trade. Sometimes these were individuals or small groups who had come to barter their buffalo robes for lead and gunpowder, while others had built up sophisticated business ventures with the Santa Fe Trail traders. The Wyandotte chief William Walker would lease an entire warehouse in Independence on his Tribe's behalf.[59]

African Americans also played a prominent part in the evolution of these Missouri outfitting towns. Despite the fact that Missouri, which had entered the Union as recently as 1821, was a slave state, by midcentury a small but significant population of freemen and women lived and worked there.* Among their many thriving enterprises was a highly successful wagon-manufacturing business belonging to an African American couple, Hiram and Matilda Young, which in one year alone (1860) produced three hundred wagons and six thousand ox yokes.[†] Emily Fisher, also a former slave, managed one of Independence's best hotels on behalf of her owner, Adam Fisher. Fisher, who was also Emily's father, had manumitted her when she was in her early forties, and when he died, he left the hotel to Emily in his will. She continued to run her hotel with great success, opening its doors to Black and white guests alike (almost unheard of for the times), thereby becoming Independence's first African American businesswoman.

It was in this richly diverse and energetic potpourri of nationalities and ethnicities that settlers now found themselves. Inevitably, it did not always go well. The overlanders may have brought large amounts of business with

---

*Some 3,572 in 1860.

†This remarkable man and woman had both started life as slaves in Tennessee. Hiram Young was so skilled as a carpenter that he had been able to save up enough money to buy both his own freedom and that of his wife, Matilda. The Youngs employed both white and Black men in their business ventures, many of the latter being slaves from the surrounding plantations. By paying their Black workers equal wages to that of their white employees, they made it possible for many of these enslaved people to buy their own freedom, as the Youngs themselves had done. The census of 1860 ranked Hiram Young as one of the wealthiest men in Jackson County, with real estate valued at thirty-six thousand dollars and personal property at twenty-thousand dollars. See Shirley Ann Wilson Moore, *Sweet Freedom's Plains*. Also, memorabilia in the Independence Jail Museum.

them, but they also made these border towns edgy places, magnets for gamblers, conmen, swindlers, and desperados of all kinds. Whisky flowed "more freely . . . than is altogether safe in a place where every man carries a loaded pistol in his pocket."[60] Settlers, many of whom carried their life savings with them, were frequent victims not only of scams (perhaps the "backwoodsmen" encountered by Francis Parkman had learned a thing or two after all) but also of "holdups, assaults, and even murder."[61] Former slave Mary McDonald, traveling overland with her husband, would take the precaution every night of burying all her money and valuables in a tin box under the ground.

In fact, robbery was perhaps the least of the potential difficulties faced by African Americans. Unlike whites, free to travel wherever and with whomever they wished, Black settlers enjoyed no such privilege. Whereas the great April assemblage on the banks of the Missouri River was, for most whites, undoubtedly the easiest part of their journey, for Blacks it was potentially the most dangerous.

Like all slave states, Missouri had been quick to pass laws that controlled every aspect of the lives of its Black population. Freemen and women, even successful business owners such as the Youngs and Emily Fisher, were required to carry a license or risk being apprehended as runaway slaves. Free African Americans from anywhere else in the United States were prohibited from entering Missouri unless they had papers to prove their citizenhood in another state. Even if they had found a wagon outfit willing to take them (as many of them did, often for a flat fee that would cover their board and sleeping arrangements), they too ran the very real risk of being apprehended and losing their freedom.*

Under these conditions, simply arriving at the frontier was an undertaking fraught with danger. Since a recaptured slave could fetch between twenty-five and one hundred dollars (and would be sold on for many times

---

*The Missouri Supreme Court had ruled that "in all slaveholding States color raises the presumption of slavery, and until the contrary is shown, a man or woman of color is deemed to be a slave." See Shirley Ann Wilson Moore, *Sweet Freedom's Plains*.

that amount), slave hunting presented rich pickings for bounty hunters. Heavily armed bands of these "border ruffians" regularly patrolled the Missouri and its environs with packs of bloodhounds, looking for prey. One former slave would later recall the sheer terror these men inspired. "I remember some tough men driving like mad through our place many times, with big chains rattling. We called them slave hunters. They always came in big bunches. Five and six together on horseback."[62] The auction blocks in Saint Joseph, and on the steps of the courthouse in Independence, did a brisk trade, their auctioneers "ratt[ling] away as if [they] were selling a steer."[63]

It was a situation that made African Americans highly vulnerable, not only to slave hunters but also to other unscrupulous whites. In 1853, Carlotta Gordon Pyles, a recently manumitted slave from Kentucky, attempted to travel through Missouri with her husband, Harry, together with eighteen members of their extended family.[*] This sizeable party was to be accompanied by Carlotta's former owner, Frances Gordon, but even the presence of a white woman on their journey was not enough to keep them safe. Mrs. Gordon had also arranged for a white minister, an Ohioan sympathetic to their plight, to join them.

At first all went well. The party traveled from Kentucky through Illinois, finally arriving safely by river steamer at Saint Louis, Missouri. Once across state lines, however, their nerves became increasingly frayed. Even as free Blacks, since they could not as yet claim residency in any other state, much less provide the required papers, the entire Pyles family could be apprehended at any time. So fearful for their safety did they now become that Frances Gordon decided to engage another man, Nathan Stone, as a bodyguard to escort them all safely across the state. The fee was agreed at one hundred dollars (the equivalent today of over three thousand dollars), but when the morning came for them to set off, Stone refused to move until he had extorted a further fifty dollars, threatening to expose the Pyles and

---

*Kentucky law prevented Carlotta from staying on in her home state after her manumission.

"turn them over to slaveholders in Missouri" if they did not comply. To her eternal credit, Frances Gordon paid up.[64]

WHITE SETTLERS, EVEN IF they were aware of these dangers, rarely refer to them. They were in any case too busy with their own affairs to pay them much heed. Once any last-minute preparations had been completed, two more major tasks now awaited them before they could finally be on their way.

The first was to cross the Missouri itself, no small undertaking with all their wagons and livestock in tow. "All are on the stir to get to the wharf before the other company gets here and now begins the scene of danger," Keturah Belknap wrote in her memorandum. "The river is high and looks terrific, one wagon and two yoke of oxen go over first so as to have a team to take the wagons out of the way—it is just a rope ferry. All back safe. Now they take two wagons and the loose horses. They say it will take about a day to get us over. Next the loose cattle must go as they are in a dry lot without any thing to eat. When they put the cattle on the boat they found that one of our cows was sick—she had been poisoned by eating the Jimson weeds.* She staggered when she walked on the ferry and in the crowd she was knocked over board and went under but when she came up the boat man had his rope ready and throwed it out and lassoed her and they hauled her to land."[65]

Once they were safely over the river, a further task awaited them. The custom had quickly arisen among settlers of dividing themselves up into companies, each one becoming known by the name of the man, or men, who had been voted in as leaders. Not surprisingly, the path to this particular honor did not always run smooth. "They have had quite a time with the election of officers," Keturah Belknap wrote drily, "every man wants an office." Each newly formed company would now decide upon a set of rules,

---

*Also known as "devil's snare," jimsonweed is a plant species in the nightshade family and highly toxic.

an informal covenant agreed by all in advance, which all members of the company undertook to observe on the journey.

Finally, after all the long months of anticipation, they were off at last. In quasi-military style, the day would begin with a roll call, to which "everyone is expected to answer to his name," Keturah wrote. Then "the order is for the first one hitched up to 'roll out,' so we are ahead on the lead today—then the Beathers [their neighbors from Illinois] next, but tomorrow we will be behind."

The first part of their journey, turning north along the feeder trails from the Missouri settlements as far as the Platte River and then due west across the prairies, was, as the missionaries Eliza Spalding and Narcissa Whitman had discovered more than a decade ago now, easy traveling. There was enough water and plenty of grazing, and at this point their own supplies were still plentiful. As Sarah Damron Owens had noted in 1843, the feeling of elation at having at last started out was infectious, making the atmosphere more like a holiday or a Sunday school outing. "It is so jolly to be going across the continent," wrote another young woman at the beginning of her journey west; "it is like a picnic every day for months; I was always sorry picnic days were so short, and now it will be an all summer picnic."[66]

Ever practical, Keturah had soon got to work to make things comfortable, baking batches of corn bread on her skillet each evening, and once even using her supply of dried apples to make "mince pies." She soon learned some of the tricks of the prairie housekeepers' trade. At night she would milk her remaining milch cows (the cow poisoned by the jimsonweed had eventually been used as part of a trade to get them over the river and had been left behind), "and strain the milk in little buckets and cover them up and set them on the ground under the wagon and in the morning I take off the nice thick cream and put it in the churn . . . and after riding all day I hav a nice roll of butter."

Not for nothing were the wide-open prairies compared to a sea. One woman, who made the journey to Oregon when she was a little girl of nine, remembered how "not being accustomed to riding in a covered wagon, the motion made us all sick, and the uncomfortableness of the situation was increased from the fact that it had set into rain, which made it impossible to roll back the cover and let in the fresh air. It also caused a damp and musty smell that was very nauseating. It took several weeks to overcome this 'sea-sickness.'"[67]

A landscape that looked flat and smooth in the distance was anything but. Breaking their way through the heavy sagebrush "was so hard on the lead team of oxen that their legs were soon bruised and bleeding, so each wagon had to take its turn at the head of the train for half a day, then drop to the rear." Then there were the prickly pears to contend with. "We children were barefooted and I can remember how we limped across that desert, for we cut the soles of our feet on the prickly pears," wrote one overlander of 1845. It was not only the humans who suffered, but the livestock too. "The prickly pears also made the oxen lame, for the spines would work in between the oxen's hoofs."[68]

But they saw wonders too. After many weeks of traveling, the monotonous and almost-featureless expanse of prairie gave way to a chain of strangely shaped bluffs and rock formations: Chimney Rock, "like some vast giant leaning against the distant clouds, standing sentinel at the entrance to an enchanted fairy-land," and Scott's Bluff, which seemed to one romantically inclined observer "as if the wand of a magician had passed over a city, and like that in the Arabian Nights, had converted all living things to stone. Here you saw the minarets of a castle; there, the loop-holes of bastions of a fort; again the frescos of a huge temple . . . while at other points Chinese temples . . . made it appear as if by some supernatural cause had been dropped in the suburbs of a mighty city."[69]

But even the sight of marvels such as these was not always enough to keep up their spirits entirely. As the journey progressed, the holiday elation soon wore off. The company rules, generally signed up to before the start of the journey, could not always prevent disagreements, fights, or sometimes worse from breaking out. The bad behavior of just one member of the company could seriously endanger the lives of the entire company.

When the Bonney family—husband, wife, and seven children—traveled to Oregon in 1845, it was a Texan named Jim Kinney who did the damage. Kinney, in the Bonneys' view, was "a typical southerner. He had long black hair, long black moustache, heavy black eyebrows, and was tall and heavy, weighing about 225 pounds." He also had a violent temper "and was a good deal of a desperado." Everyone in the party, even his own wife, was afraid of him.

One day, they came across a man (his Tribe is not named), and when Kinney saw him, he called to his driver to stop his ox team. "Going back to the wagon he got a pair of handcuffs and started back to where the Indian was. The Indian had no idea Kinney meant any harm to him." When Mr. Bonney asked him what he was going to do with him, Kinney replied, "'Where I came from we have slaves. I am going to capture that Indian and take him with me as a slave.'" Seeing the look of horror on the faces of his companions, he added, "'I generally have my way. Any man that crosses me, regrets it. I had to kill two or three men already because they interfered with me. If you want any trouble you know how to get it.'"

The rest of the party could only look on as the Texan jumped off his mule and beat the man over the head. "[He] put up a fight but was no match for Kinney. In a moment or two Kinney had knocked him down and gotten his hand cuffs on him and dragged him to the hack."

The plea that he was endangering the lives of the entire party by this unprovoked attack, and that the man's Tribe would surely take their revenge when it was discovered, fell upon deaf ears. "He would not obey the train rules but he was such a powerful man and apparently held life so lightly that no one wanted to cross him."

To their dismay, Jim Kinney then told his wife to hand him his black-snake whip, which, clearly being every bit as afraid of him as the rest of the party, she did. When the company finally moved on, Kinney rode behind, slashing his captive across his naked shoulders with the black-snake whip as he went. Finally, the man threw himself on the ground "and was pulled along by the neck. Kinney kept slashing him to make him get up, till finally the Indian got up and trotted along behind the hack."

They traveled on like this for ten days, with Kinney riding behind the man, still whipping him across his naked shoulders in order to, what he called, "break his spirit." After that he did not tie his captive up at night, boasting that he would rely on the hound dog he had brought with him, which he had often used in Texas to hunt down runaway slaves. "He said if the Indian ran away the dog would pick up his trail and he could follow him and kill him to show the other Indians the superiority of the white man. He said he had killed plenty of negros and an Indian was no better than a negro."

Happily, on this occasion at least, Kinney got his comeuppance. After three weeks of this abuse, the captive escaped, taking with him a blanket as well as Kinney's favorite rifle, worth one hundred dollars, his powder horn, some lead, and three hams. The Texan's rage was terrible to behold—"I never saw a man in such a temper in all my life"—but the man was never seen again. "Everyone in the train rejoiced that the Indian had escaped but they all appeared to sympathize with Kinney for they were afraid of being killed if they showed any signs of satisfaction."[70]

FOR MARY RICHARDSON WALKER, too, the stresses of the six-month overland journey were far more than the merely physical (although just the thought of "how comfortable father's hogs were" compared to her own filthy, wet, diarrhea-stricken condition was often enough to make her cry). The psychological strains of the journey among almost-total strangers would prove far harder to bear.

In 1838, Mary Richardson Walker became one of four missionary women who, when the success of the Whitman-Spalding expedition became known, elected to follow them to Oregon.* Like Eliza and Narcissa before her, Mary had married a man she barely knew in order to achieve her dream of becoming a missionary, "a tall and rather awkward gentleman" called Elkanah Walker. Despite some understandable misgivings, not to say panic, at the thought of what she was about to do—"I almost felt in the morning as if I wanted to throw the bargain off on to someone else"—the couple married on March 5, 1838.

Just a month later, Elkanah and his newly pregnant wife set off for Oregon. Mary's emotional state, one that she would battle on an almost-daily basis in her diary, is poignantly revealed in an entry made shortly after her marriage. "Nothing gives me such a solitary feeling as to be called Mrs. Walker," she wrote sadly. "It would sound so sweet to have someone now and then call me Mary or by mistake say Miss Richardson. But that one expression, Mrs. W., seems at once to indicate a change unlike all other changes. My father, my mother, my brothers, my sisters all answer to the name of Richardson. The name W. seems to me to imply a severed branch."[71]

Unlike both Narcissa Whitman and Eliza Spalding, however, neither of whom were much given to introspection in their diaries, Mary Richardson Walker wrote often, and vividly, about her feelings on the journey. In addition to the dislocation of having left everything familiar behind her, she was also struggling to get to know a man she barely knew.

"Tuesday, April 24th. Rested well on my ground bedstead and should feel much better if Mr. W. would only treat me with more cordiality. It is so

---

*The others were Sarah Gilbert White Smith, Myra Fairbanks Eells, and Mary Augusta Dix Gray. The latter's husband was the William Gray who had attached himself to the Whitman-Spalding expedition of 1836. On witnessing the enthusiastic reception that the missionaries had been given at the Rendezvous of '36, Gray had determined to return east and bring back his own bride-to-be. The following year, 1837, he left the annual Rendezvous ahead of the fur-company caravan, against all advice to the contrary. Exactly as the mountain men had predicted, Gray was ambushed by Lakota at Ash Hollow, in present-day Nebraska, and narrowly escaped with his life (all four of his Native American companions were killed). Mary Dix was William Gray's second choice of wife. The first had hastily broken off her engagement at the sight of two bullet holes in her prospective bridegroom's hat.

hard to please him I almost despair of ever being able. If I stir it is forward-ness, if I am still, it is inactivity. I keep trying to please but sometimes I feel it is no use. I am almost certain more is expected of me than can be had of one woman."

The misgivings she had about her new husband were matched only by those she felt about the rest of their party, particularly the three other mis-sionary couples, William and Mary Augusta Gray, Asa and Sarah Smith, and Cushing and Myra Eells. The stresses and strains of this thoroughly ill-matched party were evident from the very outset. "I never saw such a cross party before," Mary wrote. Asa Smith was "as short as pie crust" and "acted hoggish" by taking more than his fair share of food, while Mrs. Smith "tried my patience talking about Gray as she calls [him] all the time. I wish she could see how much like him only worse she acts."

The fact that they were sharing a tent with only the flimsiest of curtains between them only added to the general tension. The appalling weather conditions did not help anyone's temper, and soon it became clear that it was not only Mary who was having doubts. Even at the beginning of May it was bitterly cold. On the sixth she wrote: "Last night a frost. Ice in the pail . . . Had no idea that we were to experience so much wind and cold. Some of our company expressed regret that they have undertaken the jour-ney, I suspect more from aversion to the toil than real dread of sin."

The fluctuations of Mary's mood depended to a great extent on that of her husband, whom she was pitifully anxious to please. "May 7th: Mr. W took an emetic & some calomel. My own health good. Should feel quite happy if my dear husband were as well & in such good spirits as myself. Our company still have a good deal of unpleasantness about them."

But her own constitution was suffering too. By June she was "consider-ably out of health." She was bled, and, not surprisingly, "came near fainting" as a result. Combined with her pregnancy, then still in its vulnerable early stages, it made her not only sick but exhausted and prey to dark thoughts. "Very tired," she wrote wearily on June 6. "Everything almost excites my fears. It would be so bad to be sick in such circumstances. . . . Think bleeding did me good tho it reduced my strength more than I expected."

Pregnancy and ill health, however severe, were never reasons enough to stop the wagon train. Even under these most testing of conditions, Mary was still riding up to forty-five miles in one day. Small wonder that she was haunted by thoughts of what might go wrong. Supposing she miscarried? Or went into early labor?

Sabbath, June 10: "My health is at present rather feeble & I find it difficult to keep up a usual amount of cheerfulness. If I were to yield to inclination I should cry half the time without knowing what for. My circumstances are rather trying," she added hopelessly. "So much danger attends me on every hand. A long journey before me, going I know not whither, without mother or sister to attend me, can I expect to survive it all?"[72]

(It is hardly surprising that women sometimes snapped. "While I am writing I have an exciting experience," Keturah Belknap wrote. "Geo[rge] is out on guard and in the next wagon behind ours a man and a woman are quarreling she wants to turn back and he wont. So she says she will go and leave him . . . with the children and he will have a good time with that crying baby. Then he used some very bad words and said he would put it out of the way—just then I heard a muffled cry and a heavy thud as tho something was thrown against the wagon box and she said 'Oh you've killed it' and he swore some more and told her to keep her mouth shut or he would give her some of the same.")[73]

Mary Richardson Walker is unusual in that she mentions her condition at all. Taboos surrounding pregnancy and childbirth were so great that few women ever talked about it, even in their most private diaries. It gives an added poignancy to those, like Mary, who did occasionally voice their anxieties.

---

*She adds later that the baby was not killed.

Perhaps partly to do with these taboos, which would have prevented any useful discussion, it does not seem to have occurred to anyone that a woman's pregnancy might be reason enough not to set off on a grueling 2,200-mile trek. Babies were born so frequently on the trail that their arrival was almost commonplace, despite the fact that many were brought into the world under unspeakably awful conditions. One woman, pregnant herself, described how one of her fellow travelers gave birth in a storm so violent that rain had flooded all the wagons. "Within a tent, during the storm, were nurses *wading* around a bedside placed upon chairs ministering to a mother and new-born babe."[74]

More typical, however, was a casual one line, often uttered by the new mother herself, to the effect that her baby had been born, with no previous mention at all of her condition. Other members of the family seem to have been kept equally in the dark. "On 22nd May we were surprised by the arrival of another little sister," wrote nine-year-old Catherine Sager.

A photograph exists of Catherine Sager, taken in her late middle age, when her overland journey to Oregon would have been no more than a distant childhood memory. With a mass of glossy brown hair (probably a hairpiece) piled on top of her head and a neat lace comforter pinned with a brooch at her neck, there is not much to distinguish the portrait from that of any other woman of her time and place. It is only her piercingly level gaze and a certain doggedness about the set of her mouth that give any indication of the extraordinary and turbulent events to which she bore witness.

Catherine Sager traveled to Oregon in 1844. Her parents, Henry (originally Heinrich) and Naomi Sager, were a Virginian couple of Swiss German descent. They had six children: John (fourteen), Francis (twelve), Catherine (nine), Elizabeth (seven), Matilda (five), and Louisa, aged just three. Their seventh child, Henrietta—the surprising arrival of May 22—was, like so many children, born on the trail.

Disasters in various forms had plagued the Sagers from the outset. First, the team of oxen pulling their wagon ran up a too-narrow embankment and the wagon overturned, almost killing Naomi, who "for a long time lay insensible" on the ground. Luckily, on this occasion there was no real damage done and soon they were on their way.

It was not long before disaster struck again. Catherine was playing on the front of the wagon when the hem of her dress became caught in one of the axle-handles, throwing her under the wheels of the wagon and badly crushing one of her legs. "Seeing me clear of the wheels, [Father] picked me up and carrying me in his arms ran to stop the team, which had become unmanageable from fright. A glance at my limb dangling in the air as he ran, revealed to himself the extent of the injury I had received, and in a broken voice he exclaimed, 'My dear child, your leg is broken all to pieces.'"[75]

News of the accident quickly spread along the train of wagons, and a halt was soon called. Fortunately, among the settlers there was a Dutch doctor, Dr. Dagen, who was able to set her leg, but Catherine would be forced to remain inside the wagon for the rest of their journey.

Catherine and her mother, still weak from her recent confinement, were not the only ones to suffer. Camp sickness—in this case, probably typhoid—now broke out throughout the company and Henry Sager and the two eldest children, John and Francis, all came down with it. While the family was in this already thoroughly weakened state, disaster struck for the third time. In an effort to run off four buffalo that had come between their wagon and the one behind, Henry seized his gun and gave chase, but the exertion proved too much for him. It soon became apparent to his stricken family that their father was dying. "He himself was fully aware that he was passing away and he could not be reconciled to the thought of leaving a large and helpless family in such circumstances as they were placed," Catherine would recall. "Looking upon me as I lay helpless by his side, he said, 'Poor child! What will become of you?'"

Later that day, their company's leader, Captain Shaw, came to see him. He found Henry weeping bitterly. "He informed the Captain that his hour had come, and his heart was filled with anguish on account of his family." His wife was still very ill, and his children were all so young, with one (Catherine herself) likely to be crippled for a long time to come. The fact that the Sagers had no other relatives, either in the company or in Oregon, and a long journey still before them only added to his anguish. "He begged the Captain in piteous tones to take charge of them and see them safely through. The Captain assured him that he would do as he requested him, to the best of his ability. Father expired the next morning, and was buried on the bank of the Green River, his coffin consisted of two troughs hastily dug out of the trunk of a tree."[76]

Responsibility for the entire family now devolved upon Mrs. Sager. Still weak from the birth of her baby just three months previously, she now began to sink completely. "The nights and mornings were bitter cold; and the exposure to which she was necessarily subject produced a violent cold. But although consumed with fever and afflicted with the sore mouth that was the forerunner of the fatal camp fever, she refused to give up, but fought bravely against disease and sickness for the sake of her children."

On September 1 they reached Fort Hall. Although Mrs. Sager was not confined to her bed, she was still "in too feeble a condition" to do much. Soon she was delirious. "Her suffering was intense," her daughter recalled, "unable to make her wants known, and traveling over a road so dusty that a cloud of dust covered the train all day." To screen her as much as possible, a sheet was hung up across the entrance to the wagon, "making the air within close and suffocating." In this state of delirium, she babbled "continuously" about her husband; sometimes, to the great distress of her children, as if she believed he were actually present. In these long, rambling conversations she would beseech him "in piteous tones to relieve her of her sufferings." As the hours went on, she became unconscious, "making only a low moan."

The kindhearted women of the train continued to care for Naomi Sager as much as they could. They took the baby, Henrietta, and at the end of the day when the wagon train came to a halt they would stop by to help wash the dust from her face "and otherwise make her comfortable." But it was no use.

"The day she died we traveled over a very rough road, and she moaned pitifully all day," her daughter remembered. "When we camped at night, one of the women came in as usual to wash her. To her inquiry if she wished her face washed, she made no reply as she had done at former times; and the woman, supposing her to be asleep, washed her face, and then taking her hand to cleanse it, she discovered that the pulse was nearly gone and instantly called some others. She lived but a few moments more and her last words were, 'Oh, Henry, if only you knew how much we have suffered.'"

The Sager children buried their mother that same day. A grave was dug beside the road, with a bed of willow brush laid on the bottom. The corpse, sewn up in a sheet, was then placed inside, and on top a second layer of willow brush; then the earth was filled in. A headboard with her name and age was fixed beside the grave. "The teams were then hitched to the wagon and the train drove on, leaving her to her long sleep."

Within the space of just three weeks the Sager children had lost both their parents. What would become of them now?

For the remainder of the journey, the seven orphans were treated with extraordinary kindness by the rest of their company, particularly by Captain Shaw and his wife. The baby was taken on entirely by one of the women, and the rest were looked after, "in fact literally adopted," by the remaining company. "When our flour gave out they gave us bread as long as they had any, even dividing their last loaf with us." But it was not the same as being cared for by their parents.

The Sagers seem to have been unusually accident-prone children. One night, three-year-old Louisa almost froze to death when she rolled out of the wagon and onto the ground; another sister caught fire "and would have burned to death had it not been for the timely aid of the Doctor"; and later in the journey, in the middle of a hurricane, twelve-year-old Frank accidentally blew himself up when he poured too much gunpowder onto their fire in an effort to get it started (amazingly he survived, losing only his eyebrows and eyelashes in the resulting explosion).

It was in this absolutely pitiful state that, toward the end of October, they finally reached their destination, the haven that for weeks "had been a subject of our talk by day and formed our dreams at night." This haven was none other than the Whitman Mission.

The Sager children had survived their terrible ordeal, but only just. On her deathbed, Mrs. Sager's last request had been that her family should all be kept together. Everyone else in the company knew that this was an impossibility. Who would take on seven children, the youngest a five-month-old baby, still so small and weak that she seemed certain to die?

Captain Shaw, who had taken over the responsibility for the children after Mrs. Sager died, knew that there was only one faint hope. Knowing the Whitmans from his previous journeys to Oregon, when he was within reach of their mission he had ridden ahead to appraise Narcissa of the children's story, and to see if she could help. She had agreed immediately but said that she could only take on the girls. The Sagers were now faced with yet another agonizing parting.

A lifetime later, Catherine Sager would remember that moment with searing precision. Their cart had pulled up at "a large, white house surrounded by palisades." As though in a dream, she had looked toward it and had seen Captain Shaw conversing with Mrs. Whitman. "Glancing out through the window she saw us, and turning to her he said, 'Your children have come; will you go out and see them?'" He then came out and told the boys to help the girls out and to find their bonnets. "Alas, it was easier to talk about bonnets than to find them," and it was only after "a considerable search [that] one or two were found."

It was almost more than the traumatized children could bear. "Here was a scene for the pen of an artist," Catherine would recall. "Foremost stood the little cart with the tired oxen lying near. Sitting in the front end of the cart was John weeping bitterly. On the opposite side stood Francis with his arms resting on the wheels and his head resting on them sobbing out loud. On the near side the little girls stood huddled together, bareheaded and barefooted, looking first at the boys and then at the house, dreading we knew not what."

The captain's wife, Mrs. Shaw, would later recount how "she never saw a more pitiful sight than that cartload of lonely orphans going to find a home among strangers."

When Narcissa Whitman came out of the house at last, they were confronted by "a large, well-formed woman, fair complexioned, with beautiful auburn hair, nose rather large, and large grey eyes. She had on a dark calico dress and a gingham sunbonnet; and as we shyly looked at her we thought that she was the prettiest woman we had ever seen." She spoke kindly to them, "but like frightened sheep we ran behind the cart, peeping out shyly around at her."

Seeing Catherine's lameness, Narcissa took her by the hand to help her, and "took my little sister with the other hand," the others following behind. As they reached the steps of the house, Captain Shaw turned to her and asked her if she had any children of her own. "Pointing to a grave at the foot of a hill not far off, she said 'All the child I ever had sleeps yonder' and remarked that it was a great pleasure to her that she could see the grave from the door."

When they were all inside, Mrs. Whitman seated herself in her armchair. She placed the youngest on her lap, and "calling us around her she asked us our names and all about our parents and the baby, often exclaiming as we related our artless story: 'Poor children!'"

"While thus engaged Dr. Whitman came in from the mill, and stood in the door looking as though surprised at the large addition so suddenly made to his family. Indeed, we were a sight well calculated to excite surprise," Catherine remembered, "dirty and sunburnt until we looked more like Indians than white children. Adding to this, John had cropped our hair, so that it hung in uneven locks and added to our uncouth appearance." When Narcissa saw her husband in the doorway she laughed and said simply, "Come in, Doctor, and see your children."

In the end, in what must have seemed like nothing short of a miracle to the rest of the company, Narcissa agreed to adopt not just the girls, but the boys too. What none of them could have known, as they gathered around her chair that autumn day, was that this was just a reprieve. An even greater tragedy—more desperate, and more violent still—was waiting for them, sounding faintly, like a roll of thunder in the distance.

5

THE WHITMAN MISSION

W hen the Sager children arrived at the Whitman Mission, grieving and destitute, it seemed to them like little short of paradise.
It was now eight years since Narcissa and Marcus had first
arrived in Oregon. On leaving Fort Vancouver in the winter of 1836, they
had decided upon a place called Waiilatpu, on the banks of the Walla Walla
River not far from the Hudson's Bay Company's fort, where their intention
was to minister to the Cayuse, a neighboring Tribe to the Nez Percé.* By
1844, the humble adobe cabin they had first built had been torn down and
replaced with another much bigger house. Surrounding it was a prosperous
settlement, almost a village, spread out over thirty fenced acres of Cayuse
Tribal land.

Catherine Sager would recall her amazement on her arrival there, when
instead of the expected log houses "occupied by Indians and such folks as

*Partly due to the hostility that Henry Spalding still evinced for Narcissa, the Spaldings had
gone on to build their own separate mission, at Lapwai, a hundred and twenty miles distant,
among the Nez Percé.

we had seen about the forts" they saw that "large, white house surrounded by palisades." Nearby was another large adobe dwelling, originally built for William Gray but now used as a granary. There was also a grist mill, a mill pond, a blacksmith's shop, two large corrals for their substantial herds of cows and horses, corn cribs, a harness house, a smoke house, and a poultry yard. Large irrigation ditches had been placed all around the property. Marcus had also built a sawmill about twenty miles away and had written to the Mission Board requesting a threshing mill for his wheat and a corn thresher, articles that arrived in 1847.

From the windows of their new home, the Sagers would have been able to look out on Narcissa's neatly planted orchard of seventy-five apple trees, some of which, that very autumn, were already bearing fruit. A nursery of young peach trees, currant bushes, and locust trees were waiting to be planted nearby.

Not only time but considerable resources had been spent on achieving this level of prosperity. Not everyone approved. Henry Spalding, whose far-humbler mission at Lapwai would never achieve anything like this apparent affluence, was one. "I am astonished that anybody should let their eyes pass over the station at Waiilatpu with its mill, blacksmith shop & its large & commodious dwelling houses put up at great expense & with the aid of much hired help," he wrote in a letter to the board in October 1842. "One completed by an accomplished workman with large window blinds & richly painted doors, floors & many nice tables, settees, &c &c, richly painted & varnished, servants &c, scores of cattle, horses, & hogs, without being at all alarmed for the future, but as soon as the eye caught a glance of my old log-cabins, nothing could be seen but the germ of a costly establishment."[77]

For all Henry Spalding's sour views about the inappropriate opulence of the mission at Walla Walla, the Whitmans' attempts to bring the Christian faith to the Cayuse had started with much optimism on both sides. The Cayuse were taught prayers, and Narcissa had made good efforts to start a school for the children, teaching them to sing (something at which she had always excelled). "A strong desire is manifest in them all to understand the truth & to be taught," she wrote. She also made attempts to teach the women to spin, weave, and sew but found them "too proud to be seen usefully employed." The truth was that her energies were spread too thinly, over too many other tasks, ever to amount to much (although Marcus, as a medical doctor, would at the beginning prove to be more useful).

An abyss of cultural misunderstanding lay between the two sides. Whereas the missionaries thought they were going to convert and thereby "civilize" the poor "benighted heathen," the Cayuse and the Nez Percé themselves had a very different understanding of what the Whitmans could provide.

It is important to remember that the Cayuse had not simply allowed the Whitmans to walk uninvited onto their lands. As early as 1835, on Marcus's first expedition to the Rocky Mountains, both the Cayuse and the Nez Percé had actively encouraged the missionaries to come to them, as the ecstatic welcome they received at the Rendezvous suggests. Like many other nations throughout the continent, the Cayuse saw them as powerful spiritual leaders, perhaps not unlike their own medicine people. The mission they would establish would be "a concrete expression" of the newcomers' largesse—both material and spiritual—and of their willingness to share their power.[78]

For all these cheerful beginnings, mutual disillusionment was quick to set in. From Narcissa's point of view, the main bone of contention was a practical one. The Cayuse, she claimed, brought fleas and lice into her house and made it impossible for her to keep her house clean. "At present the Indians have full liberty to visit the kitchen," she wrote on February 18, 1837, just a few months after moving to Waiilatpu, "but as soon as we are able to prepare a separate room for them they will not be allowed to come in any other part of the house at all."

Keeping the Cayuse, the very people she had come to help, out of her home soon became an obsession. In another heartfelt letter to her mother, she explained: "The greatest trial to a woman's feelings is to have her cooking and eating room always filled with four or five or more Indians—men—especially at meal time—but we hope this trial is nearly done for when we get into our other house we have a room there we devote to them especially, and shall not permit them to go into the other part of the house at all. They are so filthy they make a great deal of cleaning wherever they go, and this wears out a woman very fast. We must clean after them, for we have come to elevate them and not to suffer ourselves to sink down to their standard. I hardly know how to describe my feelings at the prospect of a clean, comfortable house, and one large enough so that I can find a closet to pray in."

The Whitmans had tried to persuade the Cayuse to build their own house for worshipping in, but they had refused. The Whitmans were there to serve them, not the other way round, and they soon made their position clear. "They said they would not do it, but would worship in our new house. . . . We told them our house was to live in and we could not have them worship there for they would make it so dirty and fill it so full of fleas that we could not live in it."[79]

Accustomed to communal living, the Cayuse not only did not understand Narcissa's need for privacy but were also deeply offended by her attempts to bar them from her home. Narcissa did eventually get her "clean, comfortable house," but it came at a price. "The missionary work is hard, up-hill work, even the best of it," she wrote. "There are no flowery beds of ease here."[80] Very soon, such friendly feelings as the Cayuse had at first shown toward the couple began to trickle away. They became at first suspicious and then increasingly hostile, many believing that Marcus was trying to poison them with his medicines. Narcissa, in particular, was seen as "proud, haughty, and far above them," and in the events that would later unfold, a special kind of vituperation was saved for her alone.

It is impossible not to feel sympathy for Narcissa. The circumstances she found herself in—isolated from everything she held dear, chronically overworked, and so far from home that letters from her mother and sisters took

as long as two years to reach her—were enough to have broken anyone.*
Added to this, in June 1839 the Whitmans' only child, two-year-old Alice,
had drowned in the Walla Walla River.† Afterward, Narcissa seems to have
experienced some kind of breakdown, both mental and physical, from which
it took her many years to recover. There must have been many times when
she bitterly regretted her decision to go west. Writing to her father some
years later, she confessed that trying to bring up her adopted children "in a
heathen land . . . is the nearest like a hell on earth of anything that I can
imagine."[81] The truth was that from the very outset Narcissa had neither the
energy nor the natural sympathies to deal in any meaningful way with the
very people she had set out, by her own lights, to "save." "We need help very
much," she wrote to her sister Jane.

The arrival of the second missionary party—the Walkers, the Eells, the
Grays, and the Smiths, who landed, quite literally, on their doorstep in the
autumn of 1838—must at first have seemed like the hand of Providence at
work. In fact, the newcomers would prove more of a burden than a benefit.

The Grays soon moved to the Spalding mission at Lapwai, but the other
three couples had little option but to stay with the Whitmans until their
own accommodation could be built. A total of nine adults and three chil-
dren‡ had somehow to be squeezed into the Whitmans' existing house (their
original cabin measured just thirty feet by thirty-six feet). After December,
when Mary Richardson Walker was expecting her confinement, there

---

*As they did in fact almost destroy her fellow missionary Sarah Gilbert White Smith, who
had to be evacuated from the Smiths' mission at Kamiah in 1842, a broken woman in both
health and spirits.
†Her death profoundly affected all the missionaries. "The death of our babe had a great affect
upon all in the mission," Narcissa would later write. "It softened their hearts toward us, even
Mr. S[palding]'s for a season. I never had any difficulty with his wife" (letter of October 10,
1840, quoted in Whitman and Spalding, *Where Wagons Could Go*).
‡A single man, Cornelius Rogers, had also attached himself to the '38 expedition, although
he was never a full member of the mission. He returned East in 1841. As well as her own
child, who was then still living, Narcissa had already adopted two other children: Mary Ann
Bridger, the daughter of the famous mountain man Jim Bridger, and Helen Meek, the daughter of another well-known fur trapper Joe Meek and his Nez Percé wife.

would be the additional chaos of a new baby to contend with. The proximity of so many people—and ones who so far as the Whitmans were concerned were not only complete strangers, but not especially sympathetic ones at that—caused a great deal of tension. Narcissa, not surprisingly, found the strain almost unbearable.

"Mrs. W in a sad mood all day, did not present herself at the breakfast table. Went out of doors, down by the river to cry," Mary Walker recorded in her diary.[82] Sometimes Narcissa would disappear into her own room for the entire day. "I know not, I am sure, what she wishes or thinks," she added, obtusely, "but I think her a strange housekeeper. It is hard to please when one cannot know what would please."[83]

It was only in her letters home that Narcissa could give full vent to her thoughts and feelings. "Could dear mother know how I have been situated ... I know she would pity me. I often think how disagreeable it used to be to her feelings to do her cooking in the presence of men—sitting about the room. This I have had to bear ever since I have been here—at times it seemed as if I could not endure it any longer. It has been all the more trying because our house has been so miserable and cold—small and inconvenient for us—so many people as have lived in it."[84]

The already-complicated relationships among the incoming missionaries only added to the strain. The one thing it might be expected all could agree upon—the manner in which they worshipped—had immediately become a bone of contention. In the church tradition in which Narcissa had been raised, women were encouraged both to pray and sing in public—indeed, Narcissa had been much admired for her beautiful singing voice—but this presented a problem for the newcomers, who thought it immodest in the extreme for women to pray in public. A second difficulty arose over the communion wine. The Whitmans, who were teetotal, preferred to use grape juice; the others insisted on wine. In addition, Elkanah Walker choked everyone with his tobacco smoke, a habit that Narcissa excoriated.

By December, she was "nearly exhausted both in body and mind, in the labor and care of our numerous family."

Dispiriting infighting among the missionaries continued for many years, a situation complicated by the presence nearby of Catholic missionaries preaching a different and rival form of Christianity.* So many aggrieved letters of complaint made their way back to the American Board in Boston that even they began to have serious doubts about the desirability of the missions. In September 1842, a letter arrived dismissing the Spaldings from their post and giving instructions that the missions at Waiilatpu and Lapwai were to be closed. The Whitmans would be allowed to stay, but they were to move from Waiilatpu to Elkanah and Mary Walker's newly established mission at a place called Tshimakain.

Marcus Whitman was determined to change their mind. It was for this reason that he had gone back East and had, on his return journey, been able to help save Sarah Damron Owens's company from starvation. His epic, record-breaking six-month ride to Boston over the winter of 1842–43 would subsequently become famous in the history of the West.

Marcus's argument to the board would have nothing to do with the spiritual succor of the Cayuse—with whom in any case they had made little headway: during their entire mission they would fail to make a single convert—but with the white settlers, more and more of whom were arriving in Oregon with each passing year. The mission at Waiilatpu, in Narcissa's words, was not only "emphatically situated on the highway between the states and the Columbia River," but also the first settlement the emigrants would come to after crossing the Blue Mountains, perhaps the most dangerous and physically demanding stretch of the trail. Almost as soon as they

---

*A tragicomic twist to this unseemly and sometimes positively hostile rivalry between Protestant and Catholic missionaries for control over Native American souls was their use of a visual teaching aid known as a "ladder," in which various episodes in biblical history—Noah's ark, Solomon's temple, the Crucifixion, and so forth—were shown chronologically, in pictures. In the Catholic version, Protestant "heretics" such as Luther, Calvin, and Henry VIII were shown on the bottom step of this eschatological ladder, burning in hell. The Protestant missionaries, not to be outdone, made their own version in which the "heretics" had been replaced by the Pope. What the Cayuse made of this is anyone's guess.

had built their mission it had become a resting place for all those who were too exhausted, or ill, or otherwise destitute to move on.

No one was better placed to see the implications of the emigration than the Whitmans. The case Marcus put to the board was a compelling one. Christianity was not to be brought to Oregon by trying to convert its Native American Tribes directly, but by imposing it on them from above. "I have no doubt our greatest work is to be to aid the white settlement of this country to found its religious institutions," Marcus wrote.[85] He believed that it was "a part of the onward movements of the world and therefore more to be molded than to be turned aside."[86]

The board had not been the only ones who wanted the missionaries out of Oregon Territory. From the early 1840s the Cayuse had begged the Whitmans to leave, but their pleas fell upon deaf ears. Instead, they could only watch while Marcus and Narcissa went to extraordinary lengths to help an invading army of strangers, intent on taking their land. Not only did they resupply the settlers from their own stores, but they allowed large numbers of them to rest and recuperate at Waiilatpu, sometimes even taking them into their own house.

The board had allowed the missionaries to stay, but they continued to have their doubts. In a letter dated April 6, 1846, the board secretary, David Greene, wrote to Marcus: "Still we are not quite sure that you ought to devote so much time and thought to feeding the emigrants, and thus make your station a great *restaurant* for the weary pilgrim on their way to the promised land."[87]

What the board perhaps did not know was that the previous year, Marcus Whitman had gone still further when he intervened to stop a party of Cayuse warriors intent on barring the settlers' path and forcing them to turn back. Sarah Cummins, an overlander of that year, was witness to the tense standoff at the Grande Ronde Valley, just short of the Blue Mountains.

"Ere the twilight faded, and as it was apparent that great numbers of the Indians were gathering within range, Dr. Whitman began to talk to the

chief of the Walla Wallas. The chief made no reply but shook his head de-
fiantly. The chief of the Cayuses now spoke vehemently in the style of true
Indian eloquence. The Doctor spoke again and again, and the chief still
replied, still defying us to go on. Then Dr. Whitman rose to almost
super-human height and, in a stern voice, told them in emphatic terms that
the Great Father of the 'Bostons' would send men to defend these travelers,
and that shiploads of soldiers and guns would arrive to kill all the Indians
who molested his people on their way to the distant valley."[88]

Not only did Marcus Whitman use all his powers of persuasion to see off
the Cayuse; he also succeeded in taking their chief hostage overnight to pre-
empt any possible retaliation. The next day, after "a night of terror to us all,"
the settlers went freely on their way. If there had been any doubt in the Tribe's
mind as to who the Whitmans were there to help, this surely confirmed it.

BY 1847, WHEN THE Whitmans had been in Oregon just over a decade,
approximately eleven thousand settlers had made the journey west, the majority of them to Oregon. Of these a small but significant number were
African Americans, of which most (but not all) were brought there as slaves.
Oregon had not yet entered the Union (that would not happen until 1859),
but the settlers had already unofficially organized themselves into a territory.* Its popularly elected Provisional Government—voted in by a group of
just a hundred settlers in 1843—was quick to take steps that would profoundly influence what kind of place Oregon would become.

It soon became clear that white settlers wanted it all for themselves. In
1844, laws were passed in which it was declared that Oregon would not

---

*Oregon was not officially recognized as a territory—the precursor to statehood—until 1848.
Its request for statehood was delayed many times, mostly due to a long-standing debate over
whether it should enter the Union as a slave or a free state. When Oregon finally entered the
Union in 1859, it was only the southwestern portion of the territory that was included. The
rest of Oregon Territory would eventually become present-day Washington State, Idaho, and
parts of Montana and Wyoming.

permit slavery and would therefore be "free"; simultaneously, it also created a number of Black Exclusion laws making it illegal for any African Americans to reside there.* Section 4 of the law read: "And that when any free negro or mulatto shall have come to Oregon, he or she ... shall remove from and leave the country within the term of two years for males and three years for females." This particularly, and most brutally, applied to African Americans who had arrived in Oregon as slaves but were then freed by their owners. Former slaves would have just six months to leave the territory. Clause 4 of the law stated categorically that "if any such free negro or mulatto shall fail to quit the country as required by this act, he or she may be arrested ... And shall receive upon his or her bare back not less than twenty nor more than thirty-nine stripes, to be inflicted by the constable of the proper county."[89]

Six months later this notorious clause was retracted, and its instigator, Peter Burnett (the very same man who from his wayside soapbox had encouraged white settlers to follow him to Oregon with his colorful claims that the pigs there ran around ready-roasted), would claim that he had made "a mistake," but the fact was that other Black Exclusion laws, in which flogging was replaced by "bonds for good behavior," very quickly took their place.[90]

For all this, the promise that they would find freedom in the West was a powerfully motivating factor for many enslaved Blacks who traveled west with their owners. In a land that was as yet sparsely populated, the new laws were in any case very hard to enforce, and occasionally they even worked in their favor.

In the same year that the Sagers traveled to Oregon, Colonel Nathaniel Ford was also making the journey west. From his home in Missouri he had taken with him three of his slaves, including a married couple, Robbin

---

*Oregon country was still disputed territory between the US and Great Britain at this time. The settlers recognized that these "Organic Laws" were provisional and only effective until such a time as the United States should "extent its jurisdiction over us." The border with Britain was finally settled peacefully, along the forty-ninth parallel, in 1846.

and Polly Holmes, whom he had promised to free when they arrived. Ford took his time about it. At first he had no trouble in keeping the Holmeses in a state of semi-bondage, and it was only after five years that he finally honored his word and manumitted the couple, together with their newborn baby.

Their remaining four children, three of whom had been born in Oregon, were not so lucky. Ford refused to give them up, claiming that the children were still his property (one of these children, Harriet, subsequently died as a result of the treatment she had received while under Ford's daughter's "care"). It was only by taking their former owner to court, under a suit of habeas corpus, that Polly and Robbin were finally able to secure their children's freedom. In 1853, almost ten years after they had arrived in Oregon, their case was finally heard. Judge George H. Williams (a free-soil Democrat from Iowa) ruled that "these children, being then (by the voluntary act of Ford) in Oregon, where slavery could not legally exist, were free from the bonds of slavery," and he awarded custody to their parents.[91]

And still the settlers kept coming. Every autumn a small army of people poured past the Whitmans' homestead, intent on staking their claims on the rich pastures of the Cayuse's ancestral lands. "The poor Indians are amazed at the overwhelming numbers of Americans coming into the country," Narcissa wrote. "They seem not to know what to make of it." Those who were too weak or sick to travel on now wintered over at the Whitman Mission, which, as the years drew on, only increased its general air of prosperity and abundance.

Even Narcissa had moments of insight into what this state of affairs must have looked like to the Cayuse. In one of the last letters she ever wrote, she observed: "It is difficult for them to feel but that we are rich and getting richer by the houses we dwell in and the clothes we wear and hang out to dry after washing from week to week, and the grain we consume in our families."

The emigration of 1847, in which two thousand hopefuls had set out to try their fortunes in the West, had been a particularly brutal one. The difficulties of the journey had been compounded by the fact that not only was this year set to have an unusually early and severe winter, but it also saw the outbreak of a particularly virulent form of measles.

In November, fifty-six men, women, and children, many of them still desperately ill, were crammed into the various houses and farm buildings at the Whitman Mission. These, added to Marcus and Narcissa's extended family of sixteen,* made up a total of seventy-four people living at the mission at Waiilatpu.

The measles epidemic had hit the 1847 wagon trains hard, but it was as nothing compared to what it now did to the Cayuse. The Tribe were no strangers to white disease, but this measles outbreak would prove particularly devastating. Already in a depleted state due to the death of many of their animals in the harsh winter, the disease ripped through their communities with shattering consequences. Marcus Whitman did his best to treat them, but while he had some success with his white patients, no amount of medicine could save the Cayuse, who had no immunity to the virus. Many of them died, including almost all their children. Three of these were the children of the Tribal chief, Tiloukaikt.

Keturah Belknap and her family were just sitting down to their supper—"a ham bone and beans"—when they heard the news. Their company had just arrived at Ash Hollow, in present-day Nebraska, and all had spent an exhausting day in the difficult maneuver of disconnecting the wagons from their oxen and then hauling them by hand down a steep hillside

---

*Over the years the Whitmans would foster sixteen or more children for periods of up to a year. At the time the Sager orphans arrived in 1844 there were another five children already living with them: alongside Mary Ann Bridger and Helen Meek, Henry and Eliza Spalding's daughter, also called Eliza, was there so that she could attend Narcissa's school; in addition to these three little girls, there was a half-Spanish, half–Native American boy whom they had named David Malin, brought to Narcissa half-starved and covered in lice, and a nephew of Marcus Whitman's, fourteen-year-old Perrin Whitman, who had accompanied his uncle when he returned west in 1843.

of "solid rock steps." It was a mild evening, and Keturah was glad of the opportunity to rest, do a little washing and cooking, and enjoy a nearby supply of sweet water, when suddenly, out of nowhere, she heard the pounding of many horses' hooves approaching.

"Just as we were ready to sit down to supper Joe Meek and his possie of men rode into camp," Keturah recorded in her memorandum. "They were going to Washington D.C. to get the government to send soldiers to protect the settlers in Oregon and they told us all about the Indian Massacars at Walla Walla called the 'Whitman Massacre.' [Joe Meek and his posse] had traveled all winter and some of their men had died and they had got out of food and had to eat mule meat so we gave them all their supper and breakfast . . . on the whole we are having quite a time—some want to turn back and others are telling what they would do in case of an attack."[92]

The Whitman Massacre, as it would become known, had taken place on November 29 the previous year. Although the news of it would spread like wildfire along the emigration trains, and occasioned much panic among the settlers—a great number of whom wrote about it in their diaries—it was some time before the lurid details became known.

The general atmosphere at Waiilatpu had been sour for some time. The Whitmans had already received intimations that trouble was coming their way, and everyone in the house that day was tense. A Cayuse named Stickus, who was always particularly friendly to the Whitmans, had just the day before advised Dr. Whitman that a mixed-race man, Joe Lewis, had been telling the rest of the Tribe that the missionaries were trying to poison them with their medicines in order to take their land and horses for themselves. He had warned the Whitmans, in no uncertain terms, to leave the area "until my people have better hearts."[93]

That afternoon there was a knock at the Whitmans' door. It was Tilou-kaikt, the Tribal chief, whose three children Dr. Whitman had helped bury that very morning, asking for medicine. When Narcissa saw him, she called out to her husband, who was sitting reading in their private parlor. As he went out to greet him, the chief tried to force his way past the doctor into the family quarters but was at first prevented from doing so. Marcus went into the kitchen, where his medicine cupboard was, telling Narcissa to lock the door behind him. Both Mary Ann Bridger and John Sager, who were recuperating from measles, were sitting in the kitchen at the time, John "winding a ball of twine." As Dr. Whitman turned to open the cupboard, Tiloukaikt came up and struck him from behind with a tomahawk. Somehow, Marcus managed to stagger outside, but he was immediately shot at by another Cayuse waiting there. Tiloukaikt followed, striking him again and again in the head and face. John now reached for his own pistol but was shot dead. Mary Ann, who had been hiding behind the stove, managed to climb out of a window and ran round to the back of the house screaming, "The Indians are killing Father and John!"

Dr. Whitman did not die immediately. Narcissa and another woman, Mrs. Hall, who had come running into the house, unbolted the door and brought him into the sitting room, where they laid him out on the floor, bleeding profusely. Narcissa tried to staunch the flow with a towel and some ashes from the fire. "Mrs. Whitman went to the sash door and looked out. . . . She stood there watching, when Frank Iskalome, a full-blooded Indian, shot her in the left breast. Sister Elizabeth [Sager] was standing beside her and heard her exclaim, 'I am wounded; hold me tight.' The women took hold of her and placed her in a chair; then she began to pray that 'God would save her children that were to be orphaned and that her dear mother would be given strength to bear the news of her death.'"[94]

Somehow they managed to get her upstairs, but after hiding there for a while they were eventually persuaded to come downstairs by another Cayuse, Tamsucky, who promised that they would not be hurt. Narcissa, who had been laid out on one of the beds, was bleeding so badly that she had to be helped down the stairs and placed on a sofa. Sometime after this, an order was given to bring her out of the house. Since she could not walk, two men carried her out, still lying on the sofa. One end was carried by one of the settlers, a man named Rogers, who had been hiding inside the house with the others; the other end was taken by Joe Lewis. "When they had gotten out of and a short distance from the house in an open space, Joe Lewis dropped his end of the settee. Mr. Rogers looked up quickly and must have realized what it meant; but he was shot instantly and fell and an Indian tried to ride his horse over him. . . . Then an Indian came to Mrs. Whitman and took his whip and beat her over the face and head and then turned the settee over in the mud. I am convinced that she did not last long after being beaten and thrown face down in the mud, with the blankets and settee on top of her."[95]

In all, eleven people lost their lives at the time of the Whitman Massacre. Of the extended Whitman family and their numerous wards, four were killed outright by the Cayuse: Marcus and Narcissa Whitman and the two Sager boys, Frank and John. Two of their other adopted children, Helen Meek and Louisa Sager, already very ill, died shortly after of a combination of measles and exposure. The four surviving Sager sisters, Mary Ann Bridger, Perrin Whitman, David Malin, and Eliza Spalding were held, along with the remaining settlers, at the Waiilatpu mission for a month until their release was finally negotiated.

Matilda Sager remembered the journey taken by the traumatized children, eight days by river in an uncovered boat from Fort Walla Walla to Fort Vancouver, where they found refuge at last with Marguerite McLoughlin. The only one of the Whitmans' surviving children who did not escape was their little adopted son, David Malin, then aged six or seven. In an act of incomprehensible cruelty, the rescuers refused to allow him onto the boat, on the grounds that he was Canadian (he was in fact half-Spanish and half–Native American). "The last look I had of him," Matilda wrote, "was when we rowed away from Fort Walla Walla, leaving him standing on the bank of the river crying as though his heart were breaking."[96]

The Whitman Massacre would prove to be yet another turning point in the history of the West. For the eleven people who were killed it was a personal tragedy; for the children, particularly the two Sager brothers John and Frank, and for their little sister Louisa, it will always seem a particularly poignant fate given what they had already lived through. For the four surviving Sager sisters—Catherine, Matilda, Elizabeth, and Henrietta—it was a trauma from which they never really recovered.*

For the Cayuse it was a catastrophe of unparalleled proportions. The work of a handful of renegades now brought the vindictive wrath of the settlers upon an entire people—a grim pattern that would so often be repeated in white dealings with Native American Tribes—and would mark the end of their life as they had known it. Within weeks a militia of over five hundred men, later supported by US Army troops, was gathered together, all eager for revenge. As the Cayuse would see it, "the whites from down the Columbia had made war upon them, and killed many more of their people than had been killed at the mission." They said that they had begged the whites to leave, because their disease (measles) was killing them, "and that they only killed them to save their own lives."

The Reverend Henry Perkins, a Methodist who had also set up a mission in Oregon, and who knew the Whitmans well, would later give this searing account of the events that had led up to the massacre. "While [the settlers] were rapidly coming in year by year & occupying their rich lands, they looked upon the Doctor as the head of the concern," he wrote in a letter to Narcissa's sister. "They saw him entering no protest—making no remonstrance, but rather aiding and abetting—planning & directing, & all the family of course including Mrs. W. concurring apparently in their displacement. . . . They wanted their *lands*, their *homes*, the *graves of their fathers*, their *rich hunting grounds & horse ranges*. They did not look upon the man or men who would connive at the usurpation of all these as their real friends. They looked upon the Doctor & his wife as not missionaries to them but to the Americans. . . . The result could hardly have been otherwise than what it was."[97]

---

*They all went on to live eventful lives, perhaps none more picaresque than that of the youngest, Henrietta. Having been born on the Oregon Trail, lost her mother and father, and then, three years later, both her brothers and her adoptive parents, she went on to marry twice "and was reported killed at Red Bluff, California, in 1870, when an assailant aiming for her husband, shot her instead." She was just twenty-six years old. Catherine, Elizabeth, and Matilda Sager, *The Whitman Massacre of 1837.*

But Henry Perkins's was a minority view. Not content with the indiscriminate revenge killing of many scores of Cayuse, most of whom had taken no part in the massacre at Waiilatpu, some three years later a second attempt was made to punish the actual culprits, whom, it was believed, had never been apprehended.

An anonymous but allegedly "well-known" Army officer who was present in Oregon at the time was so disturbed by what happened that he would later write his own account, which was published some years later in the *Army and Navy Journal*. "The history of that affair was never written ... by any unprejudiced person," he wrote. "The elders of the tribe had thought that they ought to be satisfied [by the revenge killings that had already been carried out]. As they were not, [five] of their principal men had volunteered to go back with the governor to Oregon City to be tried for the murder.... They knew they were going among those who thirsted for their blood and that they were going to their death, and that death the most ignominious that can be accorded to the red man, as they were going to be hung like dogs."

The men "were not restrained in any way ... and walked with their heads held erect, and with the bearing of senators ... amid the jibes and jeers of a brutal crowd, to the jail.... There was no power on earth that could have made them falter in their determination ... to die like men for the salvation of their tribe." It was, the Army officer wrote, "a given" that they would be found guilty, even though "it was more than suspected that the witnesses (who claimed to recognize them) were never near the mission at the time of the massacre."*

"Without a murmur of a sign of regret, and with a dignity that would have impressed a Zulu with profound pity, these men walked to the gallows and were hung while a crowd of civilized Americans—men, women, and

---

*At least one of them, the chief Tiloukaikt, was genuinely guilty; the others are thought to have been men who simply volunteered for the good of their Tribe.

children of the nineteenth century—looked on and laughed at their last convulsive twitches.

"We have read of heroes of all times, but never did we read or believe that such heroism as these Indians exhibited could exist. They knew that to be accused was to be condemned . . . just as surely as a poor woman accused of being a witch [would] have been executed in Salem . . . two hundred years ago."

The jury who found them guilty, he wrote, "are sunk into oblivion that is the fate of those who are born without souls."[98]

The Cayuse Wars, as the conflict became known, spluttered on for another five years. The already-depleted Cayuse, who had lost half their people and almost all their children in the measles epidemic brought in by the settlers, were never a match for their adversaries, either in numbers or in firepower. In 1855 they conceded defeat. Under the Treaty of Walla Walla, the Tribe, a seminomadic people, now ceded 6.4 million acres of their ancestral homelands in exchange for a reservation* of just a quarter of a million acres and the promise of annuities in the form of goods and supplies, most of which would prove either inadequate to their needs or were never forthcoming.

---

*It exists today. The Confederated Tribes of the Umatilla Indian Reservation includes the Umatilla and Walla Walla peoples, as well as the Cayuse.

Unnamed woman on a paint horse

6

CALIFORNIA

Since the earliest days of the emigration, California had for many surpassed even the promised land of Oregon in its allure. In *The Emigrants' Guide to Oregon and California*, Lansford Hastings had extolled it as an alternative to the Pacific Northwest in typically extravagant terms. "In my opinion, there is no other country in the known world possessing a soil so fertile and productive, with such varied and inexhaustible resources, and a climate of such mildness, uniformity and salubrity," he wrote; "nor is there a country known which is so eminently calculated by nature herself in all respects to promote the unbounded happiness and prosperity of civilized and enlightened man."

That the trail to California, while initially covering much of the same route, was longer, more dangerous, and, at this point, even less well trodden than the Oregon Trail, was not regarded as any kind of impediment. Neither was the fact that in 1845, the year that Hastings's guide was first published, California was not American, but Mexican sovereign territory.* War between the US and Mexico over the latter's rich but sparsely populated

---

*Mexico had achieved independence from Spain in 1812.

northern province now seemed certain, and the US expected to win. Besides, in Hastings's opinion at least, the Californian people "were scarcely a visible grade in the scale of intelligence above the barbarous tribes by whom they are surrounded."[99]

One of these so-called "barbarous tribes" was the Northern Paiute.* Traditionally a peaceful people, the Paiute did not own horses, and before the arrival of whites most had never even seen a firearm; they were instead brilliantly well adapted to surviving in some of the harshest and most unhospitable terrain in North America. They had expert knowledge of how to trap and gather wild food, including desert rodents and insects, and, most importantly, how to extract edible roots and bulbs from the land. The early settlers gave them the derogatory name of "Diggers" and held them in the greatest contempt.

"I was a very small child when the first white people came into our country," recalled the Northern Paiute Tribeswoman Sarah Winnemucca. "They came like a lion, yes, like a roaring lion, and have continued so ever since, and I have never forgotten their first coming."[100]

At the time of Sarah Winnemucca's birth, sometime around 1844 (she was never sure of the exact year), the Northern Paiute roamed over a vast area of what is now northern Nevada, parts of eastern California, and southern Oregon, much of which fell directly in the path of what would, from the early 1840s, become known as the California Trail. Sarah—whose Tribal name was Thocmetony, meaning "shell flower"—would go on to achieve many things in her lifetime, becoming a lecturer, a teacher, a US Army interpreter, and, most importantly, a tireless campaigner for the rights of her people and the author of what is thought to be the first autobiography ever written by a Native American woman, but her childhood was spent leading the traditional life of her people.

---

*This is the name given to the Tribe by whites; they called themselves the Numa, which means "People." The Northern Paiute should not be confused with the Southern Paiute, whose language is entirely different.

Reading *Life Among the Piutes*, one has the impression that Sarah wrote just as she would have spoken, and as a result her book has an extraordinary directness, particularly in her descriptions of her childhood.*

Sarah's father was a spiritual leader who had the ability to charm antelope. In the winter, when the antelope moved in their herds, he would take a drum and then mark out a special circle around which wigwams would be placed, leaving only one small opening. Two men holding torches made of sagebrush would be sent out as messengers to the antelope. The women, children, and old men would sit with Sarah's father while he played his drum: "we were told ... to keep thinking about the antelopes all the time, and not to let their thoughts go away to anything else." On the fifth day the antelopes were charmed, "and the whole herd followed the tracks of my people and entered the circle ... coming in at the entrance, bowing and tossing their heads, and looking sleepy under a powerful spell. They ran round and round inside the circle just as if there were a fence all around it and they could not get out, and they stayed there until my people had killed every one. But if anybody had dropped anything, or had stumbled and not told about it, then when the antelopes came to the place where he had done that, they threw off the spell and rushed wildly out of the circle at that place."[101]

In their creation myth, the Paiute believed that at the beginning of the world there were four children, two white and two dark. At first, they were a happy family, but eventually they began to quarrel. Their parents were very much grieved by this and decided to separate them. "So the light girl and boy disappeared ... and their parents saw them no more." The Paiute believed that the white nation that had grown up from these two children would one day send an emissary to them "to heal all the old trouble."

---

*As Sarah's friend and editor, Mrs. Horace Mann, who helped to prepare her book for publication, wrote in her preface: "In fighting with her literary deficiencies she loses some of the fervid eloquence which her extraordinary colloquial command of the English language enables her to utter, but I am confident that no one would desire that her own original words should be altered." See *Life Among the Piutes*.

When the first white settlers appeared among them, the Tribe—and Sarah's grandfather in particular—greeted them with joy. "My people were scattered at that time over nearly all the territory now known as Nevada," Sarah would recall. "My grandfather was chief of the entire Paiute nation, and was camped near Humboldt Lake, with a small portion of his tribe, when a party . . . was seen coming. When the news was brought to my grandfather, he asked what they looked like? When told that they had hair on their faces, and were white, he jumped up and clasped his hands together, and cried aloud, 'My white brothers—my long-looked-for white brothers have come at last!'"[†102]

He took some of his men and went to the settlers' camp. "Arriving near them, he was commanded to halt in a manner that was readily understood without an interpreter." Despite her grandfather's signs of friendship—he threw down his robe and put his hands up to show that he was not carrying any weapon—they refused to allow him to approach. "He knew not what to do. He had expected so much pleasure in welcoming his white brothers to the best in the land, and after looking at them sorrowfully for a while, he came back quite unhappy." Undeterred, Sarah's grandfather and his men followed the emigrant party for several days, camping near them at night "and traveling in sight of them by day, hoping in this way to gain their confidence. But he was disappointed, poor dear old soul!" Sarah recalled. "I can imagine his feelings," she added, "for I have drunk deeply from the same cup . . . and with the help of Him who notes the sparrow's fall, I mean to fight for my down-trodden race while life lasts."[103]

The next year a second emigration passed through Northern Paiute territory, and they too camped near Humboldt Lake. With them, Sarah's grandfather would have more success. "During their stay my grandfather

*Although this is the term that is used by Sarah Winnemucca, it has been pointed out that the status of "chief" was not one generally in use among the Northern Paiute.
†It is possible that this was the Biddleston-Bartwell expedition, the very first small emigrant train to travel overland to California in 1841. They were a splinter group from a larger company traveling the Oregon Trail.

and some of his people called upon them, and they all shook hands, and when our white brothers were going away they gave my grandfather a white tin plate—it was so bright," she recalled. "They say that after they left, my grandfather called for all his people to come together, and he then showed them the beautiful gift which he had received from his white brothers. Everybody was so pleased; nothing like it was ever seen in our country before. My grandfather thought so much of it that he bored holes in it and fastened it on his head, and wore it as a hat. He held it in as much admiration as my white sisters hold their diamond rings or a sealskin jacket."

The following spring, yet more "white brothers" arrived. Among them were two mysterious figures "that [were] burning all in a blaze." When Sarah's grandfather asked for more details, he was told that "it looked like a man; it had legs and hands and a head, but the head had quit burning, and it was left quite black. There was the greatest excitement among my people everywhere about the men in a blazing fire." It was only much later that this mysterious apparition was revealed to be two African Americans wearing red shirts.

The following autumn yet more settlers came, in still greater numbers. "It was this time that our white brothers first came among us," Sarah Winnemucca wrote. "They could not get over the mountains, so they had to live with us. . . . You call my people blood seeking," she went on. "My people did not seek to kill them, nor did they steal their horses—no, no, far from it. During the winter my people helped them. They gave them such as they had to eat. They did not hold out their hands and say: 'You can't have anything to eat unless you pay me.' No—no such word was used by us savages at that time."

For all the help that the Paiute had given the settlers, it was not long before the tide began to turn against them. Slowly, with each passing emigration, they began to realize that these so-called "white brothers" had no very brotherly feelings toward them at all. Even her grandfather, who would become known to settlers as Captain Truckee, began to have his doubts when he saw the leader of one of the trains "whipping the negroes who were driving his team. That made my grandfather feel very badly."

Sarah's first sightings of white people filled her with terror. It was their appearance that seemed so strange to the Paiute children: the whites were not like humans, she wrote, "but more like owls than anything else. They had hair on their faces, and had white eyes, and looked beautiful." Soon, frightening stories began to circulate that would only add to her fear. "The following spring . . . there was great excitement among my people on account of fearful news coming from different tribes, that the people whom they called their white brothers were killing everybody that came in their way, and all the Indian tribes had gone into the mountains to save their lives. . . . There was a fearful story they told us children. Our mothers told us that the whites were killing everybody and eating them. So we were all afraid of them. Every dust that we could see blowing in the valley we would say that it was the white people.

"What a fright we all got one morning to hear some white people were coming. Every one ran as best they could. . . . My aunt overtook us, and she said to my mother: 'Let us bury our girls, or we shall all be killed and eaten up.' So they went to work and buried us, and told us if we heard any noise not to cry out, for if we did they would surely kill and eat us. So our mothers buried me and my cousin, planted sage brushes over our faces to keep the sun from burning them, and there we were left all day.

"Can anyone imagine my feelings buried alive, thinking every minute that I was to be unburied and eaten up by the people that my grandfather loved so much? With my heart throbbing, and not daring to breathe, we lay there all day. It seemed that the night would never come. . . . At last we heard some whispering. We did not dare to whisper to each other, so we lay still. I could hear their footsteps coming nearer and nearer. I thought my heart was coming right out of my mouth. Then I heard my mother say, 'T'is right here!' Oh, can anyone in this world ever imagine what were my feelings when I was dug up by my poor mother and father?"[104]

But there was worse news to come. While they were hiding out in the mountains, "the people that my grandfather had called our white brothers came along to where our winter supplies were. They set everything we had left on fire. It was a fearful sight. It was all we had for the winter, and it was all burnt during that night. My father took some of his men during the night to try and save some of it, but they could not; it had burnt down before they got there."

This party of settlers was the last to come through Northern Paiute territory that year. "This whole band of white people perished in the mountains, for it was too late to cross them," Sarah Winnemucca remembered. "We could have saved them, only my people were afraid of them. We never knew who they were, or where they came from. So, poor things, they must have suffered fearfully."

THE PARTY IN QUESTION was the Donner-Reed party, who had set out for California in 1846. Contrary to what Sarah Winnemucca's Tribe believed, not all of them died in the mountains that year. One of the survivors was a young girl of thirteen called Virginia Reed, whose family was among the very first to have been inspired by Lansford Hastings's wildly inflated tales of a land of milk and honey beyond the Sierra Nevada. In the memoir that she later wrote she gives an account of the mindset that was probably true of most emigrants making their way across what was then still known as "Indian Territory," and that explains, to some degree at least, the extraordinary hostility they felt toward the Native Americans.

"Let me say that we suffered vastly more from fear of the Indians before starting than we did on the plains," Virginia wrote, recalling how when she was a little girl her grandmother used to tell "Indian stories" in the long winter evenings. This grandmother had had an aunt who had been taken prisoner "by the savages" in Virginia and had been held captive for five years before she made her escape. "I was fond of these stories, and evening after evening would go into grandma's room, sitting with my back close against the wall so that no warrior could slip behind me with a tomahawk. I would coax her to tell me more about her aunt, and would sit listening to the recital of the fearful deeds of the savages, until it seemed to me that everything in the room, from the high old-fashioned bedposts down even to the shovel and tongs in the chimney corner, was transformed into the dusky tribe in paint and feather, all ready for the war dance. So when I was told that we were going to California and would have to pass through a region peopled by Indians, you can imagine how I felt."[105]

In fact, the likelihood of being killed by "the savages" was, in the early days of the emigration, vanishingly small. (For the two decades between 1840 and 1860, 362 settlers were killed by Native Americans, while whites were responsible for the killing of 426 Native Americans.)[106] As would so often prove to be the case, the reality of their encounters with Indigenous people proved very different. Tamsen Donner, traveling in the same wagon train as the Reed family, expressed her astonishment at how easy the beginning of her journey was. "We feel no fear of Indians," she wrote in a letter to a friend on one of their stops on the Platte River. "Our cattle graze quietly around our encampments unmolested.

"I never could have believed we could have traveled so far with so little difficulty. The Indians frequently come to see us and the chiefs of a tribe breakfasted at our tent this morning. All are so friendly that I cannot help feeling sympathy and friendship for them." She then added, "Indeed if I do not experience something far worse than I yet have done, I shall say that the trouble is all in the getting started."[107]

Virginia Reed's account, however, illustrates perfectly how misunderstandings could occur. Their wagon train had stopped at Fort Laramie, where they had celebrated the Fourth of July "in fine style," pitching camp earlier than usual so as to be able to prepare a special dinner and, at an appointed hour, drinking the health of their friends back home in Illinois with a special bottle of "good old brandy" that had been given to her father as a parting present. Virginia had by now completely lost her fear of "Indians," so when they encountered a band of "Sioux,"* whom she believed "were on

*The word Sioux was a blanket term for a group of related and allied people, including the Lakota; see "A Note on Native American Names."

the warpath, going to fight the Crows or Blackfeet," she was not in the least perturbed, finding them "fine-looking Indians" and much admiring the goods—buffalo robes and beautifully tanned buckskin, pretty beaded moccasins and ropes made of grass—with which they tried to persuade her to trade for her pony.

"The Sioux were several days in passing our caravan, not on account of the length of our train, but because there were so many [of them]"; so great a number in fact that "they could have massacred our whole party without much loss to themselves." But despite the fact that they were passing by so peacefully, some of their party became alarmed. Rifles were cleaned out and loaded "to let the warriors see that we were prepared to fight," she wrote, "but the Sioux never showed any inclination to disturb us."

Their initial fear was soon transformed into something more mundane: annoyance. Unlike the Northern Paiute, the plains Tribes had a long tradition of trading with whites, and they would have considered the settlers passing through their lands as fair game. They were also understandably curious about them, and the Reed family's peculiar two-story wagon and its contents (of which more later) was a particular source of fascination. "They were continually swarming about trying to get a look at themselves in the mirror," Virginia would remember. Much later, when the family was forced to abandon their wagon, leaving it "like a monument on the Salt Lake desert," the glass was still miraculously unbroken. "I have often thought how pleased the Indians must have been when they found this mirror which gave them back the picture of their own dusky faces."[108]

Not all her impulses were so benign. The "Sioux" had been so insistent about wanting to buy her pony, Billy, that for a while she had been forced to take a place in the wagon instead of riding him—her greatest pleasure while traveling across the prairies. To pass the time, and curious to see how far back the line of warriors extended, she picked up a field glass that was hanging near her on a peg, "and as I pulled it out with a click, the warriors jumped back, wheeled their ponies and scattered." Thoroughly pleased with this effect, she boasted to her mother that "I could fight the whole Sioux tribe with a spy-glass, and as revenge for forcing me to ride in the wagon." After that, whenever they came near, she "would raise the glass and laugh to see them dart away in terror."

Virginia Reed was lucky in that her thoughtlessness did not create a far more serious problem. While both she and Tamsen Donner might have become somewhat blasé, the vast majority of settlers, most of them brought up on exactly the same fireside tales as those told to Virginia by her grandmother, remained extremely fearful. The men, in particular, almost all of whom carried guns, were more likely to shoot first and ask questions later.

Francis Parkman, who was staying at Fort Laramie in the same year that the Donner-Reed party passed by, saw the difficulties immediately. The "timorous mood" of the settlers, he observed, exposed them to real danger. "Assume in the presence of Indians a bold bearing, self-confident yet vigilant, and you will find them tolerably safe neighbors." The "Sioux," he realized astutely, "saw clearly enough the perturbation of the emigrants and instantly availed themselves of it." Simple curiosity—wanting to look inside the wagons and admire themselves in a looking glass—often turned into something more troubling. The men "became extremely insolent and exacting in their demands." It had become "an established custom with them to go to the camp of every party, as it arrives in succession at the fort, and demand a feast. Smoke's village* had come with the express design, having made several days' journey with no other object than that of enjoying a cup of coffee and two or three biscuits. So the 'feast' was demanded, and the emigrants dared not refuse it."

He described how the settlers "stared open-mouthed at their savage guests," who had arranged themselves in a semicircle. "One evening they broke to pieces, out of mere wantonness, the cups from which they had been feasted; and this so exasperated the emigrants that many of them seized their rifles and could scarcely be restrained from firing on the insolent mob

---

*The Lakota band with which Parkman was traveling

of Indians."[109] Parkman predicted, with some prescience, that a military force would soon be necessary to keep the peace.

While attacks by Native Americans, in these early stages of the emigration, occurred only very rarely, the fear of it was a universal anxiety, often played on by unscrupulous whites to further their own interests. Keturah Belknap, who was not fooled for a moment, gives this example in her memorandum. When her company had been on the road about four weeks, and were within reach of the Pawnee villages, she remarked that the company was now extra vigilant, not only to guard themselves and their livestock "from prowling tribes" but also, and particularly, from the renegade whites "that are here to keep away from the law": "they seem to have their eyes on a good horse and follow [it] for days—then if they are caught will say they got him from the Indians. By paying them something they would give the horse up, [trying] to make us believe that they were sent out there to protect the emegrants."[110]

Horse- and cattle-rustling outlaws were by no means the only ones who preyed upon the settlers' fear of attack. Others, with far bigger plans, found it both convenient and highly lucrative to do so too. Ironically, it was by exaggerating the danger from Native people in Oregon that these "entrepreneurs"—a motley collection of mountain men turned guides, traders, and land speculators—were able to manipulate many settlers into changing course and trying their luck in California instead.

The situation was complicated further by the fact that, even by the mid-1840s, there was still a good deal of misinformation, not only about the route west, but also about the competing claims of the two destinations. "The confusion and uncertainty in the minds of the emigrants as to which was the best route to take" was clear even to an eleven-year-old, Lucy Ann Henderson Deady, who together with her family was making her way west in the same year as the Donner-Reed expedition. "There were so many people who claimed to know all about it that gave such contradictory reports that the emigrants did not know whom to believe," she wrote. "A good many of the emigrants had started out with the intention of going to

California, while others, meeting California boosters at Fort Laramie or Fort Bridger, changed their original plans and took the California Trail in place of going on to the Willamette Valley [in Oregon]. Some of the emigrants disposed of their wagons at Fort Laramie and started for California with packhorses. All sorts of reports were circulated. Some said you had to buy the land in California, while in Oregon it was free. Others said Oregon had the best climate, but it was much easier to go to California."[111]

One of these California "boosters" was the former mountain man Caleb Greenwood. He was employed by a man named John Sutter, a Swiss German who had founded a small settlement in California. With big dreams of founding "A New Helvetia" (a New Switzerland), an agricultural empire on the eastern border of what was then still Mexico, Sutter was the first of many to seek a utopia in the West. But even utopias needed flesh-and-blood settlers to make them work. In order to entice emigrants to his settlement, Sutter employed Greenwood to meet the yearly emigration at Fort Hall and persuade them to change their route.

Greenwood, who was originally from Nova Scotia, had been a fur trapper all his life. At the time when he was working for Sutter he was said to be over eighty years old. The Bonney family were among one of the settler trains that Greenwood met at Fort Hall in 1845. At first sight, Greenwood had seemed like "a very picturesque old man." Dressed entirely in buckskin, he wore a long, heavy beard and used "very picturesque language." He was also a shrewd salesman. "He called the Oregon emigrants together the first evening we were at Fort Hall and made a talk. He said the road to Oregon was dangerous on account of the Indians." Having got the assembled crowd thoroughly rattled, Greenwood then proceeded to describe how easy the alternative route to California was; "there was an easy grade and crossing the mountains would not be difficult." Then came the hard sell. "He said that Captain Sutter would have ten Californians meet the emigrants who would go, that Sutter would supply them with plenty of potatoes, coffee, and dried beef. He also said he would help the emigrants over the mountains with their wagons and that to every head of a family who would settle near Sutter's

Fort, Captain Sutter would give six sections of land of his [Mexican] land grant." In addition, Greenwood finished with a flourish, "the climate is better, there is plenty of hunting and fishing, and the rivers are full of salmon."

Caleb Greenwood's well-rehearsed patter had an instant, electrifying effect. The discussion that followed lasted almost all night. "Some wanted to go to California, others were against it." The leader of their company, Samuel Barlow, tried to use his authority to forbid anyone from leaving their train. He argued (correctly, as it turned out) that there was a great deal of uncertainty about land titles in California, "and that we Americans should not want to go to a country under another flag." They should not waste their time and risk everything merely "to help promote Sutter's land schemes." Others argued that California would soon be American territory (also true), while still others thought that "Mexico would fight to hold it and that the Americans who went there would get into a mix-up and probably be killed." There was so much disagreement that the meeting "nearly broke up in a mutiny."

The old trapper appeared first thing the next morning and spoke to them: "All you who want to go to California drive out from the main road and follow me." Despite his promise that "you will find there are no Indians to kill you," the others watched them go with dismay. "Goodbye, we will never see you again. Your bones will whiten in the desert or be gnawed by animals in the mountains." The Bonney family were not to be deflected: theirs was the first of eight wagons that now split from their company and followed the mountain man. "After driving southward for three days with Caleb Greenwood, he left us to go back to Fort Hall to get other emigrants to change their route to California," leaving them with his three sons "to guide us to Sutter's Fort."[112]

With experienced guides to see them through, the Bonneys had no difficulty in finding their way to California. Many others, trying to find their way alone and with no experience of the trails, would not be so fortunate. Although since the beginning of the century it was known that there was a trail west across the Rockies, the distances were so vast, and the terrain so varied, that there was still a great deal of confusion over the exact route. Despite its name, the Oregon Trail was never a single trail, but rather an entire network of pathways, in some places sometimes a mile or more across. The situation was complicated further by the various "cutoffs" that now began to appear. While some of these were the result of genuine attempts to find better, shorter routes, others were engineered, and then heavily promoted, by those with agendas of their own.

In the same year that the Reed family left Independence for California, Tabitha Brown, the sixty-six-year-old widow from Brimfield, Massachusetts, was headed for Oregon, together with her married son and daughter and their spouses and her thirteen grandchildren. Shortly after passing Fort Hall they met that "rascally fellow" who hoped to persuade them to follow him along a different route. The man (who is unnamed) assured them that he had found "*a near cut-off,* [and] that if we would follow him we would be in the settlement long before those who had gone down the Columbia." To anxious settlers, already exhausted by their journey, the idea of shortening their route was a very enticing one. As it turned out, it nearly killed them.

"Our sufferings from that time no tongue could tell." Assuring the party that he would clear the road before them, "that we should have no trouble rolling our wagons after him," the "rascally" guide soon disappeared altogether. "He robbed us of what he could by lying," Tabitha recalled, leaving them to cross "sixty miles of desert without grass or water, mountains to climb, cattle giving out, wagons breaking, emigrants sick and dying, [and] hostile Indians to guard against by night and by day to keep from being killed, or having our horses and cattle arrowed or stolen." The cutoff took them hundreds of miles south of Oregon, through what is now Nevada and California,* during which time Tabitha and her family lost almost

---

*It would later become known as the Scott-Applegate Trail. It had been surveyed earlier that year by a group of men led by Levi Scott and including two brothers, Lindsay and Jesse Applegate, who had been hoping to find a safer route to southern Oregon. It was on their return to Fort Hall that they had met with the settlers and persuaded a hundred and fifty of them to divert from the usual route.

everything they had, including all their livestock (not, as they had feared, to Native American "depredations" but to thirst and exhaustion), most of their wagons, and almost all their supplies. Her grandchildren, the youngest of whom was seven, came so near to starving that her son-in-law tried to shoot and eat a wolf, "but he was too weak and trembling to hold his rifle steady."[113]

Tabitha Brown and her family survived their ordeal, but many others in their party did not, dying "without any warning from fatigue and starvation." At least two were killed and robbed by men she believed were Native people. Tabitha did not reach her destination, Salem in Oregon, until mid-December, nine months after she had set out. The letter she later wrote, describing her family's tribulations, and including her own role in saving her brother-in-law Captain John Brown's life when the two became separated from the rest of their party, would become one of the most famous documents in Oregon history and earned Tabitha Brown the title of the "Brimfield Heroine."

Although Tabitha Brown and her huge extended family did eventually make it safely through, many settlers who took a chance in this way were not so fortunate. Of all the many cutoffs that might lure settlers away from the tried and tested routes, however, none would achieve more notoriety than the one that became known as the "Hastings Cutoff."

At this time, all overlanders heading to California did so by traveling along the Oregon Trail as far as Fort Hall. Here the trail split, one branch now leading southwest through Nevada to the Sierra Nevada. In his *Emigrants' Guide*, Hastings proposed that another route was possible. By leaving the trail at Fort Bridger, two hundred miles short of Fort Hall, settlers could head southwest to the Great Salt Lake and then head directly due west over the desert all the way to California. This route, Hastings claimed, would cut as much as three hundred miles off the journey. If Hastings gave few other details of this proposed shortcut, it was hardly surprising: he had never actually traveled it.

The year 1846, when the Donner-Reed party set out for California, had seen some interesting new developments in Hastings's life. Still only a young man of twenty-seven, during his time in California he had been impressed, and inspired, by John Sutter's plans for a New Helvetia. Soon, Hastings had big plans of his own: "plotting a California boom, and laying out a town near Sutter's Fort."[114] Like Sutter, he too had a vested interest in persuading prospective emigrants to choose California over Oregon. "If settlers could not be trusted to find California, then California—in the person of Lansford Warren Hastings—would go and find settlers."[115]

The Donner-Reed company knew from the outset that their destination would be California. Their party consisted chiefly of three families, "the other members being young men, some of whom came as drivers." The Reeds, a family of nine, came from Springfield, Illinois. The father, James, was of Irish extraction, although he claimed Polish nobility among his ancestry and had been a successful cabinetmaker until his business was all but destroyed by the recession. His wife, Margaret, was Scots Irish. Margaret had been a widow with a young daughter, Virginia, when she married James Reed, and he had adopted his stepdaughter. The Reeds had three children of their own: Virginia's half-sister Patty and two younger half brothers, James and Thomas. They were also accompanied by Virginia's grandmother and by their maidservant of many years, Eliza Williams, and her brother, Baylis. The Donner family was composed of two brothers, George and Jacob, and their wives, Tamsen and Elizabeth. The Donners, of German descent, had once been prosperous farmers but they too had been hard hit by the recession. Between them, the Donner and the Reed families numbered thirty-one people, including twelve children.

Of the estimated thousand settlers who set off west in 1846, the Reeds would always stand out from the rest on account of their extraordinary wagon. This contraption had been specially made to their own design, "and I think I can say without fear of contradiction," Virginia Reed wrote, "that nothing like our family wagon ever started across the plains." Theirs was certainly one of the strangest vessels ever to hit the trail. Unlike the regular wagons, which were essentially simple farm carts with canvas toppings, the "Pioneer Palace Car" was an enormous beast, two stories high. The entrance was made to one side, through which "one stepped into a small room, as it were, in the center of the wagon." To keep Grandma nice and warm, a tiny sheet-iron stove was placed in the center of this "room," with a chimney pipe running from it up through the center of the canvas roof. A circle of tin was placed on top of the exit hole to prevent the canvas cover from catching fire.

The magnificent Pioneer Palace Car was fitted inside with every modern convenience. To both sides were spring seats, with (allegedly) comfortable high backs, "where one could sit and ride with as much ease as on the seats of a Concord coach." In order to make the second story, wooden boards about a foot wide were fixed over the wheels on either side, extending the whole length of the wagon, and this provided the foundation for the "large and roomy second story in which were placed our beds."

Beneath each seat were compartments for storing articles that might be needed on the long journey, such as "a well filled work basket and a full assortment of medicines, with lint and bandages for dressing wounds." The pièce de résistance was a looking glass donated by some of "mama's young friends, in order, as they said, that my mother might not forget to keep her good looks."

The oldest member of their group was Virginia's maternal grandmother. Despite being seventy-five and bedridden, Grandma Keyes had proved deaf to all attempts to persuade her not to undertake the journey, and it was largely with her comfort in mind that the Pioneer Palace Car had been designed. "Our little home was so comfortable, that grandmama could sit reading and chatting with the little ones, and almost forget that she was really crossing the plains."

In addition, they had two extra wagons, each heavily loaded with enough provisions to keep them going through the first Californian winter. They also took a cooking stove, and "knowing that books were always scarce in a new country," an entire library of "standard works."

Virginia Reed described their departure from Springfield with particular poignancy. "Grandma Keyes was carried out of the house and placed in the wagon on a large feather bed, propped up with pillows," her sons still imploring her "to remain and end her days with them," but she was resolute. All their family and friends had turned out to wave them off, including all Virginia's "little schoolmates who had come to kiss me goodbye." Her father shook hands all round, while "mama was overcome with grief." They had been joined by the two Donner families the night before, and now, as the party of nine wagons turned its oxen toward Independence, they were processed triumphantly out of the town. Some of their friends camped out with them the first night, while some of Virginia's uncles stayed with the party for several days before bidding them a final farewell. "Could we have looked into the future and have seen the misery before us, these lines would never have been written," Virginia wrote. "But we were full of hope and did not dream of sorrow. I can now see our little caravan . . . my little black-eyed sister Patty sitting upon the bed, holding up the wagon cover so that Grandma might have a look of her old home."*

At Independence, the two families joined forces with forty other wagons. George Donner was elected to be the leader. The first part of their journey went smoothly, until somewhere on the trail after South Pass they met a man called Wales Bonney traveling the other way. Bonney (who, in a strange twist of fate, would turn out to be a cousin of the Bonney family who had been lured to California by Caleb Greenwood at Fort Hall) carried with him a letter from Hastings, which he had been encouraged to show to as many overlanders as possible, in which Hastings advertised the fact that he himself was waiting up ahead at Fort Bridger to guide the settlers along his proposed new route.

When the party reached Fort Bridger, however, Hastings had already left with another group of settlers. At this point, the company could still have taken the old route to Fort Hall, but yet more vested interests—this time those of the owners of the fort, Jim Bridger and his partner Louis

---

*Sadly, Grandma Keyes did not live long. She died on May 29, just six weeks into the journey, and was buried, like so many others, beside the trail.

Vasquez—now came into play. Bridger and Vasquez, both former mountain men, had established their trading post and general store in 1843. Placing it directly on the emigrant trail, their intention was to sell supplies to passing settlers, and in the first season they had done a booming trade. The following year, however, yet another "cutoff"* had been found that bypassed them altogether, and by 1846 the trail to Fort Bridger was largely defunct. Hastings's proposed new route, which would once again bring settlers past their store, was the perfect solution to their problem. In fact, so perfectly did the men's ambitions coincide that there were rumors of payoffs, some (including Virginia Reed) convinced that Hastings was offering financial incentives to Bridger and Vasquez to promote his route, others believing that it was the other way around.

Whatever the truth of the matter, Jim Bridger wasted no time in persuading the company that they should indeed proceed as planned. "Mr. Bridger informs me that the route we mean to take is a fine level road with plenty of water and grass," James Reed wrote. The "only bad part," he assured his fellow travelers, was a forty-mile drive through the desert by the shore of the Great Salt Lake. James fell for it: Vasquez and Bridger were "the only fair traders in these parts," he declared, unlike the other independent trappers "who swarm here during the passing of the emigrants, [and who are] as great a set of sharks as ever disgraced humanity."[116] But the truth was, as his daughter would recall, he "was so eager to reach California that he was quick to take advantage of any means to shorten the distance."

Not everyone in their party was quite so sure, and much time was lost in debating the relative merits of the two routes. Eventually, the party split. "The greater portion of our company went by the old road and reached California safely." A splinter group of eighty-seven people, including the Donner and Reed families, would choose the other path.

On the morning of July 31, Virginia Reed and her family parted with the rest of their company and, "without a suspicion of impending disaster,"

---

*The Greenwood Cutoff had been forged by none other than Caleb Greenwood in 1844.

set off in high spirits on the Hastings Cutoff. A few days on this new and almost untried route were enough to show them that the road was not at all as it had been represented. The fact that Lansford Hastings himself was leading another party, slightly in advance of theirs, initially gave them confidence, but one day they found a note left by the wayside "warning us that the road through Weber Canon was impassable and advising us to select a road over the mountains, the outline of which he attempted to give on paper."

The directions Hastings had attempted to scribble out were so hopelessly vague that three of the men, including Virginia's father, rode on ahead to try to find Hastings and persuade him to come back and show them the way himself. Hastings refused. Instead, he came back just some of the way "and from a high mountain endeavored to point out the general course."

Knowing of the difficulties that were being experienced by the party ahead of them, they decided to cross toward the lake. "Only those who have passed through this country on horseback can appreciate the situation," Virginia Reed wrote. "There was absolutely no road, not even a trail." Almost immediately they became ensnared in canyons so steep it looked at first as though they would have no choice but to abandon their wagons altogether. Eventually, by almost superhuman efforts, in which every single yoke of oxen in the entire party was required to heave each individual wagon up the sides of the canyons, they managed it and emerged on the shores of the Great Salt Lake. Beyond it lay hundreds of miles of scorching, almost-featureless white desert. Instead of taking just a week, as Hastings had promised, this small stretch of their journey had taken an entire month.

But there was no going back. If they were to cross the Sierra Nevada before winter set in, they had no more time to lose: cross the desert they must.

7

————— · —————

TRAPPED

The Great Salt Lake and the salt flats that stretch beyond it are among the most desolate places on earth. Even today, to travel across this desert wilderness on a modern six-lane highway is a daunting prospect. The salt flats yawn across a space that seems limitless, absolutely white, absolutely flat, treacherously soft, the horizon eaten away by dancing mirages.

It was a sight that filled Virginia Reed with dread: "a dreary, desolate, alkali waste" in which not a living thing could be seen; "it seemed as though the hand of death had been laid upon the country."[117] Although the company had been given to believe that they would have to travel just forty miles across this desert, it was in fact many times that distance. In order to make up some of the time they had lost in the canyons, for three days and two nights they labored painfully onward without a break, "suffering from thirst and heat by day, and piercing cold by night." On one night the cold and wind were so bitter that Virginia believed that if it were not for the fact that her father placed all five of their dogs around his children for warmth, they would have died of exposure.

Although they had stocked up—as they thought—with an ample supply of water and grass for their livestock, it was not enough. Very soon their oxen and other livestock began to collapse from exhaustion and thirst. The Reeds at this point had eighteen head of cattle with them, an investment that was essential to their plans for a new life in California. In desperation, Virginia's father sent his drivers off with them to a water source he had eventually been able to find ten miles away, but at the first scent of water the steers, crazed with thirst, had stampeded and were lost from sight. Despite the fact that every man in the company turned out to help them find the livestock, only one was ever found.

A further week had now been lost in this fruitless hunt. The Reed family, who had been by far the wealthiest of the group, were now in a frighteningly vulnerable state. All but one of their oxen were long dead (poisoned by drinking alkaline water at Bridger's fort), and now all their cattle, except for one steer, were gone too. "My father and his family were left in the desert, eight hundred miles from California, seemingly helpless." Had it not been for the fact that they were lent two yoke of oxen by others in the company they would have been completely stranded. As it was, these together with their one ox and one steer yoked together might just be able to pull one of the smaller wagons. The once-magnificent Pioneer Palace Car, with its sprung seats, comfortable feather beds, and even its looking glass, still miraculously unbroken, was now abandoned to the desert winds. All their possessions, except for the few things they were able to cram into the smaller wagon, were cached in the desert.

An inventory of all their provisions was now made, from which it was clear that no one in the company had enough food left to last them until they reached California. Two volunteers, Charles Stanton and William Mc-Cutchen, now set out alone, ahead of the rest of the company, to try to reach Captain Sutter, at Sutter's Mill, on the western side of the Sierra Nevada, and ask him for help.

The rest of the company limped painfully on. On October 5 they reached Gravelly Ford, on the Humboldt River. It was here that "a tragedy was enacted which affected the subsequent lives of more than one member of our company." A fight broke out between Milton Elliott, the Reeds' driver, and another teamster, John Snyder. In Virginia Reed's version of the story, this had occurred when Snyder began to beat his oxen around the head with the butt end of his whip. When James Reed tried to calm him down, an altercation ensued. Snyder "struck my father a violent blow over the head with his heavy whip-stock." Mr. Reed, in what he would later claim was self-defense, pulled out a hunting knife and stabbed him.

The wound proved fatal. Although James Reed would always claim that he had only acted in self-defense, the other members of the Donner party did not accept this as an excuse, and a council was held to decide what his punishment should be. In the heat of the moment, some thought he should be lynched or hanged right there and then, but, happily, saner voices prevailed. Instead, in a judgment that under the circumstances was almost as harsh, it was decided that he should be banished into the desert. "It was thought more humane, perhaps, to send him into the wilderness to die of slow starvation or be murdered by Indians," Virginia Reed wrote. "My father was sent out into an unknown country without provisions or arms—even his horse was at first denied him. When we learned of this decision, I followed him through the darkness . . . And carried him his rifle, pistols, ammunition and some food."

The rest of the Reed family had no choice but to stumble on without him. For all that theirs was a pitiful situation, it was better than that of some of the others. One couple, the Eddys, having lost everything they had, including their yoke of oxen, were forced to walk. Eleanor Eddy carried her baby daughter in her arms while her husband William shouldered their three-year-old boy and their sole remaining provisions: "three pounds of sugar, some bullets, and a powder horn." Another of their company, William Pike, was accidentally shot in the back with a pistol and died soon after, suffering "more than tongue can tell." All this while the Sierra Nevada, the largest contiguous mountain range in North America,* was getting ever closer—the last great obstacle that remained between them and their dream.

---

*The Rocky Mountains are collections of geologically distinct chains.

What they saw, as they rode slowly onward, filled them with new fear. Even though it was only the middle of October, snow had already begun to fall. Winter had set in a whole month earlier than expected. "All the trails and roads were covered," Virginia Reed remembered, "and our only guide was the summit which it seemed we would never reach."

There was only one event during this time to cheer them. One day, Charles Stanton suddenly appeared before them at the head of a mule train, bringing them not only the promised supplies, including flour and fresh meat, but also two Mexicans to help guide them over the mountains. Although Stanton's companion on the mission to resupply the company, William McCutchen, had been too ill and exhausted to attempt to recross the mountains, Stanton brought the welcome news that James Reed had also made it safely to Sutter's Mill.

Since 1841, several passes across the Sierra Nevada had been known to settlers, but it was not until 1844 that one had been found wide enough for a wagon to pass through. Even then it had proved a physically excruciating task: the wagons had had to be completely emptied, their tops removed, and the wagon bases hoisted over the ridges, before being repacked on the other side. Now, in the cold and the snow, with time running out, it seemed all but impossible.

"Despair drove many nearly frantic," Virginia wrote. "Each family tried to cross the mountains, but found it was impossible. When it was seen that the wagons could not be dragged through the snow, their goods and provisions were packed on oxen and another start was made, men and women walking in the snow up to their waists, carrying their children in their arms and trying to drive their cattle." But it was no use. Even with the Mexicans from Sutter's Mill to help them, the trail could not be found. Eventually, a halt was called.

At this point Charles Stanton went on ahead with the two guides to inspect the way himself. When he came back, he reported that he had found what he thought might be the pass, but a crossing would only be possible if no more snow fell. "He was in favor of a forced march until the other side should be reached, but some of our party were so tired and exhausted with the day's labor that they declared they would not take another step; so the few who knew the danger that the night might bring yielded to the many, and we camped within three miles of the summit."

It was a disastrous decision. That night was one of heavy snow. "Around the campfires under the trees great feathery flakes came whirling down. The air was so full of them that one could see objects only a few feet away," Virginia would recall. "The Indians (Mexican guides) knew we were doomed, and one of them wrapped his blanket about him and stood all night under a tree. We children slept soundly on our cold bed of snow with a soft white mantle falling over us so thickly that every few moments my mother would have to shake the shawl—our only covering—to keep us from being buried alive."

The next morning it was clear to everyone that their worst fears had been realized. Whatever chance they had had of crossing the mountains before winter set in was now gone. Although they were only a hundred miles short of their destination, and just three miles short of the pass, there was nothing for it but to wait the winter out.

Eighty-one people were now trapped in the Sierra Nevada. Of these, more than half were children under eighteen, and a quarter were aged under five. The party now split up into two camps. One of the other families with the Reeds, the Breens, were fortunate in that they were able to use a cabin that had been built by the Murphy-Schallenberger company two years previously on the shore of a lake, then known as Truckee Lake (named after Sarah Winnemucca's grandfather).* It was very small, had no door, and only had branches for a roof—altogether a damp, miserable space, but at least it provided them with some kind of shelter. The others hastily built two other

---

*Seventeen-year-old Moses Schallenberger and two companions had built this doorless shelter in 1844. They had volunteered to remain at Truckee Lake when winter snows prevented their wagons from crossing the pass. The three were left in charge of half the party's wagons and goods, while the rest of the party, unencumbered, made it safely over the pass. The three men had endured many similar privations to the Donner-Reed party, but perhaps because all survived, and there were no women and children involved, their story is far less well known.

double cabins nearby. These refuges were known as the "Breen Cabin," the "Murphy Cabin," and the "Reed-Graves Cabin" after the four principal families who sheltered there. Stanton and the two Mexicans, Luis and Salvador, took shelter with the Reeds.

The rest of the party, including the two Donner families, were altogether less fortunate. They camped in a small valley just below the lake, now known as Alder Creek Valley. "The snow came on so suddenly that they had no time to build cabins, but hastily put up brush sheds, covering them with pine boughs."

It was clear to everyone that the remaining cattle, brought with such painful effort across the salt desert, would not survive the winter. These were now slaughtered, and the meat was cut up and buried in the snow to preserve it. All the Reeds' cattle, except for one steer, had been lost in the Great Salt Lake, so Margaret Reed made an arrangement with one of the other families, promising to pay them back in kind, with two cows for each one, when they reached the California valley.

It was the beginning of November when they first made camp by the lake; the conditions were not now likely to improve until at least March. Huddling together in their makeshift huts, they were now faced with the prospect of four months of brutal winter cold. "The misery endured . . . in our little dark cabins under the snow would fill pages and make the coldest heart ache." Food, such as they had, was rationed to almost nothing. "Poor little children were crying with hunger, and mothers were crying because they had so little to give their children." Some chewed twigs and the bark from trees in a desperate attempt to quell their hunger pangs. Others killed their dogs and ate them.

Before long, most were so weak they could scarcely walk. Even the men had barely strength enough to gather wood. Storms, sometimes lasting as many as ten days at a time, raged around the fragile huts, and "some mornings snow would have to be shoveled out of the fireplace before a fire could be made." When the weather made it impossible to go out to gather firewood, they were reduced to cutting chips from the log walls.

Christmas Day was approaching, but to the now-starving families "its memory gave no comfort," Virginia Reed remembered. But on the day itself, "which passed without observance," something happened that must have seemed at the time like nothing short of a miracle. "My mother had determined weeks before that her children should have a treat on this one day." She had hidden away a cache of a few dried apples, some beans, a length of tripe, and a small piece of bacon. "When this hoarded store was brought out, the delight of the little ones knew no bounds. . . . And when we sat down to our Christmas dinner mother said: 'Children, eat slowly, for this one day you can have all you wish.' So bitter was the misery relieved by that one bright day, that I have never since sat down to a Christmas dinner without my thoughts going back to Truckee Lake."

This tiny reprieve did not last long. The snow was now so deep that it was higher than the roofs of the huts. As they huddled together for warmth, it was clear to everyone that they were no longer on a short allowance but were actually starving to death. Their bodies began to show the classic symptoms: "cheekbones and ribs and shoulder blades protruded. Muscle-bound arms shriveled to sticks. Joints ached. Buttocks grew so bony that sitting became painful. Skin dried and scaled to the rough texture of parchment."[118] Looking at the gaunt faces of her children, Margaret Reed could bear it no longer and "determined to make an effort to cross the mountains."

Margaret was not the only one desperate enough to attempt to cross the mountains in the midwinter snows. Several other forays had already been made by the famished settlers, "but all who tried were driven back by the pitiless storms." On December 16, a group of seventeen people—ten men, five women, and two children, the youngest of whom was ten—had set off in an attempt to reach Sutter's Mill and get help. Led by William Eddy, they had been wearing snowshoes crudely fashioned from ox bone and rawhide and had taken supplies with them which, with strict rationing, they hoped would last them six days. But they had never returned, and nothing was known of their fate.

Much later, they would learn that of this group of seventeen, known as the "Forlorn Hope" party, seven had survived. Those who made it through to Sutter's Mill included two men and all five of the women. Instead of the six days that they had predicted, it had taken them a month. Under these conditions, there had only ever been one means of survival. While everyone in the party was still alive, various gruesome options were discussed: one suggestion was to cast lots to decide who would be killed and eaten; another was that two of the men should fight a duel, the one to be killed agreeing in advance that his body might be consumed by the others. But both these plans were rejected. In the end, the first of the party to be cannibalized was a man named Patrick Dolan. One evening, Dolan had lost his head completely. Tormented by the effects of severe hypothermia, he had stripped off all his clothes and boots and run from their makeshift shelter, out into the frozen night. The others had tried to wrestle him back to their fire, but it was too late. When Dolan died shortly after, his body was quickly cut up and consumed by the rest. The others in the party who died in quick succession after that were also cut up and eaten. Some of their bodies were roasted and devoured on the spot; other parts were preserved in strips for later occasions.

It was only toward the end of their appalling ordeal, and by now suffering the most extreme psychological and physical torments brought about by near starvation, that they considered murder. The Graves family would later maintain that William Eddy tried to lure Mary Graves away from the rest so he could kill her. Another of the group (and, apart from Eddy, the only other man to survive), William Foster, was also said to have suggested murdering three of the women for food. But since all the women survived, neither of these accusations could ever be proved. In the end, it was only the two Mexican guides, Luis and Salvador, who would suffer this fate. Already harrowed by extreme exposure, they were found to be "collapsed and near death." William Foster took his gun and shot them both through the head.[119]

Back at Truckee Lake, of course, the rest of the company knew none of this. When no help seemed to be forthcoming, Margaret Reed feared the worst. All she knew was that if she did not do something, her children were going to die. Leaving the younger ones behind in the care of the Breens, on January 4, 1847, she took Virginia and her two servants, the maid Eliza and their teamster Milt Elliott, and set off to find help.

For a while all went well. Milt had fashioned himself a pair of snowshoes and the others followed in his tracks. In their already-weakened state, walking through the snow was such debilitating work that sometimes Virginia had to crawl up the steeper inclines on her hands and knees. Eliza gave up on the first day and returned alone to the camp. The others staggered on for another four days, climbing "one high mountain after another only to see others higher still ahead."

One night they fell into an exhausted sleep, "lulled by the moan of the pine trees" all around them and "the screams of wild beasts heard in the distance." The next morning they awoke to find that the heat of the fire had melted the snow all around them, that their little camp had sunk many feet below the surface, and that they were "literally buried" in a well of snow. "The danger was that any attempt to get out might bring an avalanche upon us, but finally steps were carefully made and we reached the surface." Virginia now found that one of her feet had become so badly frostbitten that to climb any farther was impossible. There was nothing for it but to return to camp. As it turned out, they reached it just in time, "for that night a storm came on, the most fearful of the winter, and we should have perished had we not been in the cabins."

The failure of their rescue attempt was the bitterest of blows. Margaret Reed, mother of four children, the youngest of whom, Thomas, was only three, now had to face the fact that her children would almost certainly starve to death or, worse, that she herself would die and leave them alone.

Others had already begun to die. The first of the Reed party to go was Eliza's brother, Baylis, who had been in delicate health even before they left Springfield. Next, and most shocking to Virginia, was Milt Elliott—"our faithful friend, who seemed so like a brother." With what little strength they had left, she and her mother dragged his body outside, where his corpse now joined a gruesome graveyard of several others lying nearby on the snow. No one had the strength to bury their dead. "Commencing at his feet," Virginia remembered, "I patted the pure white snow down softly till I reached his face. Poor Milt! It was hard to cover that face from sight forever, for with his death our best friend was gone."

There was now no food left at all. In desperation, they took down the raw buffalo hides with which their hut had been roofed, but the meagre scrapings they were able to get from them, when boiled, "were simply a pot of glue." With no covering left on their hut, they took shelter with the Breens. Virginia believed that she was only kept alive by the kindness of Mrs. Breen, who when she saw that Virginia could not eat the hide, slipped her small pieces of meat from her own supply.

Unlike the Reeds, the Breens were Catholic, and prayers were regularly said by them, both night and morning. One night, when she was sure that all was now lost, Virginia went down on her knees and prayed. "All at once I found myself on my knees with my hands clasped, looking up through the darkness, making a vow that if God would send us relief and let me see my father again, I would be a Catholic."

Shortly after, it must have seemed to her as though her prayers had been answered. On the evening of February 19, shouts were heard through the gathering dusk. "Mr. Breen clambered up the icy steps from our cabin, and soon we heard the blessed words, 'Relief, thank God, relief.'"

The rescue party, which had set out from Sutter's Mill, was a group of men led by Captain Reason Tucker. All this while James Reed had been at Sutter's Mill, frantically worried about the safety of his family. When their wagon train had not arrived the previous autumn, and fearing the worst, he had already made one rescue attempt but had been turned back by the adverse weather conditions. His subsequent efforts had been hampered for altogether different reasons. In April 1846, war had finally broken out between Mexico and the US. When James Reed had finally arrived at the mill, Captain Sutter had told him that all the able-bodied men who might have been able to make up a rescue party had "gone down the country with Frémont to fight the Mexicans." Sutter had advised him to go to Yerba

Buena (soon to be renamed San Francisco) and make his case to the naval officer in command there. While he was away, the "Forlorn Hope" party had limped into Sutter's Mill. Theirs was a shocking tale. As Virginia Reed put it: "Their famished faces told the story."

In the absence of James Reed, John Sutter himself had arranged for the relief party that had now reached them. The feelings of the survivors can barely be imagined. "But with the joy, sorrow was strangely blended," Virginia Reed remembered. "There were tears in other eyes than those of children; strong men sat down and wept. For the dead were lying about on the snow, some even unburied, since the living had not had strength to bury their dead."

A few days later, on February 22, a party of twenty-three of the strongest survivors, including Margaret Reed and her four children, started out—the rest being too weakened from starvation even to attempt such a journey. They had not gone far before it became clear that two of Virginia's siblings, Patty and Tommy, were simply not strong enough, "and it was not thought safe to allow them to proceed." There was nothing for it but to send them back to the cabins to await the arrival of their father, with the next relief party. "What language can express our feelings? My mother said that she would go back with her children—that we would all go back together. This the relief party would not permit." One of the coleaders of the rescue party, Aquilla Glover, gave her his most solemn promise that if her husband (who, they believed, would be following soon after) did not come, he would return himself to save them. "It was a sad parting—and a fearful struggle. The men turned aside, not being able to hide their tears. Patty said, 'I want to see papa, but I will take good care of Tommy and I do not want you to come back.' Mr. Glover returned with the children and, providing them with food, left them in the care of Mr. Breen."

They now fell into a pattern of travel that must have seemed oddly familiar to Virginia. Their rescuers forged the way ahead in their snowshoes, making tracks for the others to follow in. The only one who could not manage this was Virginia's little five-year-old brother, James. "In order to travel he had to place his knee on the little hill of snow after each step and climb over." Margaret Reed did her best to coax him along, "telling him that every step he took he was getting nearer papa and nearer something to eat."

At night they lay down on the icy snow to sleep, "to awake to find our clothing all frozen, even to our shoe-strings." During the day the sun reflected so dazzlingly against the white snow that it was painful to their eyes, while its heat melted their frozen skirts, "making them cling to our bodies." In this painfully slow way they stumbled on, in single file, exhausting hour after exhausting hour.

After two days, John Denton, who had been a teamster for the Donner family, gave out. He declared that it was simply impossible to go on and asked that the others continue without him. "A fire was built and he was left lying on a bed of freshly cut pine boughs, peacefully smoking." Later, when the second relief party finally found him, "poor Denton was past walking." A little poem was found by his side, "the pencil apparently just dropped from his hand."

It was not long before disaster struck yet again. In order to lighten their packs, on their journey to the cabins Captain Tucker had ordered that the provisions needed for the return journey should be cached in a certain place by hanging them from a tree. When they returned to the hiding place, they found to their consternation that wild animals had found and either destroyed or eaten everything that was there. "And again, starvation stared us in the face."

Once again, in a way that must have seemed nothing short of miraculous at the time, help was at hand. Just in time they were found by the second relief party, fourteen men who had finally been mustered by James Reed. Some of the party, recounted Virginia Reed, were traveling ahead of the others, "and when they saw [us] coming, called out: 'Is Mrs. Reed with you? If she is, tell her Mr. Reed is here.' We heard the call; mother knelt on the snow, while I tried to run to meet papa."

There was no time to lose. Learning that his remaining two children, Patty and Tommy, were still at the cabins, James Reed "seemed to fly over the snow," reaching Truckee Lake in just two days, on March 1. To his inexpressible relief, Patty and Tommy were still alive, although "the famished little children and the death-like look of all made his heart ache."

Leaving seven days of provisions and three of his men behind to look after those who were too weak even to stand, James Reed now set off with a party of seventeen—"all that were able to travel." They had not advanced more than a few miles before a storm broke. "One who had never witnessed a blizzard in the Sierra can form no idea of the situation." Virginia's father and his men worked frantically throughout the night to build a makeshift shelter for the dying women and children, the shrieking of the storm mixing with the "cries of the half-frozen children, and the lamenting of the mothers." At times the force of the tempest burst forth with such violence "that he felt alarmed on account of the tall timber surrounding the camp."

As Captain Tucker had done, James Reed had cached provisions for the return journey along the way. Just before the storm had set in, three men had been hastily sent to retrieve them, but they were too late and were unable to make their way back through the blizzard. "Thus, again, death stared all in the face.... At one time the fire was nearly gone; had it been lost, all would have perished."

The storm lasted for three days and three nights. By this time James Reed was completely snow-blind, and he would have died had it not been for the exertions of two of his men, William McCutchen and Hiram Miller, "who worked over him all night."

The storm did eventually die out, and once more they were on their way, Hiram Miller carrying little Tommy in his arms. For a while, Patty was able to walk alongside them, but soon it became clear that she was at the end of her strength: "Gradually everything faded from her sight, and she too seemed to be dying." In Virginia Reed's account, it was only thanks to the fact that her father now found "some crumbs [of bread] in the thumb of his woolen mitten," which he was able to give her, having first warmed and moistened them between his own lips, that she was saved. From here, the men took it in turns to carry her to safety.

In total, four separate relief parties made their way over the Sierra Nevada that winter. Of the eighty-one men, women, and children who had become trapped in the mountains, only forty-two survived. Almost all of them had, by the end of their ordeal, been reduced to eating the bodies of their dead in order to survive. Of the thirty-one in the Donner-Reed party who had set out from Springfield the previous April, only eighteen reached their destination, west of the Sierra Nevada. Among them, miraculously, was the entire Reed family.

"Words cannot tell how beautiful the spring appeared to us coming out of the mountains from that long winter," Virginia Reed wrote in her later account. "I remember one day, when traveling down the Napa Valley, we stopped at noon to have lunch under the shade of an oak. . . . I wandered off by myself to a lovely little knoll and looked up and down the green valley, all dotted with trees. The birds were singing with very joy in the branches over my head, and the blessed sun was smiling down upon all as though in benediction. I drank it in for a moment, and then began kissing my hand and wafting kisses to Heaven in thanksgiving to the Almighty for creating a world so beautiful."

Virginia Reed wrote her version of events long afterward, but in doing so she drew on a letter that she had written just a few months after her rescue.* It is an altogether cruder, less sentimental report, but no less vivid, and perhaps closer in spirit to the thirteen-year-old survivor of those desperate months of death and survival in the Sierra Nevada.

"O Mary," she wrote to a cousin back in Springfield, "I have not wrote you half of the truble we have had but I hav Wrote you anuf to let you know now that you don't now what truble is but thank the Good god we have all got throw and the onely family that did not eat human flesh we have left every thing but I don't cair for that." She ended her letter, "We have got through but Dont let this letter dishaten anybody and never take no cutofs and hury along as fast as you can."[120]

---

*The original no longer exists, but a photostat of it, without the emendations of later editors, is preserved in the Southwest Museum Library in Los Angeles.

8

———————

GOLD FEVER

L ittle could Virginia Reed have envisaged, when she advised anyone who wanted to follow them to California not to be deterred by their story, "to take no cutofs and hury along as fast as you can," just how prophetic her words would turn out to be.

In a curious incident, and one that is easy to skim over altogether in her devastating account of starvation and cannibalism in the Sierra Nevada, she refers to a discovery made by John Denton, the Donner family's teamster. Denton was an Englishman from Sheffield, a gunsmith and "gold-beater" by trade, who had shared the Reeds' cabin. One evening, when he was trying to fashion some fire irons out of rocks by chipping pieces off them with his cane, his attention had been caught by fragments of something bright and glittering inside the stone. "Mrs. Reed, this is gold," he had exclaimed. Virginia's mother had replied bitterly that she wished it were bread, but Denton was undeterred. Chipping away at the rocks, he had soon collected about a teaspoonful of the shining particles, vowing then and there that "If ever we get away from here, I am coming back for more."[121]

But John Denton, of course, whose frozen, emaciated body was later discovered with a small buckskin pouch of gold dust still in his pocket, did not live to fulfil his wish. Just two years later, however, an estimated thirty thousand people would set out West with exactly the same dream.

On January 24, 1848, gold was discovered at Sutter's Mill. James Marshall, a carpenter from New Jersey who was working for John Sutter at the time, had spotted some flakes of gold in the river. Very soon after, other workers at the mill made similar finds. In an almost-perfect dovetailing of events, barely a week later, on February 2, the Treaty of Guadalupe Hidalgo was signed in faraway Mexico City, bringing an end to the two-year Mexican-American War. Under the terms of the treaty, a vast majority of what is now the American Southwest and West, including the whole of California, was transferred to the United States.* The combination of these two events would change Americans' perception of the West forever.

At first John Sutter was dismayed. Predicting disaster ahead for his business ventures should the news get out, he tried to keep the discovery under wraps, but to no avail. Within just two months, 273 pounds of gold had been recovered from the Sutter's Mill area. It would prove impossible to keep this treasure trove a secret any longer.

A man waving a vial of gold fragments in the saloon bars of Yerba Buena lit the tinderbox. It is estimated that by the middle of June three-quarters of the men living there had abandoned the port—including all the tall ships anchored there—and were flooding into the Sierra Nevada foothills. The Gold Rush had begun.

The Oregon Fever of the early 1840s was as nothing compared to the California "Gold Fever" that now gripped the nation. Intoxicating stories

---

*The treaty, which came into effect on July 4 that year, transferred ownership not only of California but of a vast area comprising all present-day Nevada and Utah, more than two-thirds of Arizona, half of New Mexico, and parts of Colorado and Wyoming to the US. Under the same treaty, the Rio Grande was fixed as the border for Texas. Texas, also formerly part of Mexico, and having briefly declared itself an independent republic, had entered the Union in 1845.

soon began to filter back East. Even though most of these owed more to myth than to reality, the suggestion that the wealth of Croesus could be had by merely "dipping one's hand into a sparkling mountain stream" soon took hold.[122] It was, as one historian has written, "the beginning of our national madness, our insanity of greed."[123]

Until this time, the yearly emigration to Oregon and California had numbered a few thousand at most. Now, almost overnight, the steady trickle of farmers and homesteaders making their way west became a raging torrent as gold seekers in their tens of thousands rushed in from all corners of the globe: Chinese laborers, Mexican farmers, clerks from London, tailors from eastern Europe, Spanish aristocrats, sailors from Australia. Boats set sail from almost every port in South America.

In 1848, before stories about the discovery of gold had had a chance to percolate east, four thousand overlanders set out West. The following spring, in 1849, thirty thousand set out from the Missouri borderlands and headed to California. In 1850, fifty-five thousand followed them. While a great proportion of these were single men, many families of women and children were among them. Instead of relatively modest wagon parties such as those traveled in by Virginia Reed and Keturah Belknap, so many outfits left Independence that April that the line of wagons stretched for hundreds of miles, as far as the eye could see.

"We have been eighteen days on the plains, amid the greatest show in the world," wrote one observer. "The train is estimated to be 700 miles long, composed of all kinds of people, from all parts of the United States, and some of the rest of mankind, with lots of horses, mules, oxen, cows, steers."[124] "It seemed to me that I had never seen so many human beings in my life before," wrote one woman bound for the California gold mines in 1850. At one point, where the branches of two separate trails converged along the Platte River, the sheer numbers of wagons were like nothing she had ever seen before. "When we drew nearer to the vast multitude, and saw them in all manner of vehicles and conveyances, on horseback and on foot . . . I thought, in my excitement, that if one-tenth of these teams and these

*By midcentury, tens of thousands of settlers were leaving the
Missouri "jumping off" towns every spring.*

people got ahead of us, there would be nothing left in California to pick
up."[125]

For California's Indigenous people, many of whom were already living
in semi-slavery under the Mexican mission system, and those, such as Sarah
Winnemucca's Tribe, the Northern Paiute, living on the peripheries of the
gold fields, it would mark the end of the world as they knew it.

Gold became the impetus for a new kind of emigration altogether. Now
it was not only families from relatively humble backgrounds—the "backwoodsmen," in Francis Parkman's phrase—but middle-class men and
women from prosperous homes. "On the streets, in the fields, in the work-
shops, and by the fireside, golden California was the chief topic of conversation," wrote Catherine Haun, a young bride from Iowa. The effects of the
economic depression, begun in 1837, still resonated throughout the Mississippi Valley, and, like many others, the couple were in financial difficulties. The stories of gold that were beginning to sweep eastward fell upon
willing ears. "We ... longed to go to the new El Dorado and 'pick up' gold
enough with which to return and pay off our debts," Catherine wrote, believing it was a chance to exchange their "comfortable homes—and the

uncomfortable creditors—for the uncertain and dangerous trip, beyond which loomed up, in our mind's eye, castles of shining gold."[126]

For Catherine Haun, traveling west in 1849 with her lawyer husband and his brother, the reasons for going were complex ones. Her sister, while still young, had recently died of consumption, and she too "had reason to be apprehensive on that score." Her doctor, seeing the danger of another winter of intense cold in Iowa, had advised a complete change of climate. His first recommendation was a long sea voyage, but instead he "approved our contemplated trip across the plains in a 'prairie schooner,' for even in those days an out-of-door life was advocated as a cure for this disease." Incredibly, it also appealed to the recently married couple "as a romantic wedding tour."

"Who were going? How best to 'fix up' the 'outfit'? What to take as food and clothing? Who would stay at home to care for the farm and women folks? Who would take wives and children along?"—these were the questions on everyone's lips. "Advice," Catherine remembered, "was handed out quite free of charge and often quite free of common sense."

Settlers had always tended to take too many belongings with them, and the Hauns were no exception. In addition to four servants—a cook and three teamsters—their outfit consisted of four wagons. One of these was given over entirely to barrels of alcohol for their consumption on the journey, while two others were loaded up with merchandise which they fondly hoped to sell "at fabulous prices" when they arrived at the other end. "The theory of this was good," Catherine recalled, "but the practice—well, we never got the goods across the first mountain." As was so often the case, these entirely superfluous wares would be abandoned beside the trail, for those who came after them to plunder at their will. The alcohol they buried in the ground, "lest the Indians should drink it, and frenzied thereby might follow and attack us."

In the fourth wagon, Catherine took her trunk of "wearing apparel," the contents of which she detailed lovingly in her account. These consisted of "underclothing, a couple of blue checked gingham dresses, several large stout aprons for general wear, one light colored for Sundays, a pink calico sunbonnet and a white one intended for 'dress up' days. . . . My feminine vanity had also prompted me to include, in this quasi-wedding trousseau, a white cotton dress, a black silk manteau trimmed very fetchingly with velvet bands and fringe, also a lace scuttle-shaped bonnet having a wreath of tiny pink rosebuds, and on the side of the crown, nestled a cluster of the same flowers. With this marvelous costume I had hoped to 'astonish the natives' when I should make my first appearance upon the golden streets of the mining town in which we might locate." As she remarked, with a certain self-deprecating irony: "Should our dreams of great wealth acquired over-night come true, it might be embarrassing not to be prepared with a suitable wardrobe for the wife of a very rich man!"

As it turned out, she spent almost the entire journey in the same dark woolen dress, learning, as countless other women had done before her, that it "economized in laundrying, which was a matter of no small importance when one considers how limited, and often utterly wanting were our 'wash day' conveniences. The chief requisite, water, being sometimes brought from miles away." But this hard-won knowledge was many long, toilsome months into the future.

Many women wrote about the pain and fear of parting with family and friends, but Catherine Haun's account, which she dictated many years later to her daughter, is unusually honest.

The weather in the spring of 1849 was particularly inclement. Even at the end of April there was still snow on the ground, and torrential rain had made the road almost impassable. The beginning of the Hauns' journey was painfully slow. It was not long before Catherine's courage failed her altogether. The first night they stopped at a farm, where they found a bed for the night. "When I woke the next morning a strange feeling of fear at the thought of our venturesome undertaking crept over me," she recalled. "I was almost dazed with dread." She went outside into the sunny farm-yard, where the contrast between the "peaceful, happy, restful home" before her and the "toil and discomfort" of the previous day's journey "caused me to break completely down with genuine homesickness and I bust out into a flood of tears."

"I remember particularly a flock of domesticated wild geese. They craned their necks at me and seemed to encourage me to 'take to the woods.' Thus construing their senseless clatter, I paused in my grief to recall the intense cold of the previous winter and the reputed perpetual sunshine and wealth of the promised land." Wiping away her tears, lest they betray her feelings, she added: "I have often thought, that had I confided in [my husband] he would certainly have turned back, for he, as well as the other men of the party, was disheartened and was struggling not to betray it."

They had not been traveling more than a day when their first "domestic annoyance" occurred. The cook they were taking with them had been followed by her "Romeo," who had had no difficulty in persuading her to defect. Catherine was now the only woman in their party, and by her own admission had never prepared so much as a cup of coffee for herself before. She surprised everyone, herself included, by offering to do the cooking "if everyone else would help."

Catherine Haun's doctor's recommendation of the journey west as a health cure was, on the surface of it, not quite so outrageous as it might seem. Many women wrote about the fact that their health, and certainly their appetites, were much improved by the fresh air and exercise. Catherine herself noted that, as promised, the outdoor life completely restored her health "long before the end of our journey." Another young woman, traveling that same year, described how her invalid mother, who at the beginning of the journey was so weak that she had to be physically lifted in and out of the wagon, "now . . . walks a mile or two without stopping, and gets in and out of the wagons as spry as a young girl."[127]

Middle-class etiquette sometimes followed these middle-class women, even onto the wide-open prairies. "Mr. Reade came with six young ladies to call on us this morning, also one gentleman from the Irvine train," recorded one young woman on her journey west. "They had gone down into their trunks and were dressed in civilization costumes. They were Misses Nannie and Maggie Irvine—sisters—their brother, Tom Irvine, Mrs. Mollie Irvine, a cousin—Miss Forbes, and two other young ladies whose names I have forgotten. They are all very pleasant, intelligent young people."[128]

But the sheer weight of travelers was changing the once-pristine landscape. Wagon trains that had once left the Missouri River in small, self-contained groups now surged west in numbers that suggested nothing so much as "a vast army on wheels—crowds of men, women and lots of children and last but not least the cattle and horses on which our lives depend."[129] Sometimes the wagons traveled as many as twelve teams abreast, their billowing white canvas tops glinting in the sun. This put even greater pressure on already-stretched resources such as drinking water, while the litter and waste left behind by each succeeding party made for some disgusting conditions for those who came after, such as the "unendurable stench that rose from a ravine that is resorted to for special purposes by all the Emigration."[130] One woman was so revolted by the reek of human ordure that greeted her when she arrived at one of their camps she declared to her husband that if he did not drive her to a cleaner place to camp and sleep that night "I will take my blanket and go alone."[131] Usually, however, there was simply no option but to endure it as best they could.

With so many settlers and gold seekers, the vast majority of them men, now thronging the trail, and with ever more crowded campsites, privacy was an increasing problem. "Women told of escorting each other en masse behind the wagon train to stand in a circle facing outward, holding their skirts out to provide a bit of shelter for the one taking a turn."[132]

Insanitary conditions, and lack of an adequate water supply, soon became much more than just a trial to female modesty. Disease and "fevers" of all kinds thrived in overcrowded, filthy campsites. The indignity of coping with the effects of dysentery, one of the commonest (and often fatal) ailments on the trails, must have been a particular misery for those who were afflicted by it.

Like many women, Catherine Haun took with her a well-stocked medicine box. Principal among her remedies were the well-known staples of quinine, opium, and whiskey; she also took hartshorn, an early form of smelling salts, as a bizarre antidote for snake bites (perhaps it was effective in dealing with the shock), and she used citric acid against scurvy—a few drops of which added to sugar and water "made a fine substitute for lemonade."

A cheerful glass of lemonade was likely to have been just as effective as many of the other remedies and herbal tinctures to which women often resorted on the trails. Dysentery was treated with either dried whortleberries or half a teaspoon of gunpowder; a mixture of turpentine and sugar was said to relieve stomach complaints caused by parasites; and thickened egg whites in vinegar was used as a cough syrup. The recipe for a "Worm Elixir" included a tincture made up of saffron, sage, and tansy leaves, which should then be suspended in a pint of brandy for two weeks, a teaspoon of which should be given to children "once a week to once a month as a preventative. They will never be troubled with worms as long as you do this."[133] These remedies were usually harmless enough, and often comforting; they certainly did less violence to the body than the bleedings, blisterings, powders, and pills of uncertain provenance so often prescribed by male doctors.

One of these more sinister nostrums, bluemass, was included by Catherine Haun in her medicine supplies. Bluemass was a nineteenth-century cure-all, popularly used for a wide range of ailments from toothache and constipation to the pains of childbirth, parasitic infections, and tuberculosis. Recent analysis, in a specialist British laboratory, of some of these "blue pills" has shown the basis of bluemass to have been a compound of powdered licorice (five parts), marshmallow root or althaea (twenty-five parts), glycerin (three parts), and honey of rose (thirty-four parts). However, one third of this pleasant-tasting but otherwise entirely useless concoction was a dangerously high dose of mercury, a substance so toxic to the body that its prolonged usage, far from curing anything, eventually caused symptoms ranging from loosening of the teeth and blackening of the gums to vomiting and stomach cramps, clinical depression, and renal failure.*

But in 1849, when Catherine Haun embarked on her journey, there was nothing in her medicine box that had even the smallest chance of curing the greatest killer of them all that year: cholera.

The infection had first started in the Ganges delta and had spread across Asia and finally to Europe. The global pandemic had reached the US in 1848, thought to have been brought in on a ship, the *New York*, which had arrived from London, where the disease was then raging, in December. Seven passengers had died on board; the ship was put into quarantine, but it was too late. Five thousand people died in New York City alone.

Soon the disease had spread all over the United States, with the Mississippi Valley being particularly hard hit. Settlers, many of whom, like Catherine Haun, had decided to travel west to escape the diseases and unhealthy climate in the East, would become the very means by which the pathogen would spread.

The crowded and insanitary trails, where families ate, slept, and defecated in the closest proximity to their neighbors and traveling companions, created perfect conditions for the disease to proliferate. "Today we have passed a great many newmade graves & we hear of many cases of cholera . . . we are becoming fearful of our own safety," wrote Mrs. Francis Sawyer. Two weeks later, her worst fears had been realized. "Dr. Barkwell . . . informed us that his youngest child had died on the plains. . . . The trials & troubles of this long wearisome trip are enough to bear without having our hearts torn by the loss of dear ones."[134]

---

*The symptoms of mercury poisoning were sometimes known as "Mad Hatter Syndrome," after the character in Lewis Carroll's *Alice's Adventures in Wonderland*: in Victorian England, mercury was commonly used in the process of hat making. Bluemass, which delivered up to a hundred and twenty times the World Health Organization's acceptable daily intake of mercury, is thought to have been the cause of Abraham Lincoln's wild rages and periods of deep depression (Royal Society of Chemistry, March 22, 2010).

Wood from abandoned wagons was often used to fashion makeshift coffins, causing one woman to glance nervously at the sideboards of her own conveyance, "not knowing how soon it would serve as a coffin for one of us." There are records of burials lying in rows, fifteen or more across, and some diaries do little more than record the proliferation of wayside graves.

May 17th	. . . Saw two graves
May 18	There were two old graves close by saw two more at some distance saw one new grave
May 27th	started at six, saw three old graves and two new ones . . .
May 30th	Saw several graves today one with inscription . . .
	We counted 5 graves close together only one with inscription
June 1	Graves now are partly dug up
June 7th	7 new graves today
June 9th	Most graves look as if they were dug and finished in a hurry
June 16	Men digging a grave for a young girl. It is common to see beds and clothing discarded by the road not to be used again. It indicates death.
June 20	A young lady buried at [Independence] Rock today who had lost mother and sister about a week ago[135]

There is barely an account of the 1849 journey that does not mention similarly disturbing sights. Graves were sometimes recorded with the same obsessive attention as miles traveled, as in this chilling record kept by a woman traveling with her family from Illinois to Oregon in 1852:

June 25	. . . Passed 7 graves . . . made 14 miles
June 26	Passed 8 graves

June 29	Passed 10 graves
June 30	Passed 10 graves . . . made 22 miles
July 1	Passed 8 graves . . . made 21 miles
July 2	One man of [our] company died. Passed 8 graves made 16 miles
July 4	Passed 2 graves . . . made 16 miles
July 5	Passed 9 graves . . . made 18 miles
July 6	Passed 6 graves . . . made 9 miles
July 11	Passed 15 graves . . . made 13 miles
July 12	Passed 5 graves . . . made 15 miles
July 18	Passed 4 graves . . . made 16 miles
July 19	Passed 2 graves . . . made 14 miles
July 23	Passed 7 graves . . . made 15 miles
July 25	Passed 3 graves . . . made 16 miles
July 27	Passed 3 graves . . . made 14 miles
July 29	Passed 8 graves . . . made 16 miles
July 30	I have kept an account of the dead cattle we have passed & the number today is 35
Aug 7	We passed 8 graves within a week . . . made 16 miles
Sept 7	We passed 14 graves this week . . . made 17 miles
Sept 9	We passed 10 graves this week . . . made 16 miles
Oct 1	We have seen 35 graves since leaving Fort Boise[136]

Even more unnerving, if possible, was the sight of gravediggers actually at work. Or the poignant sight, often recorded, of graves being dug before the victim was even dead, "so as to save time."

Even those who survived could find themselves in a pitiful situation, and women were particularly vulnerable. While Catherine Haun's company was among the very few to escape the scourge, one day a "strange white woman" with torn clothes and disheveled hair, carrying a little girl in her arms, came rushing out of the wilderness into their campsite. The woman was in a state of near collapse, "trembling with terror" and barely able to walk from hunger. The little child, who at the sight of them "crouched with fear and hid her face within the folds of her mother's tattered skirt," appeared just as traumatized.

At first the woman was too distressed to give any account of herself "but was only able to sob: 'Indians,' and 'I have nobody nor place to go to.'" The Haun party took her in, and after some food and a night's rest, they were finally able to hear her story. The woman, who was from Wisconsin, was called Martha. It transpired that she had been traveling in a family group made up of her husband, their two children, and her brother and sister. When her husband and sister had contracted cholera, the other family members had made the fatal mistake of separating themselves from the rest of their company in order to look after them. "The sick ones died and while burying the sister, the survivors were attacked by Indians, who, as she supposed, killed her brother and little son.'"

Martha and her little girl had walked for three days through the wilderness trying to find help. She had seen another emigrant train in the distance but had convinced herself that there were "Indians" in the vicinity between them and herself and found it necessary to conceal herself behind trees and boulders in order to avoid them. At one point she had been forced to take a detour "miles up the Laramie [River]" in order to find a crossing place, but the swift current "had lamed her and bruised her body."

In fact, the greatest danger she faced was not attack by Native people but starvation and exposure. Martha had survived by eating raw fish, which she

---

*While nothing is known about the fate of the brother, the little boy was later recovered, safe and sound, traveling only a few days behind her in another emigrant train, having been traded to them for a horse.

caught with her hands, and, on one occasion, a squirrel that she had killed with a stone. Finally, on the third day, attracted by the sound of voices and firelight coming from the Hauns' camp, "in desperation she braved the Indians around us and trusting to darkness ventured to enter our camp."

Martha remained with the Hauns' wagon train all the way to Sacramento, California. She had pleaded with them to take her back to Independence, but they had now come too far to make a return there possible, and she was reconciled to "a long and uncertain journey with strangers." Two days into their resumed travel they found her deserted wagon, from which the horses and all her clothes had been "stolen by the Indians."

If Martha's clothes had indeed been stolen by Native Americans, rather than simply picked over by other settlers, it was likely to have had fatal consequences. The cholera brought by the overlanders spread with devastating rapidity among the plains Tribes who lived, hunted, and traded along the westward-bound trails. It was not only the settlers' stinking campsites and rudimentary graveyards—where bodies had on occasion been buried so hastily that heads and limbs were sometimes still visible sticking out of the ground—that became a source of infection. Almost anything belonging to the settlers—their wagons, supplies, and equipment abandoned or cached by the roadside, soiled clothing and bedding, and even food—could potentially carry the contagion (which is spread by feces). Perhaps most terrible of all, however, was the contamination of their water sources. Infected people washing, bathing, and defecating on the banks of rivers and streams soon turned the life-giving resource into deadly poison.

At first, many Native people turned to the settlers themselves for help, often approaching wagon trains to ask for medicine, which in turn exposed them still further to infection. "Many died of the cramps," reads a Lakota winter count for that year, its pictograph showing the agonized body of a man dying from diarrhea and dehydration, cholera's most deadly symptom. That summer, a party of the Army Corps of Engineers, heading along the North Platte, came across a group of five tipis abandoned near the river.

Approaching cautiously, they found that the tipis were in fact tombs, in which the dead bodies of a number of Lakota had been ritually laid out. Most poignantly, in the smallest tipi they found the lovingly arranged body of a young teenage girl "richly dressed in leggings of fine scarlet cloth," her decomposing body "wrapped in buffalo-robes."[137]

But as the contagion spread ever more quickly, there was often no time to dress and paint their dead. The remarkable Hunkpapa historian Josephine Waggoner, who spent several decades of her life recording her people's oral history, gives a vivid description of the sense of panic that gripped them as the disease, previously unknown among them, struck with all the terrible force of a storm. "It came up from the south with the hot winds, which drove the malady into sweeping flames as though it were a prairie fire," she wrote. "It took the weak and strong, the young and the old; it was a raging epidemic."

While the disease started along the Platte River, where the overlanders were most numerous, it soon spread north, ripping through village after village. Presenting, at first, "with a bilious attack," within a few hours "the sufferers would be seized with all the symptoms of cholera." Usually, death followed within a matter of hours. "The well ones forsook the sick, mothers forsook their children who took it. A panic struck the whole tribe; they fled north, leaving those that died rolled in blankets or robes. Whole villages were swept away; there were tents and camps that were left standing where whole families had died and no one left alive to bury them.

"The odor from the dead bodies could be scented for miles and above the deserted tents buzzards were sailing; sometimes flocks of crows flew out of the tops of the tents. This was the desolate time remembered by those who survived the epidemic. Those who were seeking help were shot at when they came anyways near the well ones. In this way, some came to a quicker end." Josephine Waggoner had been told this by the wife of the great Lakota chief Spotted Tail. "Mrs. Spotted Tail was a survivor; she told the conditions that existed at that time."[138]

Red Cormorant Woman

Susan Bordeaux Bettelyoun, who in her later life would collaborate with Josephine Waggoner on her own account of the history of her people,* gives an even more graphic description of the devastation caused by the cholera epidemic. Susan was the daughter of Red Cormorant Woman, a Brulé Lakota, and a woman greatly honored in her band. In 1841 she had married the French American fur trader James Bordeaux. The two had met on the North Platte River, where Red Cormorant Woman's band often camped in order to exchange goods with the fur traders and trappers, many of whom, like Susan's father, were of French descent. James Bordeaux operated a trading post and road ranch just eight miles east of Fort Laramie, on the North Platte River. Susan's early childhood was spent living in close proximity to the emigrant road, and she witnessed firsthand the growing tide of white migration. Although Susan herself was born in 1857, well after the cholera epidemic, many years later she would record her family's memories of the havoc it wreaked. "As a small child I was not talkative, but very observant and could remember well incidents and faces and names. Any stories or tragedies related to me were never forgotten.

"During the time of cholera, which had reached Laramie by 1849 it was a very dry year. There had been no rainfall all spring and summer. The disease seemed to be in the air and even in the dust. The cholera broke out in places all over so suddenly and without warning that no one knew what to do; even running water brought on the disease. People were afraid to drink water."

The disease did not only spread among the Lakota. "It was among all the tribes in the remotest parts of the Rocky Mountains. Thousands of

*The Oglala and Brulé (Sicangu) Lakota.

Blackfeet were reported to have died from it; the Snake Indians, the Crows, were greatly reduced in numbers. Some of these, it was told, killed their dying and then killed themselves. People fled from each other as the disease made its appearance. No one stopped to bury the dead." Sometimes holes were cut in the ice, and the dead were thrown in these. "It was reported that many suicides were committed here. Those that lost loved ones jumped right into these holes preferring a watery grave." According to Susan Bordeaux, the Mandan were reduced from three thousand people to just thirty adults, while half the Rees and the Gros Ventres died. In 1849 alone, the Sicangu lost one in every seven of their people. "All up and down the Yellowstone and the Missouri there were thousands of Cheyennes and Assiniboines lying unburied." Even Tribes as far north as Canada were affected. "In all parts of the West there was no one spared; no matter what tribe they belonged to, they were being swept off the face of the earth. It was the most heartrending circumstance. . . . It was common for a long time for a hunter to find skeletons any place, a few years after, lying where the sick had been dragged away and left, the bones bleached as white as driven snow."[139]

When she saw that the cholera was coming, Susan's mother, Red Cormorant Woman, had locked up their ranch and taken all her children and some other relatives who were staying with her to the house of a neighbor, another French American trader, Joseph Robidoux. Robidoux ran a successful blacksmith shop, right on the Oregon Trail at Horse Creek, near Scott's Bluff. So far, the disease had not reached Robidoux's ranch. Then, one day at noon, while they were eating their dinner, they heard a strange sound. As it came closer, they realized it was a man singing his death song.

"A rider came to the door and said, 'Be on the lookout. This man coming, singing, is White Roundhead. He is coming armed to kill every white man that he sees.'" White Roundhead had lost his entire lodge of four or five tents to the disease. "Blaming the white people for bringing such a scourge into the country, he was out for revenge." Susan's uncle, Swift Bear, took his gun and stepped outside, "firing above the man, who was coming along the edge of the creek bank. Every once in a while, White Roundhead was doubled up with the cramp. He kept on coming with his gun in his hand and bows and arrows strapped to his back, although he was warned not to come any farther. By this time the white men were out with their guns and, as he did not heed the warning, he was shot as he stopped with a cramp again."

Like White Roundhead, Susan's Brulé grandmother, Ptesanwiŋ, would also become the sole survivor of her band.* Like all the other Lakota, her band had fled north as soon as they heard that the cholera was coming. But it was too late—the disease was already among them. "Each night's camp there were less and less in number, as the people were buried all along the way. Some of them were in the throes of death who were to die anyway so were left behind. By the time they reached the Niobrara River [in northern Nebraska], the whole band had passed away." Only Ptesanwiŋ and one of her brothers, Brave Eagle, were left alive.

For a while they lived in separate tents on the banks of the river. Winter had come early, making it impossible to travel any farther. "My uncle was busy trailing deer every day in the snow, and brought home the deer. He said to my grandmother, 'You dry all this meat and make pemmican; it may be hard to find deer when this snow leaves. It is not very far from here to where some of our people are on White River—it is straight north of here. You could not lose your way even if you were to travel alone.'"

Ptesanwiŋ worked hard to dry the meat as fast as her brother, Brave Eagle, could bring it in. "One day, she heard a shot as she was cooking breakfast. When she went into my uncle's tent he had dressed himself in his best clothes, had painted himself for death, and the gun with which he had shot himself was still smoking."[140]

---

*She was born in 1797 and lived to be ninety years old.

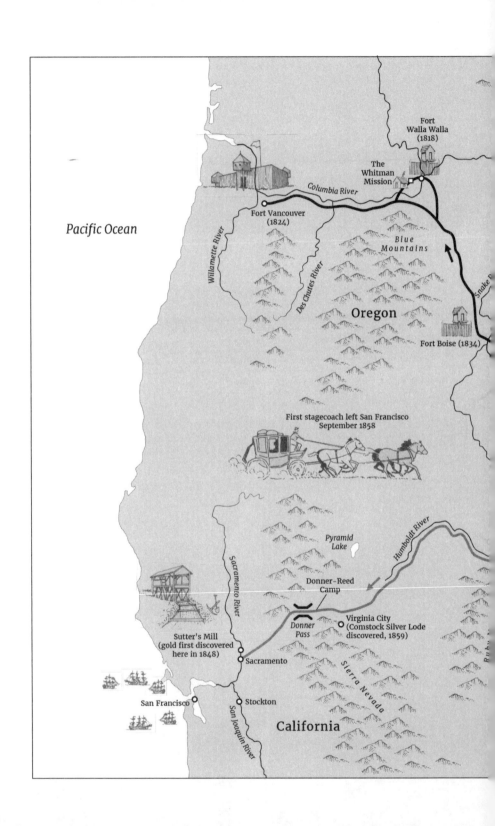

Fort
Walla Walla
(1818)

The
Whitman
Mission

Columbia River

Fort Vancouver
(1824)

Pacific Ocean

Willamette River

Des Chutes River

Blue
Mountains

Oregon

Snake R

Fort Boise (1834)

First stagecoach left San Francisco
September 1858

Pyramid
Lake

Humboldt River

Sacramento River

Donner-Reed
Camp

Sutter's Mill
(gold first discovered
here in 1848)

Donner
Pass

Virginia City
(Comstock Silver Lode
discovered, 1859)

Sacramento

Ruby M

Sierra Nevada

San Francisco

Stockton

San Joaquin River

California

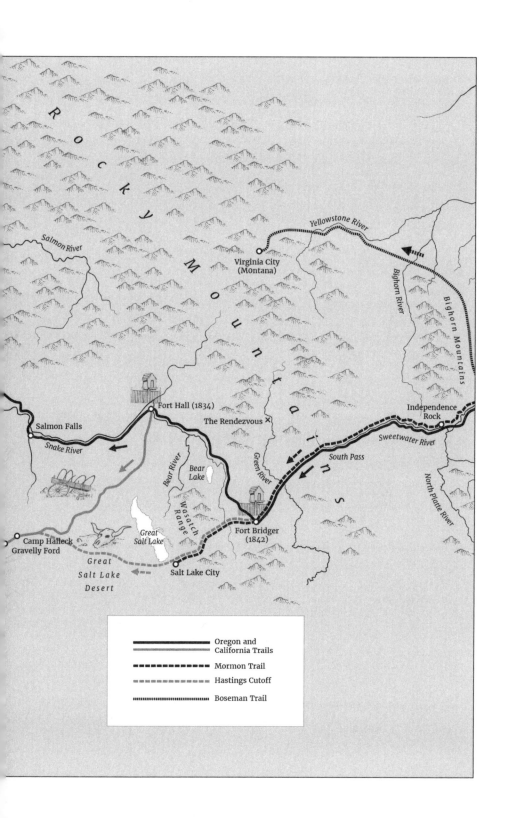

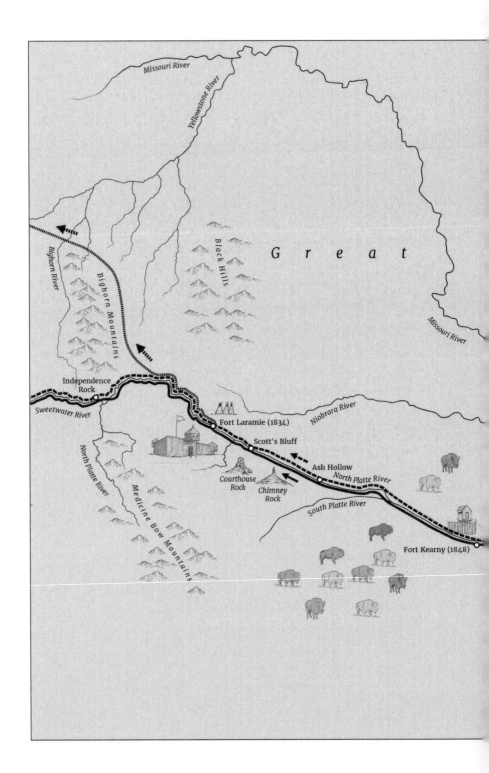

Missouri River

Yellowstone River

Bighorn River

Bighorn Mountains

Black Hills

G r e a t

Missouri River

Independence
Rock

Sweetwater River

Fort Laramie (1834)

Niobrara River

Scott's Bluff

North Platte River

Medicine Bow Mountains

Courthouse
Rock

Chimney
Rock

Ash Hollow

North Platte River

South Platte River

Fort Kearny (1848)

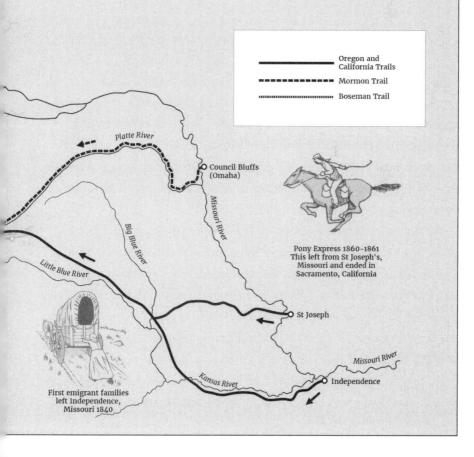

P l a i n s

Oregon and
California Trails

Mormon Trail

Boseman Trail

Platte River

Council Bluffs
(Omaha)

Missouri River

Big Blue River

Little Blue River

Pony Express 1860–1861
This left from St Joseph's,
Missouri and ended in
Sacramento, California

St Joseph

First emigrant families
left Independence,
Missouri 1840

Kansas River

Missouri River

Independence

9

THE MINES

Almost overnight, the Californian port of Yerba Buena had changed from a sleepy little pueblo into "a bawdy, bustling bedlam of mud-holes and shanties."[141] In 1847, when the US flag had first been raised, the port had a population of around seven hundred inhabitants. Just three years later, and newly renamed San Francisco, the settlement could boast of a permanent population of at least twenty-five thousand, most of whom were adult males under forty.

By any measure, San Francisco was an extremely precarious place for a woman to be, a vast shantytown of leaky canvas tents connected by rudimentary thoroughfares in which the mud ran so deep that horses and mules regularly drowned in it. Sanitation was nonexistent. Rats the size of terriers bit out chunks of men's cheeks and earlobes as they lay sleeping. Housing was so scarce that rocking chairs, and even table tops, were hired out at fifty dollars a night. Tall ships at anchor in the bay, most of which had been abandoned by their crew who had rushed, en masse, to the gold fields, were requisitioned as the city's first boardinghouses and saloons.

In this hellhole, gold was king. Prices skyrocketed. A humble boiled egg cost one dollar, sometimes more; a single apple could sell for as much as five dollars. Blankets were sold for forty dollars each; a pair of good-quality boots could not be found for under one hundred dollars. Laudanum was priced at one dollar a drop. A common iron tack for fastening a cloth partition was, literally, worth its weight in gold.[142]

Even the most basic services were all but impossible to find. Mary Ellen Pleasants, an African American cook from New Orleans who arrived by sea in San Francisco in 1850, was besieged by a crowd of men before she had even left the wharf, all desperate to employ her. Eventually she agreed to sell her services to the highest bidder—allegedly for a phenomenal five hundred dollars a month. Laundry facilities were so few and far between, and of such dubious quality, that the richest miners sent their clothes by clipper to Canton and Honolulu to be laundered—a round trip of three to six months.* Others, returning from the gold fields, had their teeth pulled out and solid gold plates installed instead (making a fortune for dentists; Henry D. Cogswell was rumored to have retired with savings of about $2 million). As the *New York Evening Post* wrote, late in 1849, "the people of San Francisco are mad, stark mad."[143]

As San Francisco grew, saloon bars and gambling dens proliferated. According to one estimate, there were perhaps as many as a thousand of the latter, men standing in lines three or four deep "for the privilege of reaching the board." Rent on one of the most prominent of these, the El Dorado, although little more than a canvas shack, is said to have brought forty thousand dollars a year to its owners.

The greatest scarcity of all, however, was women. In the first year of the Gold Rush there are thought to have been only three hundred living in San Francisco, as opposed to twenty-five thousand men.[144] The sight of one of

---

*Much as women after the French Revolution would send their white muslin dresses to the Caribbean to be bleached.

these "petticoated astonishers" was so rare that it was said that crowds formed just to catch a glimpse of them, and this gave rise to some entertaining stories. When an auction of city lots was in progress in a Montgomery Street building, "a man poked his head into the auction room and shouted: 'Two ladies going by on the sidewalk!' Whereupon the entire crowd immediately poured out of the auction room and rushed out into the street to watch them pass by."[145]

Of these three hundred women, perhaps two-thirds were prostitutes, mainly Mexicans and women from other Central and South American countries. Others soon arrived to join them, traveling there from other parts of the US. San Francisco soon possessed a red-light district that was larger than those in most American cities, even those several times its size. Brothels, from the humblest shacks to the most expensive houses of accommodation, proliferated alongside the saloons and gambling dens. Sometimes they doubled up. The El Dorado, in particular, would gain fame as one of the city's most elegant brothels. The walls were covered with "costly painting[s], extremely lascivious in character," of women in various positions of abandonment, with "furniture and fittings of rococo elegance. At one end was a raised platform from which an orchestra played. At the other end was a bar, behind which was a huge mirror of fine cut glass."*

Working women were soon arriving from as far away as Europe. In October 1850, the *Pacific News* announced that "nine hundred women of the French demi-monde, carefully chosen from the bagnios of Paris and Marseille for their beauty, amiability and skill, were expected."[146] The numbers were almost certainly an exaggeration, and in the end only fifty arrived, but it was very possibly at this time that this well-known ditty was composed:

---

*It was here that the US's most famous bartender, "Professor" Jerry Thomas, the inventor of the "Blue Blazer" and the "Tom and Jerry," began his long career. The Blue Blazer was hot whiskey mixed with sugar, poured from one silver-plated tankard into another so that, when lit, a spectacular blue flame fired up along the trajectory.

The miners came in forty-nine
The whores in fifty-one
And when they got together
They produced the native son.

Into this dangerous, dirty, gold-crazed maelstrom, one day in 1849, stepped a slight, blonde-haired young woman called Louise Clappe. Nothing in Mrs. Clappe's highly educated, ferociously literary, solidly middle-class former life could possibly have prepared her for life in San Francisco, far less for that of the mining fields to which she was headed.

Born plain Louise Smith in 1819, in New Jersey, her family later moved to Massachusetts, where Louise attended the prestigious Amherst Academy.* Its unusually broad and ambitious curriculum, open to girls as well as boys, included "mental philosophy" (as opposed to "natural philosophy," which we would now call science), Latin, botany, and geology, which would account for the unusual degree of erudition she would later bring to her writing. Louise had other ambitions too. "You must know I am a regular Nomad in my passion for wandering," she wrote to a friend as early as 1839,† declaring her avowed intention to set forth "at no distant period for the Far West."[147]

Ten years later she would realize that dream. When Louise was twenty-nine, relatively old for the time and well on her way to becoming "another example of that awesome phenomenon, the New England literary spinster,"[148] she married Fayette Clappe, a medical student five years her junior.

Fayette Clappe was a youth "of fine personal appearance," a fact that at first made up for his faults in other areas. A "changeable, unsettled young man" who was prone to losing his way, and making plans that did not work

*The same establishment that was attended only a few years later by the poet Emily Dickinson, whose grandfather had been one of the founders.
†Alexander Hill Everett, a writer, diplomat, and editor of the *North American Review*, whom she met and fell into conversation with when they were both passengers on a stagecoach.

out, he would later sink one thousand dollars—a vast sum—into a mining claim that turned out to be worthless (a mistake in which he was hardly alone). For all his faults, they must have made a handsome couple. Louise Clappe, as described by a friend, was "small, fair, and golden-haired," delicately beautiful, and "not physically strong."[149] But there her weakness ended. Her own description of herself as being a "shivering, frail, home-loving little thistle," and even "a half-dying invalid" (it has been suggested, again by unkind critics, that what she mostly suffered from was hypochondria), is totally belied by the exuberance—the sheer élan—of her letters home. "When I make up my mind to it," she wrote, "I can be as willful as the gentlest of my sex."[150]

In 1849, among their many other ailments, the couple caught "Gold Fever." They were among the first prospectors to sail to California. Arriving by sea, on board the "good ship *Manilla*," they lived for about a year in San Francisco and then later in Plumas, near Marysville. In 1851 Fayette's ill health, which included jaundice and many recurrences of unspecific "agues" and fevers (possibly malaria), caused them to move again, this time to a small mining community, Rich Bar, high in the upper reaches of the Feather River Canyon.

Mining towns were not usually known for their health-giving properties, but the couple clearly believed the mountain air would do him good. It was decided that Fayette would set himself up there as a doctor.* Their friends in San Francisco were horrified. It was inconceivable to them that "a lady" could possibly live in a crude mining camp. Mrs. Clappe, on the other hand, and in the true spirit of a nomad, declared herself "perfectly enchanted" by the idea.

The twenty-six letters that she wrote to her sister Molly during this time (1851–52) were later gathered together and published in the *Pioneer*, a California monthly magazine, under the nom de plume "Dame Shirley." Her

---

*He had never finished his medical studies but by some mysterious means had acquired his doctor's certificate "in absentia."

extraordinary eye for detail, her wit, and above all her tolerance for the miners themselves, living out their "coarse, barbarous life" under often brutal conditions, make her letters one of the best accounts ever written of "the strangely effervescent qualities" of life in an early mining camp.*

The story of how gold was first discovered at Rich Bar is typical of its kind. It had all started with a rumor ("one of those vague 'Somebodies'—a near relation of the 'They Says'—had discovered mines of a remarkable richness in a northeasterly direction"), which in this case began in the nearby mining station of Nelson's Creek, situated on the Feather River. Once this "golden rumor" had been set afloat, a large company of prospectors had immediately packed up their goods and chattels—these generally consisting of "a pair of blankets, a frying-pan, some flour, salt pork, brandy, pick-axe and shovel"—and headed off to the "new Dorado."

"They 'traveled and traveled and traveled,' as we used to say in the fairy stories, for nearly a week in every possible direction, when one evening, weary and discouraged, about one hundred of the party found themselves at the top of that famous hill, which figures so largely in my letters, whence the river can be distinctly seen. Half of the number concluded to descend the mountain that night, the remainder stopping on the summit until the next morning."

Of the men who went down immediately to the bottom of the ravine, a few ventured on several miles farther than the others. They were rewarded the next day when, on turning over a large boulder in the riverbed, they discovered beneath it "quite a sizeable piece of gold." From a small panful of dirt they had soon extracted $256 worth of gold. Before nightfall, the entire bar had been "claimed."

---

*Her contemporaries certainly thought so. It was widely believed that the editor and short-story writer Bret Harte had stolen some of his best material from her letters—a bitter irony, given that it was also well known that he had always snubbed all her attempts to contribute to his magazines and anthologies. Her work, a contemporary wrote, was "as much ahead of Bret Harte's stories as champagne is ahead of soap suds." See Rodman Wilson Paul, "In Search of Dame Shirley."

In those first heady days it must have seemed as though the entire river ran with gold. Within two weeks the same two men who made the first discovery were in possession of six thousand dollars' worth. Two others took out thirty-three pounds in one eight-hour stint—"the best day's work that has been done on this branch of the river." On another occasion, a single panful of dirt delivered up a treasure trove of fifteen hundred dollars.

When Louise Clappe arrived at Rich Bar, at first glance the location seemed to her "charmingly fresh and lovely. Imagine a tiny valley," she wrote, "apparently hemmed in by lofty hills, almost perpendicular, draperied to their very summits with beautiful fir trees." But there the romance of it ended. Rich Bar was precariously balanced on a spit of land measuring just eight hundred yards by thirty yards. In this tiny space, in little more than a week, five hundred miners had set up camp for the summer.

At the center of the "town" there was a "street," down either side of which about forty tenements of various shapes and sizes had been crammed in: "round tents, square tents, plank hovels, log cabins . . . The residences varying in elegance and convenience from the palatial splendor of 'The Empire' down to a 'local habitation.'"[151] Within days of a digging being found, "the monte-dealers, those worse than fiends, rush vulture-like upon the scene and erect a round tent, where, in gambling, drinking, swearing and fighting, the *many* reproduce Pandemonium in more than its original horror, while a few honestly and industriously commence digging for gold, and lo!, as if a fairy's wand had been waved above the bar, a full grown mining town hath sprung into existence."[152]

The Clappes first stayed at the Empire, at the time the only two-story building in "town." For all the grandeur of its name, the Empire was a crudely thrown-together edifice made from planks "of the roughest possible description; the roof, of course, is covered with canvas, which also forms the entire front of the house, on which is painted in immense capitals, the following imposing letters: THE EMPIRE." This "impertinent apology for a house" had cost its original owners an exorbitant eight thousand dollars— reflecting the fact that when it was built, all the materials necessary had been brought by mule across the mountains from Marysville at a cost of forty cents a pound.

Its original owners had been "a company of gamblers," and the Empire also doubled up as a brothel. The two prostitutes (or, as Dame Shirley put it in her flowery way, "two of those unfortunates, who make a trade—a thing of barter—of the holiest passion, when sanctified by *love*, that ever thrills the wayward heart of poor humanity") had left in a few weeks. The miners, she claimed (somewhat improbably), had eschewed the company of these "daughters of joy," looking "only with contempt or pity upon these, oh, so earnestly to be compassionated creatures!" Whatever the real story, the women were gone, "absolutely driven away by public opinion." The disappointed gamblers had sold the "hotel" for a few hundred dollars to the present owners, Mr. and Mrs. Bancroft.

Mrs. Clappe describes this establishment in loving detail. "You first enter a large apartment, level with the street, part of which is fitted up as a bar-room, with that eternal crimson calico, which flushes the whole social life of the 'Golden State,' with its everlasting red." In the center of a "fluted mass" of the same red calico "gleams a really elegant mirror, set off by a back-ground of decanters, cigar vases and jars of brandied fruit." The whole, she assured her sister Molly, "forming a *tout ensemble* of dazzling splendor."

In the center of the room stood a table covered with a green cloth, "on which lies a pack of monte cards, a backgammon board, and a sickening pile of 'yallow kivered' literature."* Several uncomfortable-looking benches completed the furniture. The remainder of the room doubled up as a general store, "where velveteen and leather, flannel shirts and calico ditto—the latter starched to an appalling state of stiffness—lie cheek by jowl with hams, preserved meats, oysters and other groceries, in hopeless confusion."

From the saloon bar, four steps led up into a parlor, "the floor of which is covered by a straw carpet." This room contained "quite a decent looking

---

*"Yellow-covered," meaning sensational or lurid popular novels, so called after the yellow covers with which they were often bound.

glass, a sofa fourteen feet long, and a foot and a half wide, painfully suggesting of an aching back—of course covered with red calico, (the sofa, *not* the back,)—a round table with a green cloth, six cane-bottom chairs, red calico curtains, a cooking stove, a rocking chair, *and* a woman and a baby, of whom more anon—the latter wearing a scarlet frock, to match the sofa and curtains."

A second small flight of steps led from the parlor to the upper story, where on each side of a narrow entry were four tiny bedrooms (eight feet by ten feet). Here, "your eyes are again refreshed with a glittering vision of red calico curtains, gracefully festooned above wooden windows, picturesquely lattice-like." These bedrooms were furnished with little tables covered with oilcloth, and bedsteads so heavy "that nothing short of a giant's strength could move them."

The Clappes did not stay long at the Empire in Rich Bar. Within a few weeks they had moved to a second mining camp, Indian Bar, just a short distance away. Indian Bar was, if possible, even tinier than Rich Bar, boasting no more than twenty tents and cabins, including those made up of nothing more substantial than "calico shirts and pine boughs." By the time the couple arrived, the entire level had been so completely worked over that there was not a blade of grass, nor any living green thing, to be seen. Instead, every conceivable space not taken up by the makeshift tenements was covered with mining holes, "on the edges of which lie the immense piles of dirt and stones which have been removed from the excavation."

Although the valley was so narrow that for three months of the year the sun did not reach the camp at all, Louise made the best of it. The surrounding scenery, with its fir-clad mountains soaring above them, "the summits of which are broken into many beautifully cut conical and pyramidal peaks," was, she wrote, "infinitely more charming" than that of Rich Bar, and the river itself, a vivid emerald green, ran musically along the valley bottom.

For the first time, the couple now acquired their own home, a rudimentary log cabin, about twenty feet square, situated immediately behind the only "hotel" in the camp, the Hotel Humbolt (spelled, she noted, without the *d*). Despite the tiny size of Indian Bar, the Humbolt boasted some surprising amenities. While the sound of clinking glasses and the swaggering air of some of the drinkers in the saloon bar made it "no place for a lady," it also had "a really excellent bowling alley, and a bar room sufficiently big for the miners to dance upon, and, above all, a cook who can play the violin."

"Enter, my dear," she wrote to her sister Molly, "you are perfectly welcome; besides, we could not keep you out if we would, as there is not even a latch on the canvas door." Inside the cabin, the walls had been hung with lengths of gaudy chintz in a rose pattern, "from the largest cabbage, down to the tiniest Burgundy . . . arranged in every possible variety of wreath, garland, bouquet, and single flower." A curtain of this same chintz divided off the sleeping quarters, which included a bedstead "that in ponderosity leaves the Empire couches far behind." The fireplace was crudely built of stones and mud, while the mantelpiece was a beam of wood cunningly covered with strips of tin taken from various cans, "upon which still remain in black hieroglyphics the names of the different eatables which they formerly contained." It was here that she would store her library of books, which included Shakespeare, Spenser, Coleridge, Shelley, Keats, and, delightfully, the seventeenth-century celebration of the art of fishing, Izaak Walton's *The Compleat Angler*.

Mrs. Clappe soon got to work to make herself comfortable. "My toilet table is formed of a trunk elevated upon two claret cases," she wrote to her sister, "and by draping it with some more of the blue linen neatly fringed, it really will look quite handsome, and when I have placed upon it my rosewood work-box, a large cushion of crimson brocade and some Chinese ornaments of exquisitely carved ivory, and two or three Bohemian glass cologne stands, it would not disgrace a lady's chamber at home."

The washstand was another trunk covered with a towel, with a large vegetable dish for a bowl. From Marysville she had brought with her "a handsome carpet, a hair mattress, pillows, a profusion of bed linen, quilts, blankets, towels, &c., so that in spite of the oddity of most of my furniture,

I am in reality as thoroughly comfortable here as I could be in the most elegant palace."

Their four chairs were brought from the Empire. While she would have preferred to have three-legged stools made up, since the floor of their cabin was so uneven "that no article of furniture gifted with four legs pretends to stand upon but three at once, so that the chairs, tables, etc., remind you constantly of a dog with a sore foot," she quickly discovered that it would be impossible to find anyone to make them for her. "So you see," she wrote to her sister, "that even in the land of gold itself, one cannot have everything that [one] desires.

"How would you like to winter in such an abode? In a place where there are no newspapers, no churches, lectures, concerts or theaters; no fresh books, no shopping, calling nor gossiping little tea-drinkings; no parties, no balls, no picnics, no *tableaux*, no charades, no latest fashions, no daily mail, (we have an express once a month), no promenades, no rides nor drives; no vegetables but potatoes and onions, no milk, no eggs, no *nothing*? Now I expect to be very happy here. This strange old life fascinates me.[153]

"In good sooth, I fancy that nature intended me for an Arab or some other Nomadic barbarian, and by mistake my soul got packed up in a Christianized set of bones and muscles. How shall I ever be able to content myself to live in a decent, proper, well-behaved house?"

Rich Bar and Indian Bar, like all the mining camps, were home to an extraordinarily diverse community. "From happiest homes, and such luxuriant lands, has the golden magnet drawn its victims." On Rich Bar and Indian Bar alone Louise would find Swedes, Italians, Germans, French, Spanish, English, Irish, Chinese, and Sandwich Islanders, as well as the Mexicans so recently dispossessed of their lands. They ranged from "'the General,' the largest and tallest and—with one exception, I think—the oldest man [he was fifty] upon the river, who . . . wears a snow-white beard of such immense dimensions in both length and thickness, that any elderly Turk would expire with envy at the mere sight of it"[154] to a young Spanish surgeon from Guatemala, "a person of intelligence and education." Others were doctors, lawyers, scholars and farmers, and even church ministers. Many were barely more than schoolboys, such as the five or six "intelligent, hardworking, sturdy young men" who invited her to a dinner party, feasting her on beef, ham, mackerel, potatoes, and "splendid new bread made by one of the gentlemen of the house."[155]

Among her favorite acquaintances, however, was a former peddler from the US, "Yank," who ran the local general store. "Yank," she wrote, was "quite a character in his way . . . and is a great friend of mine." Deliveries of food to the mining camps were brought laboriously across the mountains by "mule-back express" from Marysville, making the cost of the most basic foodstuffs even higher than in San Francisco. Despite this, Yank's store was surprisingly well provisioned. "He is an indefatigable 'snapper-up of unconsidered trifles,' and his store is the most comical *olla podrida* of heterogeneous merchandise that I ever saw. There is nothing you can ask for but what he has,—from crowbars down to cambric needle; from velveteen trowsers up to broadcloth coats of the jauntiest description. The *quality* of his goods, it must be confessed, is sometimes rather equivocal. His collection of novels is by far the largest, the greasiest, and the 'yellowest kivered' of any to be found on the river." Once, Yank even produced a stick of sealing wax from his shelves with which she was able to mend a broken chess piece.

The man for whom she had the most admiration, however, was Ned, "the Paganini of the Humbolt." Formerly a ship's cook, Ned was an African American (a "light-mulatto") of many talents. As well as playing the violin, Ned had the happy facility of being able to conjure up a feast with practically no ingredients.

The day the couple moved into their log "palace" cabin on Indian Bar, he prepared a "coronation dinner" for them that neither would ever forget. "'You see, Sir,' said Ned, 'when the queen arrives (with Ned, as with the rest of the world, "a substitute shines brightly as a queen, until the queen be by," and I am the only petticoated astonishment on this Bar), *she* will appreciate my culinary efforts. It is really discouraging, sir, after I have exhausted my

skill in preparing a dish, to see the gentlemen devour it with as much unconcern, as though it had been cooked by a mere bungler in our art!'"[156]

The dinner proceeded as follows:

FIRST COURSE: Oyster Soup

SECOND COURSE: Fried Salmon, caught from the river

THIRD COURSE: Fried Oysters

VEGETABLES: Potatoes and Onions

PASTRY: Mince Pie, and Pudding, made without eggs or milk

DESSERT: Madeira, Nuts and Raisins

WINES: Claret and Champagne

COFFEE

Ned had not overrated his culinary powers. "The dinner, when one considers the materials of which it was composed," Mrs. Clappe wrote, "was
really excellent." The soup "was truly a great work of art," the fried oysters
"dreamily delicious." And as for the coffee, "Ned must have got the receipt
for making it from the very angel who gave the beverage to Mahomet."

Ned himself waited on them, dressed in a sparkling new flannel shirt, "a
benign and self-satisfied smile" lighting up his face, "such as *should* illuminate the features of a great artist, when he knows that he has achieved
something, the memory of which the world will not willingly let die. In
truth he needed but white kid gloves, to have been worthy of standing behind the chair of Count d'Orsay himself, so grand was his air, so ceremoni-
ous his every motion, that we forgot we were living in the heart of the Sierra
Nevada; forgot that our home was a log cabin of mere primitive rudeness;
forgot that we were sitting at a rough pine table, covered with a ragged piece
of four cent cotton cloth, eating soup with iron spoons!"

But Ned's greatest talent was his skill in playing the violin. "Ned and one
of his musical cronies, a white man, gave me a serenade the other evening,"

Louise wrote. "As it was quite cold, F[ayette] made them come inside the cabin. It was the richest thing possible, to see the patronizing, and yet serene manner, in which Ned directed his companion what marches, preludes, etc. to play for the amusement of that profound culinary and musical critic, 'Dame Shirley.'"

Louise Clappe went to considerable lengths to claim respectability for many of the miners, but for all the acts of gentlemanliness, the "coronation dinners" and displays of musical prowess by Ned, the "Paganini of the Humbolt," she could not quite hide the fact that a mining camp was, more often than not, a brutal place to be.

On holidays, when large amounts of alcohol were consumed, even in the smallest of camps the revelry could reach a dangerous pitch. In one of her letters, "Dame Shirley" described the festivities one Christmas Eve. "About dark, we were startled by the loudest hurrahs, which arose at the sight of an army of India-rubber coats (the rain was falling in riversful) each one enshrouding a Rich Barian, which was rapidly descending the hill," she wrote to her sister Molly. "At nine o'clock in the evening, they had an oyster and champagne supper in the Humbolt, which was very gay, with toasts, songs, speeches, etc. I believe that the company danced all night; at any rate, they were dancing when I went to sleep, and they were dancing when I woke the next morning. The revel was kept up in this way for three days, growing wilder every hour. Some never slept at all during that time. On the fourth day, they got past dancing, and, lying in drunken heaps about the bar-room, commenced a most unearthly howling;—some barked like dogs, some roared like bulls, and others hissed like serpents and geese. Many were too far gone to imitate anything but their own animalized selves."

Of course, she added, there were some respectable men "who kept themselves aloof from these excesses; but they were few, and were not allowed to enjoy their sobriety in peace. The revelers formed themselves into a mock vigilance committee, and when one of these unfortunates appeared outside, a constable, followed by those who were able to keep their legs, brought him before the Court, where he was tried on some amusing charge, and *invariably* sentenced to 'treat the crowd.' The prisoners had generally the good sense to submit cheerfully to their fate."[157]

IT WAS INTO THIS turbulent, drunken, highly competitive and often violent world that women who came to the Californian gold fields were plunged—a tiny minority in a sea of men. While Louise was the only (in her own phrase) "petticoated astonishment" on Indian Bar, she was by no means the only woman in the mining camps. While some of these, like Louise herself, had arrived by sea, most had traveled overland, and the journey had taken its toll. "The poor women arrive, looking as haggard as so many Endoran witches; burnt to the color of a hazelnut, with their hair cut short and its gloss entirely destroyed by the alkali."[158]

The speed and determination with which they got down to work was astonishing. One woman, whose husband had died of cholera after just six hours of illness en route, had arrived in the mining camps with nine small children to support and no way home. Louise had come across her taking in ironing, the board for which she had improvised out of her only remaining piece of furniture, the seat of a chair.

Very occasionally, a few brave women tried mining themselves. Louise had herself made a brief attempt to become a "mineress," but it was not a success. "I wet my feet, tore my dress, spoilt a new pair of gloves, nearly froze my fingers, got an awful headache, took cold, and lost a valuable breast pin." But generally speaking, they had more success elsewhere. Some, such as the African American Mary Ellen Pleasants, set themselves up as cooks; others would earn good livings as laundresses. A Mrs. B—, mentioned by Louise Clappe, was alleged to have earned nine hundred dollars in just nine weeks by taking in miners' washing. The real money, however, was in boarding-houses.

By 1851, according to Louise Clappe, California "might be called the Hotel State, so completely is she inundated with taverns, boarding houses etc."—and women were quick to take advantage. In Rich Bar, the three other women in "town," apart from Louise herself, were all engaged this way. Mrs. Bancroft, "a gentle and amiable-looking woman" of about twenty-five years of age, ran the Empire. "She is an example of the terrible wear and tear to the complexion in crossing the plains, hers having become, through exposure at that time, of a dark and permanent yellow, anything but becoming." She had left behind an eight-month-old baby and two other small children "to cross the plains in search of gold." When Louise arrived, Mrs. Bancroft was cooking supper for some half a dozen people, while a two-week-old baby lay in his "champagne basket" at her feet.

In addition, there was Mary Stanfield, popularly known as the "Indiana Girl" (so called after the name of her father's hotel, the Indiana House). Mary was "a gigantic piece of humanity" who wore the thickest kind of miners' boots and "has the dainty habit of wiping her dishes on her apron." The first white woman to arrive in Rich Bar, Mary was said to have hidden much gold dust under the floorboards of the Indiana House, entrusted to her for safekeeping by the miners. And another Mrs. B—, "as small as the 'Indiana Girl' is large," kept a third boardinghouse known as "The Miners' Home" and tended the bar there. "Voilà, my dear, the female population of my new home—splendid materials for social parties this winter, are they not?"

Like the unnamed woman ironing laundry for miners on the seat of her chair, Luzena Stanley Wilson had arrived in California with little more than her wagon and the clothes she stood up in. Even a tent was a "luxury" that her family could not afford. The mining camp, later known as Nevada City (now a ghost town), was then merely "a row of canvas tents [lining] each of the two ravines ... alive with moving men"—a daunting sight for a woman. Undeterred, Luzena went to work immediately to clean up her family. "I scrubbed till my arms ached, before I got the children back to their natural hue.... I remember filling my washbasin three times with fresh water before I had made the slightest change apparent in the color of my face."

Only then would she get down to the real work. "As always occurs to the mind of a woman, I thought of taking boarders," Luzena would recall.

"There was a hotel nearby and the men ate there and paid $1 a meal. . . . With my own hands I chopped stakes, drove them into the ground, and set up my own table. I bought provisions at a neighboring store and when my husband came back at night, he found . . . twenty miners eating at my table. Each man as he rose put a dollar in my hand and said I might count on him as a permanent customer."

"El Dorado," as she called her establishment, was soon catering to between seventy-five and two hundred boarders a week, for which each paid twenty-five dollars. Soon, she was hiring cooks and waiters to help her with the work.

As the Indiana Girl had done in Rich Bar, Luzena would often take the miners' gold into safekeeping. "Many a night have I shut my oven door on two milk-pans filled high with bags of gold dust and I have often slept with my mattress lined. . . . I must have had more than two hundred thousand dollars lying unprotected in my bedroom."[159] Luzena also loaned out money, at an exorbitant 10 percent a month, but such prosperity was not to be had for long. Eighteen months later, a fire destroyed the entire settlement, and she and her family—along with eight thousand miners—were left homeless again.

Many African American women would also find their way to California during the Gold Rush years. A tantalizing glimpse of a lone Black woman "tramping along through the heat and dust" near the Humboldt Sink, the arid, abandoned-wagon-strewn desert just east of the Sierra Nevada, on her way to California in 1850 is to be found in white overlander Margaret Frink's description. She was carrying "a cast iron bake stove on her head with her provisions and a blanket piled on top—all she possessed in the world—bravely pushing on for California."[160]

Although this lone woman seems to have been a voluntary emigrant, most African Americans arrived in California as slaves. In 1850, after California achieved statehood as a "free state," many of these former slaves would become freemen and women. Perhaps no one exemplifies the energy and enterprise of these women better than an African American slave named Nancy Gooch. Her story also encapsulates some of the bitter struggles Black settlers would have to confront, even in the relatively "free" land of California.

Born in Maryland in 1811, Nancy later moved to Missouri, where she became the property of a man named William Gooch. In 1849, William succumbed to "Gold Fever," and when he set out for California he took both Nancy and another of his slaves, Peter, with him. Nancy and Peter had a three-year-old child, Andrew,* whom they were forced to leave behind in Missouri. Despite their great anguish at being separated from their child, the couple became among the first African Americans to travel to California.†

The following year, when California joined the Union, both Nancy and Peter gained their freedom. They immediately set about making independent lives for themselves. Peter worked in mining and construction. Nancy took on domestic work, cooking and doing laundry for miners. Little by little they bought up small pieces of farmland, eventually amassing 320 acres, including the original site of Sutter's Mill, where the Gold Rush had first begun. Their greatest dream, however, was to be able to buy their son's freedom. Peter, who died in 1861, did not live to see his son again, but Nancy eventually succeeded in saving the necessary seven hundred dollars. Although by the time she did so slavery had been abolished, in 1870, more than twenty years after their separation, Nancy was able to use her savings to bring her son—now a grown man with a family of his own—to join her in California.

But all that was far in the future. Back in the mining camps of Rich Bar and Indian Bar, Louise Clappe was witnessing change of a different kind. In May 1852, she wrote to tell her sister of how in the space of just a few days, several hundred new prospective miners had arrived on the bar. To the original Humbolt were now added the Oriental, the Golden Gate, and the

---

*It is likely that Andrew, who would always be known as Andrew Munroe, was sold on to another family named Munroe.
†They would formally marry in 1857.

Andrew Munroe (pictured here in a top hat) and his family at Sutter's Mill

Don Juan, as well as four or five other boardinghouses. Drinking saloons were springing up in every direction. "On Sundays, the swearing, drinking, gambling and fighting, which are carried on in some of these houses, are truly horrible."[161]

"Justice" was handed out summarily, and viciously, to anyone who was thought to have erred. A "Committee of Vigilance," who called themselves the "Moghuls," was set up, who "paraded the streets all night, howling, shouting, breaking into houses and throwing people into the river"—which did nothing other than enhance the precariousness of existence. Men accused of stealing were "tried" by a "folk-moot" of miners and immediately hanged if opinion went against them. Foreigners were regularly murdered with impunity.

The increased competition made for some ugly scenes. Gone were the days when gold was to be had simply by dipping a hand into a mountain stream. On Rich Bar, a resolution was made that no foreigner was to be allowed to prospect there—a decision that Louise found "selfish, cruel, and narrow-minded in the extreme."[162] The rest of the overwhelmingly male population of California did not agree. In one of the first laws passed by the state legislature, a tax of twenty dollars a month was levied on all foreigners—far more than most of them were able to pay. There was much violence, even a duel fought, in which an Englishman was shot and killed.

The summer of 1852 was the turning point in Louise Clappe's mining experiences. Increasingly, her valiant attempts to put the best face forward, to see idiosyncrasy and humor—the flakes of gold, if you will—in the base metal of the mining camps, began to fray. She tried to focus on the glories of the season, and in her rambles through the hills found syringa, lilies, wild roses, and irises "of every hue and color," but in vain. She had "seen the elephant," she wrote, "experienced the ultimate possibilities of the situation; had passed through a most difficult experience, and had hit hard luck via a manner seemingly inevitable."[163]

After only a few years, the surface gold, so abundantly available in the early days of the rush, was all gone. It is estimated that between 1849 and 1860 half a billion dollars' worth of gold was extracted from the California hills—but the madness that came with it had left behind an ugly legacy. One thing was for sure: wherever gold or silver was found, Americans rushed in, towns sprang up, and Native people very quickly found themselves outnumbered in their own lands.

10

WHITE BROTHERS

Louise Clappe's descriptions of "the strangely effervescent" quality of life in the California gold mines could not conceal the violence and bloodshed that the discovery of gold brought with it. Of all the Native Americans whose lives were affected by the western emigrations, none would suffer more than the nations of California.

Even without the destruction caused by the mining camps, the coming of settlers had, within a remarkably short time, deeply impacted the delicate environmental balance of the land on which Indigenous people depended for their livelihood. Settlers shot their game and fished their rivers and lakes; their cattle and other livestock ate their seed. The overlanders also brought their sicknesses with them—diphtheria and typhoid and cholera—infecting the waters of the Humboldt River.

It was not only the terrain along the emigrant trails themselves that was despoiled. Within the space of a few short years whole towns sprang up, crops were planted, saw and grist mills were erected. Even Sarah Winnemucca's people, the Northern Paiute, were affected. In the Sierra Nevada, the mountain wilderness in which so many of the Donner-Reed party had starved to death just a few years previously, the pines that they harvested annually for nuts were cut down by miners, thereby destroying one of the Tribe's most prized sources of food. Everywhere that the new settlements took root, the resources that Native Americans depended on were either depleted or destroyed. For Indigenous leaders such as Sarah Winnemucca's grandfather Captain Truckee, some degree of assimilation into this new, white world now seemed the only option available.

Some years previously, Captain Truckee had traveled to California, probably as a guide, with the explorer and military commander John C. Frémont during the time of the Bear Flag Revolt, a short-lived rebellion in which a small group of American settlers had risen up against the Mexican government and declared themselves an independent republic. In recognition of his services, Frémont had given him a letter of commendation, and this he had been able to use to good effect among the incoming settlers, who had often rewarded him with gifts of food and clothing.

Despite growing evidence to the contrary, Captain Truckee remained enthusiastic about the general benevolence and generosity of the incomers. With this in mind, in the spring of 1850, when Sarah was about six, he gathered together a band of about thirty of his people from their lands near the Humboldt Sink and took them with him across the Sierra Nevada to California, with the intention of seeking work among the newly arrived white ranchers. In time, he believed, they would eventually be able to acquire some horses for themselves, which would be a great boon to the Tribe. Among those who accompanied Captain Truckee to California were Sarah's mother, Tuboitonie, and her five children.

For all her grandfather's continued enthusiasm for his "white brothers," Sarah's first encounters with whites were traumatic. The terrible memory of the time when she had been buried alive by her mother in an attempt to save her from the "white owls" had never faded. Perhaps connecting this description of whites with the Cannibal Owl, "a Paiute bogeyman who, in a well-known tale, carried away crying, misbehaving children, pounded them into a tender pulp, and ate them with relish,"[164] the first time Sarah met white people she was overcome with terror.

"'Oh, mother, what shall I do? Hide me!'

"I just danced around like a wild one, which I was. I was behind my mother. When they [the white settlers] were coming nearer, I heard my grandfather say,—

"'Make a place for them to sit down.'

"Just then, I peeped round my mother to see them. I gave one scream, and said,—

"'Oh, mother, the owls!'

"I only saw their big white eyes, and I thought their faces were all hair.

"My mother said,—

"'I wish you would send your brothers away, for my child will die.'

"I imagined I could see their big white eyes all night long. They were the first ones I had ever seen in my life."[165]

At least some of Sarah's encounters with white people, particularly with women, would prove to be benign ones. Their party eventually arrived in Stockton, already a thriving community on the San Joaquin River in California's Central Valley, and she was given some bread to eat by one of the settlers. Soon after, Sarah became so ill that at first her family thought the food had been poisoned. "I do not know how long I was sick, but very long," she remembered. "I was indeed poisoned, not by the bread I had eaten, but by poison oak. My face swelled so that I could not see for a long time, but I could hear everything. At last, one came that had a voice like an angel. I really thought that it must be an angel, for I had been taught by my father that an angel comes to watch the sick one and take the soul to the spirit land. I kept thinking it must be so, and I learned the words from the angel (as I thought it). I could not see for my eyes were swollen shut. These were the words: 'Poor little girl, it is too bad!' It was said so often by the pretty sweet voice, I would say it over and over when I was suffering so badly."

The "angel" was a white woman who had come to visit Sarah every day. Her own little girl, about the same age as Sarah then was, had recently died.

"The first thing she did she put her beautiful white hand on my forehead. I looked at her; she was, indeed, a beautiful angel. She said the same words as before. I asked my grandpa what she was saying. Then he told me what she meant by it. I began to get well very fast, and this sweet angel came every day and brought me something nice to eat."

It was in Stockton, too, that Sarah and her family were able to witness for themselves some of the extraordinary things her grandfather had talked about after his previous journey west. One of these marvels was the house, three stories high, belonging to one of his "friends." "We have to climb up three times to get to the top," her grandfather had told them, whereupon the rest of the band had all laughed, "as much as to say my grandpa had lied. He said, 'You will not laugh when I show you what wonderful things my white brothers can do. I will tell you something more wonderful than that. My brother has a big house that runs on the river, and it whistles and makes a beautiful noise, and it has a bell on it which makes a beautiful noise also.'"[166]

Sarah's first experience of the interior of a settler homestead filled her with wonder. "Oh what pretty things met my eyes," she recalled. "I was looking round the room, and I saw beautiful white cups, and every beautiful thing on something high and long, and around it some things that were red. I said to my sister, 'Do you know what those are for?' for she had been to the house before with my brothers. She said, 'That high thing is what they use when eating, and the white cups are what they drink hot water from, and the red things you see is what they sit upon when they are eating.'" She watched in amazement as the white family all came and sat around "that high thing, as I called it. That was the table. It was all very strange to me, and they were drinking the hot water as they ate." Later, she and her brothers were all invited to eat at the same "high thing." "I was quiet, but I did not eat much," she recalled. "I tasted the black hot water; I did not like it. It was coffee that we called hot water."

For all these relatively benign experiences, the fact was that anywhere that had been settled by emigrants, particularly areas such as mines or ranches where there was a preponderance of men, were increasingly dangerous places for Indigenous women to be. Sarah's elder brothers, Tom and

Natchez, found work on a ferry crossing, while some of the women, including Sarah's mother and her elder sister Jane, were employed as domestics on the ranch belonging to some of Captain Truckee's "friends," two men named Scott and Bonsal. Once the women were settled, her grandfather announced his intention of going into the mountains with the rest of his band, to look after some cattle and horses belonging to the ranchers. Sarah's mother, Tuboitonie, tried to persuade her father not to leave Jane behind when he went, but he refused, believing that his womenfolk would all be safe.

As soon as Captain Truckee was gone, a reign of terror began. Jane, who was "young and very good-looking," suffered almost constant harassment from the hired hands on the ranch. "The men whom my grandfather called his brothers would come into our camp and ask my mother to give our sister to them," Sarah recalled. "They would come in at night, and we would all scream and cry; but that would not stop them." Even her uncles and brothers, Sarah wrote, "did not dare say a word, for fear they would be shot down."

"We used to go away every night after dark and hide, and come back to our camp every morning," but even these precautions were not enough. One night as they were getting ready to leave for their hiding place, five men came into their camp. "The fire was out; we could see two men come into the tent and shut off the postles outside. My uncles and my brothers made such a noise!" Sarah recalled. "I don't know what happened; when I woke, I asked my mother if they had killed my sister. She said, 'We are all safe here. Don't cry.'

"'Where are we, mother?'

"'We are in a boarding-house.'

"'Are my uncles killed?'

"'No, dear, they are all near here too.'

"I said, 'Sister, where are you? I want to come to you.'

"She said, 'Come on.'

"I laid down, but I could not sleep. I could hear my poor sister's heart beat" all night long.

In her later life Sarah would come to count many white people among her friends (and would later marry a white man), but the experience on the ranch left her mother and sister with a lifelong mistrust of them. "I cannot for my life see why my father calls them his white brothers," her mother lamented. "They are not people; they have no thought, no mind, no love. They are beasts, or they would know I, a lone woman, am here with them. They tried to take my girl from me and abuse her before my eyes."

In the early years of the Gold Rush, most of the emigrants headed straight for the mines, but it was not long before white settlements were appearing east of the Sierra Nevada as well. "The Paiutes, and other tribes west of the Rocky Mountains, are not fond of going to war," Sarah Winnemucca wrote. "I never saw a war dance but once. It is always the whites that begin wars, for their own selfish purposes." But when two little girls were abducted, even this most peaceful of nations was pushed beyond endurance.

The children, both twelve years old, had gone out into the woods to dig for roots. When they did not come back, the alarm was raised and a search party quickly organized. Trails were found that led to the house of two traders, the Williams brothers, who ran a whiskey shop and provision store on the Carson River. The brothers denied that they had ever seen the girls and even invited the search party to go into the house and look around. When they did this, they found nothing.

The family had all but given their daughters up for dead when, a few days later, one of them rode up to the Williamses' cabin. Seeing that the man was riding a good horse, the brothers tried to buy it from him, offering him guns and ammunition as a trade. When they attempted to shortchange him, he tried to take his horse back. In the altercation that ensued, the traders set their dog on him. "When bitten by the dog he began haloing, and to his surprise he heard children's voices answer him, and he knew at once that it was the lost children."

He went away and raised the alarm, and a group of men, including Sarah's brother Natchez, went up to the cabin to confront the brothers. Yet again they denied everything, but eventually, after the girls' brother knocked one of the Williamses down with his gun, the others stooped down and raised a trap door. "The father first peeped down, but could see nothing; then he went down and found his children lying on a little bed with their mouths tied up with rags. He tore the rags away and brought them up. When my people saw their condition, they at once killed both brothers and set fire to the house. Three days after the news spread as usual. 'The blood-thirsty savages had murdered two innocent, hardworking, industrious, kind-hearted settlers.'"

Other white settlers in the area sent word to California asking for troops, and when none were available, a vigilante group of a hundred and sixty volunteers gathered together, "and without asking or listening to any explanation" demanded that the girls' rescuers be handed over. "But my people would not give them up," Sarah wrote, "and when the volunteers fired on my people, they flew to arms to defend the father and brother, as any human beings would do in such a case, and ought to do. The war of 1860 began in this way."

The Pyramid Lake War, as it came to be known—more a series of cat-and-mouse skirmishes between the two sides—lasted three months. The peace treaty that eventually followed resulted in the creation of the Pyramid Lake Reservation. The Northern Paiute, a people who had once roamed freely over a vast area of the Nevada and Utah deserts, stretching well into the eastern foothills of the Sierra Nevada, were now confined to a piece of land just sixty miles long and fifteen miles wide.

IN THE EARLY YEARS of the Gold Rush, the geographical distance of the Northern Paiute from the California gold mines had given them at least some measure of protection from white settlers. The Tribes who lived in California, west of the Sierra Nevada, however, had no such protection.

Although the US Army had, as yet, almost no presence along the emigrant trails, safeguarding the route to the gold fields quickly became a national priority. In response, and enabled by an Act of Congress, the Army now began to provide overlanders with rifles, handguns, and ammunition—all at cost price. Heavily subsidized in this way, entire companies of forty-niners made their way to California, bristling with weaponry. "Wagons . . . rolling along toward the Pacific, [were] guarded by walking arsenals." Some groups organized themselves along paramilitary lines, "armed, equipped, and uniformed after the manner of military companies." One company from Charleston, Virginia, issued every man with a rifle, a double-barreled shotgun, and a brace of pistols. "These men were so afraid of being attacked by Indians that they even hauled a cannon across the United States. In total, emigrants headed to California between 1848 and 1852 spent more than $6 million on knives and pistols alone."[167]

Settlers and gold miners alike had little sense of the vast difference between powerful, numerous nations such as the Lakota and their allies on the central plains, who had spent much of the previous century amassing their own arsenals of guns and horses, and the numerically far smaller, less bellicose Tribes in California. Like Sarah Winnemucca's people, the Northern Paiute, these were mostly hunter-gatherers with no history of raiding or warfare. Many had nothing more than bows and arrows with which to defend themselves.

The influx of foreigners onto their land was both sudden and overwhelming. Only too soon, Native people in California found themselves not only outnumbered but also bearing the full brunt of the settlers' lust for gold. With their traditional hunting and gathering resources severely under threat, at first some voluntarily joined in the mining activities. But the miners soon began to see any non-whites as dangerous obstacles to wealth. Native Americans who worked in the mines were killed to rob them of their gold, and their attempts to defend themselves were crushed. The slightest incursions on white property brought the most cruel and severe retribution. Men who were only suspected of having stolen cattle were indiscriminately run down and killed. "Whenever anything was stolen, the so-called Christian miners would invariably say, 'Kill every d— Indian you can find.'"[168] Often they needed no provocation at all. The killing of any whites as was inevitably the case in this increasingly savage environment, brought down acts of revenge that were nothing short of genocidal.

Gold seekers did not only come along the emigrant trails from the East. The most murderous among them came from the north, from Oregon Territory. According to one estimate, about two-thirds of the male population of Oregon, almost all those "capable of bearing arms," left for the gold mines of California in the summer and autumn of 1848. Fresh in the minds of many, with disastrous consequences for any Indigenous people in their way, was the massacre of the Whitman family just one year previously. In addition to their lust for gold, the Oregonians were motivated by what the historian Benjamin Madley has called a "murderous hostility" toward the Native people they found farther south. "The Oregonians, especially, hunt them as they would wild beasts," wrote one commentator. "An Oregonian will leave a richer place to wreak his vengeance on one of a race that he has learned to regard as his foe, by the outrages they have committed upon the whites in Oregon."[169]

Many of the new settlements paid bounties for Indian scalps.* Among the most bloodthirsty, it was regarded almost as a sport.† "In 1850 we saw the scalps of Diggers‡ hanging to tentpoles," reported one local California newspaper. "The Oregon men who first settled that part of the State thought it sport to kill a Digger on sight, as they would a coyote."[170] Others simply flipped a coin (to decide their fate).

In 1849, some of the worst of this violence was visited upon the Nisenan people, whose lands lay in and around Sutter's Mill in the western foothills of the Sierra Nevada, where gold had first been discovered. While

*Mount Shasta City, in Northern California, paid five dollars for every head brought to its city hall—just one example among many.
†While modern society still tends to believe that scalping was an American Indian activity, the practice as carried out by whites goes back to colonial times. In California between 1846 and 1873, scalping was an almost exclusively white practice. "Scalping served as a way to inventory killing, collect macabre trophies, and express a profound disdain for victims." See Benjamin Madley, *An American Genocide*.
‡As previously noted, a derogatory term for an Indigenous person.

attempting to rape some Nisenan women, a group of Oregonian miners had shot and killed several Nisenan men who had been trying to protect them. Soon after, several white miners were killed in retaliation. The violence quickly escalated, triggering a chain of events that John Sutter himself would later describe as "a war of extermination against the aborigines."

A prospector named Theodore Johnson, who arrived at Sutter's Mill about this time, left this description. "A war party of ten or twelve men, including the two Greenwoods, went out, well mounted, to attack a neighboring rancheria of Indians, and avenge the murder. . . . As they galloped away . . . Old Greenwood shouted, 'Be sure, boys, you bring me a squaw!'" whereupon one of Johnson's party "jocosely added, 'Bring me a scalp!'"[171]

On this occasion, the "war party" killed four Nisenans, took several more prisoners, and burned down their rancheria. But even this was not enough to satisfy the miners, who had concluded that "the only way to put an end to the murders was to . . . wipe out the tribe." When another Nisenan was later captured, "his life was spared on the condition that he should guide the whites to their rancheria." Another war party was made up, this time of about twenty men, most of them from Oregon. Once again, Theodore Johnson was an eyewitness. According to his account, the men were all "well mounted and equipped . . . Each man carried besides his inseparable rifle, a long Spanish knife . . . and many were also provided with a brace of pistols or bowie knife, worn in the red Mexican sash around the waist. Old Greenwood shouted, 'Mind the scalps and the squaws for me, and be sure to bring 'em all in, boys,' and away they went at a thundering *lope*."[172]

In all, the posse gunned down and killed about thirty people. "Each Oregonian had about thirteen shots a piece, I do not suppose the battle lasted more than one minute." The Nisenan "warriors" trying to defend their people had been armed only with bows and arrows. Despite this, their chief had fought until he was shot three times, "rising each time to his knees and discharging his arrows," until he finally dropped down dead.

After the massacre, between forty and sixty traumatized Nisenans from the same rancheria were taken prisoner. They were later spotted by Johnson as they were marched through a nearby ravine. "Warriors and boys, squaws with papooses tied to boards and slung at the back, all were prisoners," he observed. "Clustered together like sheep driven to the slaughter, they hastened through the gorge with uncertain steps, the perspiration rolling off their faces now pale with fright." Perhaps trying to rationalize this brutal act by portraying them as less than human, he added: "Many of them were quite naked, and the men and boys especially looked more like ourang-outangs than human beings."[173]

More chilling still was Johnson's description of the vigilantes themselves. "Every man's rifle lay across the pommel of his saddle, and dangling at both sides hung several reeking scalps. Among them was a dashing young mountaineer named John Ross, who had two scalps for his share, and sticking in his sash was the red-sheathed bowie knife, which I had sold him a few days previously for an ounce of gold dust. Used previously to sever the rinds of pork, or shovel in rice and frijoles, it had now been 'wool gathering,' or collecting wigs [i.e. scalps] for old Greenwood's fancy stores."[174]

The atmosphere of brutality soon seeped into the white community as a whole. "Many of these men are so violent that they denounce everyone who advances any reason why a wholesale slaughter should not be made," explained one shopkeeper. Even James Marshall, the man with whose discovery at Sutter's Mill the Gold Rush had first begun, was powerless against the vigilantes. Eventually, most of the Nisenan prisoners, except for seven "warriors," were released. When Marshall tried to stand up for one of the remaining prisoners, he was nearly shot down himself by one of the "ruffians," and "given five minutes to leave the place."[175]

The "murderous violence" that had at first largely been confined to the Coloma area around Sutter's Mill soon spread throughout California. Their numbers already hugely depleted by European diseases, and by the oppressive mission system imposed on them by their previous conquerors the Spanish, the Native people were now hunted down like wild animals through the mountains, first by vigilante groups but later by state-sponsored militias. Men were butchered, their women raped and killed. Small children were used for target practice.* One white settler chose to kill children with a revolver instead of a high-caliber shotgun because the latter "tore them up so bad."[176]

Survivors' accounts of these extermination raids on their villages are, for obvious reasons, extremely rare, but devastating ones do occasionally surface. Sally Bell,† whose nation the Sinkyone was from Northern California, was one of the few survivors of the Needle Rock Massacre, in which a vigilante group not only destroyed her village but wiped out her entire family. She was a small child at the time of the massacre. No warning was given.

"My grandfather and all of my family—my mother, my father, and we [children]—were around the house and not hurting anyone. Soon, about ten o'clock in the morning, some white men came. They killed my grandfather and my mother and my father. I saw them do it. I was a big girl at the time. Then they killed my baby sister and cut her heart out and threw it in the brush where I ran and hid. My little sister was just a baby, just crawling around. I didn't know what to do, I was so scared that I guess I just hid there a long time with my little sister's heart in my hands. I felt so bad and I was so scared that I just couldn't do anything else."[177]

In terror, Sally ran into the woods, where she hid for a long time. Together with a small handful of others who had also managed to escape, she survived by eating berries and roots. They were too afraid to light a fire, even when the weather was cold. "We didn't have clothes after a while, and we had to sleep under logs and in hollow trees because we didn't have anything to cover ourselves with, and it was cold then—in the spring. After a long time, in the summer, my brother found me and took me to some white folks who kept me until I was grown and married."‡[178]

---

*In June 2019, the Governor of California, Gavin Newsom, issued a formal apology to California's Native American communities. As historians of the period have long seen it, he called the past atrocities they had suffered a genocide.

†A grove of redwood trees at the Sinkyone Wilderness State Park is now named in her honor.

‡Before 1848 it is estimated that there were a hundred and fifty thousand Native Americans in California. By 1870, there were fewer than thirty thousand. See Madley.

11

FORT LARAMIE

The Gold Rush had implications that would echo far down the emigrant trails to the East. No one was more aware of this than Susan Bordeaux, the daughter of Red Cormorant Woman and James Bordeaux, whose extended family lived all their lives in and around Fort Laramie, at the very heart of the events that were about to unfold.

Before this time, the only permanent white inhabitants on the plains were the fur traders, the majority of them, like James Bordeaux, French Americans. Some, like the Bettelyoun family (one of whose sons Susan would eventually marry), were of Dutch origin. In all, Susan estimated that there were about three hundred of these men and their families living along the Platte River and its tributaries. As the trade in fur declined, they turned their hands to ranching, opened general stores, and ran smithies to service the settlers, while others acted as guides. As the Hudson's Bay factors had done, almost all married Native American women, with whom they had large families, and the plains Tribes considered them as kin. Their offspring were so numerous that they even made up their own band, the Laramie Loafers.

An artist's impression of the many Lakota lodges surrounding Fort Laramie in 1840, at the very beginning of the emigrations west

"There [was] perfect peace among the Indians and the fur traders who had mingled with them in the hunting grounds," Susan Bordeaux wrote. Vast herds of buffalo roamed the prairies, making it one of the richest regions in the world, and furnishing the Indians' every need. "The country was dear to them. The waving grass, the sparkling streams, the wooded hills were filled with life-giving foods that the red man appreciated more than gold."[179]

Even before the emigration began, many different kinds of travelers had been welcomed into this hybrid world on the Laramie plains. "There were rich English lords who were traveling for adventure, to kill big game in the mountains . . . rich French gentlemen and some of Spanish blood who wanted to get some of the thrill of hunting that the West furnished in those days." Although the accommodation was rough and "no one received much courtesy or attention," many of these visitors had taken shelter in the Fort Laramie stockade. "Supper was dished out in a pie plate. Meat and bread was the bill of fare. Sorghum molasses was a luxury, but it was served once in a while, and a big tin cup of coffee." At night, they slept on the floor, wrapped in buffalo robes.

Throughout the 1840s, as settlers started to arrive in increasing numbers, Susan's family adapted. The fort, where her father acted for many years as agent for the American Fur Company under Jim Bridger, was soon functioning as a kind of roadhouse. "Emigrants and travelers were constantly coming or going, [and] a great many of these stopped at Laramie to eat." The food consisted mainly of wild meat—deer, elk, buffalo, and antelope— which was brought in daily by hunters. "The cooking was not so fancy, but it took a lot to feed so many. . . . The long table was always full, coffee was always piping hot, with hot biscuits and meat, which was sometimes jerked meat."

In 1849, when the fort was sold to the US Army, Susan's father started his own grocery store at Sarpy's Point, eight miles below Fort Laramie. Trade was brisk. Sometimes he exchanged his own chickens, cows, and pigs for the settlers' exhausted horses. The overlanders also offloaded a great deal of their unnecessary furniture, "and it was not a surprise to see some of the finest marble-topped tables, bureaus, tables, stands, and colonial carved chairs in some of the humblest of log cabins along the Oregon Trail."[180]

Wherever the fur traders were, there was always music. "Pretty near every Frenchman could play," Susan would recall, and among them there were many who were "artists with the violin." Looking back, it seemed to her as if men like her father "were born for gaiety and music; it is life with them and they are never as happy as when the music was on the air and a crowd of people were moving to its rhythm." Even in later years, when the troubles came and this vibrantly cross-cultural world faced its greatest existential threat, the fiddles came out at the slightest excuse. At Fort Laramie there were dances every week. "There were quite a number of half-breed girls, all dressed up in bright calico with ribbons in their hair and on their waists, that could fly around in a quadrille as well as anybody, stepping to the music in their moccasined feet. There were many little girls that were in the swing as well as myself."

Sometimes even the emigrant men and women would join in, playing the music and dancing with the rest. It was the only sport that the "old timers" enjoyed. "Many times some of the older men were called out to the center to step off a jig to fast music and they could be sure to do it to perfection." Stick candy and ginger snaps were passed around, and "we were just as happy and enjoyed it as much as if we were dancing in marble halls with chandeliers with their brilliant rays, as the candles' light we loved."

But the arrival of the "gold-crazed" settlers changed everything. They came "like a living avalanche sweeping before it all that the Indian prized," Susan wrote. "The devastation of the game! Many of these emigrants knew they were on Indian soil. They were armed to the teeth. A great many started shooting before they were attacked, which caused the Indians to attack, to scalp and mutilate, resolving to stay the tide of the encroachment at any cost."[181] One way or another, a solution had to be found.

Even before the Gold Rush, as early as 1846, Lakota leaders had petitioned the US government for compensation for the damage done by settlers. Policymakers in Washington, on the other hand, had "looked straight through the plains nomads into New Mexico and California, where the imperial stakes were highest."[182] So far as anyone knew, the great wilderness at the heart of the continent contained no extractable wealth. Except for the golden corridor that linked their brand-new state of California, now arguably the richest place on earth, to the rest of their country, Americans did not yet need the plains. Now, the umbilical cord had begun to look dangerously exposed.

Along the entire 2,200-mile emigrant route there were only two military posts: the former trading post at Fort Laramie and another modest fortification, Fort Kearny, about halfway along the Platte River. Until now, the risk of settlers being attacked while en route had remained vanishingly small.* Most of the plains Tribes had welcomed the chance to trade with

---

*Between 1840 and 1860, Native Americans killed 363 whites on all emigrant trails—just eighteen per year, representing only 4 percent of all deaths on the road. Settlers were twenty times more likely to die from accidents and disease. See Benjamin Madley, *An American Genocide.*

them. But increasingly, the overlanders were being seen as a threat. Not only had the cholera epidemic they brought with them had devastating consequences, but the settlers' livestock had all but exhausted the rich pastureland along the Platte River. The vast buffalo herds on which the plains Tribes depended, once one of the wonders of the world, were beginning to thin out. In the words of one Indian Office agent: "What then will be the consequences, should twenty thousand well-armed, well-mounted, and the most warlike and expert in war of any Indians on the continent, turn out in hostile array against all American travelers through their country?"[183]

In an effort to address these problems, and to defuse the growing tensions, a great council was called. The result was the Fort Laramie Treaty. In the autumn of 1851, a massive assemblage of Lakota, Cheyenne, Arapaho, and Shoshone gathered at Horse Creek, near Susan Bordeaux's family ranch. It had taken the US government's Indian Office*—which, perhaps tellingly, was a division of the War Office—two years to plan. At the council, US government agents fully acknowledged the damage caused by overlanders. They offered an annuity of goods worth fifty thousand dollars, to be distributed every year for the next half century, if the plains Tribes would agree to keep within certain geographical boundaries. In return, the Tribes were to allow the construction of roads and military posts along the Platte River and to permit the safe passage of any settlers making their way along them. These terms were agreed to, but with the stipulation (absolutely critical, as it would turn out) that the proposed borders would not affect their right to hunt wherever they wanted—a stipulation that was acknowledged at the time by the US agents. The treaty, in the Tribes' understanding, "in no way implied surrender of sovereignty or lands."[184]

The Horse Creek Treaty (later renamed the Fort Laramie Treaty) of 1851 lasted three years. One of its immediate consequences—and surely an unintended one so far as the Native signatories were concerned—was a

---

*This had been created by the secretary of war, John C. Calhoun, in 1824 as the Bureau of Indian Affairs.

flood of yet more settlers. In the spring of 1852, seventy thousand overland-ers departed from the Missouri jumping-off points, a greater emigration than had ever before been seen on the plains, even at the height of the Gold Rush. In the same year, Indian Office agents informed the Tribes that the promised annuities had been reduced from a period of fifty years to ten. Not surprisingly, the reaction was one of outrage. The valleys along the Platte River, once a haven for buffalo and other game, were now little better than "mile wide dust highways." The unthinkable fact that the herds they de-pended on might one day disappear altogether began to dawn.

In the end, it was not a buffalo but a lame cow that would destroy the uneasy truce brought about by the Fort Laramie Treaty. The failing animal belonged to a group of Mormon settlers who were passing close to the fort. "Now, it was a custom of the Indians when anything was abandoned not to claim it anymore," Susan Bordeaux wrote, "so, supposing that the poor skinny cow which had been traveling hundreds of miles had been thrown away," it was shot by a man named High Forehead, the guest of a Brulé chieftain, Mato Oyuhi (Scattering Bear), who was camping with his band a few miles away from Fort Laramie. When the news reached the fort, a twenty-four-year-old Army officer, Lieutenant John Grattan, volunteered to ride out to "crack it to the Sioux." Grattan, who had only graduated from West Point the year before, was not only arrogant but filled with what the Army chaplain at Fort Laramie would later describe as an "unwarrantable contempt of Indian character."[185] In vain, Susan Bordeaux's father tried to reason him out of it. "My father told Grattan that he was doing a foolish thing. 'Why don't you let the old cow go,' he said. 'It was laying there with-out food or water and would soon die. It was too lame to walk—its feet were worn through to the flesh. It was shot by some boys who wanted a piece of skin.'" Grattan refused to listen.

Accompanied by twenty-nine heavily armed volunteers and two howit-zer cannons, Grattan rode off to the Brulé camp, situated not more than a quarter mile from the Bordeaux ranch, to demand that High Forehead be handed over for punishment. When Mato Oyuhi, who had already offered the settlers one of his own horses in recompense for the dead cow, refused to hand over his guest, the young lieutenant ordered his troops to open fire on the village. The chieftain, who had turned around and was walking back to his tipi, was shot three times in the back.

For all Lieutenant Grattan's boast that he could "whip the combined force of all the Indians of the prairie" with just thirty men, only one of them would make it back to Fort Laramie: the wounded man was found by Swift Bear, one of Susan's uncles, at a spring near the Bordeaux ranch. When the rest of Grattan's men were found, their bodies had been mangled almost beyond recognition, their heads crushed and their limbs cut off. So contemptuous had the Brulé warriors been of the unnecessary violence shown by the soldiers that they had exposed their genitals to the dismembered bodies—a Lakota way of shaming them forever. Grattan's corpse, which had twenty-four arrows in it, had been so badly mutilated that he was only identified by his pocket watch. Susan Bordeaux's father would later help to bury the bodies. In the ferocious August sun, they had already begun to swell and bloat. "Bordeaux said the dead had all turned black before he got them buried."[186]

Retaliation was swift and brutal. A veteran US Army general, William S. Harney, was summoned by the War Department and given orders to "subdue" the Lakota. Harney, insisting that the American Indians "must be crushed before they can be completely conquered,"[187] assembled an army of six hundred men, and in August the following year he marched up the Platte River.

Harney soon learned that there was a Brulé village camped at a place called Ash Hollow on a tributary of the Platte River known as Blue Water Creek, within sight of the emigrant trail and about halfway between Fort Kearny and Fort Laramie. When he heard the news of the approaching army, Susan Bordeaux's father sent a message to one of the chiefs, Iron Shell, warning him to move away. Iron Shell told the messenger to tell James Bordeaux not to worry as he was not going to fight. "He was going to surrender to save trouble as the Indians were not prepared for battle and would not do so."[188]

Accordingly, when some of the Brulé chiefs—including Iron Shell, Spotted Tail, and Little Thunder—saw Harney's troops approaching, they attempted to parley with him. The men rode out, carrying a white flag as "an insignia of truce." Their band had had nothing to do with the murder of Grattan's troops, the perpetrators of which had quickly flown north, where they could not be found. When they saw that the general intended to fight, they asked for an hour to remove the women and children from the camp, but according to some of the survivors, who would later tell their stories to Susan Bordeaux, Harney's men did not wait. "Now, I have heard Iron Shell and Spotted Tail and others tell that there was no mercy shown— the firing of the guns started right away as the chiefs started toward the army carrying the white flag."[189]

The fighting, which took place over an area that extended for more than five miles across the plains, was not so much a battle as a rout. Little Thunder was shot and wounded almost immediately. "Men, women and children were shot right down and badly strewn on the prairies everywhere, trampled under the feet of the sharp-shod cavalry horses."

One of the women who was present at what would become known as the Battle of the Blue Water was Cokawiŋ, "a fine-looking, stately Indian woman" who was the warrior Iron Shell's mother-in-law. Many years later she would describe her experiences to Susan Bordeaux. "When she saw that there was to be no peace, she started to run without a thing, not even her blanket." The other women, many of them already wounded and bleeding, tried to crawl under the overhanging weeds and grasses along the banks of the river, but Cokawiŋ kept on running. When she looked back, she saw a soldier taking aim behind her. "If she had not turned around that instant, he would have shot her right in the middle of the back, but by turning, the shot tore her stomach wide open just below her belt." The bullet ripped her open, making a wound about six inches across. "She was disemboweled, a gaping wound, and her bowels protruded from her wound as she fell." Thinking that she was dead, the soldier moved on, looking for others to kill.

Seeing a nearby buffalo wallow, somehow Cokawiŋ managed to crawl into it and cover herself with long grass. Tearing off one of the sleeves from her robe, she stuffed it into her wound to staunch the blood. "There she lay all day listening to the guns roar and to the hoofbeats of the horses, the shouting and yelling of the soldiers who came so near at times she thought she would be discovered. Once in a while she could hear a Sioux war cry.... It was a desperate time with her people; in her anxiety she almost forgot her wound."

Eventually, she realized that her people had retreated. Harney's army had taken seventy captives, all of them women, children, and old men who had been too weak to run away. As dusk fell, the soldiers began to herd them away from the battlefield. As Cokawiŋ cautiously emerged from her hiding place, all she could see were dead bodies and dead horses in the deserted valley. "There was not a soul on the bloody battle ground."

Night was falling, and all this time Cokawiŋ had been without either food or water. Now she saw a little skunk wandering around, "sniffing this and that way." Although she said she pitied the animal, it was the only food in sight. She caught and skinned it and then cooked it on a fire that she made with her flint. Although the soldier's shot had torn open her stomach, she could see that her bowels had not been perforated. Somehow, she fashioned a rudimentary bandage for her wound with a strip of skunk skin.

Knowing that it would be sure death if she stayed where she was, Cokawiŋ began to walk in the direction taken by Harney's army. Despite her wound, she walked all night, resting many times. Toward morning, when she had walked almost five miles, she began to see the faint outline of the soldiers' camp. "Way to the north, beyond the Platte, were signal fires along the hills," built by the retreating warriors to guide any stragglers who were left behind and did not know the direction of the retreat. "The reflections flamed in the gray dawn." But it was too late for Cokawiŋ to join them.

"Cokawiŋ, the mother-in-law of Iron Shell, nearly reached the camp, she could dimly see the sentries walking their beat back and forth." She knew then that she had only one option. "Cokawiŋ said that it took a lot of courage; it was like facing death. She began to sing a death chant. In Indian life there are songs for everything, but to sing your own death chant is an awful thing—it takes a brave person." Singing her own death chant, Cokawiŋ walked into the camp and gave herself up.

Although the extent of the battlefield made it difficult for Harney's army to count the numbers of the dead, one estimate put it at eighty-six, among them many women and children. General Harney would thereafter be referred to by to the Lakota as "The Butcher" and "The Woman Killer."

"This was the beginning of the Sioux battles with the US soldiers," Susan Bordeaux wrote, troubles that would last for the next twenty years. "In the beginning, the trouble began with the killing of a lame cow belonging to a Mormon"—an unfortunate affair, she explained, that should never have happened. "The Mormon should have been made to take payment of horses as long as his cow was too worn out to travel." The Fort Laramie Treaty of 1851 was dead in the water. When soldiers on scouting expeditions encountered any hunters, they had no compunction in killing them and taking their scalps "as trophies to take back East." For their part, the plains Tribes now began to raid the emigrant trails, running off their horses and their cattle, "and war was declared against all invaders."

The world of peaceful coexistence between the white fur traders and the American Indians was about to be shattered forever. The Laramie plains were an increasingly dangerous place to be, not only for overlanders, but also the people who lived there, even the mixed-race families such as Susan Bordeaux's. Although some of the "friendlies," including many of her Lakota relatives, were able to keep the worst of the trouble from the more hostile northern bands at bay, they did not succeed entirely. "It was nothing to find a lone Indian dead and scalped, or a soldier dead and also minus his scalp." Even James Bordeaux, for so long accepted as kin by his wife's Brulé relatives, "being a white man with plenty of good horses, was no better to them than the Mormons who were on constant string along the Oregon Trail westward."

12

UTOPIAS

While all went west to make a better life for themselves—some to find gold, others lured by the promise of land—the Mormons were looking for wealth of a different kind. Excoriated by some, and feared by others, throughout the 1850s an estimated seventy thousand made their way to the Great Salt Lake basin in Utah, to found a utopian city in the deserts of the West. Those who were too poor to provide themselves with wagons would walk the entire route, pulling their possessions behind them in handcarts.

Among these handcart pioneers was Priscilla Merriman Evans, a young Welshwoman from Tenby in Pembrokeshire. The second daughter in a family of eight children, Priscilla was seventeen when she converted to Mormonism.

"After the death of my mother we were very lonely, and one evening I accompanied my father to the house of a friend, where, by chance, two Mormon Elders were holding a 'cottage meeting.' I was very much interested in the principles they advocated," she wrote, "despite seeing that my father was very worried, and would have taken me away, had he known how.

When he became aware that I believed in the Gospel as taught by the Elders, I asked him if he had ever heard of the restored Gospel. He replied sarcastically, 'Oh, yes, I have heard of Old Joe Smith, and his Golden Bible.'"[190] Despite her father's opposition, Priscilla believed that she had "found the truth." "When I heard the Elders explain it, it seemed as though I had always known it, and it sounded like music in my ears."

"Old Joe Smith," or Joseph Smith, was born in Vermont in 1805. When he was still a very young man, Smith claimed to have had a series of visions. In one of these, an angel named Moroni had directed him to a place where a number of golden tablets lay buried deep in the ground. These tablets, which Joseph Smith transcribed, were believed to have been written by a hitherto unheard-of prophet, Mormon, containing the history of an ancient people. The church that Smith went on to found, the Church of Jesus Christ of the Latter Day Saints, was believed by his followers to be a restoration of the Christian Church to its original and "true" form, as it had existed in the days of the apostles, and as described in the golden tablets. Smith also claimed that God had given him, and him alone, divine authority to lead the church back to its true Christian roots. More specifically, Joseph Smith had been instructed to found a "New Jerusalem," a shining city of the righteous and godly, where all new believers should gather.

The fact that no one other than Joseph Smith himself ever set eyes on the "Golden Bible" presented no intellectual difficulties to his followers. Not surprisingly, it presented a great many difficulties to almost everyone else. From the beginning, Joseph Smith and his followers were both reviled and feared, not only for their unorthodox views, but also for their desire to live in a community apart from others, and for the increasing power of their charismatic leader.

In the early years of his movement, Joseph Smith had made several attempts to found his "New Jerusalem," attracting both converts and bitter opponents in equal measure. He and his followers moved first to Kirtland, Ohio, with an outpost in Jackson, Missouri, but the Missourians, alarmed at the large numbers of converts pouring into their lands, soon ran them out of town. In 1837, a financial scandal caused the church in Kirtland to regroup again, and this time Smith and his followers headed to Far West, in Caldwell County, Missouri, only to be forcibly expelled once more after the governor declared that all Mormons were to be "eliminated" and driven from the state.

For all the controversy surrounding his new religion, Joseph Smith continued to collect enthusiastic converts, many of them from abroad. In 1839, Smith and his followers, now some eight thousand strong, migrated east again, this time to the small town of Commerce, Illinois, where they at last succeeded in building a temple. They renamed the town Nauvoo. Here, yet again, Smith found himself in trouble. A short-lived local newspaper, the Nauvoo Expositor, published an article in its first (and only) issue, exposing the fact that Smith had secretly begun to advocate a form of polygamy to be enjoyed by the senior men in the church, known as the "apostles." Smith's "vicious principles" were "taught secretly and denied openly," the editorial claimed, and now others, too, were set to adopt these same "abominations and whoredoms."[191] In short, it accused Joseph Smith, in extremely plain terms, of being a sexual predator. In fury, Smith found the newspaper printing press and destroyed it. Not long after, on June 27, 1844, while being held at the country jail in Carthage, Illinois, he and his brother Hyrum found themselves surrounded by an angry lynch mob, and both were killed.

Joseph Smith himself never succeeded in founding a permanent New Jerusalem. This would eventually be achieved by Smith's successor, Brigham Young.* Realizing that their longed-for utopia would only be possible in isolation, Young had set his sights west. In 1847, a party of 143 men, three women, two children, and three Black slaves made the journey along the emigrant trail, where they eventually found sanctuary on the edge of the Great Salt Lake in Utah—the place that is known today as Salt Lake City.

---

*In the bitter fight over the succession that followed Smith's death, Brigham Young was only one among a number of contestants, and the Mormon Church splintered into several denominations. Young became the second president of the Church of Jesus Christ of the Latter Day Saints, three and a half years after Smith's death.

For all the harshness of the land, the city flourished. "Saints"began to flock there, not only from the US but from all over Europe, where Mormon elders had carried out a vigorous proselytizing campaign. Shortly after her conversion, Priscilla had met one of these elders, a man named Thomas Evans. Although he was just twenty-one, Thomas was already an accomplished speaker and had a fine tenor singing voice. Soon the couple were not only engaged but had determined that they would follow Joseph Smith's dictates and travel to join their fellow "Saints"in the unimaginably far-distant deserts of Utah.

The Evanses would need all their convert zeal to hold true to their decision. "About that time the Principle of the Plurality of Wives was preached to the world," Priscilla wrote, adding that the news, when it reached Tenby, had "caused quite a commotion in our branch." Another young woman, who like Priscilla was also engaged to marry a Mormon and follow him to "Zion," came to her with tears in her eyes and said, "'Is it true that Brigham Young has nine wives? I can't stand that. Oh, I can't stand it." I asked how long it had been since I had heard her testify that she knew the Church was true, and I said if it was true then, it is true now," Priscilla counseled her. "I told her I did not see anything for her to cry about."

Perhaps more emotionally challenging for such a young couple was the strenuous opposition of both their families. It was not only Priscilla's father who bitterly disapproved of their decision. Thomas's family, too, did everything in their power to stop the couple from leaving. "They were all well off, and his brothers said they would send him to school, support his wife, and pay all of his expenses," Priscilla wrote—but to no avail. On April 17, 1856, the couple set sail for Boston on board the SS Curling. A newly pregnant Mrs. Priscilla Merriman Evans was sick the whole way.

From Boston, the couple traveled first to Iowa City, where they remained for three weeks, waiting for their carts to be made. These carts—"small, two

---

*Young himself may well have agreed with her. When he first learned of Smith's new theory about plural marriage himself, he is alleged to have said, "It was the first time in my life that I desired the grave." He in fact had fifty-five wives, twenty-six of whom were "conjugal," by whom he had a total of fifty-nine children.

wheeled vehicles with two shafts and a cover on top . . . very much like those the street sweepers use in the cities today"[192]—were the brainchild of Brigham Young. Young had very quickly realized that for many of the new converts—rich in faith but poor in everything else—the expense of building and equipping a wagon outfit was likely to be prohibitive. The handcarts were devised as the most efficient and inexpensive way to transport large numbers of Saints across the plains to the Great Salt Lake. Like many thousands of other handcart pioneers, the Evanses prepared themselves to walk thirteen hundred miles to Salt Lake City, pulling their possessions behind them.

Although Handcart Pioneers are usually associated with the Mormon exodus west, many others, too poor to afford the ox-drawn wagon outfits, had no option but to walk.

Priscilla Merriman Evans and her husband were part of the Third Handcart Party, one of five that made the journey in 1856. Theirs was a curious company. Their fellow travelers consisted of three hundred Welsh Saints, many of whom spoke only Welsh, which Priscilla did not. "Don't you think I had a pleasant journey," she wrote, "traveling for months with three hundred people of whose language I could not understand a word?" The people who were detailed to share their tent were more curious still. These were a motley group consisting of "my husband with one leg," two blind men . . . a man with one arm, and a widow with five children. The widow, her children, and myself were the only ones who could not talk Welsh."

But there were other more pressing problems. The carts were so small, and their allowance for personal possessions so tiny—just seventeen pounds of clothes and bedding per person—that Priscilla found that she was obliged to leave most of her belongings behind. "My feather bed, and bedding, pillows, all our good clothing, my husband's church books, which he had collected through six years of missionary work, with some genealogy he had collected, all had to be left in a storehouse."† At night they slept on an old overcoat on the ground with just a shawl for covering.

Although there were five mule teams pulling the wagons that contained their tents and some of their provisions—these included extra flour and "a little coffee and bacon"—it soon became clear that they were woefully under-provisioned. The bacon and coffee were very soon used up, and "we had no use for any cooking utensils but a frying pan," Priscilla wrote. "The flour was self-raising and we took water and baked a little cake; that was all we had to eat. . . . My husband was commissary for our tent, and he cut his own rations short many times to help the little children who had to walk and did not have enough to eat to keep up their strength."

On these all but starvation rations, the entire company was expected to walk all day, pulling their carts behind them. There were no concessions for the sick, the infirm, or even the very young; far less for women who, like Priscilla, were pregnant. The captain of their company, Edward Bunker, made these conditions plain. "If there are any sick among you, and are not able to walk, you must help them along, or pull them on your carts." No one, Priscilla noted, rode in the wagons (which were for provisions only).

---

*He had lost it at age seven in an accident in a forge, where he had been apprenticed as an iron roller.
†The storehouse later burned down, and they never saw any of their possessions again.

Instead, "strong men would help the weaker ones, until they themselves were worn out, and some died from the struggle and want of food, and were buried along the wayside. It was heartrending for parents to move on and leave their loved ones to such a fate, as they were so helpless, and had no material for coffins. Children and young folks too, had to move on and leave father or mother or both."

If Priscilla, although pregnant, had not a word of self-pity to say about herself, it was perhaps because Thomas, with his wooden leg, had a much worse time of it. "My husband, in walking from twenty to twenty-five miles per day, [had pain] where the knee rested on the pad; the friction caused it to gather and break and was most painful. But he had to endure it, or remain behind, as he was never asked to ride in a wagon."

The Evanses survived their journey, but only just. When they arrived in Salt Lake City at last, they were met with prayers, hymns, and general rejoicing, but Priscilla was almost beyond caring. By now six months pregnant, her feet were bleeding, her clothing was in rags, she was at the point of collapse, "and so weak we were nearly starved." But at least she lived to tell her tale. Two more handcart parties had left Iowa that year but had fatally delayed their departure. The Fourth Handcart Party was caught in a blizzard in Wyoming, and large numbers of them died of cold and starvation before any backup from Salt Lake City could reach them.

IT WAS NOT ONLY the followers of Joseph Smith who believed they would find a utopia in the West. In 1856, the same year that Priscilla Evans left for Salt Lake City, her contemporary, Miriam Davis Colt, set out with her husband on one of the odder quests in the history of the West.

The Kansas Vegetarian Colony was the brainchild of an Englishman named Henry Stephen Clubb.* Clubb was the founder and first president

---

*Clubb had emigrated from Britain to the US in 1853. He was, among other things, an abolitionist and a journalist.

of the Vegetarian Society of America. Having done a reconnaissance of some land just west of the Missouri border, Clubb's plan was to attract a group of like-minded people—about a hundred in all—who would form a colony together. This utopia would not be so much about spiritual rewards as physical and intellectual ones. Potential colonists had to agree to abide by certain rules, carefully set out in Clubb's constitution. These included not only abstaining from alcohol and the flesh of animals, but also "to assemble together frequently . . . for the discussion of agricultural, physiological . . . and other sciences [to avoid] the dullness and monotony of country life."

The scale of the colony was an ambitious one. Clubb foresaw not only grist mills, stone quarries, and brickyards, but printing presses, machine shops, and orchards. All this would be paid for by the colonists themselves, who would buy shares in Clubb's company. The pièce de résistance, the crowning jewel at the heart of all Clubb's proposals, was the city he hoped to build there. The weirdly modern-sounding Octagon City would feature an octagon-shaped town square, radiating from which would be eight roads. Between each road, the members of the commune would build not only octagonal-shaped farmhouses but also octagonal-shaped barns and an octagonal-shaped communal building with sixteen farms grouped around it.

Miriam's husband, William Colt, had long been a practicing vegetarian. When he learned of Clubb's plans he proceeded to sell their farm and purchase shares in the newly formed "Vegetarian Company" and sent all his money, "as directed," to the Company Secretary, Mr. H. S. Clubb.

"We are going to Kansas," Miriam wrote in her journal on January 5, 1856. "The Vegetarian Company that has been forming for many months, has finally organized, formed its constitution, elected its directors, and is making all necessary preparations for the spring settlement. . . . We can have, I think, good faith to believe that our directors will fulfil on their part; and we, as settlers of a new country, by going in a company will escape the hardships attendant on families going in singly, and at once find ourselves surrounded by improving society in a young and flourishing city."

Seven members of the Colt family planned to be part of this social experiment: Miriam and William and their two children, William's parents, and his "good fat sister" Lydia. Their outfit was quickly fitted up, and at the beginning of May they set out, their wagon groaning beneath the weight of "eight trunks, one valise, three carpet bags, a box of soda crackers, 200lbs flour, corn meal, a few lbs. of sugar, rice, dried apple, one washtub of little trees, utensils for cooking, and two provision boxes." Whatever other private thoughts Miriam might have had about it all, she at least looked forward to living in a more "genial clime" (they had spent the previous seven years in Montreal), with people "whose tastes and habits will coincide with our own."

At first the auguries seemed good. The spring weather was favorable and the landscape beautiful—"Will our Kansas scenery equal this?"—and she was struck particularly by the "sweet odor . . . from the blossoms of the crab apple trees that are blooming in sheets of whiteness along the roadside." There was also much-needed camaraderie with their fellow travelers, as "we ladies, or rather, 'emigrant women'" chatted around the campfire: "We wonder if we shall be neighbors to each other in the great 'Octagon City'?"

It was with a gathering sense of excitement that they drew near to the allotted place. "Full of hope, as we leave the smoking embers of our campfire this morning," she wrote on May 12. "Expect tonight to arrive at our new home."

When Priscilla Evans and her husband arrived in Salt Lake City, they were greeted not only with prayers, hymns, and general rejoicing but also with something more sustaining. Kind neighbors had been detailed to take the exhausted travelers into their own homes, giving them food and shelter until the they had recovered from their ordeal. No such welcome was on hand to greet the Colt family. Although they had sent three men in an advance party to announce their coming, and Miriam expected every minute to see the secretary of their society, Henry Stephen Clubb, "with an escort to welcome us into the embryo city," nothing of the kind was forthcoming. "No escort is seen! No salute is heard!" Instead, like a presage of things to come, a fine drizzle had begun to fall as they moved "slowly and drippingly into town just at nightfall—feeling just a little nonplussed on learning that our worthy, or unworthy, Secretary was out walking in the rain with his *dear* wife."[193]

The colony they were expecting to find, and had indeed already paid for, the much-vaunted Octagon City, was nowhere to be seen. The family left their wagons and made their way, through the dark and the rain, to a large campfire around which could be seen a number of men and women cooking their suppers. More suspiciously, "not a house is to be seen. In the large tent here is a cook stove—they have supper prepared for us; it consists of hominy [grits], soft Johnny cake (or corn bread, as it is called here), stewed apple, and tea. We eat what is set before us, asking no questions for conscience sake."

Apart from the conspicuous lack of buildings, there were other signs that all was not well. Some of the women told Miriam that they were sorry to see her come to that place, "which shows us that all is not right." Weary and dispirited, they found beds where they could, some in tents and some in their wagon.

The next day, May 13, Miriam took up her journal again. "Can anyone imagine our disappointment this morning, on learning from this and that member, that no mills have been built; that the directors, after receiving our money to build mills, have not fulfilled the trust reposed in them, and that in consequence, some families have already left the settlement?"

It was not only the promised mills that were not forthcoming. When they went to look over what should have been "the city grounds," they found that it contained a single extremely small log cabin measuring sixteen feet by sixteen feet, "mudded between the logs on the inside, instead of on the outside." The cabin had neither door nor windows, and the oak shingles for the roof, although they were over three feet long, were only "about as wide as a sheet of fools cap paper." Perhaps most dispiriting of all was the sight that daylight afforded them of the other families, most of them now living like refugees in a makeshift camp around the perimeter: "some living in tents of cloth, some of cloth and green bark just peeled from the trees, and some wholly of green barn [i.e. branches], stuck up on the damp ground, without floors or fires." There were, she noted, only two stoves in the entire campsite.

In these less-than-utopian conditions, Miriam and her family had no choice but to make the best of it. Although it was now the middle of May, the weather had turned cold and windy, with a steady drizzling rain. They had taken up residence in the partially built communal octagon, but despite her husband's valiant attempts to make what improvements he could, it remained "dark, gloomy, cheerless, uncomfortable, and cold inside." "The prairie winds come whizzing in," reads her journal entry for May 13. "Have hung an Indian blanket at the door, but by putting trunks and even stones onto the end that drags, can hardly make it answer the purpose of a door."

More difficult still was the fact that she had to cook everything on an open fire. "Have a fire out of doors to cook by; two crotches driven into the ground with a round pole laid thereon, on which to hang our kettles and camp pails, stones laid up at the ends and back to make it as much as it can be in the form of a fireplace, so as to keep our fire, ashes and all, from blowing high and dry, when these fierce prairie winds blow." Anyone who tried to cook in these conditions was scorched by the flames, so much so that "the bottoms of our dresses are burnt full of holes now, and will soon be burnt off."

It was dispiriting work. "I have cooked so much out in the hot sun and smoke that I hardly know who I am, and when I look in the little looking glass I ask, 'Can this be me?' Put a blanket over my head, and I would pass well for an Osage squaw. My hands are the color of a smoked ham, and get so burnt that the skin peels off one after another." "If we stay here," she added, only half in jest, "we must needs don the Bloomer costume."

First advocated by a popular health periodical, the *Water Cure Journal*, bloomers* had initially been worn by women in public in 1851, but outside sophisticated urban areas such as New York, where they were first adopted, they would have been regarded with a suspicion bordering on disgust. For Miriam they were, literally, a lifesaver. "Am wearing the Bloomer dresses

---

*These usually took the form of a short skirt with pantaloons underneath, closely modeled on those worn by Turkish women. The temperance advocate and journal editor Amelia Bloomer did not invent the eponymous "bloomers" but was one of their earliest champions.

now; find they are well-suited to a wild life like mine," she wrote in her journal on May 30. Any scruples she might have had were dissolved by the newfound freedom. "Can bound over the prairies like an antelope, and am not in so much danger of setting my clothes on fire while cooking when these prairie winds blow."

Just a few days later, a tremendous thunderstorm threatened to overwhelm their still-fragile living quarters. "The thunder tumbled from the sky, crash upon crash . . . the rain came in torrents, and the wind blew almost tornadoes." When they heard the storm approaching, the Colts had dressed, wrapped themselves tightly in their blankets, "and made ready to protect our children from the rain that was then dripping through the roof." Putting all the bedding that they had around them, and "all we could see to get by the glare of the lightning (could not keep a candle lit)," they huddled together under their umbrellas and sat the storm out as best they could.

The next morning dawned cloudless and bright, the sun rising "as majestically as though there had been no war in the elements through the night." But a terrible scene met their eyes. "The rain had dissolved our mud chinking, and the wind had strewed it all over and in our bed, on our clothes, over our dishes, and into every corner of the house. Have had all our sheets to wash, beds and blankets to dry in the sun and rub up, our log walls to sweep down, our shelves and dishes to clean, and our *own selves* to brush up. 'Such is prairie life,' so they say."

Not everyone was so philosophical. For many, prairie life had already proved too much. Several of their colony were already packing up and heading back East. Just two days after the storm "our young and very much respected Mr. Sober has left the settlement, and gone back to his home in Michigan," she wrote; "disappointment has darkened every brow."

The Colt family were not yet ready to give up. Under the Vegetarian Company's terms and conditions, which were made possible by a government scheme, individual members of the company had each been able to lay claim to 240 acres of land—160 acres of timber and 80 acres of prairie. Miriam's husband, her father-in-law, and her sister-in-law Lydia were all claimants; taken as a whole, the family now owned, or believed they owned, a substantial 720 acres of potential farmland. It was too valuable an asset to give up on so soon.*[194]

They spent their days deciding on the site of what they hoped would be their future home, eventually plumping for an idyllic spot just a little way from the clear, stony-bottomed creek that flowed nearby. Sitting in their wagon, Miriam would marvel at the view over the wide-open prairie—"not a stump, fence, stone or log, to mar the beautiful picture"—while her "hopeful husband" planted corn and garden seeds.

Never previously farmed, at first the prairie was deceptively easy to cultivate. "After the plowing, the planting is done by just cutting through the sod with an axe and dropping in the seeds—no hoeing the first year; nothing more is done until the full yellow ears are gathered in autumn time." And yet for all this, she was not quite convinced. "I do not like to hear the voice which whispers, 'This will never be,' but still it will whisper."

---

*This was made possible by the US government's Preemption Act of 1841, a forerunner of the better-known Homestead Act of 1862. The Preemption Act allowed for settlers who were living on government-owned land to purchase up to 160 acres for just $1.25 per acre, before the land was offered up for sale to the general public, if certain conditions were met. One of these was that the settlers—effectively "squatters," as they were quite openly referred to—had to have been residing on the land, and working it, for a minimum of fourteen months. Laura Ingalls Wilder's family were among these, an experience described in Wilder's most famous book, *Little House on the Prairie*. Both Kansas and Nebraska territories, which had only been incorporated in 1854, were largely settled (by whites) by this means. This took no account of the fact that these lands were already home to many Indigenous Tribes. The situation was complicated still further by the fact that a large section of "Indian Territory" immediately west of Missouri (present-day states of Kansas and Oklahoma) had been designated by the US government as a kind of "dumping ground" for the continent's original inhabitants. In 1830, President Andrew Jackson had signed the Indian Removal Act, whereby, in one of the most shameful episodes in US history, as many as a hundred thousand Native people—highly educated, slave-owning Cherokee plantation owners among them—had been forcibly relocated from Georgia and other southern states to small strips of windswept prairie west of the Mississippi and Missouri Rivers, their fertile lands expropriated to make way for cotton farming. On the forced marches, known today as the Trail of Tears, many thousands died of starvation, exposure, and disease. Thus, the Colts did not actually "own" their land at all, which was still rightfully, and legally, Osage Tribal land. See Frances W. Kaye, "Little Squatter on the Osage Diminished Reserve: Laura Ingalls Wilder's Kansas Indians."

Although Octagon City, what there was of it, was only thirty-eight miles from the Missouri border, the settlement was still extremely isolated. The Colts were a hundred miles from the nearest grist mill and fifty miles from the nearest post office; when one of their plows broke, it was another fifty-mile round trip to the nearest blacksmith to get it mended. The work they were now faced with proved backbreaking: not only were there crops to sow but clothes to wash, cornfields to fence, rails to split, poles to cut—and, most tiresome of all for Miriam, the never-ending job of baking bread for her family every day in a tiny Dutch oven (a cast-iron cooking pot on legs) over an open fire. "Have labored really hard all day," she wrote in her journal, "and have baked only two small loaves of bread, while, in a family of seven like ours, one can be dispatched at each meal."

Morale was not helped by the fact that there was never enough to eat. Over a month after their arrival, Mr. Clubb finally showed up at the colony with some extra provisions, which he had bought at Fort Scott, the nearest settlement, fifty miles away. Despite the fact that they had been bought with the company's money, they were still charged a very high price for them. Even potatoes, at four dollars a bushel, were so expensive that the family could not afford to have even one meal of them. "I live entirely on food made of corn-hominy and milk, and Johnny-cake and milk."

There were times when anxiety for the future threatened to overwhelm Miriam. "The people say we have had our hardest time here, but it does not seem so to me. I often ask myself, 'Why do I have so many presentiments of coming sorrow?' . . . I am so impressed some nights with this feeling, that I sit up in bed for hours, and fairly cringe from some unknown terror. I tell my husband, 'We are a doomed ship; unless we go away, some great calamity will come upon us; and it is on me that the storm will burst with all its dark fury.'"

"What are we to look for, and what fear next?" she wrote on June 16. One night it was reported that Mrs. Clubb had found a rattlesnake in her bed; but the worst plague of all was the mosquitoes. "They troubled us very much at the creek today while washing. . . . Our bed being short, in the night they have a good chance to nibble away at our protruding extremities. . . . I try to keep my children covered, so they won't eat them all up before morning. As for myself, I get so infuriated that I get up, descend the ladder, make my way out into the wet grass upon the run, not minding what reptiles may be under my bare feet; then I return from my dewy bath, lie down and try to sleep, but it is almost in vain."

The whole family came down with malaria. "Dishes of water have been set near our heads, so that we could help ourselves to drink when it seemed as though we should burn up with fever. My head has ached dreadfully; am glad to crawl down the ladder, with weakened limbs get out door[s] here, sit down on a stone, lean my dizzy head against the logs of the cabin, breathe a little fresh air, see the sun go down, and ask, 'Can this be the same sun that shines [on] our Northern friends, who are enjoying blessings and comforts they know not how to appreciate?'"

So much for utopian dreams. By now, almost all the other colony members had simply given up and returned east. One of their closest neighbors, Mr. V, had arranged for a passage in an ox wagon that would take his family back to Kansas City. William Colt believed that they too should cut their losses and go with him, but his father was determined to hold out. Despite the fact that "Mother," the "good fat sister," and Miriam herself were all by now equally anxious to leave, the old man refused: "His indomitable will is not thus to be turned."

The prairie summer was scorching hot. "Today the sun comes pouring down his floods of heat again," Miriam wrote on July 4. "I can't step outside the cabin door without burning my feet. The prairie grass makes such wear and tear upon our shoe leather, that I am trying to save my own calf-skin shoes, for I see they are being worn badly now, and I shall want them more when cold weather comes; so I go barefoot inside, and slip my feet into my rubbers when I go from the cabin."

Soon, their water supply began to dry up. "The spring that was cleaned out and dug deeper, in the gulch below our cabin, is almost dry," she wrote on July 1; "the water is not fit to drink."

Even this was not enough to deter old father Colt. About four miles away from the settlement he had spotted a house belonging to some Osage, which was standing empty while they were away on their annual hunt. Knowing that the water there was still in good supply, Mr. Colt was determined to move there. Miriam and her husband debated whether to follow the old people. If they moved, they would be four miles away from their nearest neighbors. Furthermore, "if [the Osage] should return from their hunt and find us there, they would think we were intruding almost too much, and I know not what our fate would be," Miriam wrote. "We cannot stay here without water, neither can we leave the old people four miles away, alone. . . . We conclude that we must submit to the dominion of paternity, and take the result." The house turned out to be a dilapidated dwelling, built around three sides of a north-facing "piazza." Despite having no glass in the windows, it was, Miriam wrote, "a palace [compared to] the rude cabin we have left."

But it was no use. As the summer ended it was clear to all that their enterprise had been a failure. Continued bouts of malaria, the loss of their oxen, and altercations with the Osage when they returned from their hunt, whose precious resource—water—they had taken, were finally too much for them. On September 2, Miriam and William and their two children headed back East, leaving William's parents and sister Lydia behind at what remained of the Octagon City.

Of the seven members of the Colt family, only two would survive the experience. Miriam's husband and her son both died on the journey back home, probably of malaria. It was not until she reached New York City that she also learned of the deaths of her parents-in-law and sister-in-law. It was to earn money for herself and her daughter, Mema, that she wrote her memoir, giving it a title as strange and sorrowful as the experience itself: *Went to Kansas: being a thrilling account of an ill-fated expedition to that fairy land, and its sad results.*

13

CAPTIVES

While it is not known exactly how many settlers had, like both Louise Clappe and Miriam Colt, "seen the elephant," their numbers amounted to many thousands. Overwhelmed by their experiences, they simply packed up, turned their wagons around, and headed back East. For the Osage, whose land and resources the Colt family had taken over, it was a reprieve of a kind, albeit a temporary one.

Miriam had estimated that there were some four thousand Osage living near to the vegetarian colony. For all that they were generally friendly to the settlers, sometimes even visiting Miriam and her family in their cabin, the proximity of a "city of wigwams" just across the Neosho River from Octagon City was disturbing to its inhabitants, most of whom would have preferred to have their new lands to themselves. By Miriam's own admission, it was only when the Osage left on their annual buffalo hunt that she had felt really at peace: "It seems quiet and good, to have our fear removed for a time."[195] "I cannot look at their painted visages without a shudder," she wrote; "and when they come around our cabin, I sit down and take Willie on my lap, and have Mema stand by my side, with my arm around her, for fear they may steal my children from me. They point to my boy and make signs that he is pretty. 'Chintu-chinka' they call my boy, and 'Che-me chinka,' girl."[196]

Miriam Colt was not alone in her dread of her Native American neighbors. Almost all US emigrant women had been conditioned to feel this way. It was not only attack that they feared. "Indian barbarities," of the kind that were talked of at the fireside on dark winter nights, included many tales about the capture and enslavement of whites by Native people. Between the sixteenth and the nineteenth centuries, tens of thousands of whites, including many women and children, had suffered this fate, and it was perhaps stories such as these that Miriam was remembering when she hugged her children to her.

Native Americans took white captives for a number of different reasons. Sometimes it was in revenge for the death of their kinsmen; at other times it was to use them as slaves and also to replenish their own numbers if depleted by war or disease. The experience was not always as bad as was generally feared. While the rape and sexual exploitation of Native American women and children by white men was commonplace, there is little evidence to suggest that sexual violence was perpetrated against white women. An especially unpalatable truth for parents (of girls) and husbands (of young women) was that women and girls, in particular, if they were taken young enough, often assimilated very well into Tribal life. There are well-documented cases of white women who came to love their new families and refused to leave them when they were found, sometimes even running away from their rescuers to try to find their way home.

Stories such as these were particularly disturbing to nineteenth-century sensibilities. Many of these captured women had made successful marriages, borne children, and in some cases become respected leaders of their Tribes. Perhaps the most famous of these, Cynthia Ann Parker, was taken captive in 1836 by Comanche when she was nine years old. The Comanche empire, once one of the most powerful and extensive in all the Americas, spread across what is now Texas and New Mexico. Cynthia Ann was married to a

Tribal chief, Peta Nocona, by whom she had three children. One of these, Quanah Parker, went on to become a legendary Comanche leader and one of his nation's most famous warriors.* Many years later Cynthia Ann was "rescued" by Texas Rangers, and after many attempts to run back to her Comanche family, she allegedly died of grief. (More than a century later, her story would become the inspiration for one of the most famous "cowboy" movies of all time, John Ford's *The Searchers*.)

The story of Frances Slocum, while less well known, is no less dramatic. Taken captive in 1778 by the Delaware in Pennsylvania, she too was married into the Tribe and had children. Her Native name was Wet-let-a-wash. When she was eventually found by her birth family more than fifty years later, she refused to return. "No I cannot. I have always lived with the Indians. They have always used me very kindly. I am used to them. The Great Spirit has always allowed me to live with them, and I wish to live and die with them. Your *Wah-puh-mone* (looking glass) may be larger than mine, but this is my home. I do not wish to live any better, or anywhere else, and I think the Great Spirit has permitted me to live so long, because I have always lived with the Indians. I should have died sooner if I had left them."[197]

The white response to this is encapsulated in the memorial plaque to a woman who was taken captive in Massachusetts in the early eighteenth century. While her father and two brothers were later redeemed (her mother and two sisters having died), Eunice Williams refused all attempts to separate her from her Native American family. Even when she returned with them to Massachusetts, she is said to have refused to enter her former home, and her father, a Puritan minister, was obliged to deliver his admonishing sermon to her from his front garden. The plaque which was erected in memory of her reads: "Eunice Williams: married a savage and became one."[198]

---

*Quanah Parker "was the embodiment of the dynamics of ethnic incorporation . . . his rise to power illustrates the opportunities the multiethnic Comanche society offered to people who were not full-blood Comanches." See Pekka Hämäläinen, *The Comanche Empire*.

Stories such as these were passed on, often thrillingly embellished, not only by word of mouth but also in books, pamphlets, and broadsides. They even turned up as filler material in the almanacs sold by traveling booksellers, which were, until newspapers replaced them after the Civil War, "the supreme and only literary necessity" in nearly every American household.[199] Captives who survived their experiences and were eventually rescued, often after a substantial ransom had been paid, lived quite literally to tell the tale.*

From the earliest days of the colonies, captivity narratives had been devoured by a public eager for their particular brand of dark thrills. With their lurid mixture of cruelty, violence, "information" about Native people, and, as often as not, a satisfying dose of white propaganda thrown in for good measure, these narratives were escapist literature of the first order (and a close cousin to similar narratives about cutthroats, footpads, pirates, highwaymen, and courtesans that were so popular in England in the eighteenth century). If the captives were women, a hint of salaciousness was also added to the ingredients—always good for sales. By the mid-nineteenth century there were many thousands of such texts, telling the stories, often highly fictionalized, of the many hundreds of white prisoners who had endured captivity among every major Native American Tribe. Not only did these tales sell in huge numbers; they were also read multiple times. First editions of these pamphlets rarely survive, most of them having been, quite literally, "read to bits."[200]

One of the most sensational of these, and one of the bestselling captivity narratives of all time, was that of a young woman named Olive Oatman.

While no two versions of Oatman's story would ever be exactly alike, all were agreed on the circumstances surrounding her release. On a February morning in 1856, a young Indigenous woman appeared on the banks of the

---

*In 1675, a twenty-pound ransom was paid for Mary Rowlandson, who had been taken captive in Massachusetts. Twenty pounds was the average yearly income for a skilled worker.

Colorado River, just opposite one of the smallest and most isolated American forts, Fort Yuma, on the California-Arizona border. The woman's name was Spantsa. She and her companions had been traveling for ten days to reach Yuma, sometimes on foot, sometimes by floating down the river on a raft made from rushes. It was clear from her appearance that Spantsa was not a local Quechan, but a Mohave, a people who lived many miles away across the Arizona desert to the East. Like the other female members of her Tribe, she wore no clothing other than a skirt made of bark. Her face was painted, and the deeply tanned skin on her upper arms and the lower part of her face, from the corners of her mouth all the way down her chin to her jawline, was marked with intricate blue tattoos.

An officer from the fort crossed over the river on the ferry and went to meet her. Taking the exhausted young woman by the hand, he led her to the river where she washed the paint from her body, and black mesquite dye from her hair, before replacing her bark skirt with a calico dress that the officer had brought with him. When she was dressed, he took her back across the river with him and led her up a small hill to the fort, where her arrival was greeted by cheering soldiers and a volley of cannon fire.

The young woman was nineteen-year-old Olive Oatman, a white American who had been taken captive some five years previously after the wagon in which she had been traveling had been attacked by "Apaches."* While the rest of her family had been killed, Olive and her younger sister Mary Ann had been taken by the Tribe as slaves. About a year into their captivity, the two girls had been sold on to another Tribe, the Mohave. Mary Ann had died, but Olive, or Spantsa as she was now known, had continued to live with them. Early in 1856, rumors about a white woman living with the Mohave had reached the authorities at Fort Yuma. Through a Mohave intermediary, known to the military there as Francisco, a search

---

*In fact they were Yavapai, an Apache subgroup. The ethnologist A. L. Kroeber listed them as Yuman Yavapai, sometimes called Mohave-Apache or Yuma-Apache. The term *Apache* was used throughout the Southwest at this time as a blanket term for any warrior-like Native people.

party was sent out, and about a month later, Olive was finally delivered to the fort. The ransom paid for her release was a horse, three blankets, and some beads.

Olive Oatman's story caused a sensation. Within a week an article about a young American girl, "very fine in appearance" and "a lady" to boot, who had been rescued after being held for five years by "savages," had found its way into the *San Francisco Herald*. The story was picked up by newspapers in nine other states, and within a month Olive had become a media darling. Arriving in California, she found herself the object of intense, often prurient interest. Had she been raped? Had she married a Mohave and perhaps even had children by him? Although the answer to both these questions is almost certainly no, there was always enough ambiguity surrounding her story to fuel the speculative flames. Pictures of her, a dark-haired Gothic beauty with her enigmatically tattooed face, only added to her mystique. In the streets, people rushed "to see her and stare at her, with about as much sense of feeling as they would a show of wild animals."[201]

It was not only Olive's dramatic facial tattoos that captured the public imagination. There was also a gripping subplot to her story. All this time, Olive had thought that she and her sister were the only survivors of the "Apache" attack but, unbeknownst to her, her elder brother Lorenzo had also miraculously survived. Left for dead by the Yavapai, and almost expiring from starvation (he would later confess that he had considered eating his own arm), Lorenzo had managed to crawl away from the scene of the massacre and was rescued by a group of Pima. When he finally regained his health, he had gone on to conduct an extraordinary five-year campaign to find his missing sisters. It was largely due to his efforts that the military commander at Fort Yuma had been forced into action and Olive had eventually been redeemed.

But what had really happened to Olive Oatman during the time of her captivity? And had she even wanted to be "rescued"? The timid young woman, in her borrowed cotton dress, who climbed the hill to Fort Yuma that February day was more Mohave than American. A transcript of her first interview with Captain Martin Burke, the commanding officer at the fort, begins with the remarks that not only was Olive's memory of her previous life "very defective," but that she was "not able to pronounce more than a few words in English." And Olive was very clear about one thing: the Mohave had treated her well. Captain Burke had begun the interview with a direct question, to which he had received an unequivocal answer: "How did the Mohaves treat you and your sister? Answered, 'Very well.' (from her manner seemed perfectly pleased.) They had never whipped her but always treated her well."[202]

Early newspaper accounts stuck to the true version of events. Every interview that Olive gave in the early days of her return indicated that not only was she well treated by the Mohave, but she had in fact considered herself one of them. In an interview with the San Francisco *Daily Evening Bulletin*, she stated that while the Yavapais treated them as slaves, the Mohave behaved to them as kin. The chief of the Tribe, Espaniole, and his wife, Aespaneo, had taken the sisters as their adopted children, "and we were treated as members of his family."[203] She was particularly explicit about her relationship with Aespaneo. "She speaks of the Chief's wife in the terms of warmest gratitude," reported one newspaper, and when the Tribe was forced to give her up, "the kind woman . . . had cried a day and a night as if she were losing her own child."[204]

The Mohave themselves concurred with this version of events. In 1903, half a century later, a Tribal elder name TokwaOa, or Musk Melon, was interviewed by the American anthropologist and ethnologist A. L. Kroeber about these events. Not only had TokwaOa been one of Olive's companions on her journey to Fort Yuma in 1856, he had also been present during her first interview at the fort. "An old officer asked her about the bad happening (*her parents' murder*): 'How did it happen? Where did they catch you?' She told them: 'I don't know. We were too young to remember, my sister and I. I think it was somewhere this side of Phoenix; from there they took us to the mountains. Then those Mohave Indians heard about us, came, took us away and kept us both. My sister died and I was alone, but they treated me well. There was not much to eat, but I helped them, and got used to it, and got along with them. They saved my life.'"*[205]

About two weeks later, Olive's brother Lorenzo arrived at Fort Yuma, and the two were reunited. The last TokwaOa saw of Olive was her riding away from the fort behind a string of wagons. "As they came, I was close to the road," TokwaOa told Kroeber. "She got off to talk to me. I said, 'You are going?' Then her brother picked up a club and started for me, but she said: 'Don't! He is a nice man; he took good care of me.' So he threw his club away and gave me a whole box of crackers. She said: 'This is the last I shall see of you. I will tell all about the Mohave and how I lived with them. Goodbye.' We shook hands and I saw her go off."[206]

Olive Oatman did indeed tell all about her time with the Mohave, but she was not the only one who told the story. Over the years there would be many versions, each one a little further from the truth, but none would have more of an impact than that of the Reverend Royal Stratton. "Tall, fine-boned, and silver-tongued," Stratton was an itinerant Methodist preacher who had become acquainted with Lorenzo and Olive after they left California and moved to Gassburgh, a mining settlement near the Willamette Valley in Oregon. At Lorenzo's request, Stratton agreed to help the two survivors write their story. Quickly realizing the golden commercial opportunities it presented, the preacher proceeded to give an eager public exactly what it wanted. The highly sensationalized ghostwritten version of the Oatmans' story, *Life Among the Indians*, sold out in just three weeks. Six thousand copies of a second edition, *The Captivity of the Oatman Girls among the Apache and Mohave Indians*, sold out almost equally rapidly. A third edition, in which Stratton's tirades against the Native people—"degraded bipeds," "man-animals," "worse than fiends," and even "human devils"—were by now almost hysterical, would take Olive's story still further from the truth.

---

*The Mohave would have agreed. In 2005, Olive Oatman's biographer interviewed a Tribal elder, Llewellyn Barrackman. "They felt sorry for her," he said. "We have a feeling for people." See Margot Mifflin, *The Blue Tattoo*.

SO WHAT HAD REALLY happened during the five years of her captivity?

When Olive's family began their journey west, they too had believed they were on their way to paradise. The Oatmans were Brewsterites, a Mormon splinter group that believed in the claims of James Brewster. As an eleven-year-old, Brewster stated that he had had revelations from God that were remarkably similar to those experienced by Joseph Smith. This time it was not the wisdom of Mormon but of another, hitherto unknown, ancient Hebrew prophet called Esdras. With the help of his father, Brewster had had the temerity to translate and then publish "the lost books of Esdras." As well as voicing strong opposition to polygamy, the books included the astounding revelation that the Mormon Church would one day be reorganized under James Brewster himself. Not surprisingly, Joseph Smith did not take kindly to this challenge to his authority. Mormon doctrine held that only he, Joseph Smith, was entitled to receive revelations from God, and Smith denounced Brewster's claims in the Church newspaper as "perfect humbug" (or, as it might be termed today, "fake news").[207]

But James Brewster's ideas did acquire some traction. As Joseph Smith's successor, Brigham Young, had done a few years previously, Brewster convinced his followers to set out with him to the promised land. The Land of Bashan, as he called it, was a fertile, well watered, and lushly timbered valley, vaguely located somewhere between the Gila and Colorado Rivers, far to the southwest. But this paradise existed in his imagination alone.

In 1850, the year of the Brewsterite exodus, danger from Native American attacks along the Oregon Trail still existed largely in settlers' imaginations; along the more southerly route that the Brewsterites would take, it was a grim reality. The Gila Trail was a little-used alternative route to California. From Independence, Missouri, it dipped down in a southwesterly direction via Santa Fe, continuing on through what is now Arizona and New Mexico but which at the time of the Oatmans' journey was still part of Mexico. Various warring nations, principal among them the Apache, enraged by white incursions onto their land and the environmental disasters

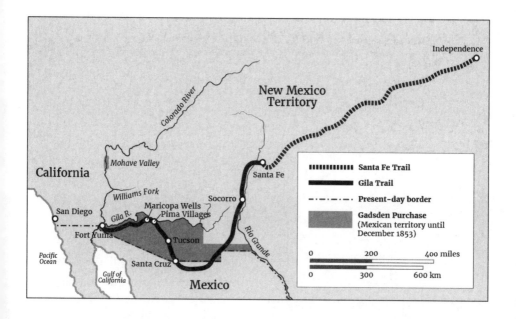

they had brought upon them,* regularly attacked and killed whites. Like the more northern Lakota bands, the Apache were formidable warriors who for two hundred years had been fighting off their white enemies, first Spanish and then Mexican. The utopia the Oatmans were heading to would lead them through territory that was, unbeknownst to them, "considered a war zone at best, a natural disaster at worst."[208]

In this state of ignorance, a party of around ninety people, including James Brewster, his parents, and five siblings, left Independence on August 9, 1850, to find the completely imaginary Land of Bashan. Among them were Olive's father, Royce, her mother, also called Mary Ann, and their seven children, ranging in age from two to seventeen. Mrs. Oatman was pregnant again. From the outset, it was an unhappy and quarrelsome company. To disagreements over how and even where they were traveling—only

---

*Fur trappers had "trapped out" most of the area. Their habit of leaving the dead bodies of skinned beaver on the riverbanks was particularly offensive to the Mohave, for whom the beaver was a sacred animal. See Margot Mifflin, *The Blue Tattoo*.

a few weeks into their journey, Brewster changed his mind about the location of the Land of Bashan, which became conveniently six hundred miles
closer than he had previously indicated—were added unedifying squabbles
over the allocation of food rations (they had not brought enough). Brewster
himself turned out to be "a contentious and unlikeable zealot," but he was
the least of their problems.

It was Olive's father who proved the most troublesome. An Illinois
farmer of Dutch origin who also fancied himself as a part-time preacher,
Royce Oatman was considered by his fellow travelers to be, variously, "a
facetious quarreler," incapable of suborning his personal needs and those of
his family to the group, and "the nucleus of all our troubles." One of them,
and the only non-Mormon in the party, wrote caustically of him: "Could we
therefore have exchanged him for the smallpox, the measure would have
had the majority vote."[209]

The party quarreled and then split and then quarreled and split again.
By January the following year, the Oatmans were in company with just two
other families. In February they found themselves in Maricopa Wells, a
drought-stricken settlement of a thousand almost starving Pima and Maricopa. The choice was whether to stay there and risk starvation themselves
or continue on to Yuma—a further 190 miles of hostile terrain. Royce Oatman decided to go it alone.

The journey that now lay ahead would take them across "a land so barren
that the legendary scout Kit Carson had said a wolf couldn't survive on
it."[210] Their outfit consisted of a single yoke of oxen and two yoke of cows,
but these animals were now in so pitiful a condition that it was doubtful
whether they would last the course. Their provisions amounted to little
more than starvation rations. Mrs. Oatman, now in the ninth month of her
pregnancy, was expecting the birth of her eighth child at any moment.
Somehow, they limped along for about eighty miles, but when they came to
more mountainous territory their animals were simply too weak to pull their
wagon, which had to be unloaded each time and half carried up every in-
cline. It was backbreaking work. "We frequently found places on our road

upon which the sun shines not, and for hours together the road led through a region as wild and rough as the imagination ever painted any portion of our earth."[211]

By March 18, when they were still only halfway to Yuma, the family was at breaking point. They had reached the Gila River, but the recent rains had swollen its waters "to an unusual width and depth," making it all but impassable. Somehow, they managed to get themselves to a narrow sandbank in the middle of the river. Night was falling, and it proved impossible to go any farther, and so it was here that the exhausted family made what would prove to be their last camp. "Let the mind of the reader pause and ponder upon the situation of that forlorn family at this time," Olive would later write. "Still unattended and un-befriended; without a white person or his habitation within the wide range of nearly a hundred miles; the Gila, a branch of which separated them from either shore, keeping up a ceaseless, mournful murmuring throughout the entire night; the wild wind, as it swept unheeding by, sighing among the distant trees and rolling along the forest of mountain peaks, kept up a perpetual moan solemn as a funeral dirge."

The next day they managed to get themselves to the opposite bank, and traveling by night "out of mercy to our famished teams" they clawed their way to the top of the next hill. "We found ourselves now upon the summit, which proved to be the east edge of a long tableland . . . lying between two deep gorges, one on the right, the other on the left," and beyond them lay a sight that must have frozen them to the heart. To the south lay "a wild, uninhabited, and uninhabitable region, made up of a succession of table-lands, varying in size and height, with rough, verdureless sides, and separated by deep gorges and dark canyons, without any vegetation save an occasional scrub-tree standing out from the general sterility. Around them, not a green spot to charm, to cheer, to enliven the tame, tasteless desolation and barrenness." To the east and north were "mountain ranges rising skyward until they seem to lean against the firmament."

More frightening than this scene of desolation was the effect it was beginning to have on their father. Until now Royce Oatman had always had "a hopeful countenance and cheerful spirit and manner, the very sight of which had a power to dispel our childish fears," but now a change had come upon him. Their father may have been a "facetious quarreler" to the rest of their party (and one whom they would happily have exchanged for the smallpox), but to his family those same qualities gave him a reassuring strength. But by now it was clear to all that he was at the absolute limits of his endurance. The night before, Olive's elder sister had heard her father weeping bitterly for a full hour. Now, he sunk down on to the ground, exclaiming, "Mother, mother, in the name of God, I know that something dreadful is about to happen!"

It was Olive who saw the Yavapai first. There were nineteen of them in all. Dressed in wolf skins, and with their bows and arrows slung across their backs, they were making their way "slowly and leisurely" up the mountain track behind them. "I was greatly alarmed," Olive wrote, "and for a moment dared not speak," but it was the look on her father's face when she pointed to them that made her really afraid. "The blood rushed to my father's face. For a moment his face would burn and flash as it crimsoned with the tide from within it; then a death-like paleness would spread over his countenance, as if his whole frame was suddenly stiffened with horror."[212]

At first the men appeared friendly, and Royce Oatman, who prided himself in his ability to "deal" with Native people, having often "censured whites for their severity toward them," did his best to play along. The men sat and smoked a pipe with him. They then asked for something to eat, but having so few rations left for his own family, this he refused.* There was a tense silence as the Oatman family made their final adjustments to the wagon, with the Yavapai looking on from a distance.

The attack was as sudden as it was brutal. "As a clap of thunder from a clear sky, a deafening yell broke upon us, the Indians jumping into the air, and uttering the most frightful shrieks, and at the same time springing

---

*It has been suggested that the reason for the attack was that, like the Pima they had encountered at Maricopa Wells, the Yavapais were starving.

toward us flourishing their war-clubs, which had hitherto been concealed beneath their wolf-skins."

Olive was struck across the head with a blow so hard that she fell to her knees; a second blow all but blinded her, and in this dazed state it was a few moments before she could take in what was happening. When she was able to turn around it was to see her father and brother lying on the ground. "My father, my own dear father!, struggling, bleeding and moaning in the most pitiful manner," while a little way off her brother Lorenzo was lying with his face in the dust, his head covered with blood, and bleeding from his ears and mouth. "I looked around and saw my poor mother, with her youngest child clasped in her arms, both of them still, as if the work of death had already been completed." Olive's younger sister, Mary Ann, then aged seven, was still standing next to the wagon, sobbing with her face in her hands. The rest lay motionless, "all upon the ground, dead or dying." At the sight of her massacred family, "a thrill of icy coldness" passed over her: "My thoughts began to reel and become irregular and confused; I fainted and sank to the earth, and for a while, I know not how long, I was insensible."

When she finally came to, Olive hardly knew where she was. "[I] thought I was probably dying. I knew that all, or probably all the family had been murdered; thus bewildered, confused, half conscious and half insensible I remained a short time, I know not how long. . . . Occasionally a low, piteous moan would come from someone of the family as in a dying state. I distinguished the groans of my poor mother, and sprang wildly toward her, but was held back by the merciless savage holding me in his cruel grasp, and lifting a club over my head, threatening me in the most taunting and barbarous manner."[213]

At that moment, Olive herself longed to die. "'O,' thought I, 'must I know that my poor parents have been killed by these savages and I remain alive!'" She begged her captors to kill her, "pleaded with them to take my life, but all my pleas and prayers only excited to laughter and taunts the two wretches to whose charge we had been committed."

It is something of a mystery why Olive and Mary Ann alone should have been spared by the Yavapai. Although it seems clear from Olive's account that they were treated as slaves during the time they spent as their captives, they would also have been two more mouths to feed and of limited use physically. It was perhaps for this reason that just a year later the two girls were sold on.

In the spring of 1852, a band of Mohave, on their annual trading visit to the Yavapai, bought the two girls, now aged fifteen and eight, exchanging them for two horses, three blankets, some vegetables, and a handful of beads.

The Mohave were a very different people to the Yavapai. Even in Reverend Stratton's heavily doctored and sensationalized version of their story, it is clear that they were treated with kindness from the start. The two girls were taken back to the Mohave village, a ten-day walk across a desiccated landscape full of "unshapen rocks" and burning sands. When their feet became too bruised to walk, pieces of leather were given to them to use as shoes, and during the cold nights Topeka, the daughter of one of the Mohave leaders, shared her blankets with them.

The sisters' "captors" had become their "guides." On the eleventh day of their journey, they came within sight of the Mohave village. Following the gaze of their guides, the two girls stood still for a few moments. What they saw was if not "the Land of Bashan" then a landscape that, after the seemingly endless desert they had just passed through, must have appeared quite close. Before them lay a narrow valley "covered with a carpet of green, stretching a distance, seemingly of twenty miles. On either side were the high, irregularly sloped mountains, with their foothills robed in the same bright green as the valley." Just a few miles away down the valley they could see smoke rising, "winding in gentle columns up the ridges." Before long, "there came into the field of our steady view a large number of huts, clothing the valley in every direction." A large number of these huts were huddled into a fold of the hills on the banks of a river (the Colorado) "whose glassy waters threw the sunlight in our face; its winding, zigzag course pointed out to us by the row of beautiful cottonwood trees that thickly studded its vicinity."

"'Here, Olive,' said Mary Ann, 'is the place where they live. O isn't it a beautiful valley! It seems to me that I should like to live here.'

"'May be,' said I, 'that you will not want to go back to the whites anymore.'

"'O yes, there is green grass and fine meadows there, besides good people to care for us,' Mary Ann replied, before suddenly recollecting herself, and adding hastily '[but] these savages are enough to make any place look ugly, after a little time.'"

Accompanied by a troop of curious children, who tripped along beside them "with merrymaking, hallooing and dancing at our side," they were taken immediately to see Topeka's father, Espaniole.* The family greeted the two girls with smiles, but their welcoming of Topeka was nothing short of joyful. "Seldom does our civilization furnish a more hearty exhibition of affection for kindred, than welcomed the coming in of this member of the chief's family, though she had been absent but a few days." They were given food to eat, and later that night, the entire village gathered for dancing and singing. Or, in Stratton's interpolation: "This was that of a company of indolent, superstitious, and lazy heathen, adopting the only method which their darkness and ignorance would allow to signify their joy over the return of a kindred and the delighted purchase of two foreign captives."

That night they lay down to sleep. Stratton once again added his own thoughts to Olive's, in his own particular brand of purple prose. "Where is the heart but throbs sensitive to the dark, prison-like condition of these two girls," he wrote, ". . . having been for nearly the whole night of their introduction to a new captivity made the subjects of shouting and confusion, heathenish, indelicate, and indecent, and toward morning hiding themselves under a scanty covering, surrounded by unknown savages." Speculating for

*Olive describes Espaniole as the village "chief," but he was most likely a *kohota*, or festival leader, responsible for overseeing celebrations. See A. L. Kroeber, "Olive Oatman's Return."

good measure "that under friendly guises their possible treachery might be wrapping and nursing some foul and murderous design."

But the foul and murderous design of Reverend Stratton's overheated imagination was not forthcoming. In fact, according to the interviews conducted by A. L. Kroeber, what Espaniole had really said was: "Let everyone help raise them. If they are sick, tend to them. Treat them well."[214] Nothing worse seems to have happened to them other than to have been taught to live as the Mohave themselves did. "In a few days they began to direct us to work in various ways, such as bringing wood and water, and to perform various errands of convenience to them."

One of the sisters' main occupations throughout their first summer was to collect "Musquite" (mesquite), which Olive describes as being "a seed or berry growing upon a bush about the size of our Manzanita." "In the first part of the season, this tree bloomed a beautiful flower, and after a few weeks a large seed-bud could be gathered from it, and this furnished what is truly to be called their staple article of subsistence." Nonetheless, the days were long, "twilight to twilight": they were expected to walk from six to eight hours a day to the place where the mesquite grew, with their baskets on their back.

More congenial work was to tend their own garden after the "chief's" wife, Aespaneo, gave them their own patch of ground, about thirty feet square, and some seed—corn, wheat, and melon seeds—to plant in it. "This we enjoyed very much. It brought to our minds the extended grainfields that waved about our cottage in Illinois, of the beautiful spring when winter's ice and chill had departed before the breath of a warmer season."

One day, some Mohave overheard the girls singing together. "This aroused their curiosity, and we were called, and many questions were put to us as to what we were singing, where we learned to sing, and if the whites were good singers. Mary Ann and I, at their request, sang them some of our Sabbath-school hymns, and some of the short children's songs we had learned. After this we were teased very much to sing to them. Several times a small string of beads was made up among them and presented to us . . .

also pieces of red flannel, (an article that to them was the most valuable of any they could possess,) of which after some time we had several pieces. These we managed to attach together with ravelings, and wore them upon our persons. The beads we wore about our necks, squaw fashion."

Gradually, the Oatman sisters were becoming Mohave. Before long, beads and decorations were not the only things that made them look like "squaws." "One day, while we were sitting in the hut of the chief . . . there came two of their physicians attended by the chief and several others, to the door of the hut. The chief's wife then bade us go out upon the yard, and told us that the physicians were going to put marks on our faces." The "physicians" proceeded to prick their skin "in small regular rows on our chins with a very sharp stick, until they bled freely. They then dipped these same sticks in the juice of a certain weed that grew on the banks of the river, and then in the powder of a blue stone that was to be found in low water, in some places along the bed of the stream, (the stone they first burned until it would pulverize easy, and in burning turned nearly black,) and pricked this fine powder into these lacerated parts of the face."

In Stratton's version of this event, the tattooing is specifically linked to the Mohave fears that the girls would try to escape. "They told us this could never be taken from the face, and that they had given us a different mark from the one worn by their own females, as we saw, but the same with which they marked all their own captives, and that they could claim us in whatever tribe they might find us." But the reality was quite different. The tattoos were indeed an identifying mark, but the Mohave only ever tattooed their own people, never their captives. The ceremony that Olive describes was a sign that both she and her sister had been fully and willingly accepted into the Tribe.

Unlike Olive, Mary Ann did not live to tell her own tale. She died, probably of starvation, about three years after they had first arrived among the Mohave.* A drought had caused the Tribe's crops of wheat and corn to fail.

---

*Olive gives two separate dates for the death of Mary Ann. In Stratton's version, she gives it as 1853; in her interview with Captain Burke, she gave it as 1855.

Reduced to living on mesquite "mush," they were, Olive wrote, "barely able to keep body and soul together." When it became clear that Mary Ann was dying, a crowd gathered round her: "Some of them would stand for whole hours and gaze upon her countenance as if enchained by a strange sight, and this while some of their own kindred were dying in other parts of the village."

Principal among these was Aespaneo. "She came up one day . . . and bent for some time silently over her. She looked in her face, felt of her, and suddenly burst out in a most piteous lamentation. She wept, and wept from the heart and aloud. I never saw a parent seem to feel more keenly over a dying child. She sobbed, she moaned, she howled. And thus bending over and weeping she stood the whole night."

By the next morning, it was clear that the end had come. Surrounded by members of the Tribe, Aespaneo, and Olive herself, Mary Ann "sank to the sleep of death as quietly as sinks the innocent infant to sleep in its mother's arms."

There are many contradictions in Stratton's version of Olive Oatman's experiences among the Mohave but none more glaring than the account of what happened next. In Stratton's retelling of events, after Mary Ann's death, Olive claimed that she too wanted to die, terrified that the "savages [would] by cold, cruel neglect, murder me by the slow tortures of starvation." Just a few pages later, however, she is recounting, in clear, simple language, very far removed from Stratton's overwrought prose, how the "chief's" wife, Aespaneo, now "came again to the solace and relief of my destitution and woe."

Olive was by now near starving herself, so faint and weak that she was hardly able to walk, "and had . . . concluded to wait until those burning sensations caused by want of nourishment should consume the last thread of my life." Just as she was preparing herself for the inevitable, Aespaneo came to her with some corn gruel that she had prepared in a bowl made from a hollow stone.

"I marveled to know how she had obtained it," Olive wrote. "This woman, this Indian woman, had uncovered a part of what she had deposited against spring, had ground it to a coarse meal, and of it prepared this gruel for me. I took it, and soon she brought me more. I began to revive. I felt a new life and strength given me by this morsel, and was cheered by the unlooked-for exhibition of sympathy that attended it. She had the discretion to deny the unnatural cravings that had been kindled by the small quantity she brought first, and dealt a little at a time, until within three days I gained a vigor and cheerfulness I had not felt for weeks. She bestowed this kindness in a sly and unobserved manner, and enjoined secrecy upon me, for a reason which the reader can judge. She had done it when some of her own kin were in a starving condition ... and when deaths by starvation and sickness were occurring every day throughout the settlement. Had it not been for her, I might have perished."

As it was, Olive survived the famine. The next year, the rains came again and brought with them a time of renewed plenty for the Mohave. "[I] really imagined myself happy for short periods," she wrote. That same year, another event occurred which, had she so desired it, might have made her happier still. A party of whites arrived in the Mohave Valley.

Lieutenant Amiel Whipple led his Pacific Railroad exploration party through the valley in February 1854. Whipple had been sent by the company to map a route from the Mississippi River to the Pacific Ocean through what was now, after the Gadsden Purchase of the previous year, no longer a northern Mexican badland but officially US territory.* A keen amateur ethnologist, Whipple brought with him a group of more than a hundred men, not only soldiers and guides but engineers, cartographers, geologists, meteorologists, and even astronomers, all of whom were energetically engaged in measuring and mapping their new terrain (still news to the Mohave) and the people who lived there. One of his team was a German

---

*This land was not incorporated into the US until December 30, 1853. Under the Gadsden Purchase, a 30,000-square-mile block of land south of the Gila River, comprising what is now southern Arizona and the southwestern part of New Mexico, was acquired from Mexico because the US wanted to build a southern transcontinental railroad, the Southern Pacific Railroad, which it did between 1881 and 1883.

draftsman, Baldwin Mollhausen, who became the first person ever to draw the Mohave. Mollhausen also wrote about them extensively in his journal, taking almost as much of an interest in the Native people they came into contact with as Whipple.

One of the things that struck both men was the incredible physical beauty of the Mohave. The men, in particular, Whipple wrote, moved "with the dignity of princes." Men with "brilliant eyes flashing like diamonds— looked even taller than they were from the plumes of swans', vultures', or woodpeckers' feathers that adorned their heads. Some wore as their sole garment a fur mantle, made of hares' or rats' skins, thrown over their shoulders; but one outshone the rest of the company, having picked up an old waistcoat that had been thrown or bartered away by some of our people, and now displayed it for the completion of a costume that had hitherto consisted only of paint."[215]

Whipple and his men remained in the valley about a week. It is all but impossible that Olive would not have known about the expedition. While it was not the first time that the Mohave had been in contact with whites, the arrival of so many of them in the valley was an extremely unusual occurrence. Furthermore, it was one that the Mohave appeared to thoroughly enjoy. There was an almost carnival atmosphere during the week that the expedition was there. As yet unsuspecting of the devastating effect this would later have on their way of life, the Mohave traded freely with Whipple's men, joined them in games of archery and hoop rolling, and allowed them to roam freely along the river and through their fields, occasionally even to visit them in their houses. Throughout the entire visit, the Mohave "ranged about the camp in picturesque and merry groups, making the air ring with peals of laughter." At no time was there any suggestion that there was a white woman living among them, and nor

---

*American Indians were nothing if not sartorially inventive. In the same year, many hundreds of miles north, an Oglala winter count for 1854–55 records that a Pawnee warrior had been killed wearing a suit of steel armor, probably a relic of a Spanish conquistador. See Waggoner, *Witness*, appendix 5.

did Olive—or Spantsa* as she now was—make any attempt to contact them.

It is possible that she was simply hidden away for the duration of the visit—possible, but not likely. In one of the first interviews that she gave to a newspaper, the *Los Angeles Star*, on her return, Olive told the reporter that "the Mohaves always told her she could go to the white settlements when she pleased but they dared not go with her, fearing they might be punished for having kept a white woman so long among them, nor did they dare let it be known that she was among them."[216] Even if she had been forced into hiding, it is strange that Stratton makes no mention of a near-rescue having been thwarted by Mohave villainy. The most likely explanation seems to be that of A. L. Kroeber. "Was she perhaps at the time a more or less willing abettor in being concealed, but later, when with white people, was ashamed of this complaisance? Or again Stratton may have suppressed the fact of her knowledge, if she admitted it to him: it would have contradicted the tenor of his book, whose keynote is Olive's misery among the degraded savages."[217]

There are many other facts about the Mohave that the Reverend Royal Stratton either suppressed or would have done had he known of them. In sexual matters, the Mohave were considered "notoriously outspoken and uninhibited." The mountain man Jedediah Smith had said of them: "No Indians I have seen pay as much deference to women as these. . . . Here they harangue the multitude the same as men."[218] The women were as sexually uninhibited as the men. When they saw the Whipple party's long beards, of which the men themselves were not a little proud, they burst into peals of laughter, and "put their hands to their mouths, as if the sight of us rather tended to make them sick." A century and a half later, a Mohave scholar suggested that because they were unaccustomed to men's facial hair, "the women thought the beards made the men look like talking vaginas."[219]

---

*Olive was also known as Aliutman, an elision of "Olive" and "Oatman."

Olive Oatman's Mohave nickname, Spantsa, meaning "rotten" or "sore" vagina, also gives the modern historian pause for thought. Native American scholars believe that it could have been because she was unusually sexually active, "implying that she was having so much sex that she was 'sore' and had a vulgar smell ('rotten') or that she was with someone so virile he was wearing her out."[220] Whatever the truth, the utter impossibility of her ever admitting to such a thing, or even discussing it, once she was returned to white society is beyond doubt.

The story of Olive Oatman would have a remarkable afterlife, becoming the subject of plays, paintings, short stories, novels, and even a sculpture. Throughout the 1880s and 1890s, the "Tattooed Lady" became a staple feature of circuses and vaudeville acts. In the following century a version of her story would appear in the television series *Death Valley Days*, in which Ronald Reagan played the part of the Fort Yuma commander Martin Burke, here reimagined as Olive's rescuer. More recently still, in 2011, another television series, *Hell on Wheels*, featured a traveling player whose face is marked with identical blue tattoos.*

For all this, or perhaps because of it, we will never now know what Olive's true thoughts and feelings really were. In her own lifetime it was Stratton's version—"at once pious and titillating . . . and a clear refrain for white supremacy"—that sold. Under the reverend's Svengali-like influence, Olive had quickly become a captive of another kind. Part media darling, part circus freak, over the next six years she would spend many months "on the road," giving talks about her experiences and displaying her tattoos to a fascinated public—and selling Stratton's version of her "Five Years Among the Indians!"

---

*For a more detailed discussion of Olive Oatman's literary afterlife, see Margot Mifflin's excellent *The Blue Tattoo*.

A promotional photograph of Olive Oatman, taken shortly after her "rescue" from captivity among the Mohave

14

HELL ON WHEELS

There was only one person who might have known what Olive's true thoughts and feelings were about her time among the Mohave, and she was, if possible, an even more notorious figure than Oatman herself.

When Olive had first arrived in Yuma, there were perhaps only two or three other white women living there. While newspaper accounts of the time reported that she had been looked after at the fort by a Mrs. Twist, the wife of Lieutenant Reuben Twist, more recent research has shown that the person who took it upon herself to care for Olive during the two weeks she spent there was not Mrs. Twist at all, but a woman named Sarah Bowman.*

Sarah Bowman was a woman of many talents and even bigger personality. Throughout her long and vigorous career she was, variously, an Army camp follower, entrepreneur, cook, innkeeper, and battlefield heroine. At the

---

*An Army officer, Edward Tuttle, who knew Sarah Bowman well in the 1860s, identified her. See J. F. Elliott, "The Great Western: Sarah Bowman, Mother and Mistress to the U.S. Army."

time when Olive was taken into her care, she was running a thriving business as the madam of the local brothel.

Of all the clichés that beset the history of the American West, the "whore with a heart of gold" is perhaps the most egregious and very rarely survives any serious scrutiny. Sarah Bowman, however, is an exception. But then Sarah Bowman, "the greatest whore in the West," was exceptional in every way. Six feet two in her stockinged feet, and weighing in at more than two hundred pounds, she bore a vivid scar down one cheek, "a souvenir from the blow of a Mexican saber at the siege of Matamoros." No one who saw her ever forgot her. "Today we are reinforced by a renowned female character, a giantess . . . over seven feet tall," wrote one frontiersman on first making her acquaintance. "She appears here modest and womanly not withstanding her great size and attire. She has on a crimson velvet waist[coat], a pretty riding skirt and [her] head is surmounted by a gold laced cap of the Second Artillery. She is carrying pistols and a rifle. She reminds me of Joan of Arc and the days of chivalry."[221]

Nicknamed "The Great Western," or sometimes simply "the Western" for short, after the largest British-owned steamship then in existence, Bowman was born sometime around 1812 in Tennessee but grew up in Missouri. Although she could neither read nor write, she learned to speak fluent Spanish from her time as an Army camp follower during the Mexican-American War and could give any man a run for his money. "They called her old Great Western. She packed two six-shooters, and they all said she shore could use 'em, that she had killed a couple of men in her time."[222]

Everyone who met Bowman loved to tell stories about her and her larger-than-life exploits. In 1846, at the beginning of the Mexican-American War, she was present at Fort Brown (in present-day Texas), just across the Rio Grande from Matamoros. Here she set up her kitchen tent in the middle of the compound, refusing to leave it even when under enemy fire. After a bullet pierced her bonnet and another hit the bread tray she was carrying, she declared that she was ready to man the ramparts with her own musket if the Mexicans should storm the besieged fort, earning for herself

*Sarah Bowman, imagined here in the saloon bar of
one of her several "places of resort" (brothels)*

another nickname, "the heroine of Fort Brown." At the US victory celebrations after Matamoros was taken, a special toast was made to her: "The
Great Western—one of the bravest and most patriotic soldiers at the siege
of Fort Brown."

A year later, at the Battle of Buena Vista, a breathless scout came running in with the news that the US Army was about to be "whipped" by the
Mexican general Santa Anna. Bowman was not having any of it: "She just
drew [him] off and hit him between the eyes and knocked him sprawling;
says, 'You damned son of a bitch, their ain't Mexicans enough to whip old
Taylor.'" Then she added, 'You just spread that report around and I'll beat
you to death.'"[†223]

With the signing of the treaty of Guadalupe Hidalgo, the troops prepared to march west to occupy their newly acquired territories New Mexico
and California. The major in charge informed Bowman that if she would

---

*General Zachary Taylor.
†The teller of this tale would add that this was "a story the boys tell, I don't know whether
it's true or not," but clearly the Western was the kind of woman to whom stories stuck.

marry one of the dragoons and be mustered in as a laundress, she could go too. "Her ladyship gave the military salute and replied, 'All right, Major, I'll marry the whole squadron and you thrown in but what I go along.' Riding along the front of the line she cried out, 'Who wants a wife with fifteen thousand dollars and the biggest leg in Mexico! Come, my beauties, don't all speak at once—who is the lucky man?' Finally, Davis of Company E said, 'I have no objection to making you my wife, if there is a clergyman here to tie the knot.' With a laugh the heroine replied, 'Bring your blanket to my tent tonight and I will learn you to tie a knot that will satisfy you, I reckon.'"[224]

No one knows what happened to Davis of Company E, but by the mid-1850s Sarah had met and married another lover, Albert Bowman. Originally from Brunswick, in Germany, her new husband was fifteen years her junior. It was while she was married to Albert that, sometime in the mid-1850s, Sarah had arrived in Yuma.

Fort Yuma was infamous as being the worst and most isolated US Army garrison in the entire country—and the bar was not high. It more than earned its sobriquet, "Hell's Outpost." As Sarah Bowman liked to say, "there was just one thin sheet of sandpaper between Yuma and hell."

The summers were so roastingly hot that one hundred degrees Fahrenheit was considered quite bearable. One often-repeated story was of a man who ventured out in the middle of the day, only to be discovered later as nothing more than a huge grease spot and a pile of bones on the parade ground. Another story, equally "hackneyed to army ears," was of the soldier "famous for his wickedness, who, having died, reappeared, and was seen hunting for his blankets: the inference being that the warm place to which he had been assigned was not hot enough for one accustomed to Fort Yuma's climate."[225] Apart from the intolerable heat, soldiers were plagued by ants, biting gnats, and malaria-carrying mosquitoes from the Colorado River. Scorpions nested in their shoes, and they were so poorly paid that the desertion rates were among the highest in the land. As one of the lieutenants stationed there noted in a letter to a friend: "Our principal occupation at present is drilling, riding, 'rogueing' Squaws and drinking ale—the weather being too hot for whiskey."[226]

This desolate spot marked the end of the Gila Trail. Although many travelers would have passed through the settlement—prospectors heading for the gold fields, scientists, traders, and cattle and sheep herdsmen—there were few permanent white residents other than a small number of US Army personnel manning the fort and the men who worked the ferry (former mountain men having wrested this job from the local Mexicans). It was, as the saying goes, no place for a lady. But the pistol-packing Sarah Bowman fit right in.

Although Albert Bowman, a former dragoon, had recently been discharged from the Army, it was not long before his wife was making herself indispensable at the fort. "The officers have hired the Great Western to keep a mess for them, or rather board them, and she came up [to the fort] after dark with bag and baggage," the commander at the time, Major Samuel Heintzelman, wrote in his diary not long after her arrival. Soon, Sarah was well entrenched, not only "keeping mess" for several Army officers and the resident doctor but cleaning Heintzelman's house and giving oyster dinners for his men (of which the mournful Heintzelman wrote "and everybody in camp but me was invited").

Like everyone else who met her, Sarah fascinated Heintzelman, who wrote about her frequently in his diary. "She looks 50, and is a large, tall, fearless looking woman," he noted, adding that he did not think that she intended to stay long at Yuma. He was mistaken. Not many people would have seen "Hell's Outpost" as a business opportunity, but Sarah Bowman did. Keeping house for officers and throwing oyster suppers did not keep her happy for long. Soon she was making plans to set up on her own, just across the river on Mexican soil.

Although she would at first try to pass off the house she built there as her own private residence, it was clear to all that this would be what was euphemistically called "a place of resort." The Great Western was an old hand at running establishments of this kind. During the Mexican war she had done so with great success twice before, once in El Paso, in Texas, and again in Saltillo, in Mexico. Dancing, drinking, and gambling were the principal entertainments on offer; and, inevitably given the all-male clientele, it was not long before women were also on the menu. Major Heintzelman did not approve, but he knew that there was little he could do. "I was sorry I agreed to go," he wrote of a visit there, "but when you are in Rome you must do as Rome does."

His lieutenants had no such scruples. "I have just got a little Sonoran [Mexican] girl for a mistress," wrote one. "She is seventeen and very pretty. . . . For the present she is living with The Great Western, and comes up nights to my room. The Great Western you remember . . . Among her other good qualities, [she] is an admirable pimp. She used to be a splendid-looking woman and has done 'good service,' but she is too old for that now."[227]

While some of these reminiscences may have grown in the telling, there was never any doubt about Sarah Bowman's essential goodness of heart. One man, who as a boy used to take eggs and other supplies to her house, and be rewarded with meals, described her simply as "a hell of a good woman."[228] Over the years, Sarah had adopted a number of destitute children, including at least three Mexicans, not only caring for them but also teaching them skills to support themselves into adulthood. Although no details remain of her dealings with Olive Oatman, the Great Western— "kindly and considerate to all, and of great strength and force of mind"— was in many ways the ideal person to watch over the timid young Mohave woman during the first few weeks of her reentry into the world of whites.

The Oatmans' strange story certainly remained on Bowman's mind for many years after Olive left Yuma. In a tender postscript to their briefly linked lives, one autumn, while traveling to Tucson, Arizona, Sarah took it upon herself to tend to the forgotten graves of Olive Oatman's slaughtered family, instructing her "peons" to remove their bones from a pile of rocks on top of a hill and overseeing their reinterment near the road.[229]

The Great Western died as dramatically as she had lived. In 1861, at the beginning of the Civil War, she moved to another Army post back East, so as to be nearer the action. When she died, five years later, from the bite of a venomous spider, she was given a full military funeral: an escort, a flag-draped coffin, and a three-gun salute.

DURING THE CIVIL WAR (1861–65), which engulfed the East and South of the country for four long years, the emigration slowed considerably.* When the war finally came to an end, there would be a movement west like never before: hundreds of thousands of demobilized soldiers, recently emancipated slaves dreaming of the chance to carve out new lives for themselves, and a new influx of immigrants from abroad, hungry for land and work—all would be lured to the territories beyond the Missouri River.

Even before upheavals brought about by the Civil War, the West had seen many changes. In 1858, the Patee House Hotel opened in Saint Joseph. Boasting that it was the "Largest and Finest" hotel west of the Mississippi River, the Patee House's luxurious facilities included a billiards room, a reading room, and an elegant dining room offering all "the Delicacies of the Season" on its extensive menu. As well as individual parlors for ladies and gentlemen, there was a huge saloon, decorated with velvet sofas, damask curtains, and paintings on the walls, extending over most of the second story. The floors and stairs were covered in rich red Brussels carpet. Each individual bedroom had running water and was illuminated at night with gas lamps—almost unknown luxuries for the times. Perhaps most remarkable of all, however, was a small room on the ground floor—the headquarters of a brand-new business venture.

Amid much fanfare, the Pony Express opened for business on April 3, 1860. Using teams of relay riders, messages and letters could now be carried the 1,966 miles from Saint Joseph, Missouri, to Sacramento, California, by courier. A journey that had taken the first overland settlers upward of six

---

*Around six thousand settlers made their way west during this time. See Lillian Schlissel, *Women's Diaries of the Westward Journey.*

months was now telescoped into a daring dash of just ten days.* But the venture, extraordinary as it was, was short-lived. Just a year and a half later, telegraph poles had been erected from coast to coast, eliminating the need for the Pony Express, which closed for business in October 1861.

The greatest change of all, however, would be brought by a new technology more powerful still than the telegraph. In 1862, two railroad companies, the Central Pacific Railroad and the Union Pacific Railroad, received charters from the US government, and when the Civil War ended they began what would be one of the most ambitious industrial enterprises of the age: laying 1,775 miles of railway track from Omaha, Nebraska, on the Missouri River, to Sacramento, California. When completed, the transcontinental railroad would unite the East and the West like never before.

In order to lay the railway track, a series of base camps, roughly seventy miles apart, were built across the once-pristine prairies. Primarily intended to provide services for the Union Pacific's eight thousand railroad workers, these makeshift "towns" sprang up almost overnight, sometimes disappearing again almost as quickly as the railway workers moved on.

Julesburg, on the border of present-day Colorado and Nebraska, appeared in a matter of weeks over the summer of 1867.† The "town" covered some three hundred acres and, at the height of the Union Pacific's activities,

---

*Local legend has it that the riders rode their horses directly into the hotel building to collect their satchels full of mail. Altogether the riders are estimated to have carried 30,835 letters, at a cost of five dollars per half ounce.

†Julesburg had formerly been an important overland station on the Oregon Trail, but in 1864 it had been attacked and burned to the ground by a war party led by Chief Spotted Tail, in revenge for the killing of a large number of peaceful Cheyenne at Sand Creek. Hundreds of volunteer soldiers led by Colonel John Chivington had razed the sleeping village to the ground, killing and brutally mutilating 150 people, most of them women, children, and the elderly. One pregnant woman had her stomach ripped open, and even the fetus had been scalped. Most of the dead were hideously dismembered. The soldiers had kept not only the scalps of their victims but also their body parts—women's breasts, hearts, fingers, noses, and even their genitals—and used them as decoration on their hats and saddles. It was an act of senseless barbarism that would not only spark short-term reprisals such as the attack on Julesburg but also radicalize a generation of outraged Cheyenne and their Lakota allies. Chivington was never brought to trial.

contained some twelve hundred dwellings, of which (so the joke went) nine hundred were saloons. "Over the streets, that had scarcely ceased to be paths in the wilderness, Government [wagon] trains passed, bound to distant frontier forts," wrote one emigrant woman on passing through. "Railway employees, with long lines of wagons containing implements and necessaries for the great work going on farther west; ox-trains, en route for the gold regions, transporting merchandise; drivers flourishing long whips, and shouting with all the force of their powerful lungs—kept up a varying percussion; and the vile exhilarant called whisky was freely used, and aided much in causing the wild excitement."[230]

While some railroad towns, such as Cheyenne, would survive as "cow towns," others quickly dwindled into insignificance as soon as the construction workers moved on, becoming little more than ghost towns. Julesburg, "the city of prodigy, that passed from infancy to old age in the short space of a few weeks, vanished like morning dew, and the ground was almost deserted in three months from the time of commencement."[231]

All, in their day, shared a reputation for lawlessness and vice. Elizabeth Custer, the wife of George Armstrong Custer, left a vivid description of one railroad town, Hayes City, on the later Kansas Pacific Railway, when her husband's regiment was stationed nearby. "The railroad having but just reached there, the 'roughs,' who fly before civilization, had not yet taken their departure," she wrote. "There was hardly a building worthy of the name, except the station house. A considerable part of the place was built of rude frames covered with canvas; the shanties were made up of slabs, bits of driftwood, and logs, and sometimes the roofs were covered with tin that had once been fruit or vegetable cans, now flattened out. A smoke rising from the surface of the street might arrest your attention, but it indicated only an underground addition to some small 'shack,' built on the surface of the earth."

According to Elizabeth Custer, Hayes was "a typical Western place," where carousing and general lawlessness were incessant, and where pistol shots were heard so often "it seemed a perpetual Fourth of July, only without the harmlessness of that pyrotechnic holiday. The aim of a border ruffian is so accurate that a shot was pretty certain to mean a death, or, at least a serious wound for someone. As we sat under our fly in camp, where all was order, and where harmony reigned, the report of pistol shots came over the intervening plains to startle us. The officers, always teasing, as is so apt to be the case with those who are overflowing with animal spirits, would solemnly say to us, 'There goes a man to his long home'; and this producing the shudder in me that was expected, they elicited more shivering and sorrowful ejaculations by adding, as the shots went on, 'Now, there goes a woman; two were shot last night.'" The soldiers, she added, "knew so much of the worthlessness of these outlaw lives that it was difficult to arouse pity in them for either a man's or a woman's death in the border towns."[232]

It was not only the railway employees who landed in the new towns. So many single men gathered together, and isolated for many months at a time in the remote wilderness, presented plenty of opportunities for others, both men and women. Almost as soon as the Union Pacific Land Office had opened its doors on a new site, a swarm of professional card sharps, gunmen, saloon owners, pimps, and prostitutes followed in its wake, "a carnivorous horde, hungrier than the native grasshoppers, eager to devour the men's weekly pay."[233] In a term coined by newspaperman Samuel Bowles, this phenomenon became known as "Hell on Wheels."

When the Union Pacific's employees packed up and moved west again to another depot, "Hell on Wheels," like a circus troupe or a traveling fairground, was quick to follow.* "By day disgusting, by night dangerous," the Hell on Wheels towns offered everything from dentistry and hardware supplies to dance halls, gambling, and women of easy virtue. Its centerpiece was the big tent in which brass bands brayed continuously day and night. This vast edifice, forty feet by a hundred feet, was in essence a mobile "place of resort," similar in kind, but on a much larger scale, to Sarah Bowman's

---

*The first "Hell on Wheels" town was near Fort Kearny, in Nebraska Territory. Before completion of the railroad, they also included Julesburg, Cheyenne, Laramie, Green River, and Benton. Curiously, the Central Pacific Railroad, which began laying railway tracks east from Sacramento, does not seem to have attracted the same kind of activities.

Keystone Hall, a temporary edifice not unlike a circus Big Top,
was the centerpiece of the "Hell on Wheels" railway town.

various enterprises, and with all the same amenities. "The big gambling hall had extra lights, extra attendants, extra tables; and the great glittering mirror-blazing bar with glistening bottles, paintings, and row after row of polished glasses. The rest of the space was devoted to tables for faro, monte, roulette, or whatever game of chance the reckless cared to try."[234]

In Julesburg there had even been a theater, "where a motley audience dressed in every conceivable fashion, and of every grade of character but the pure, came together nightly to witness melodrama no less startling than their own lives," commented one shocked emigrant woman. "If ever the preaching of the gospel might claim a field rife in iniquity ... surely this was the one."[235]

The railroads would bring with them iniquities far greater than the theater. Prostitution was a fact of life everywhere that large groups of single men gathered together: in mining communities, around US military garrisons—and the new railway towns would be no exception.

Prostitution was grim, brutal, and widespread. Contrary to the popular myth, it is hard to find any evidence that these women were held in any particular esteem by their clientele, while the gaudy glamour of the saloon bar or the "urbane brothel, patronized by courtly gentlemen," the trope of dime novels and countless westerns, has long been exposed for the romantic fiction that it is.[236] In the railway towns in particular, working women were more likely to operate out of makeshift booths, known as "cribs," or, perhaps saddest of all, from mobile brothels known as "cat wagons."

Men came up with many different euphemisms to describe the women they frequented. These "soiled doves" or "sporting women," as they were sometimes known, occasionally gained notoriety enough to acquire their own sobriquets. The history of the West is full of women with flamboyant names—Big Nose Kate, Squirrel Tooth Alice (so called because she kept prairie dogs as pets), the Queen of the Blondes, and even the Great Western herself—but since most of their stories rely heavily on hearsay, it is hard to separate the truth from the fantasies that surround them. Even Calamity Jane, who like the Great Western was a known Army camp follower, is reputed to have turned her hand occasionally to the trade, having once been employed by Dora DuFran, a well-known madam operating in Deadwood, South Dakota. The letters and diary that she wrote, in which she drove stagecoaches, shot "Indians," and won ten thousand dollars in a poker game, and which were later published by a woman claiming to be her daughter, have been convincingly shown to be fakes.*

Occasionally, madams such as Dora DuFran and Sarah Bowman ran thriving businesses and died wealthy women, but more often than not, prostitutes were young or poor, usually both. The vast majority of them

---

*The author of the diaries, Mrs. Jean Hickok McCormick, claimed to be the daughter of Calamity Jane and Wild Bill Hickok. In fact, Calamity Jane, whose real name was Martha Canary, never met Wild Bill. Nor did she ever take part in Buffalo Bill Cody's Wild West show, as her "daughter" would claim. It may be true, however, that she once rode horses for the Pony Express and on at least one occasion joined forces with a band of outlaws who pulled off a successful gold heist—stories which, curiously, never made it into her "diary."

scratched out a living along the fault lines of a constantly shifting frontier, from which the only exit was often a violent one, either by someone else's hand or their own.

In Hayes City, there were thirty-six deaths over a single summer. "The citizens seemed to think no death worthy of mention unless it was that of someone who had died 'with his boots on,'" Elizabeth Custer wrote. "There was enough desperate history in the little town that one summer to make a whole library of dime novels."[237]

EVEN BEFORE THE COMING of the railways, tensions along the Oregon Trail had been mounting. After the Grattan incident, and with the brutal reprisals that had followed, "all the Indians were rebellious," Susan Bordeaux wrote. "They saw that they were being robbed and that there was no protection for an Indian."

After the Harney massacre, many had retreated north, away from the central plains—not, as the US government officials complacently imagined, in defeat, but to regroup, rearm, and radically expand their sphere of influence. Under warriors such as Red Cloud, High Backbone, Crazy Horse, and a newly emerging leader, Sitting Bull, not only did they stockpile horses, guns, and ammunition, but they met together and strategized. They also grew in numbers, absorbing bands from other Tribes such as the Cheyenne and the Arapaho, in the process becoming "the largest, richest and safest Indigenous domain in North America." By the early 1860s the Lakota were as many as twenty thousand strong. "Americans did not know it yet, but Lakotas had overshadowed them in the deep interior in diplomatic reach and sheer military might."[238]

The Lakota had seen firsthand the environmental destruction caused by the emigrant road across the central plains, and they were determined that the same would not happen in their heartland, either in the Black Hills or in the fertile river valleys farther east—Powder River country. They had also heard troubling stories from their eastern kin, the Dakota, who had thought to make peace with the whites. Having sold off their land and agreed to give up hunting, the Dakota's territory had been overrun by white settlers and their promised annuities pocketed by government agents. Almost all had sunk into crippling poverty. A Dakota uprising, known as the Minnesota Massacres, had been brutally suppressed. Stories such as these would only add to the Lakota leaders' bitter opposition to the white brand of peace and everything they knew it would bring with it: "reservations, farming and alien mores and beliefs."[239] By 1864, they were ready for war. Now, after months of planning, "the war council decided to force a mass battle with the [whites]."[240] They would fight not as a fragmentary group of individual bands but as an empire.

The recent discovery of gold in Colorado and Montana had only added to the pressure. As early as the summer of 1857, all seven of the Lakota bands had met in council in the Black Hills, the Lakota's spiritual and temporal heartland far to the north of Fort Laramie, at which they had vowed to protect their land and their way of life. If gold were found here too, it would spell disaster for both. The council was agreed that "any Indian who should show the gold fields in the Black Hills to white men, should die, and the whites thus made aware of the presence of gold there should also die, for fear that their country be taken from them."[241]

Farther south, on the Oregon Trail, the US Army was now a greater presence than ever before, as more troops were sent and new garrisons were built, as Susan Bordeaux put it, "to protect the emigrants and miners against the Indians on their own land." Some mornings the Bordeaux family awoke to find "a city of white tents" surrounding them. These belonged to regiments that had been sent out to explore and survey the country, many of them heading still farther north and west, into the Lakota's fiercely protected heartland. Particularly offensive to the Lakota was the new Bozeman Trail, which led from Fort Laramie to the recently created mining town of Virginia City, Montana, and two new forts, Fort Phil Kearny and Fort C. F. Smith, which the military had built along the trail in order to protect the free flow not only of miners heading west but of the new mineral wealth flowing east—a much-needed revenue stream for a nation about to face the huge costs of reconstruction in the aftermath of the Civil War. All were flagrant violations of the terms of the 1851 Fort Laramie Treaty.

The plains Tribes knew that "their land was coveted and would sooner or later be taken. The wild game over a thousand hills that meant life to an Indian would be all a thing of the past."[242] But their opinion about how to deal with the continuing encroachment was divided. "Some were for the signing of a new treaty then being talked of," Susan Bordeaux wrote. "Others said the treaty of 1851 was the only one they wanted to live up to. The treaty signers hung around the agencies living on rations, while those who wanted to retain their land as it was pulled out on their travois to live by hunting as they had always done."

But this was not all they were doing. In 1864, Brulé, Oglala, and Cheyenne bands, united together to fight off the white settlers, began a series of systematic raids along the North Platte River, attacking overlanders, supply posts, and garrisons. The area became "a vast war zone geared to stop westward expansion in its tracks."[243] Even families such as Susan Bordeaux's, fur traders who had lived for so long in harmony with their Native American neighbors and had been allowed to hunt and trap along all the streams "whenever they wished without any molestations in their goings or comings," were no longer safe. That spring, "just when the plowing of corn was taking place," an attack was made along the Little Blue River. "For three hundred miles, homes were burned, horses, cattle, and even women and children were captured."[244]

Among the captives taken by the Cheyenne was a woman called Lucinda Eubanks and her child. The following year, two Lakota from the Mnikhowozu band, Two Face and Black Foot, arrived at Fort Laramie, bringing the two captives with them, with the intention of claiming the reward that had been offered for their return.

The two men had visited the fort the previous summer with their band and had "quite a talk" with one of the lieutenants there, a man named Fleming. They had assured Fleming that they were "good Indians and had come from the north and had never fought a white man" and that their only reason for being in the area was to hunt. Two Face had even asked for a written recommendation that he could show any US soldiers he might meet as they went about their hunt. "With this 'Good Paper' in his possession, he and his band left Laramie, following the river east." Unfortunately, only a few days later, Two Face had lost this letter of recommendation, which was subsequently recovered and taken back to the commanding officer at the fort.

When Two Face and Black Foot arrived at Fort Laramie, bringing Lucinda Eubanks and her child with them, instead of receiving the promised reward, they and ten others were immediately taken prisoner. After the briefest of court martials, the arresting officers, who were both drunk at the time, sentenced Two Face and Black Foot to be hanged. "They were placed in the guardhouse till a scaffold was built. In vain did Mrs. Eubanks plead for the life of Two Face. This tall, handsome man had won her heart. She begged the commanding officer to spare his life. 'He was good to me!' she cried, but to no avail."[245] Singing their death songs, they went to the scaffold.

It was not only the injustice of their sentence that angered the Lakota. With an armed sentry on permanent guard nearby, no one could go near the bodies to take them away for burial. Instead, Two Face and Black Foot were left hanging on the scaffold, next to the rotting corpse of another man, a Cheyenne named Four Antelope, who had also been sentenced to death a month previously, accused of stealing a horse. "The Cheyenne was hanged with the ball and chain with which he was manacled, and it was not long till the body was decayed and the ball, from its weight, pulled the limb off."

Susan Bordeaux remembered seeing the bodies many times, swinging in the wind. "Four Antelope wore a red handkerchief clasped with a large silver medallion such as were given to the men at the Treaty [of Fort Laramie]. In the spring sunshine, as the body turned and swung, this medallion glistened and shone like a looking glass. It seemed to be sending signals of distress to the tribes. The emigrants passing along the road which ran nearby could easily see him."[246]

Isolated incidents such as these, for all their senseless cruelty, were indicative not so much of US Army strength as of its failures.

The series of battles, sieges, skirmishes, raids, and bungled attempts (on the part of the US) at peace talks that ensued over the next few years would collectively become known as the First Sioux War. Almost all civilian traffic along the Bozeman Trail ceased during this time, travel and freighting along the Oregon Trail also, while hostilities along the Platte River meant that even the building of the Pacific Union railway all but ground to a halt, "its 11-million-acre federal land grant suddenly rendered useless," as raiding parties derailed trains, ransacked freight cars, and shot at surveying crews.

Despite the US tendency to declare victories when there were none, the truth was that the Lakota had won the war. As General William Tecumseh Sherman would declare, "fifty of these Indians can checkmate three thousand of our soldiers." The Lakota had proved a formidable fighting force. Their sheer numbers, their extraordinary equine maneuverability, and their superior knowledge of the terrain over which they were fighting meant that the US government had no choice but to treat with them.

In 1867 an Indian Peace Commission was established to carry out negotiations, which took place at both Fort Laramie and the new railroad town of North Platte over several weeks that autumn and then again the following spring. Even the more moderate chiefs, such as Spotted Tail and Swift Bear, were now "anything but moderate." Peace, if it came at all, would be on Lakota terms. Particular grievances were the Bozeman Trail and the extension of the Union Pacific railroad west of North Platte, both of which disturbed the buffalo. It was clear, too, that the detested military forts along the Bozeman Trail would have to be dismantled. As one negotiator, a former trader, put it, if the US did not agree to these things, "no argument, no presents, no amount of money, no matter how large, will ever satisfy these Indians."[247] "All the things that anchored US power in the West—roads, rails, steamboats, soldiers, forts, even annuities—fell under threat when

Lakota delegates doggedly articulated their key demand: the preservation of their territory, the bison, and the traditional Lakota way of life."[248]

The new Fort Laramie Treaty was signed in 1868. Under its terms, a territory for the Lakota, the Great Sioux Reservation, was now clearly defined. Although slightly smaller than the area demarcated under the Horse Creek Treaty of 1851, it stipulated that the lands east of the Bighorn Mountains and north of the North Platte River, while lying just outside the boundaries of the reservation, were to be sovereign Lakota lands where "no white person or persons" could ever settle. In the Bighorn Mountains, the Lakota watched soldiers marching out of Fort C. F. Smith and Fort Phil Kearny. When they had finally gone, their warriors burned the forts to the ground.

In return, the Union Pacific would be allowed to resume the construction of its railway along the North Platte River as planned.

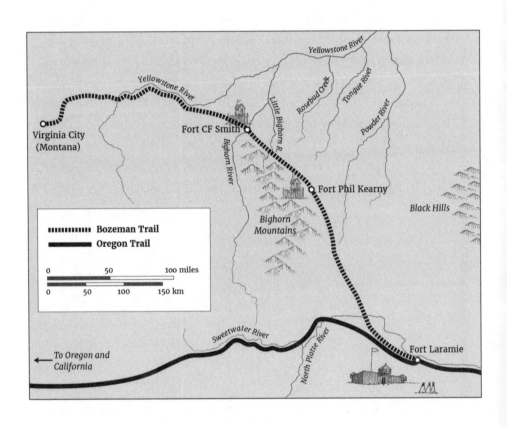

Yellowstone River

Yellowstone River

Virginia City
(Montana)

Fort CF Smith

Little Bighorn R.

Rosebud Creek

Tongue River

Powder River

Bighorn River

Fort Phil Kearny

Black Hills

Bighorn
Mountains

Bozeman Trail
Oregon Trail

0   50   100 miles
0   50   100   150 km

Sweetwater River

To Oregon and
California

North Platte River

Fort Laramie

15

MILITARY WIVES

lthough it was barely thirty years since Narcissa Whitman and Eliza Spalding had made their first groundbreaking journey across the Rocky Mountains, the US was a profoundly different place from what it had been at the beginning of the emigration. The country that would arise, phoenix-like, from the ashes of the Civil War would become ever more industrial, more aggressive in its imperial ambitions, and vastly bigger than it had been at the beginning of the emigration. The addition of Oregon, Texas, and the other lands ceded by Mexico after the Mexican-American War, together with the Gadsden Purchase, had between them increased its landmass by almost 70 percent. The US now had both the financial and administrative capability to begin turning what had once been only "imperial abstractions" into all-out state-sanctioned violence.[249]

Forts and military outposts proliferated throughout these new territories. In the post–Civil War years, between 1865 and 1890, more than eighty-five new garrisons were built as the US government turned its attention west. The numbers of military men stationed along the emigrant trails also increased, from around 8,400 to more than double that figure.[250] In their wake, many more women now moved west. Military wives, cooks, laundresses, and camp followers of many different kinds would all now carve out lives for themselves along the ever-shifting American frontier.

Frances Anne (or Fannie) Boyd was a young bride of nineteen the first time she set out, alone, to join her soldier husband out West. She was, by her own admission, a "delicately nurtured woman" who had lived in the city all her life, and she considered her hometown, New York, "the only habitable place on the globe." Even San Francisco, where she was initially headed, seemed to her "as far away as China." While realizing that wives were good for their men's morale, the US Army made no special provision for them, and Fannie would spend the next twenty years of her life dutifully following her husband to the newly minted US territories of Nevada, Arizona, New Mexico, and Texas, making the best she could of some of the remotest and most isolated military outposts the Army had to offer.

While many military wives would leave records of their experiences, Fannie's level but optimistic gaze, her good grace under appalling conditions, and her genuine sympathy for her husband's men make hers one of the best of its kind. "I have always had, and always shall have, a tender, sympathetic feeling for American soldiers," she wrote in *Cavalry Life in Tent and Field*. "In fact, most of the kindly help which made life on the frontier endurable for me came from those men."[251]

While Fannie came to love the West, her initial experience of military life would test her down to the last fiber. Her first posting was to Camp Halleck, a tiny military outpost in a remote part of eastern Nevada, where her husband, Orsemus—a Civil War veteran even though he was barely out of his teens—had been sent with part of his regiment, the Eighth Cavalry, "as a sort of advance guard and protective force for the contemplated Pacific Railroad."[252]

Fannie's experience of traveling in the West in 1868 was already unimaginably different from how it had been when Virginia Reed and her
family had trudged their way, slowly and painfully for many months, across
exactly the same terrain, albeit in the opposite direction, just two decades
previously. While the transcontinental railway (the western section of it still
held up by Lakota "hostilities") would not be completed until the following
year, the introduction of the stagecoach had already revolutionized travel
along the emigrant roads.*

Traveling by day and night, at an average speed of ten miles an hour,
stagecoaches were three times faster than the old settler wagon trains. Their
drivers, known as "bullwhackers" or "whips," prided themselves on being
able to complete the journey from the Missouri to Sacramento, California,
in as little as three weeks.

Stagecoach drivers were "the rock stars of their generation." Famously
ruthless, hairy, and hard-drinking, these kings of the road were both revered
and feared by their passengers in equal measure. "His hirsute and unclean
appearance indicates a cat-like aversion to water," wrote one fascinated passenger. "He is more profane than the mate of a Mississippi River packet,
and, we have his word for it, 'ken drink more whiskey.'"[253] But for all their
dubious personal habits, the drivers were smartly turned out. "Each was
issued with a gum coat, a buffalo robe, a pair of blankets, a blue overcoat of
the type worn by Civil War soldiers, a pair of flannel overalls, a fur muffler,
a shawl, a buffalo coat, a breech-loading Wesson rifle, a Colt revolver, and
'plenty of ammunition.'"[254] Those who worked for Ben Holladay's Overland
Stage were positive dandies, their uniforms consisting of "high boots with
western heels, velvet-trimmed corduroy trousers, a wool-lined overcoat, a
wide-brimmed sombrero, and the ubiquitous long whip for use on his

---

*The first company to complete the entire overland journey, from Leavenworth, Kansas, to
California, was the Pioneer Line. It took thirty days and cost the eye-watering sum of two
hundred dollars.

teams."[255] These whips, which were made of sixteen-foot-long pieces of rawhide, would retort like pistol shots over the heads of their galloping teams.*

It was into the hands of one of these ferocious, whip-cracking bull-whackers that Fannie Boyd committed herself in the early part of 1868. Having arrived in California by sea (which, by overlanding across the Panama isthmus, was now a mere three weeks on board a Pacific Mail Steamship Company vessel), she picked up the stagecoach in Cisco, in the western foothills of the Sierra Nevada.

Stagecoaches may have been the fastest and most modern way to travel, but it did not necessarily make them either safer or more comfortable than the humble ox-drawn wagon. Fannie's first impression was of "a large vehicle with thorough-braces instead of springs" and a "roomy interior" that suggested comfort. "Alas!" she wrote. "Only suggested! Possibly no greater discomfort could have been endured than my companion and self underwent that night. Those old-fashioned stagecoaches for mountain travel were intended to be well-filled inside, and well-packed outside. But it so happened that instead of the usual full complement of passengers, one other woman and myself were all."[†256]

Leaving Cisco at noon, they did not reach Virginia City,‡ on the eastern side of the Sierra Nevada, until ten o'clock the next morning. "A pen far more expert than mine would be required to do justice to the horrors of that night." All night long the terrified women found themselves peering "into endless precipices, down which we momentarily expected to be launched, for the seeming recklessness of our driver and the extreme narrowness of the roads made such a fate appear imminent.... We did not expect to find ourselves alive in the morning, and passed the entire night holding on to

*The sound is caused by a sonic boom.
†Fannie Boyd never explains who her companion was, although it seems likely that she may have been the wife of another, unnamed, Army officer.
‡This was Virginia City, Nevada, not to be confused with Virginia City, Montana, at the end of the Bozeman Trail.

anything that promised stability. An ordinary posture was quite impossible: we had either to brace ourselves by placing both feet against the sides of the vehicle, or seize every strap within reach."

Long before morning, all devices "except the extreme one of lying flat on the bottom of the coach and resigning ourselves to the inevitable" had failed. "Every muscle ached with the strain that had been required to keep from being bruised by the constant bumping, and even then, we had by no means escaped."

Toward evening, when they emerged on the eastern side of the Sierra Nevada, they came to a beautiful lake in the heart of the mountains. The place, Fannie explained, had been "made famous by the frightful sufferings of the Donner party." The former Truckee Lake had recently been re-named in their honor. Donner Lake was now a picnic spot. Although barely twenty years had passed since the Donner party's ordeal and Vir-ginia Reed's extraordinary trek to safety through the icy mountains, their story was already part of western mythology; so well known, and so often described by other writers, Fannie Boyd noted, "that a passing mention will suffice."

The two women spent the following night in Virginia City. Once a muddy "bar" of the kind that "Dame Shirley" had so vividly described, Vir-ginia City was now a metropolis that could rival San Francisco in size and luxury. In 1859, the discovery of the Comstock Silver Lode, the first of its kind in the US, had sparked another mining bonanza, bringing in miners and other settlers by the thousands. In the city were not only the tunnels and bore-shafts of innumerable mines but an entire metropolitan infra-structure necessary to support its fifteen thousand inhabitants: mills, lumber yards, two schools, three theaters, and no fewer than forty-two saloons. It even had its own stock exchange. The hundreds of horse and mule teams that were needed to transport the ore meant that traffic jams, sometimes lasting hours at a time, were a daily occurrence, exacerbated by as many as half a dozen stagecoach lines, such as the one Fannie Boyd had traveled with, that now served Virginia City, each one arriving loaded down with "passengers, capitalists, miners, 'sports,' thieves, robbers, and adventurers of all kinds."*[257]

The miners spent their money lavishly, building luxurious mansions for themselves, wearing fine clothes, and spending their nights at the theater or the opera.† The beautiful pine trees, once a staple food source for Native people such as Sarah Winnemucca's Northern Paiute, were long gone. Game from their hills, salmon from their rivers and lakes, and beef grazed and fattened on their pastures now appeared on the silver-decked dining tables of the newly rich.

---

*The wealth created by the silver mines gave rise to an unusual variety of jobs for women in Virginia City. Census figures show that as many as a hundred seamstresses and dressmakers catered for the wives of the newly rich, among whom nothing less than Parisian-style high fashion would do. Further census data shows that as well as traditional occupations for women such as teaching and laundering, women in Virginia City worked as merchants, waitresses, cooks, saloon and restaurant operators, an opium den operator, a bookkeeper, a book folder, a fortune-teller, a peddler, an upholsterer, a hairdresser, a house painter, a dairy operator, and a laborer. While women were almost entirely excluded from mining activities, in 1871 a group of women opened their own mine on B Street. A mine tunnel dug by women was so unusual that the *Territorial Enterprise* wrote two surprisingly supportive articles about them. "We do not see any reason why women should not engage in mining as well as men," it wrote. "If they can rock a cradle, they can run a [mining] car; if they can wash and scrub, they can pick and shovel. Although some gentlemen friends of the ladies are attempting to persuade them from continuing work, they are determined, and we are pleased to see it." Forth Ward School Museum, Virginia City.

†The same frontier "roughs" who panned for gold, herded cattle, and made up the vigilante groups could become almost pitifully starstruck when faced with one of their stage darlings. The arrival of the beautiful Jewish actress Adah Isaacs Menken in Virginia City in 1863 was greeted with almost hysterical fervor. Menken was one of the superstars of her day. Her melodramatic performances included *Mazeppa, or The Wild Horse of Tartary*, adapted from a poem by Lord Byron. This involved a display of horsemanship in which she rode onto the stage on a horse before galloping up a runway, enclosed on either side with cardboard cutouts of craggy mountains. Opinions varied as to her equestrian skill—which since she had to be strapped onto the horse backward, and in a semirecumbent position, was perhaps not very great—but this did not matter so much as the thrilling fact that she was (for the times) practically naked. Menken's stage attire varied according to each of her particular acts. They included "The French Spy" and "Pirates of the Savanna," but many were of the "captive eastern slave" variety and were clearly designed to show off her legs. One particularly notorious "costume," and one in which she was frequently photographed, consisted of nothing more than tightly fitting underwear—in itself a sensational piece of performance art. For weeks before her arrival, posters in which Menken's half-naked body was draped dramatically over the back of a rearing black stallion adorned the walls of every saloon bar and gambling den.

While pleased to find herself in "a real mining town," Fannie was too exhausted by her journey to seek out any of these pleasures during her overnight stop. Instead, on leaving her breakfast table the following morning to resume the journey she was unpleasantly surprised to find that the stagecoach, practically empty the previous day, was now full of other passengers.

From being "tossed about like balls," the two women now had to suffer "the very extreme of our previous night's journey." Inside the stagecoach there was a front and a back seat, and between the two a middle bench, facing backward; together, they left "not an inch of space unoccupied." Somehow squeezing themselves in among the other passengers, they settled themselves as best they could and set off again. The passengers were so packed in together that it was not even possible to move their feet "without asking our vis-à-vis to move his at the same time, as there was not an inch of space unoccupied." They traveled like this for five whole days, "without the slightest change of any sort."

Although the "rough frontiersmen" who were now their traveling companions did their best to make this situation more endurable, it was an impossible task. After the two women had sat bolt upright and all but sleepless for two days and two nights, the passengers facing them proposed, "with many apologies, that we should allow them to lay folded blankets on their laps, when, by leaning forward and laying our heads on the rests thus provided, our weary brains might find some relief." The women gratefully assented, only to find that "the unnatural position rendered sleep impossible, so decided to bear our hardships as best we could until released by time."

From catapulting along the narrow mountain passes at breakneck speed, the pace of the stagecoach now changed to a crawl. Being the middle of winter, the vehicle frequently found itself bogged down in a deep, clinging mud that made regular progress impossible. Their only respite was when the coach stopped at a staging post, to change horses and to allow the passengers to get something to eat, with the result that they "breakfasted at midnight and dined in the early morning." In any case, Fannie wrote, the food was "frontier food" and all but inedible: "biscuits almost green with salterus, and meats sodden with grease, which disguised their natural flavors so completely that I often wondered what animals of the prairies were represented."

If Fannie had hoped that the situation would improve when they finally left the mountains, she was soon disappointed. The terrors of the mountain precipices were exchanged for "the endless monotony" of the plains of Nevada. To Fannie's untutored eye, there was nothing to be seen but sagebrush, "a low, uninteresting shrub ... as its name indicates, a dingy sage-green in color: nothing else could be seen, not only for miles and miles, but day after day, until the weary eye longed for change."

As the days and sleepless nights lapsed into one another, the journey took on an almost-hallucinatory quality. "At dusk imagination compelled me to regard those countless bushes as flocks of sheep, so similar did they appear in the dim light, and I was unable to divest my mind of that idea during our entire stay in Nevada." In vain, she counted the revolutions of the wheels, which appeared to get slower and slower with each passing mile. Like children, the passengers took it in turn to ask the driver the querulous question, "How long before we reach the next station?"

Even when they did finally reach the next stop, there was little comfort to be had. "The names of our stopping places were pretentious to such a degree that days passed before I was able to believe such grand titles could be personated by so little. I also noticed that a particularly forbidding exterior, and interior as well, would be called by the most high-sounding names."*

But arrive, eventually, she did: not in Camp Halleck, which was still a hundred miles farther east, but at another military outpost, Fort Ruby, where she found Orsemus waiting for her. After five grueling days in a stagecoach "I no longer felt particularly young," Fannie wrote. "Experience and the loss of sleep had aged me." And yet even she was taken aback when one of the station employees asked her husband: "How did the old woman stand the trip?"

---

*As any backpacker will know, it is a phenomenon alive and well in far-flung places even today.

"I listened intently for his answer," Fannie wrote, "fully expecting to see the man severely rebuked, if not laid flat; but Mr. Boyd understood human nature better than I, and in the most polite tones replied: 'Thank you, very well indeed.'"

The Boyds completed the remaining hundred miles to Camp Halleck, a further four days of traveling through heavy snow, in the back of a mule-drawn government ambulance, "in this case the most uncomfortable one I have ever seen."*

On the first of these days, toward evening, in the middle of nowhere, the ambulance came to a sudden stop. "I doubt if any mortal was ever more amazed than I when told we were to go no farther," Fannie wrote. "Not a sign of habitation was in sight! Nothing but broad plains surrounded us on all sides! Not even a tree could be seen, and the four mules had to be hitched to our ambulance wheels, as tiny bushes were not, of course, [suitable] for such a purpose."

At this point, even the cheerful Fannie must have had many misgivings. This was her first experience of camping out. The Nevada desert, at night, is cold and unimaginably vast. As she lay down to sleep, a vertiginous feeling of aloneness came over her: "The knowledge that except one tiny dot in the wilderness—our ambulance—we had no resting place, gave me a curious homeless feeling that was indeed cheerless."

Later, bedded down in the back of the ambulance, her sleep was continually disturbed by the antics of the four mules. "Sometimes one mule would be seized with the ambitious desire to break away; this would rouse the

---

*It is a measure of the phenomenal speed with which the railroad was built that when the Boyds left Camp Halleck a year later, the tracks had been laid to within twelve miles of the place. The couple were able to travel by train (albeit a construction train) all the way back to San Francisco, although the freight car was so uncomfortable, and became so packed with railroad employees, that the atmosphere "soon became intolerable," Fannie wrote. "The road-bed was so new and the jolting so alarming, I concluded that a stage ride would have been preferable, as we could at least have seen what was before us. . . . I felt almost glad to have taken what had become so completely a memory of the past—a stage-ride over those grand old mountains."

other three, who would each in turn attempt to stampede, and but for the driver's timely assistance it is difficult to state what might have happened, as our vehicle was not sufficiently strong to withstand such violent wrenches."

Fannie Boyd's only experience of the Army before this point had been when she had watched her husband graduate from West Point, the prestigious military academy in New York State. Somehow, she had imagined that every Army post would be exactly like it and that "however far we might travel such a home would always be found at our journey's end." But when she finally arrived, battered and sleep-deprived, at Camp Halleck, it proved to be about as far from "beautiful West Point" as could be imagined.

The Boyds' new home, and the place where Fannie would live for the next year, turned out to be a cluster of rudimentary tents, barely more sophisticated than a mining camp. Their living quarters were formed of two wall tents pitched together "so the inner one could be used as a sleeping and the outer one as a sitting room." The two sections were divided by a calico curtain, and a carpet of old grain sacks covered the floor. Almost the entire space in the inner tent was taken up by a pine bunk that did service as a double bed. The outer tent was dominated by a huge fireplace (absolutely necessary when the temperatures fell to more than thirty-three degrees below zero), leaving only just enough room for them to sit down, and requiring "constant watchfulness to avoid setting one's clothing on fire."

These living conditions may have seemed rudimentary, but she soon realized that they were positively palatial when compared to the living arrangements of the rank-and-file soldiers, miserably quartered in dugouts—literally holes dug in the ground. To Fannie's unaccustomed and horrified eyes, they were "places in which only animals should have been sheltered."

New York, at this point, must have seemed very, very far away. Lying in bed on her first night at the camp, she was surprised to hear "familiar airs, played upon a very good piano" coming from somewhere nearby. "It seemed impossible that there should be a fine musical instrument such a distance from civilization, particularly when I remembered the roads over which we had come, and the cluster of tents that alone represented human habitation," she wrote. The sound turned out to be not some kind of aural hallucination but the captain's wife, playing on a piano that had somehow been transported to the middle of the Nevada desert. The instrument "added greatly to her happiness, and also to the pleasure of us all, though its first strains only intensified my homesick longings."

But Fannie was nineteen and in love with her husband, and, as she put it, "young people are not easily discouraged." One happy day she received the news that her household goods, "a modest supply of dishes and cooking utensils" that she had bought from a departing Army officer at Fort Ruby, had finally arrived. "An ominous sound which greeted our ears as we opened the boxes rather dismayed us," Fannie recalled, "but we were not prepared for the utter ruin that met our eyes. What had not been so brittle as to break, had been rendered useless and unsightly by having been chipped or cracked; and as we took out the last piece of broken ware I concluded that what was left might be sold in New York for a dollar." When they compared the residue with the inventory, they discovered that half their goods were missing.

The same fate befell their chairs. Of the six they had been expecting, for which they had paid the princely sum of fifty dollars, only one arrived. "When we asked about the other five, the man replied that the roads were so bad, our chairs, having been placed on top of the load, were continually falling under the wheels, and finally, broken in pieces, had been left to their fate," Fannie recalled. "We, however, suspected that they had served as firewood." After the first pangs of this new misfortune had worn off a little, they made a joke of their fifty-dollar chair, "claiming a great favor was bestowed upon anyone allowed to occupy it."

She soon found that her housekeeping "was simplified by absolute lack of materials." What matter if they had no plates, if there was barely any food to put on them? Their food was confined to the usual soldiers' rations. Every bit as basic as those of the early wagon trains, these consisted of bacon, flour, beans, coffee, tea, rice, sugar, soap, and condiments. Their only luxury was dried apples, "and with these I experimented in every imaginable way until the last of my efforts to disguise them utterly failed, and we returned to our simple rations."

Occasionally they were able to acquire other supplies, but only at a cost. The nearest trader's store was two miles distant and this, Fannie wrote, "was a matter of congratulation" rather than otherwise, as when they did occasionally splurge, the frontier prices were so inflated "we felt as if eating gold."

The high prices kept them "poor and hungry for years." A dozen eggs cost a fantastic two dollars; canned goods, a dollar each; and all these had to be paid for either in gold or silver as, like everywhere in the West, "greenbacks," or paper money, were not accepted. "I had always disliked to offend anyone; but remarking one day that the flavor of wild onions* which permeated the only butter we could procure, and for which we paid two dollars and a half a pound, was not exactly to our taste," she seriously offended the person who made it. "I rejoiced thereat when she refused to supply us with any more, feeling that a lasting economy had been achieved without any great self-denial."

Even to this lonely outpost, a mail coach arrived once a week. It brought them not only letters, but reading material—their greatest luxury—in the form of serial stories in magazines. There was one particular story in which both she and Orsemus became deeply engrossed, "the heroine of which was cast on a desert island, where I thought only her lover's presence could reconcile her to the absence of supplies" (a story that clearly resonated with her own). "But after we had become most deeply interested," she wrote, "five weeks passed during which not a single number was received, and we were left to imagine the sequel." This state of affairs continued with such regularity that in the end they began to believe "that we were furnishing light

---

*Certain kinds of wild herbs, particularly if eaten by the cows in the early spring, had this effect: it also affected the taste of milk and even meat. In Texas, especially, Fannie noted, "the flavor was abominable."

literature to the poor inhabitants of some lonely stage station on the road; and in that belief we tried to find consolation for our own losses."

There were other consolations, too, chief among which was the time she was able to spend with Orsemus. She became an admirable cribbage player, and when interminable winter finally gave way to spring, they often went for rides together—Fannie on the steadiest old horse that could be found for her, whom they named "Honest John"—stopping to catch trout in the abundant streams full of meltwater. She delighted, too, in the wildflowers, which were of "endless beauty and variety." Even Camp Halleck, so dismal when she had first arrived, turned out to be situated on a stream in a grove of cottonwood trees and proved to be "far more beautiful than I had ever imagined."

Summer came, bringing trials of another kind. The sun was so searingly strong that it could penetrate the thin canvas of their tent, until her face was as burned "as if I had been continually out of doors." Venomous and biting creatures of all kinds also found their way into the tents, including snakes, tarantulas, scorpions, and plagues of biting gnats so microscopically small that no amount of netting could keep them out. "I had never before, nor have I ever since, seen any insect in such quantities, nor so troublesome and annoying." On one occasion she found a colony of wasps nesting in their canvas roof, swarming "in countless numbers above our heads, going in and out through the knotholes in our rough pine door, buzzing about angrily whenever we entered hastily—in fact, disputing possession with us to such a degree that I dared not open the door quickly."

Throughout these various trials, Orsemus, to whom she had been married for just two days before his regiment sent him west, proved to be a thoughtful and attentive husband. "I was highly diverted by the efforts my husband made to find presents for me, and shall never forget the peculiarity of his gifts." These included a box of a dozen apples, for which he had paid the tremendous price of a dollar; a sewing machine, which, although it had cost the equivalent of a month's pay, turned out to be "entirely out of order, and represented nothing in the way of usefulness." And, most eccentric of all, a donkey.

Unlike the sewing machine, which had been almost ruinously expensive, Orsemus had bought the donkey because it was extremely cheap, "and so docile a child might ride it." The animal, whom they called Burro, despite being very small, had a bray "that was a marvel of strength and volume" and turned out to be something of a nuisance. "If military orders were being read, Burro kept up an accompaniment which drowned out all other sounds; and in his apparent loneliness, the poor fellow had a way of seeking human companionship, and would appear at our doorstep and lift up his voice in a manner that made us feel the roof must rise above our heads in order to allow the fearful sound to escape."

Unlike some of her other postings, in which Fannie would find herself the only woman for fifty miles or more, there were several other military wives at Camp Halleck, as well as a smattering of ranchers, mostly Mormons, living nearby. Although she claimed to have made friends with some of them, it is clear that she was sufficiently different from them in both background and education that the friendships did not go far, and she seems to have regarded them as something of a curiosity: "Their wives interested us greatly," she wrote, considering them "perfect specimens of frontier women."

But the conditions of frontier life, no matter what a woman's background or resources may have been, were nothing if not a leveler. "No one could envy others, for all were in the same boat, with no comforts whatsoever." Fannie would observe several times during her twenty years as a military wife, and perhaps with a tinge of schadenfreude, the efforts of some of the richer military wives to throw their money at the problem. In Fort Bayard, in southwest New Mexico, she observed the arrival of a young bride married to a recent graduate of West Point. "That little lady had all the ambition and pride in a refined way of living that arose naturally from having spent her early life amid luxurious surroundings," Fannie recalled. "She had passed several years in the gayest capitals of Europe, had imbibed most extravagant ideas from fond and indulgent parents, had scarcely ever known an ungratified wish, and was therefore less prepared for the actual realities of life, as developed at Fort Bayard, than anyone else I have ever known."

Just as Fannie had done on her arrival at Camp Halleck, the newcomer clearly expected all military stations to be alike. In addition to twelve enormous trunks full of smart clothes (doomed never to see the light), she had brought with her from New York "the most luxurious outfit ever seen on the frontier." This included magnificent carpets, curtains, furniture, and ornaments, many of them from W. & J. Sloane, the fanciest and most expensive department store of its day—more fit for a palatial New York apartment than for garrison quarters in the hills of New Mexico.

Unaware of the weather conditions, the "little bride" proceeded to lay her carpets directly on the mud floor and hang up her expensive curtains in the windows, and she had soon "decked the interior to look like a perfect fairy bower." When the first summer storm came, just as Fannie had predicted, the rains flooded right through the house, until the "fairy bower" was ankle-deep in mud: "The pretty white curtains were streaked and discolored beyond recognition, the carpets covered with mud, while the pictures and ornaments were unrecognizable."

"Her experience was pitiable," Fannie explained. "Having an abundance of money, she naturally supposed it would purchase some comforts; but money was no use there, and, indeed, seemed only an aggravation."

This was particularly so when it came to sending east for fashionable clothes—which were, in any case, of questionable use on the frontier. Like Fannie's kitchen chairs, and even her magazine stories, they would arrive either damaged or needing alterations which only a skilled hand could carry out. Shoes hardly ever arrived in pairs. Everything involved "almost incredible waiting" and was never what was expected.

Most Army wives soon learned to live, of necessity, "with the greatest unconcern regarding fashions," but everyone, even Fannie, loved a new bonnet. After two years on the frontier, and when "some head covering became an absolute necessity," she sent east for a new one. When her parcel finally arrived, she opened it to find, instead of the "plain little hat, dark and useful" that she had ordered, "a very gaudy, dashing piece of millinery, that would have been suitable for the opera but was altogether out of place on the frontier." To a twenty-dollar bonnet was added the ruinous cost of the express charges for transporting it. "For that entirely useless arrangement, I had to pay forty-two dollars," she noted ruefully, "and then had no bonnet, for I never wore it."*

However gently born the wife of a military officer might have been, when it came to domestic matters—cooking, cleaning, and laundry—she usually found herself on her own. Domestic servants of the kind the Boyds had been used to in New York, if they could be hired at all, had an inconvenient way of taking one look at the primitive conditions of an Army camp and heading home as fast as possible. Double wages were expected on the frontier, but even that was not always a sufficient inducement. The rich New Yorker at Fort Bayard had brought her maid with her all the way to Santa Fe, only to be told flatly that "she did not care to go any farther from civilization."

There was another reason that female servants, single ones in particular, were so hard to keep. "Women were so scarce, and men so plenty, that no matter how old or ugly, a woman was not neglected." Knowing this, but still anxious to employ some kind of nurse for their two young children, the Boyds had persevered. On leave in New York between postings, and after much searching, they finally thought they had found the perfect candidate. "We congratulated ourselves on the servant's appearance, which was so far from pleasing that it seemed safe to take her. Had it been otherwise she would, we were sure, soon desert us for matrimony. The girl was an absolute grenadier in looks and manners; and although not absolutely hideous, was so far from pleasing that we were confident of retaining her services, so made a contract for a year."

They soon discovered the error of their belief that her plainness would be any kind of impediment to finding a suitor. They had not been at their

---

*A vast sum for the Boyds: as a lieutenant, Orsemus's monthly pay was $120, which went down to half that amount when they were either traveling or on leave. The expenses they incurred when traveling from post to post on half pay, which officers paid from their own pockets, was a perpetual source of grievance.

new posting, Fort Union, for three days before the "grenadier" received her first proposal of marriage. Discovering that he drank, she "quickly discarded him," but the damage was done. "It required but little time in which to become aware of her own value." To Fannie's dismay, in the weeks that followed her unprepossessing nanny acquired not one but "scores" of suitors for her hand.

The man who was eventually successful in winning her hand did so without ever having set eyes on his prize. Although the soldier in question had been away from Fort Union on "distant service" for several months, word had nonetheless reached him that the Boyds had brought a young woman from the East with them. In Fannie's view, this man "was brave in every sense of the word." Trusting to the old adage "Faint heart ne'er won fair ladie," "he had made the necessary preparations for their marriage while en route back to his post—even going so far as to engage a carriage at Las Vegas for their wedding trip—before he had even set eyes on her." His pluck must have pleased her, the Boyds realized, for just three days after his return "she accompanied him to Las Vegas, where they were united for life."

There was nothing the Boyds could do, although Fannie admitted that what she actually felt was relief. Quite apart from the drama of the long line of lovelorn suitors, for the five months that she had been with them "she had made my life harder in every way," Fannie wrote. "Not only had she scorned all our belongings and surroundings, but absolutely wearied me with incessant complaints over the absence of modern conveniences."

Another Army wife, Elizabeth Custer, gives an even clearer idea of what it was like to live and work in a remote frontier garrison, there being not so much an absence of "modern conveniences" as no "conveniences" at all. Like Fannie Boyd, Elizabeth Custer spent many years following her husband on his US Army postings, but there the similarity ends. The wife of Lieutenant Colonel George Armstrong Custer, Elizabeth, known to her family as Libbie, was almost as flamboyant a character as her husband. Although the several books that she would later publish about her experiences of camp life have many similarities with those of Fannie Boyd, they are very different in tone. Raven-haired, flirtatious, and more self-consciously a "lady" than the quiet and unassuming Fannie, Elizabeth's vigorous campaigning after her husband's death was in large part responsible for his later hagiography as the gallant fallen hero of "Custer's Last Stand."

The Army, Elizabeth observed, generally preferred Black servants because they were more "faithful" than their white counterparts (an observation that can be interpreted today to mean that they did not have all that much choice in the matter). The Custers, who for much of this time had their African American cook Eliza with them, were no exception. They not only valued Eliza but were also a little in awe of her. The formidable Eliza clearly had her own tried-and-tested ways of making her value felt. In the Custer household, Mondays were known as "Black Friday," as this was the day when they gave her their orders for the week, but only if it "were absolutely necessary." "It was very odd to hear a grown person, the head of the house, perhaps say, 'You tackle Eliza this time, I did it last time.'"[258]

Elizabeth and George Armstrong Custer, with their esteemed African American cook, Eliza

Eliza's efforts on their behalf were nothing short of heroic. Her tent kitchen was so rudimentary that there was no surface to work on, and she was obliged to sit on the floor, "*a la Turque*," to do everything from peeling potatoes and grinding coffee to mixing dough. The wood for making fires, usually soft cottonwood, was often so damp that it would hardly burn at all, or if it did, it gave off such billows of smoke that it hurt her eyes. Worst of all, however, were the incessant prairie winds. "No one," Elizabeth Custer wrote, "ever gets quite used to the wind of the plains," which seemed at times as if it would "blow her tent quite down."

"Mingled with everything was the fine dust which the gusts of wind blew in, or which the continual flapping of the tent-wall on the ground sifted into every dish or cooking utensil. The tea blew away while being put into the teapot, the flour rose in little puffs while being molded. . . . I have seen poor Eliza ironing on the ground, the garment over which she worked held down by stones for weights, while she swiftly and vigorously plied her iron, holding down the other part with her free hand."[259]

16

---·◈·---

CAMP FOLLOWERS

Army garrisons in the West were full of women such as Eliza. Many of them, like her, were African Americans, but others came from countries as diverse as Ireland, England, Canada, Germany, Holland, France, Denmark, Sweden, and even Italy. Others, from nearer home, included Mexican and Native American women, all of whom found employment with the military as cooks, domestic servants, nurses, and laundresses. Although they sometimes appear in passing in the accounts of military life written by the likes of Fannie Boyd and Elizabeth Custer, their low status means that they are usually invisible, and they remain largely forgotten participants in what was no longer merely an emigration but a full-blown military conquest of the West.

While women had always followed troops, most did so on sufferance. One group, however, would stand out from the rest. After an Act of Congress in 1802, laundresses were not just camp followers but fully paid members of the US military. Employed in a ratio of four laundresses to every hundred soldiers, they received regular salaries for their work, as well as housing and rations.

Although the military did not encourage their rank-and-file soldiers to marry, they nonetheless often employed couples as a package—he as a soldier, she as a laundress—and seem to have been fully accepting of the fact that they would be bringing their children with them too. Single women, also often with a family in tow, frequently married the soldiers they met en poste (although these were usually common-law arrangements). If, as sometimes happened, their husbands rose through the ranks to become officers, they became known as "half-way ladies," a derogatory term that indicated their inferior social status.

As Fannie Boyd had found, both accommodation and food supplies varied from post to post. In the hands of unscrupulous contractors, rations often arrived in a lamentable condition. It was not unusual for cooks to find rat and mouse droppings, and occasionally even an entire rodent, in their supplies, while flour and grain sacks invariably came with a rich insect life of maggots, weevils, and worms. In some postings, "the butter was simply oil, if procurable at all; the milk thin—not tasteless but with a decidedly disagreeable flavor of wild garlic and onions, and the beef dry, and with so strange a flavor we could not eat it."[260] Sometimes supplies were so out of date that they were quite simply inedible. Potatoes, unless dried or powdered, were "a mass of decay" when they arrived, while some flour biscuits baked in 1861 did not turn up until 1867 and had to be broken up with a hammer.[261]

To supplement these basics, and in the absence of any kind of fresh produce, a strange kind of vegetable "brick" or "cake," made from pressed and dried onion, cabbage, peas, celery, carrots, beets, turnips, tomatoes, and peppers, was also a staple of Army rations. Approximately nine inches by three inches across and an inch thick, these vegetable cakes, when softened in water, could be added to soups or stews in the faint hope of giving them some flavor. As Fannie Boyd would write, "I never knew a woman who, amid all those conditions of improper and insufficient food and severe heat, did not lose health and strength."[262]

And yet, despite the harsh conditions, it was not necessarily a bad life for the times. There were plenty of opportunities for the industrious.

Laundresses could take on extra washing for officers and their wives and could turn their hands to sewing and baking. If they had their own cows with them, as many did, they could also make a tidy profit selling their milk and cheese.

One especially entrepreneurial woman was a Mexican called Mrs. Nash. For ten years between 1868 and 1878, Mrs. Nash worked as a laundress at Fort Meade, in Dakota Territory.[263] Over the years, "Old Nash," as she was later known, had been married to a succession of US soldiers, at least two of whom deserted her. But like Sarah Bowman before her, Mrs. Nash (her first name is not recorded) was a woman of unusual energy and enterprise, and she soon picked herself up and started again. Elizabeth Custer, who also spent time at Fort Meade, came to know her well.

Tall, angular, and awkward in her demeanor, Mrs. Nash was by all accounts an odd-looking woman but highly skilled at her job. "When she brought the linen home, it was fluted and frilled so daintily that I considered her a treasure," Elizabeth Custer wrote. Her only fault, if it could be called that, was that she was very shy. She always brought the washing back at night, and when Elizabeth went outside to pay her, she "kept a veil pinned about the lower part of her face."[264]

One day, on receiving a report that Mrs. Nash was sick and in trouble, Elizabeth went to visit her. She arrived to be told that not only had Mrs. Nash's husband forsaken her, he had also robbed her of all her savings, which amounted to several hundred dollars. This extraordinary sum of money had been earned not only through laundering but also by baking pies for the soldiers and by sewing and altering clothes, at which she was also extremely skilled. She also frequently asked to act as a midwife to the camp women.

It was on this same visit that Mrs. Nash confided to Elizabeth something of her story. By her own account, she had lived a very rough life before signing up as a laundress with the Seventh Cavalry. At one time she had even resorted to dressing up as a man "in order to support herself by driving the oxteams over the plains of New Mexico," before the railroads had replaced that method of transporting freight and had taken away her job. From an earlier liaison she had had two children of her own, but they had both died in Mexico. "Finding the life of a laundress easier, she had resumed her woman's dress and entered the army, and thinking to make her place more secure, had accepted the hand of the man she was now mourning."

The enterprising Mrs. Nash, however, was not down for long. She soon succeeded in securing another husband, and when he absconded like the first, also stealing her savings, she consoled herself by going to the soldiers' balls "dressed in gauzy, low-necked gowns," where "notwithstanding her architectural build and massive features," she had no sooner accumulated another bank account "than her hand was solicited for the third time." This man, Corporal Patrick Noonan, was none other than Colonel Tom Custer's* batman and "the handsomest soldier in his company."

So far as the rest of the regiment was concerned, this was clearly a mariage de convenance (a marriage of convenience). "The trooper thought he had done a very good thing for himself, for notwithstanding his wife was no longer young, and was undeniably homely, she could cook well and spared him from eating with his company, and she was a very good invest- ment, for she earned so much by her industry. In addition to all these traits," Elizabeth Custer wrote, "she was already that most desirable creature in all walks of life—'a woman of means.'"

During this time, one of Elizabeth's friends at Fort Meade, a woman she refers to only as "Miss Annie," was expecting her own confinement. Terri- fied of having to rely on the post surgeon, who was young and "wholly in- experienced in such duty," although not without some misgivings the two women turned to Mrs. Nash for help.

On a visit to the laundress's little house in Laundress Row—generally a byword for filthy and primitive conditions—they were amazed by what they found. Mrs. Nash's little home was spotlessly clean and shining. "The bed was hung with pink cambric, and on some shelves she showed us silk and

---

*Elizabeth's brother-in-law.

woolen stuff for gowns; bits of carpet were on the floor, and the dresser, improvised out of a packing-box, shone with polished tins. Outside we were presented to some chickens, which were riches indeed out there in that Nova Zemblian* climate."

When the time came for "Miss Annie" to be confined, not only did the laundress turn up promptly, but she proved herself to be "as skillful a physician" as she was a nurse. "My friend used to whisper to me that when she watched her moving about in the dim light of the sickroom, she thought with a shiver sometimes how like a man she seemed." Every so often, she would come over to the bed and ask, in her harsh voice, "Are you comph?"—meaning comfortable. But "the gentle, dexterous manner in which she lifted and cared for the little woman, quieted her dread of this great giraffe."

Eventually, however, Mrs. Nash's past life of "hardship and exposure" took its toll. Becoming "ailing and rheumatic," she died soon after. Elizabeth Custer had left Dakota by this time, but later she heard the story of how the old laundress had begged the other camp women not to wash or prepare her body in any way, but simply to bury her at once, fully dressed, just as she had died. "They, thinking such a course would not be paying proper attention to the dead, broke their promise," Elizabeth wrote. "The mystery which the old creature had guarded for so many years, through a life always public and conspicuous, was revealed: 'Old Nash,' years before, becoming weary of the laborious life of a man, had assumed the disguise of a woman, and hoped to carry the secret to the grave."

When the story got out, the grieving husband was interviewed by a local newspaper, the Bismarck Tribune, which reported that "he didn't know his wife was a man" and that they had hoped to have children together. The story was soon picked up by other newspapers. The shame and harassment that he suffered caused Corporal Noonan to shoot himself two days later.[265]

---

*She is referring to the Novaya Zemlya (also known as Nova Zembla) archipelago, in the Arctic.

·

When the Custers' friend, "Miss Annie," "whom the old creature had so carefully nursed," read the report describing her death, "her only comment was a reference to the Mexican's oft-repeated question to her: 'Poor old thing, I hope she is "comph" at last.'"[266]

History, when it recognizes them at all, has not been kind to Army laundresses. Given the overwhelmingly male environment in which they found themselves, there were of course other, less wholesome ways with which women could supplement their incomes. In the past, the term laundress was taken to be synonymous with prostitute. Without either the time or skills to leave their own versions of their experiences, firsthand accounts are few, but Army records, while reporting only on a woman's misdemeanors, are revealing.

While some laundresses clearly did resort to prostitution, it was never a binary occupation, and the impression one gets is of women trying to make ends meet, with whatever means were at their disposal. One entrepreneurial African American, known to all as "Colored Susan," caused consternation at Fort Phil Kearny, Wyoming, in the late 1860s. Not only did Susan make a considerable profit out of selling her own "ardent spirits" and fruit pies (made, it was suspected, from government rations); she was also accused of luring away the officers' servants to staff what seems to have been her own private brothel. A special order dated 1866 records the written warning she received, not only for being herself "disorderly," but also for "breeding mischief in the garrison by inciting officers' servants to abandon their situations, and as an inducement setting forth the large sums of money she realizes and accumulates."[267]

While officers were encouraged to marry as it was thought to be good for their morale, in terms of the population of a military garrison as a whole, the women who were attached to them (for whatever reason) remained a tiny minority. Behind the military wives' cheerful descriptions of regimental "hops," of sewing bees and Fourth of July celebrations, there lurked a seamier side to military life that "ladies" such as Fannie Boyd and Elizabeth

Custer either excised altogether or only barely alluded to—even when it occurred right under their very noses.

Badly paid, poorly fed, and underemployed, Army ranks were filled with drifters, misfits, and desperados of all kinds, many of them fleeing the law. Desertion was rife (the get-rich-quick mining settlements being popular destinations), and according to one estimate, as many as forty in every thousand men were hospitalized for alcoholism. Twice that number committed suicide. As one commentator put it drily, even a penitentiary would appear like "a haven of rest and decent treatment" after a spell in an Army camp.[268] Under the circumstances, it was inevitable that soldiers turned to gambling, drinking, and "whoring" to pass the time.

Wherever Army camps or garrison towns sprang up, women offering their sexual services were sure to follow. Sometimes they washed up in "places of resort," such as those set up by Sarah Bowman at Saltillo, El Paso, and Fort Yuma; at other times they operated their own informal brothels, such as the Hell on Wheels "cribs" and "cat wagons" that followed railways. Sutler's stores were also places where women's sexual services could be acquired. These stores were government-controlled operations, but they were run by civilians. Situated in close proximity to the Army posts, which were themselves often constructed along the principal emigrant routes, the sutler's store was often the only place for very many miles where non-government-issued rations could be bought: coffee, soda, bacon, calico, tobacco, sweets and candies of many different kinds,* and, especially, alcohol. Often the sutler himself became a powerful local figure, and as such had no trouble in

---

*At Fort Bridger, Wyoming, a bill, dated May 27, 1865, from the Saint Louis wholesaler S. H. Bailey, "Manufacturer of Best Quality, Steam Refined CANDY," gives an idea of the astonishing range of sweets that could be bought at the sutler stores. Items on the bill include ten boxes each of Rock Candy, Small Stick Candy, Fancy Candy, and Maple Sugar Candy; forty boxes of French Kisses; forty boxes of Mint, Victoria, Grape, and Frosted Drops; forty boxes of Hearts, Stars, Rings, and Sugar Almonds; twenty boxes of Rose Almonds and Arabian Drops; thirty boxes of Lemon, Strawberry, and Vanilla Drops; and twenty boxes of Jenny Lind and Pineapple Drops. S. H. Bailey was also a purveyor of "Motto Verses, Fireworks, Fire Crackers and Torpedoes of every description, always on hand" (Fort Bridger Museum, Wyoming).

keeping a steady stream of women available along with his other supplies, so that their premises became centers of "drinking, gambling, and brawling."* If challenged, he would merely pass them off as domestic servants. No one was fooled. "Periodically, commanders would complain about unauthorized females around the sutler's store and order them from the post." These directives, and others banning the sale of intoxicating liquors, "appeared with such regularity that they were automatically ignored."[269]

That the moral conduct of soldiers was less than perfect is alluded to, in different ways, by both Fannie Boyd and Elizabeth Custer. In Fannie's account, the US Army in the late 1860s was in a particularly "chaotic state" on the Pacific coast, where the California volunteers, "though brave and hardy men," were totally unused to military discipline. "The wild lawlessness which had made California a place of terror, and that had only been subdued by the vigilance committee, was still extant, and many occurrences during our first year of army life told us there were desperadoes among us." Even when on exercise these men were "disposed to be unruly" and "would become intoxicated whenever liquor could be had." The captain in command of the company, and the first lieutenant—"two of the most illiterate men I have ever met," Fannie wrote with unusual asperity—were not much better (eventually, both would find more fitting occupation in a frontier mining town, where, her tone suggests, they clearly belonged). "My expectation of finding a new, untried, world [in which] all were ready to meet me with open hearts and hands was completely shattered."[270]

With a clear allusion to the potentially explosive sexual tensions that could arise when so many single men were locked up together, Elizabeth Custer wrote, "It was a pretty solemn business when the detail came to

---

*Sutler's stores were far less likely to be dissipated places if a woman had a hand in the running of them. The sutler's store at Fort Bridger, Wyoming, was run by Mary E. Carter and her husband William Alexander Carter, who together amassed a fortune. The couple opened the store in 1857 and later diversified into lumber, mining, livestock, and politics. After her husband's death in 1881, Mary continued to run the family store on her own, and with equal success, until the fort was abandoned in 1890.

either of the two officers whose wives were with them; but when they obtained permission to bring their wives to the regiment, it was with the understanding that their presence should not interfere with any duty . . . we three women made as little trouble as possible," she wrote. "With a whole camp of faithful soldiers, who, no matter what they did outside, would never harm their own, the wives . . . were perfectly safe."[271]

The fact that she had to write this at all implies that there were times when exactly the opposite was true. While soldiers usually took their private business outside, sometimes sexual tensions reached such a pitch that they exploded within the walls of the garrison itself. This was the case at Fort Davis, Texas, when a Corporal Taliafero, "J" Company, Ninth Cavalry, attempted a forcible entry into the sleeping quarters of Mrs. S— Kendall, whose husband was absent from the fort at the time.

It did not end well. According to the report that was later filed, "Mrs. Kendall warned the man from the window but he persisted in his efforts. Driven to distraction, Mrs. Kendall seized a revolver and just as the scoundrel had succeeded in getting his head through the window she fired, sending a bullet through his brain and killing him instantly."[272]

While cases such as this did make it into Army reports, for the most part the authorities looked the other way. Not only were officials discouraged from documenting any such events, but "the officer who tried to report such moral abuses found his path blocked." More egregious still, should such "moral abuses" come to light, the Army blamed the women themselves, claiming that they "victimized" the soldiers "by parasite pursuit that the men could not escape." Whichever way, the results were the same. The post surgeons, wrote one commentator, "had nothing to do but confine laundresses and treat the clap."[273]

WHILE FANNIE BOYD'S HUSBAND had gone out West to protect the transcontinental railroad in Nevada, Elizabeth Custer's had been detailed to the southern plains on far bloodier business.

Not only had the US government failed to fight the Lakota into submission, but the Indian Wars in general had cost them an enormous amount of money. Since the 1840s, military campaigns against Native Americans had drained the US treasury of more than $750 million. Throughout the 1860s, in particular, their encounters with the Lakota and their allies had cost an estimated $144,000 a day.[274] President Ulysses S. Grant, having wavered for many years between the policies of negotiating with the plains Tribes and making war on them, would now oversee a different strategy altogether.

Under Grant's new "Peace Policy," recalcitrant American Indians were to be appeased "until there would be so many whites and so few resources that armed resistance became impossible."[275] The instrument for doing this was the reservation. There, so the theory went, not only could Indigenous people be more conveniently counted and monitored, but they would also be "civilized." On the reservations they would learn the white man's ways but at the same time be protected from his vices (such as alcohol). On the reservations they would learn to give up the hunt—so inimical to the government's plans to build railways and provide more land for white settlers—and turn to farming instead; their children would be sent to white schools, often many hundreds of miles away from their families, where they would be given new, white names and educated by white teachers (most of them women). Above all they would become good Christians.

Before Grant's Peace Policy had come into effect, and in part the inspiration for it, Major General Philip Sheridan, a veteran hero of the Civil War, had orchestrated a brutal campaign against some of the most warrior-like of all America's Indigenous people, the Southern Cheyenne. In the winter of 1868, Sheridan set out to force the Cheyenne off their traditional hunting grounds on the southern prairies and onto their allotted reservation in Indian Territory.* He had chosen his favorite officer, George

---

*From being a landmass the size of half a continent at the beginning of the nineteenth century, the US terrain designated Indian Territory—still indicated on some contemporary maps as "Unorganized Territory"—had been shrunk to a mere fraction of that size. By 1868 it had been reduced to the area known today as Oklahoma.

Armstrong Custer, also a hero of the Civil War, and a man "insanely ambitious of glory," to spearhead his campaign.

At dawn on November 27, 1868, Custer had led a raid on a tranquil, sleeping village of as many as fifty lodges belonging to the Cheyenne peace chief Black Kettle on the Washita River, in present-day Oklahoma. To the merry strains of a well-known drinking song, "Garry Owen," eight hundred soldiers of the Seventh Cavalry had set upon the village, massacring dozens of warriors and as many as seventy women and small children, burning their tipis to the ground and destroying their winter food supplies. In what would prove an even more crippling blow, Custer had also ordered the slaughter of nearly nine hundred of their horses. Four white women who had been taken captive by the Tribe were rescued on that day,* and many Cheyenne women and children were now taken prisoner in return.

After almost every military engagement carried out by the US, Native American women became spoils of war, officers simply picking off the best-looking ones to keep as their "favorites." According to Susan Bordeaux, among the prisoners after the Battle of the Blue Water in 1855 "were many young, nice-looking women who became the property of their captors."[276] And after the massacre at Washita, Elizabeth Custer's husband, George Armstrong Custer himself, would do the same. Among the long string of female prisoners led in triumph over a hundred miles of snow to Camp Supply was a young woman called Monahsetah, the daughter of one of the southern chiefs. According to Cheyenne oral history: "When the young girls were selected for the officer tents on that cold march, she was sent to Custer."[277]

---

*One of these women had become pregnant by her captors. Elizabeth Custer noted that two years after her rescue, she had been spotted on a ranch, together with "her little Indian boy." Her white husband, despite the fact that she was thought to have married him after her rescue, now "often recalled her year of captivity with bitterness, and was disposed to upbraid her, as if she had been in the least responsible for the smallest of her misfortunes" (Elizabeth Custer, *Following the Guidon*).

Elizabeth Custer was to meet Monahsetah, but the prettified account she would later write sheds little true light on the story. Like most white women of her day, Elizabeth had been conditioned to see Native women as degraded "squaws," but it was clear, even to her, that Monahsetah was different. "She was the Princess," Elizabeth wrote (conforming to yet another stereotype), "the ranking woman among them all, being the daughter of Little Rock, who, since the death of Black Kettle in the battle of the Washita, was the highest in authority among the Cheyennes." While Elizabeth had little real understanding of the Cheyenne, Monahsetah's perceived "rank" and her good looks were both attributes to which Elizabeth (having herself a plentiful supply of both) could comfortably relate. The Cheyenne's name, she noted, meaning "The Grass that Shoots in the Spring," was "so musical that it well became the comely squaw." Monahsetah had proved herself "useful" to Custer's troops, and during the previous winter "her intelligence and judgement had been of service in the attempts that had been made to bring the tribes to surrender."[278]

For all this, Monahsetah was now a prisoner at Camp Supply and was Custer's acknowledged concubine. If Elizabeth ever knew this, she was not about to say so. Instead, she commented, without a trace of irony, that the Cheyenne "had in many other ways made herself of service to the command." In her assessment, not only was the Cheyenne "young and attractive" but "perfectly contented, and trustful of the white man's promises, and the acknowledged belle among all other Indian maidens."[279] Nor does this whitewashed account reveal that Elizabeth was well aware of the fact that the Cheyenne "maiden" had in fact been ruthless enough to have once shot her own husband in the knee rather than submit to his authority over her. It was a story that would cause Elizabeth a great deal of anxiety.[280] When she had entered the stockade to view the imprisoned women, she had been terrified that one of them "would stab her with a concealed weapon."[281]

According to Cheyenne oral traditions, Monahsetah was taken by Custer on his later winter expedition into Texas, when he was again in pursuit of her people. Eventually she became pregnant by him and gave birth to a son, Yellow Swallow.* "When Custer's wife was coming to him, the Cheyenne girl was sent back to the Indians, where this son was born toward the autumn moon. Years afterward, the traders told her that he wrote about her in a book, praising her charm, her beauty, and her grace. Not until Long Hair [General Custer] was dead did she take another man."[282]

A decade later, in the bloody aftermath of the last remaining Cheyenne resistance at Fort Robinson, some of the elders of the Tribe, "the old soured ones," would attribute the disasters that had overcome their Tribe, at least in part, to events such as these. It was because the women of the Cheyenne "had lost their virtue," they said, and given themselves to the men who killed their people, as Monahsetah had done. "To those who said she was a helpless captive, they replied that a good woman knows how to avoid marrying the man who has killed her father." And that she should not have hesitated "to use the knife."[283]

---

*Some historians believe that Yellow Swallow was in fact the child of Custer's brother, Thomas Custer. George Armstrong Custer, the theory goes, had contracted gonorrhea at West Point and was infertile. He and Elizabeth had no children.

17

MEANWHILE, BACK IN
CALIFORNIA . . .

W hile many African Americans, like the Custers' cook Eliza, would lead peripatetic lives following the drum of the US Army, others had already succeeded in making settled lives for themselves in the new territories of the West. California, particularly during the Gold Rush years, was considered "the best place for black folks on the globe" by one enthusiastic emigrant.[284] Unlike Oregon, California had not passed Black Exclusion laws, and many white Americans coming to California for the first time were confused by what appeared to them to be a lack of racial distinctions.*

While the more fluid racial order that existed in California in the early years of its statehood did not last, and the specter of slavery was never quite eradicated until after the Civil War, for all this it was in California that many African Americans would find their first, exhilarating tastes of

---

*California's early political leadership included some men of African American ancestry—a legacy of the greater racial mix that had existed when California was still part of Mexico. See Quintard Taylor, *In Search of the Racial Frontier*.

freedom—and none more so than a remarkable woman named Biddy Mason.

A black-and-white photograph of Biddy taken some time in the 1870s shows her well into middle age; a small, homely-looking woman, she stares

Biddy Mason

out at the camera with a strikingly level gaze. She wears a neat black dress, carefully buttoned up the front, with a satin bow at the neck, to which has been pinned a simple brooch. At the time when this photograph was taken, Biddy Mason was a woman of substance.

Bridget (or Biddy) Mason had been among the very first African American women ever to make the journey west. By the time of her death in 1891, at the age of seventy-three, she was one of the most prominent and respected citizens in Los

Angeles and a substantial property owner and philanthropist. First arriving in California in 1855, she was one of the first non-Mexican residents of Los Angeles, where she became a successful midwife. After ten years of working and saving she had earned enough money ($250) to purchase land and build a home for herself and her family, becoming one of the first African American women to own property in her own right.* She was also instrumental in setting up the Los Angeles branch of the First African Methodist Episcopal Church, which had its inaugural meeting in her house. Those who knew her in her exemplary and prosperous later life would never have been able to guess at the bitter hardships she had endured.

---

*Her plot of land was on a block between Spring Street and Fort Street (later Broadway), an area then slightly out of town, and "interspersed with vineyards, groves and vegetable gardens." See Dolores Hayden, "Biddy Mason's Los Angeles."

Like many African Americans in the early years of the emigrations, Biddy Mason had first gone west as a slave. Born in Georgia* in 1818, as a small child she had been given as a wedding present to Robert and Rebecca Smith, the owners of a Mississippi cotton plantation. Biddy bore three children, all girls—Ellen, Ann, and Harriet—very possibly the offspring of her owner, Robert Smith. Whatever the case, like Biddy herself, these children were Smith's property and represented a considerable addition to the family's wealth. Despite not being able to read or write, as a young woman Biddy acquired a number of crucial skills. As well as working in her owner's cotton fields, she learned how to manage livestock and became a skillful practitioner of herbal medicine. Robert Smith had a further six children with his wife, and Biddy often attended her during her confinements—an experience that would serve her well in later life.

Robert Smith was an early convert to Mormonism, and in 1848 he decided to take his family west, to follow Brigham Young's call and help build the Kingdom of the Saints.† On March 10, the Smiths joined forces with a party of Mississippi Mormons, a group of fifty-six whites and thirty-four slaves. In the Smiths' party there were nine whites and ten slaves. These included Biddy and her three children, one of whom she was still nursing, and another young enslaved African American woman, Hannah, who may have been Biddy's half-sister and who was pregnant at the time.[285]

Despite nursing a tiny baby and having two other young children to care for (Ellen and Ann were ten and four respectively), Biddy was put in charge of herding the family's livestock. This she did, for seven long months, on

---

*The census of 1860 gives her birthplace as Mississippi. This is contradicted by the 1870 and 1880 versions, both of which give her birthplace as Georgia, as does her obituary in the *Los Angeles Times*. See Dolores Hayden, "Biddy Mason's Los Angeles."

†The Mormons had outlined their prospective state, which they called Deseret, which was to include large portions of Nevada, Arizona, New Mexico, and Southern California. See Dolores Hayden, *Seven American Utopias*.

that arduous journey across the prairies and mountains to the desert salt flats of Utah.

Unlike the Pacific Territories (Oregon and California), both of which would go on to declare themselves free, Brigham Young's desert kingdom enjoyed no such prohibitions. When the Smiths arrived in Utah, Biddy and daughters all continued in their household as slaves. Three years later, the Smiths decided to move again, this time to San Bernardino, California, where they hoped to help establish another Mormon colony.* Despite warnings from Brigham Young that "there is little doubt but [the slaves] will all be free as soon as they arrive in California,"[286] the Smiths made the decision to take their slaves with them. In 1851, these comprised an extended family of thirteen: Biddy and Hannah, who between them now had ten children, and one grandchild of Hannah's, the child of her daughter, Ann.

In the same wagon caravan that left Salt Lake City for California there were a number of other enslaved people, including Elizabeth Flake, a young woman who, like Biddy, had herded her owner's livestock on the journey from the Mormon Winter Quarters (North Omaha) in Nebraska to Salt Lake City. The journey would prove life-changing for both young women. One of the teamsters on that journey was another African American, a former slave called Charles Rowan, and it is likely that it was Rowan, who would go on to be a prominent antislavery advocate, who first urged the two women to contest their enslaved status when they reached California. Elizabeth Flake, who did indeed become a freewoman when she reached California, went on to marry Charles Rowan, and like him became a prominent member of the African American community in San Bernardino and also a vigorous abolitionist.

Biddy Mason, however, was not so fortunate. Like so many other slaveholders, Robert Smith had no intention of relinquishing his property.

---

*Their intention was to make San Bernardino a way station for Mormons traveling the sea route via either Cape Horn or Panama to San Pedro and then making the overland trek, west to east, to Salt Lake City.

Although under California's new constitution slavery was expressly prohibited, it did not follow that on crossing the border, enslaved people such as Biddy and her family would automatically be free. Slaveholders who had arrived before 1850, when California gained its statehood, had been permitted to keep their slaves as indentured servants, but the reality was that many slaveholders simply ignored the law, which was considered by many to be unenforceable. Slaveholders either went unchallenged, or, if they were, the courts were overwhelmingly likely to favor their cause.

The situation was further complicated by the fact that, after several years of infighting, and as a concession to the southern slave states, in the same year that California became a free state, Congress had passed the Fugitive Slave Act, which made it easy to recapture escaped slaves. Bounty hunters who made a lucrative business of tracking down and capturing runaways (in much the same way that they were paid to collect Native American scalps, known as "hairy banknotes") operated throughout California, often openly advertising in local papers throughout the 1850s. This created a bitterly fraught situation in which many African Americans, freed by their former masters, still faced persecution and harassment, in much the same way as they still did in the Missouri River towns such as Independence and Saint Joseph.

Throughout the 1850s, however, attitudes in California had begun, slowly, to change. Just two years after the Smiths' arrival, a story appeared in the *Alta California* newspaper in which "a person by the name of Brown attempted to have a Negro girl arrested in our town a few days since as a fugitive slave, but was taken all a-back by the girl's lawyer, F. W. Thomas, producing her Freedom Papers. Brown's father set the girl at liberty in 1851, and it is thought by many that the son knew the fact, and thought to catch the girl without her Freedom Papers, but fortunately for her he did not."[287]

Sensing that there was trouble ahead for him if he remained in California, in late 1855 Robert Smith decided to move his entire family to Texas (which, like all the other southern states, would remain a slave state until after the Civil War). Any hopes that Biddy may have had of eventually gaining her freedom in California now seemed utterly dashed. "While slaves in California were free by law, it was impossible to be free and Black in Texas, since Texas law forbade the importation of free Blacks into the state, and Texans would have regarded them as slaves."[288]

Against all the odds, Biddy now found herself with two powerful allies. One of these was Elizabeth Flake; the other was another African American called Robert Owens. Owens was, by all accounts, a formidable man, a former slave who had come to California from Texas in 1850, driving an oxteam. At the time he came to champion Biddy Mason, just five years later, he was already an extremely successful businessman, a horse and mule trader who ran a thriving corral in Los Angeles, employing ten vaqueros.

Robert and his wife Minnie Owens had a particular interest in Biddy's case. Their son Charles was in love with Biddy's daughter Ellen, now seventeen, and wanted to marry her. A third man, Manuel Pepper, possibly one of Robert Owens's vaqueros, was in love with Hannah's daughter, Ann, a young woman of the same age.

Although time was running out, there was now a small but critical delay to Smith's plans to spirit his slaves away. Hannah was about to give birth to her eighth child, and the Smiths were camped out in a canyon in the Santa Monica Mountains, impatiently waiting for her confinement, after which she would be able to travel again. During this time, Elizabeth Flake and Robert Owens petitioned the local court for a writ of habeas corpus for Biddy and her family. In what must have been a moment of heart-stopping tension, a posse of mounted men—two county sheriffs, together with Robert Owens and his vaqueros—"all swooped down on the camp in the mountains and challenged Smith's right to take his slaves out of California."[289] Biddy and her family were taken to the county jail, where they were put "under charge of the Sheriff of this county for their protection," until their case would be heard.[290]

It is almost impossible to imagine the courage that was now necessary. Although she was a mature woman of thirty-eight, until this point in her life absolutely everything that Biddy Mason had ever known would have militated against taking such a step. Enslaved people were the absolute property of their owners. While laws varied across the southern slaveholding states, all followed a similar pattern. Slaves were forbidden from congregating together, even for religious worship, without white supervision. They were forbidden to bear arms, or to marry or travel without the written permission of their masters. They could own no personal property of their own, sometimes including their working tools or even the clothes they stood up in. Most crucially perhaps, they were forbidden from learning how to read or write.

In Virginia, the cotton-planting region where the majority of African Americans lived, slave literacy was a criminal offence. In Virginia, also, even free Blacks were prohibited from trying to educate themselves, and if a free Black left the state to be educated elsewhere, they were barred from ever returning. Most egregious of all, in Kentucky, it was a criminal offence for African Americans to try to defend themselves, no matter what the circumstances, against white assault. Slaves, and any children they might have, could be bought and sold, either together or separately, at the will of their owners, who often split families apart with impunity; they could be given away in lieu of debts and left in wills as part of their owner's estate. It goes almost without saying that their testimony was worth nothing in a court of law.

It is hard to imagine what Biddy Mason might have been feeling as she looked out through the bars of the jail, contemplating the prospect of having to face her owner, Robert Smith, in court. One thing she would have known, with absolute numbing certainty, was that if she lost her case, the consequences for her and her children would be catastrophic.

It is, on the other hand, absolutely clear what Robert Smith felt. The entire case that he put forward through his lawyer, Alonzo Thomas, was shot through with lies. First, he tried to argue that the petitioners were members of his family, denying outright that he was holding them as slaves. They had come with him from Mississippi to California, he argued, "with their own consent, rather than remain there, and he [had] supported them ever since, subjecting them to no greater control than his own children." It was his intention, he stated, "to remove to Texas and take them with him."

The situation for Hannah was more dangerous still. Unlike Biddy, who had been immediately taken into protective custody, the recently confined Hannah and her newborn baby had remained with the Smiths. They were therefore not only physically under his control, but highly vulnerable to his threats and intimidation. In the case put forward by his lawyer, Smith argued that Hannah and her children were "well disposed to remain with him, and the petition was filed without their knowledge and consent." His lawyer added: "It is understood, between said Smith and said persons, that they will return to the State of Texas with him voluntarily, as a portion of his family."[291]

The trial, which was later reported, in all its painful details, in the *Los Angeles Star*, took place between January 19 and 21, 1856. Presiding over the case was Benjamin Hayes, judge of the District Court of the First Judicial District, Los Angeles. In his summation, the judge set out the situation with great clarity. Robert Smith, he declared, "intended to and is about to remove from the State of California, where slavery does not exist, to the State of Texas, where slavery of Negroes and persons of color does exist, and is established by the municipal laws, and intends to remove the said before-mentioned persons of color, to his own use without the free will and consent of all or any of the said persons of color, whereby their liberty will be greatly jeopardized, and there is good reason to apprehend and believe that they may be sold into slavery or involuntary servitude."[292] Robert Smith, he noted, "is persuading and enticing and seducing said persons of color to go out of the State of California, and it further appearing that none of the said persons of color can read and write, and are almost entirely ignorant of the laws of the State of California as well as those of the State of Texas, and of their rights and that the said Robert Smith, from his past relations to them as members of his family does possess and exercise over them an undue influence in respect to the matter of their removal insofar that they have been in duress and not in possession and exercise of their free will so as to give a binding consent to any engagement or arrangement with him."[293]

The necessarily dry legalese with which Judge Hayes gives his verdict in the case of *Mason v. Smith* conveys little of the febrile atmosphere in and around the court on that day. The article in the *Los Angeles Star*, on the other hand, gives an eyewitness account of the extraordinary, nail-biting human drama.

Perhaps sensing that the case was going to go against him, Robert Smith had tried various other tactics. First, he had attempted to threaten Biddy and Hannah outright, and when that did not work he proceeded to bribe their lawyer with one hundred dollars (a huge sum) to drop the case. Their lawyer (unnamed in the *Star* article) accepted the bribe. Just one day into their trial, the two women found themselves completely abandoned in the courtroom. Under California law, Blacks, "Mulattoes," and Native people were all prohibited from testifying against whites, in either civil or criminal cases.

Without a lawyer, they did not stand a chance.

But Robert Smith had not reckoned with Judge Hayes. "I was pained by an occurrence not to be passed unnoticed," the judge wrote. "There was a motion to dismiss the proceedings, based on a note from the petitioners' attorney on the opposite side, in these words: 'I, as attorney for the petitioners, being no longer authorized to prosecute the writ, and being discharged by the same and the partner who are responsible to me, decline further to prosecute the matter.'"

Judge Hayes subpoenaed the lawyer, questioned him, and then denounced his lack of legal propriety. He then proceeded to question the women, not in court but in his private chambers. In addition to Judge Hayes himself, two disinterested "gentlemen witnesses" were present to hear their story. The conversation was reported as follows:

Biddy: "I have always done what I have been told to do; I always feared this trip to Texas, since I first heard of it. Mr. Smith told me I would be just as free in Texas as here."

Hannah's daughter, Ann, when questioned separately from Biddy, asked the judge, "Will I be as free in Texas as here?"—a question the legal experts found a poignant response to Smith's bluster that all would travel willingly.[294]

It would transpire later that Robert Smith had tried not only verbal threats but other, even worse forms of intimidation to try to force the women to give up their case. One of the Smith party, a man named Hartwell Cottrell, made a bungled attempt to snatch two of Hannah's children away from her but was prevented, and he had to flee California himself, with a charge of kidnapping against him. The turnkey at the county jail, Frank Carpenter, later gave evidence in court as to the women's terror of Smith, but, even without his testimony, it was perfectly clear to everyone in court. The judge decided that the "*speaking silence* of the petitioners" must be listened to, and that Hannah, in particular, had almost certainly been threatened. "Nothing else—except force—can account rationally for a favorable disposition in Hannah, if she had any." Her very hesitation in speaking out, he noted, "spoke a volume," and furthermore, "she is entitled to be listened to when, breathing freer, she declares she never wished to leave, and prays for protection."[295]

In his conclusion, Judge Hayes wrote: "No man of any experience in life will believe that it was ever true, or ever intended to be realized—this pleasant prospect of freedom in Texas." Robert Smith, he observed, had only "$500 and an outfit" and had "his own white family to take care of, and seemed to have no reason to transport fourteen slaves so far—unless he intended to sell them."[296]

"And it further appearing . . . to the judge here, that all of the said persons of color are entitled to their freedom and cannot be held in slavery or involuntary servitude, it is therefore argued that they are entitled to their freedom and are free forever."[297]

THERE WAS ANOTHER FORM of slavery in California, however, that for many decades yet would remain impervious to legislation. The life of the

---

*If Biddy Mason's case had come to trial just a year later, she would have lost her case. In 1857, in the now-notorious Dred Scott decision, the US Supreme Court ruled that a slave was not a person, but property, and that a slave's residence in free territory, or in a free state, did not make that slave free.

Chinese sex slave, wrote one commentator as late as the 1890s, was one "of total debasement and ill-treatment." Girls had been found "who have been burnt with red-hot irons, dragged about with the hair, and had their eyes propped open with sticks. Slaves that are resold by a contract, a document which, while unfit for publication, is a most remarkable paper, showing that the sale of a woman is looked upon in the same light as that of the lowest animals."[298]

In 1852 there were only nineteen Chinese women residing in San Francisco, compared to around three thousand Chinese men. In later years, between 1860 and

An enslaved Chinese woman, photographed in holiday attire

1880, many more would arrive, the vast majority of them smuggled in as slaves or indentured sex workers. They joined the thirty thousand Chinese men who journeyed to San Francisco in this same period, huge numbers of whom were employed in the late 1860s to do the dangerous and backbreaking work of laying the western portion of the transcontinental railway through the Sierra Nevada.* While some Chinese women traveled to California as genuine wives or concubines, most did not. These women were known as *baak haak chai*, or "one hundred men's wife."

The women arrived from China by sea, a journey that in the days before steam travel could take as many as a hundred days.† Conditions on board the boats were so primitive that many arrived half-starved or sick from long weeks in cramped, unsanitary, and poorly ventilated holds. Occasionally,

---

*These were part of a massive exodus of between ten and thirteen million people who emigrated from China at this time.
†The first voyage by the Pacific Mail Steamship Company's China line was in 1867.

women and young girls were concealed behind false partitions, but even if they had the "luxury" of traveling steerage, they were crammed together on a framework made of shelves, no more than eighteen inches apart. One journalist from a San Francisco weekly remarked that "if a few barrels of oil were poured into the steerage hold, its occupants would enjoy the distinction, so often objected to, of being literally 'packed like sardines.'"[299]

Added to this was the extreme distress that all the women suffered when the reality of their situation finally sank in, since many of them had been either kidnapped or otherwise duped into boarding the ship. Some, like Lin Yu-shih, who boarded a ship in Hong Kong, wept for days on discovering that she had been kidnapped; many others committed suicide by jumping into the sea. Others were only small children when they were trafficked and had no real idea of what was happening to them. Lilac Chen was six years old when her father sold her to a procurer. Many years later she would recall that she had thought she was going on a visit to her grandmother, becoming confused when her mother started to cry. When the ship finally sailed, leaving her alone on a deck full of strangers, she "kicked and screamed and screamed," refusing to eat, and begging to be taken home, but to no avail.[300]

In the early 1850s, when San Francisco was in its lawless infancy, and the numbers of Chinese women being trafficked were still very small, they were openly sold on the docks, the bidding being carried out in full view of the spectators, who frequently included police officers among their number. Later on, the auction sites moved to Chinatown itself, the newly burgeoning area that within a decade would be home to the largest population of Chinese outside of their own homeland.

It was here, in a place known as the "Queen's Room" on Dupont Street, that most of the auctions took place. For all its grandiose name, in reality the "Queen's Room" was no better than "a public slave mart" where women were put on display, to be bought and sold on again at the will of the slave dealers. By the time they arrived in California, the likelihood was that they had already been passed down a long line of traffickers, beginning in China itself. Traffickers were well established in almost all large Chinese cities, and these in turn had subagents "in the suburban districts, whose duty it is to kidnap the victims and forward them to the agent at the shipping ports."[301]

Often women were told that they were traveling to America to be married. Despite repeated legislative efforts to try to stem the flow of Chinese emigration—particularly what was termed "involuntary immigration" on the part of Chinese women—political will was insufficient to prevent it. "Unfortunately, the Chinese law and custom of marriage aids the kidnapper," wrote one commentator. "A wife rarely sees her husband before marriage; the affair being a business arrangement, pure and simple." Girls and young women were valued from $15 to $3,500 at auction, and consequently "every effort is made by the consignee to bring them through the ordeal successfully."

"This accomplished, the girl, who perhaps still expects to meet her promised husband, is taken to a boardinghouse, provided with a rich wardrobe and rendered as attractive as possible. She is now . . . conducted to the 'Queen's Room,' which she is told belongs to her husband and where she is to receive his friends. The girl is now really on exhibition for sale and is critically examined by high-binders, slave-dealers, speculators, brothel keepers, and others interested in the sale. Finally, a price is agreed upon and she becomes the property of some man whom she supposes to be her husband. The plot is not discovered by the credulous victim until her master hands her over to the keeper of a brothel. In four-fifths of the cases of slavery this is the method of procedure, which, it is needless to say, is invariably effective, the victim rarely if ever escaping."[302]

One particularly poignant article in the *Daily Morning Chronicle* in 1868 printed the following bill of sale:

Loo Woo to Loo Chee

Rice mats at $2..............................$12

Shrimps, 50 lbs, at 10c.....................$5

Girl... $250

Salt Fish, 60 lbs, at 10c..................... $6

———

$273[303]

Although the majority of Chinese women were brought to California to work in the sex industry, many found other forms of employment. They worked as domestic servants, laundresses, and seamstresses and in industries such as the tobacco, cigar, boot, and shoe trades. Of those who did work as prostitutes, by no means all considered themselves as victims. Many were resigned to what they saw as their fate; others looked on it as a business arrangement, sometimes even signing contracts to this effect.*

An "Agreement Paper" signed in 1875 between two Chinese women, Yut Kum and Mee Yung, was preserved in the congressional records of the day and reads as follows: "At this time there is a prostitute woman, Yut Kum, who has borrowed money from Mee Yung $470. It is distinctly understood that there shall be no interest charged on the money and no wages paid for services. Yut Kum consents to prostitute her body . . . for the full time of four years." The Agreement Paper records not only the length of time that Yut Kum should work but, with brisk practicality, the terms and conditions that were attached to her service. "If Yut Kum should be sick fifteen days she shall make up one month. If she conceives, she shall serve one year more. If during the time any man wishes to redeem her body, she shall make satisfactory arrangements with the mistress, Mee Yung." The paper also includes clauses about what should happen in the event of Yut Kum falling

---

*Census takers in 1870, instructed for the first time to describe as accurately as possible the occupations of all inhabitants, identified approximately 72 percent of the Chinese female population as prostitutes. (The historian Benson Tong [*Unsubmissive Women*, p. 97] believes it was closer to 63 percent.) The Chinese population as a whole had more than tripled in the years between 1860 and 1870, boom times for the vice industry. A Chinese official, visiting California in 1876, estimated that of the six thousand Chinese women he believed were living in the US, between 80 and 90 percent were involved in the sex trade.

sick with one or other of the "four great sicknesses" that might affect her trade: leprosy, epilepsy, conception, and "stone woman," a condition in which a woman was unable to have intercourse with a man. If she were to run away and be recovered, "then her time shall never expire." But, in the happy event that "the mistress [should] become very wealthy and return to China with glory, then Yut Kum shall fulfil her time, serving another person."[304]

If Yut Kum had remained in San Francisco to ply her trade, she would have done so within the relatively orderly confines of Chinatown. By the 1870s not only was the Chinese presence in San Francisco extremely well established, but the city as a whole was a very different place from the lawless shantytown it had been during the Gold Rush years. Throughout the 1850s two notorious gangs, the Hounds and the Sydney Ducks, had all but brought the city to its knees, and it had taken the combined efforts of two vigilance committees, one in 1851 and one in 1856, to bring the city under control. Now, places such as the Barbary Coast, and Chinatown in particular, were, if not yet exactly tourist destinations, then places it was de rigueur for the more intrepid to visit. A description of the city without a description of Chinatown and the Chinese would have been like "Hamlet without the Prince of Denmark's character."[305]

It was made all the more fascinating by the fact that there was still a delicious frisson of danger to be had. When Mrs. Frank Leslie, the wife of a wealthy newspaper proprietor, traveling in high style, visited San Francisco in 1877 with her entourage, she employed the services of a bodyguard to accompany her there. Mr. Mackenzie was a veteran detective and police officer who had served in the San Francisco police service for twenty-two years. Although he was disappointingly discreet when she tried to elicit his reminiscences from the past, when they came to Portsmouth Square he pointed to one of the buildings and remarked: "Out of that window the Vigilance Committee of '51 hung their first man."

Mrs. Leslie had not been particularly impressed by her first visit to Chinatown. Nonetheless she was fascinated by it, returning there at least four times during her visit to San Francisco. "Each little shop hangs out its sign of red and gilded paper inscribed with Chinese characters," she wrote, while the joss houses were "redolent of a pungent, delicious odor of sandalwood and Oriental perfumes." From fashionable Kearney Street, the burly Mr. Mackenzie had led them into "steep and dingy" Munro Street, and all at once they had found themselves in a different world. "Here all the houses are dingy, no two alike; all the people are poor, and although universally clean in person cultivate a squalid and odorous mode of existence . . . that makes visiting among them rather distasteful to fastidious people," she wrote. "In Dupont Street the narrow walks were scarcely lighted except by the smoky glare from the shop windows, and the silent-footed, sad-eyed passengers crept along the wall, or stepped off from the walk at our approach, more like the shades of Dante at the entrance of the Inferno than living and busy mortals."

As they made their way still farther in, they found themselves at the entrance to "a black and narrow alley, its depths hidden in tenebrous shadow, and here our guide produced and lighted two candles, whose gleam faintly illuminated the first few steps of a black and rickety staircase. Up this the guide led and we followed, walking purely by faith; since nothing was to be seen but the little patch of light, the dim roofs of houses beneath us, and, far above, the cold pure gleam of the stars. As the candlelight fell upon the wall at the left, we perceived that it was closely covered with scraps of red and gold paper inscribed with Chinese characters." It proved to be a tiny temple, its ceiling hung with lanterns, its walls with banners made from scarlet and gilded paper, and scarves and ribbons festooned across with peacock feathers.

Mr. Mackenzie's tour of Chinatown proved to be nothing if not comprehensive. They visited barber shops, the Royal Chinese Theatre on Jackson Street, and even an opium den. They ate in a Chinese restaurant. But he had saved the pièce de résistance for last. At the end of their tour, stopping at the entrance to "a dark and dismal court, whose odors seemed more sickening and deadly than those we had breathed before," he said to them:

"'I reckon I can show you as strange and tough a sight as you want to see, if you like to risk it, for the ladies.' 'This is pretty rough' said the guide; 'but say the word and I will take you in.'"

They climbed the wooden stairs and found themselves at last on a narrow balcony overhanging a courtyard. "Some Chinese women clustered at the end of this balcony staring at us, behind them was a shrine containing the Goddess of Love, with gilt paper and Joss-sticks burning in the tray before us." From the gallery they passed into "a perfect honeycomb of little rooms, dimly lighted, or not lighted at all; no doors were visible, the doorways being shaded by long, pink calico curtain, and as they blew or were drawn aside we saw every room crowded with men and a few women, smoking, drinking tea, or playing at dominoes or cards. Every room we entered was exceedingly tidy and clean, and the inmates looked remarkably neat and tidy. Some effort of decoration was visible in the way of gilt and red paper, bright-colored scarves and peacocks' feathers upon the walls, and pretty little Chinese tea-pots and other pottery upon the table and shelves. Everyone was smiling and bland as possible, and seemed overjoyed to receive a call."

As they went farther in, the rooms became smaller and more crowded. Here, "the women were mostly without beauty or grace and usually dressed in dingy blue sacks with huge sleeves, their hair drawn back and curiously puffed, coiled or plaited behind. They all wore the mechanical smile which seems part of the national character; but their faces were thin and haggard, and the paint did not disguise the wan weariness which was eating away at their lives." Many of them had signed a contract, and received "a certain sum in advance for services during a term of years or for life; the larger part of which sum goes to the broker or intermediary. These slaves—for they are so considered, and, as a general thing, are very harshly and penuriously treated—receive only a maintenance and coarse clothing during their brief period of health, and when overtaken by sickness are turned out to die in any hole they can creep into.

"Coming out of this house, we passed a row of tiny windows, breast-high to a man, looking out upon the narrow sidewalk of the court, at each of which appeared the face of a woman, the little room behind her as bright and attractive as she knew how to make it; one in especial was quite illuminated and decked with flowers and draperies, and the inmate, a rather pretty young girl, was singing in a sort of cooing little voice."

Mrs. Leslie was observant enough to notice that not all the Chinese women she saw that day were either haggard or downtrodden. One who caught her attention was a prosperous-looking "fat, good-looking woman of thirty or so, with her hair elaborately coiled, puffed and ornamented with bright gold pins"; another she spied in a gambling room seemed positively affluent: "By no means unattractive [she] wore beautiful earrings and had a large diamond ring, and on her fat and pretty arms bracelets which our guide said were twenty-carat-fine gold."[306]

As Mee Yung would do in her "agreement" with Yut Kum, there were many Chinese women who took full advantage of the opportunities offered by the vice trade: strong women with sound business minds. Perhaps the most famous of these was a woman named Ah Toy, who in her day was one of San Francisco's most prominent madams.

One of only a tiny handful of Chinese women to take up residence in San Francisco in the first year of the Gold Rush, Ah Toy began her career working alone from a small shanty just off Clay Street. By 1850 she was employing two more recently arrived Chinese women, Aloy and Asea, to work for her. A few years later, in a city directory for 1852, she is listed as the proprietor of not one but two boardinghouses (often a euphemism for a brothel), No. 34 and No. 56 Pike Street. The *San Francisco Examiner* reported (possibly with a pinch of poetic license) that white miners queued for a whole block and paid an ounce of gold just "to gaze on the countenance of the charming Ah Toy."[307]

Ah Toy soon proved herself to be a woman of considerable business acumen. Catering for white as well as Chinese clients, she is said to have been involved in running brothels not only in San Francisco, but as far away as Sacramento and Stockton too. Soon she became rich, once owning a diamond breastpin worth three hundred dollars (later stolen by one of her clients). She also knew how to use the legal system to protect herself, appearing in the courts a number of times to sue clients who had paid her with brass filings instead of gold dust,* until California law was changed to include Chinese in the same ruling that forbade African Americans and Native Americans from testifying against whites.

As the years went by, San Francisco became an increasingly difficult place for a single businesswoman, particularly a Chinese one, to operate in. Anti-Chinese legislation, together with stricter measures for social control put in place by the police, steadily encroached on her business. More detrimental still was the rise, in the mid-1850s, of criminal Chinese gangs, known as the fighting Tongs, determined to dominate all aspects of the vice trade. Very soon her business was on the point of collapse.

Sometime in 1857, Ah Toy sold her property and sailed for China. Two years later, however, she was back in San Francisco. While there is some evidence to suggest that she once again opened her own brothel, the era for independent entrepreneurship such as hers was well and truly over. Ah Toy was not heard of again until her death was announced in 1928. According to newspaper accounts, for many years she had been living quietly with her husband in San Jose, Santa Clara County, and, after his death, with her brother-in-law. She had last been sighted selling clams to visitors in Alviso (a suburb of San Jose) and had died just a few months short of her hundredth birthday.[308]

Like Ah Toy, a large number of former sex workers went on to marry, or become conjugal partners of some kind, sometimes as a second wife. The moral disgrace of having lived "a life of vice," almost without exception an insuperable barrier to white prostitutes, did not seem to apply. "For the most

---

People v. Hall, 1854. See Benson Tong, *Unsubmissive Women*.

part the Chinese did not attach the same stigma to prostitution . . . far from being considered 'fallen women,' prostitutes were seen as daughters who obeyed the wishes of the family."[309]

One such dutiful Chinese daughter was a young woman called Lalu Nathoy. Unlike most Chinese women to emigrate to America, the vast majority of whom came from the southern Chinese province of Kwangtung (Guangdong), Lalu Nathoy was born in northern China in 1853. The area where she lived was subject to bandit attacks, and when the crops failed, the bandits had forced her family to give up what little produce they had. Faced with the prospect of seeing his entire family starve, Lalu's father sold his daughter to one of the bandit leaders in exchange for seeds to plant a new crop (a not-unusual practice at the time). She was trafficked to San Francisco, and sometime in 1872 she was sold on to a man named Hong King, the owner of a saloon in the tiny mining community of Warrens in the mountains of central Idaho.

Lalu was nineteen when she arrived in Idaho. A pretty but physically tiny young woman well under five feet and "no taller than a broom," she probably looked much younger. Years later, in 1922, she gave an interview about her life. "They sell me as a slave girl," she told her interviewer. "Old woman she smuggled me into Portland [probably from San Francisco]. I cost $2,500. . . . Old Chinese man he took me along to Warrens in a pack train."[310]

There has been much speculation about Lalu's status when she arrived. Some have claimed that Hong King bought her as his concubine, but the sum of money involved, even if exaggerated, would have been a stupendous outlay for a saloon owner in an obscure mining village, and the likelihood is that Hong King expected some kind of a return on his money.* Whatever the truth of the matter, once in Idaho, not even her name was her own: from now on Lalu would be known simply as "Polly."

---

*In an admirable feat of literary detective work, author Ruthanne Lum McCunn has traced Polly Bemis's signature to a legal document of 1896. The Chinese characters (which may not have been written by her) translate as Gung Heung, meaning "a woman provided for public enjoyment." See Ruthanne Lum McCunn, "Reclaiming Polly Bemis."

There would soon be another twist in Polly's story. At some point during her time in Hong King's saloon, she met a man named Charles Bemis. As the daughter of Polly's greatest friend would later explain, "Polly was brought from China for the world's oldest profession. When taken to [Hong King's] saloon she was terrified. Charlie Bemis was present and protected her from unwanted advances."[311] According to local lore, when Bemis sustained a serious gunshot wound, Polly nursed him back to health, gaining not only his gratitude, but his love. Bemis proposed, and Polly accepted. After her marriage (history does not relate what happened to Hong King), she went on to run a thriving homestead in the mountains of Idaho with her new husband, growing her own vegetables and keeping chickens and horses.

There is another mystery connected to the story of Polly Bemis, and that is her birth name. Lalu Nathoy is so un-Chinese-sounding that there has been speculation that it was never her real name. Some recent historical detective work has shown that Lalu/Polly was in fact not Chinese at all, but Mongolian, probably a Daur, a minority people related to the Mongols and the Tungus-Manchu-speaking people, large numbers of whom settled in Han (majority Chinese) areas in the mid-nineteenth century and adopted their customs. Nathoy is an anglicized version of Nasoi. Lalu means Islam, or "long life."[312] She died, appropriately enough for her name, aged eighty, on the same ranch she had lived on for decades, a peaceful end to a tumultuous life.

LATER IN THE CENTURY, various rescue homes were set up specifically to give sanctuary to Chinese women who had been forced into prostitution. For the most part these were run by Presbyterian and Methodist women missionaries, and while it is impossible to be anything but admiring of their work, the general attitude in the homes—colored by the moral values of their day, and with a heavy emphasis on Christianity—did not always sit well with their clientele. In some of these refuges, the women were kept as virtual prisoners. And, so far as proselytizing was concerned, a religion that represented "a foreign, heterodox faith that attempted to subvert traditional Chinese society" mostly fell upon deaf ears. As Narcissa Whitman had found, all those years ago among the Cayuse, while some of these "fallen women" were "saved," the reality was that most Chinese women rejected the missionaries' attempts to convert them. Mature women, especially, were "rebellious." In the words of one Presbyterian missionary, it was "a most difficult work—to tame barbarians."[313]

18

STRONG-HEART SONGS

T he West was now a place of many overlapping worlds. The lives of
the women in San Francisco's Chinatown, or that of an African
American former slave, may have been a far cry from the pampered
milieu of Mrs. Frank Leslie when she made her much-publicized trip across
America in a private railway carriage in 1877, but all had been made possible, in their different ways, by the relentless thrust of western emigration.

By the early 1870s, railways had come to be seen as the embodiment of
the US's progress in the West, transforming the pace of change from the
slow, steady tread of the oxteam to the shriek of the steam engine. The vast
distances, the almost limitless wilderness that had afforded America's Indigenous people some measure of protection against white incursion, had
been conquered. On May 10, 1869, the transcontinental railway had finally
been completed. Amid much fanfare, the tracks of the Central Pacific Railroad's western branch and the Union Pacific's eastern branch finally joined
up on Promontory Summit in Utah. In the space of just thirty years, a
journey that had taken the first emigrants to California upward of six
months could be completed in little more than a week. Many other

railways—most notably the Kansas Pacific Railway, south of the Platte River, and the proposed Northern Pacific Railroad, through the Lakota heartland—were soon to follow.

Throughout the 1860s, the Lakota and their allies the Cheyenne had proved formidable opponents to the progress of the railways, and in the wars leading up to the second Fort Laramie Treaty of 1868 had bested the US government, forcing it to agree to their terms. But they had made one fatal concession: by acquiescing to the negotiators' insistence that they must allow the construction of the transcontinental railway, the plains Tribes effectively sealed their own demise. The railways would allow much quicker troop deployments and would also open the floodgates to many more settlers.* Between 1877 and 1887 an estimated four and a half million more emigrants would make the journey west, many of them settling on prairie land that until now had been thought too inhospitable and dry for human habitation.

The railways quickly came to be seen as "a cure-all" to the Native American "problem." As the commissioner of Indian affairs would predict, the proposed Northern Pacific Railroad, in particular, "will itself completely solve the Sioux [Lakota] problem, and leave ninety thousand Indians ranging between the two transcontinental lines as incapable of resisting the Government as are the Indians of New York or Massachusetts."[314]

Josephine Waggoner would experience firsthand the changes brought by the railroads in her birthplace, Dakota Territory. "The railroad was pushing its way westward regardless of the loss of human lives and stock," she wrote. "Its iron rails were creeping on like a formidable enemy, slow but sure." Railways may have been a symbol of progress, but they brought chaos too. Waggoner's childhood home of Bismarck grew up with all the rapidity of one of the notorious Hell on Wheels towns along the Platte River. "Gambling places, dance halls, meeting places, town trading posts where different

---

*Much of this settlement was on land that had been given to the railway companies as part of a government subsidy and was then sold on.

kinds of men congregated sprang up. Every night there was an uproar and a shooting scrape. With the arrival of the buffalo hunters, river men, plains men, gold miners, cowboys, and soldiers—all with their different ideas—there were bound to be clashes. Every day, reports of shooting affrays came to us. The hay camps were attacked by Indians. . . .The Rees stole horses and the Sioux stole horses. There had been treaties, but neither side lived up to them."[315]

There were other, even more far-reaching consequences. "The insatiable greed of land seekers and settlers would soon cover the land with home-steads, so that there would be no herds left on the prairie; the migrating herds would have no trails to follow. . . . The death chant was quivering in the air."[316] The deer and the beaver had already gone "to enrich the white man." And now the buffalo was going too.

For the plains Tribes, the buffalo were the stuff of life itself. Old Lady Horse, a woman from the Kiowa nation, described how everything her peo-ple had came from them. "Their tipis were made of buffalo hides, so were their clothes and moccasins. They ate buffalo meat. Their containers were made of hide, or of bladders or stomachs. The buffalo were the life of the Kiowas." Perhaps even more important than providing food and shelter, the buffalo were essential to their spiritual life. "A white buffalo calf must be sacrificed in the Sun Dance. The priests used parts of the buffalo to make their prayers when they healed people or when they sang to the powers above."[317]

Before the emigration began, as many as thirty million buffalo roamed the central American grasslands. By the 1860s, just twenty years later, their numbers had already been significantly depleted. The early settler trails along the Platte River Valley had caused much disruption to the herds, but this had not been the only cause. In the early part of the century, the lucra-tive trade in buffalo robes had long been a source of both wealth and power, for the Lakota in particular, and a highly effective chess piece in their geo-political maneuvering. The buffalo were also affected by drought, disease, and the huge herds of horses (the descendants of those brought by the

Spanish conquistadors) that had been painstakingly built up over a century or more by many of the bands. The coming of the railways, however, spelled wholesale disaster.

Not only did the railways affect the migratory patterns of the buffalo (and thus their fertility), but they also enabled hunters on a scale that had never previously been either seen or even imagined. The Union Pacific had hired men to hunt buffalo, to feed the hungry crews laying the railway tracks, but many more were private individuals who thought of it simply as a sport. In the past, a white hunter had been obliged to organize a full-blown expedition, often with American Indian guides, remaining with them in the wilderness for many months at a time. Now, it was not even necessary to set foot on the prairie. Now, anyone could be a hunter; anyone could boast of that ultimate trophy, simply by leaning out the window of a train.

In the early days of the emigration, herds could be as many as a hundred thousand strong. One wagon train was blocked for hours by a herd that was estimated to have been three miles wide and ten miles long. Even in the early 1870s, when Elizabeth Custer saw a herd for the first time, it was an unforgettable sight. "I have been on a train when the black, moving mass of buffaloes before us looked as if it stretched on down to the horizon," she wrote. But it was not enough just to look. "Everyone went armed in those days, and the car windows and platforms bristled with rifles and pistols, much as if it had been a fortification defended by small-arms instead of cannon," she explained, with the greatest insouciance. "It was the greatest wonder in the world that more people were not killed, as the wild rush for the windows, and the reckless discharge of rifles and pistols, put every passenger's life in jeopardy. No one interfered or made a protest with those travelers, however . . . I could not for the life of me avoid a shudder when a long line of guns leaning on the backs of the seats met my eye as I entered a car. When the sharp shriek of the whistle announced a herd of buffaloes the rifles were snatched, and in the struggle to twist round for a good aim out of the narrow window the barrel or muzzle of the firearm passed dangerously near the ear of any scared woman who had the temerity [to get in the way]."[318]

Elizabeth Custer used her opera glasses, the better to view the slaughter. "It struck us as rather odd, when taking them from their velvet cases on the barren desert of a plain, to contrast our surroundings with the last place where they were used," she wrote. "The brilliantly lighted opera house, the air scented with hothouse flowers, the rich costumes of the women, the faultlessly dressed men, the studied conventionality of the calmly listening audience, hearing ravishing music unmoved—all these recollections presented a scene about as different from that on the plains as can be imagined. Here we were, after all that glimpse of luxurious life, rolling over the arid desert."[319]

More destructive still was the arrival of the professional buffalo hunter, many scores of whom now swarmed across the prairies. At three dollars a hide, the animals were "walking gold pieces." The buffalo, according to one hunter, "was the stupidest game animal in the world." If their leader was killed or wounded, instead of taking fright and scattering away, the others would simply gather round it. One hunter reported having acquired 269 hides with just three hundred cartridges. Not so much a slaughter as a "harvest."

In the smart cities in the East there was a rage for buffalo-hide lap robes; smoked buffalo tongue had become a delicacy. Buffalo horns were made into buttons, combs, knife handles; their hooves were melted down for glue; their bones were made into fertilizer. As one military observer would write, "Where there were myriads of buffalo the year before, now there were myriads of carcasses, the air foul with a sickening stench, a vast plain which only a short twelve-month before had teemed with animal life was a dead, solitary, putrid desert."[320]

On the southern plains, hunters were soon encroaching even onto the lands that were reserved to the plains Tribes by treaty. In 1874, alarmed by the carnage, Congress attempted to pass a law to protect the herds, but

President Ulysses S. Grant refused to sign it. The link between the coming of the railroads and the demise of the buffalo herds—twin prongs in the "final solution" to the "Indian question"—was not lost on Washington.* Not only would the US government do nothing to stop the hunters; they even provided them with free ammunition. Between 1872 and 1874 alone, an estimated three million hides were shipped to the East from the southern and central Great Plains, sending the buffalo into a terminal decline.

Without the buffalo, the plains Tribes knew that they would starve. In the same year, in desperation, and in a last attempt to remain free, large numbers of Kiowa, Comanche, Southern Cheyenne, and Arapaho rose up to try to drive not only the hunters away, but all whites who had encroached onto their lands, only to be ruthlessly hunted down themselves. By the spring of 1875, all the resisting bands, by now desperate for food, had been driven back onto the reservations. The hunters returned, unchecked, and within a year the buffalo herds on the southern plains were gone.

Old Lady Horse described all of this in her deceptively simple folktale:

> So, when the white men wanted to build railroads, or when they wanted to farm or raise cattle, the buffalo still protected the Kiowas. They tore up the railroad tracks and the gardens. They chased the cattle off the ranges. The buffalo loved their people as much as the Kiowas loved them.
>
> There was a war between the buffalo and the white men. The white men built forts in the Kiowa country, and the woolly-headed

---

*As Senator William Stewart of Nevada would write in a Congressional report in 1869: "[Native Americans] can only be permanently conquered by railroads. . . . The railroads will settle the country as they progress. The water stations and freight stations built on the lines immediately become the germs of towns and centers of military operations. Farms follow the roads and a column-front of self-sustaining settlements moves slowly but surely toward the Rocky Mountains. . . . As a thorough and final solution of the Indian Question, by taking the buffalo range out from under the savage, and putting a vast stock and grain farm in its place, the railroads to the Pacific surely are a military necessity. As avenues of sudden approach to Indians on the war-path, and of cheap and quick movement of supplies to troops, they are surely a military necessity." See Pekka Hämäläinen, *Lakota America*.

buffalo soldiers* shot at the buffalo as fast as they could, but the buffalo kept coming on, coming on, even into the post cemetery at Fort Sill.† Soldiers were not enough to hold them back.

Then the white man hired hunters to do nothing but kill the buffalo. Up and down the plains those men ranged, shooting sometimes as many as a hundred buffalo a day. Behind them came the skinners with their wagons. They piled the hides and bones into the wagons until they were full, and then took their loads to the new railroad stations that were being built, to be shipped east to the market. Sometimes there would be a pile of bones as high as a man, stretching a mile along the railroad track.

The buffalo saw that their day was over. They could protect their people no longer. Sadly, the last remnant of the great herd gathered in council, and decided what they would do.

The Kiowas were camped on the north side of Mount Scott, those of them who were still free to camp. One young woman got up very early in the morning. The dawn mist was still rising from Medicine Creek, and as she looked across the water, peering through the haze, she saw the last buffalo herd appear like a spirit dream.

Straight to Mount Scott the leader of the herd walked. Behind him came the cows and their calves, and the few young males who had survived. As the woman watched, the face of the mountain opened.

Inside Mount Scott the world was green and fresh, as it had been when she was a small girl. The rivers ran clear, not red. The wild plums were in blossom, chasing the red buds up the inside slopes. Into this world of beauty, the buffalo walked, never to be seen again.[321]

---

*African American troops of the Ninth and Nineteenth Cavalries.
†In the southern part of present-day Oklahoma.

. . .

BEFORE THE EMIGRATION "THE white men in the region were only a few little islands in a sea of Indians and buffaloes," Mari Sandoz, a white writer who would record much Cheyenne oral history in her book *Cheyenne Autumn*, would write. Fewer than forty years later, in 1877, "the buffaloes were about gone and the last of the Indians driven onto the reservations— only a few little islands of Indians in a great sea of whites."[322]

Throughout the 1870s, Ulysses S. Grant's "Peace Policy" had succeeded in completing the task of moving vast numbers of Native people onto reservations. By the early part of the decade, not only the buffalo but game of all kinds had all but disappeared from the Platte Valley. Dwindling numbers of bison elsewhere resulted in much intertribal fighting: the Lakota, driven by the absolute imperative to keep the herds for their own people, usually won. Cut off from their game, and soon all but starving, smaller, less powerful nations such as the Pawnees, the Poncas, the Omahas, and the Otoe-Missourians had had little choice but to accept government rations and be relocated, many of them to distant Indian Territory. Farther to the southwest, the Shoshones and the Utes had also accepted life on their allotted reservations, as had Sarah Winnemucca's Tribe, the Northern Paiute. The same fate had befallen the Cayuse, the Miwok, and the Navajo. Major General Philip Sheridan's notorious winter campaign of 1868 in the central Great Plains had now all but destroyed the autonomy of the Southern Cheyenne and the Arapaho. They too were moved to reservations on Indian Territory.

One group, however, had remained free. While almost all other Native American nations were struggling for their survival in the "great sea of whites," the Lakota, their bands perhaps as many as thirty thousand strong, had not only held out against them, but were still both expanding and enriching their empire.

The Lakota heartland was in Powder River country, between the Black Hills and the Bighorn Mountains. Here, in these lush, well-watered valleys of the Yellowstone, Powder, Rosebud, Tongue, and Bighorn Rivers, where

the buffalo and game were still plentiful, large numbers of Lakota lived.* As
a little girl, Josephine Waggoner experienced this life firsthand when she
traveled with her mother to Powder River country in the summer of 1875,
in what would prove to be the last days of Lakota hegemony.

Like her friend and collaborator Susan Bordeaux, Josephine Waggoner
was a woman of mixed-race heritage. Hers, too, would prove to be a life of
many overlapping worlds. Her
father, Charles McCarthy, was
an Irishman who as a young boy
had emigrated with his family
from County Cork in 1840. After fighting in the Civil War—
he had marched with General
Sherman to Atlanta—he had
gone out West, along with many
other veterans, "to seek his fortune." After a short period as a
miner, he had sold on his claim,
and with the proceeds had set
up a general store at the American Fur Company's trading
post at Grand River in South
Dakota. An Indian agency had

*The historian Josephine Waggoner
(seated, center) as a child*

been set up at Grand River in 1868, and it was there that he had met Josephine's mother, Itȟatéwiŋ, or "Wind Woman," a Lakota woman of the
Hunkpapa band, buying her from her brothers as his wife.

It was not an unusual arrangement for the times. As Waggoner states in
her magisterial work *Witness: A Hunkpapa Historian's Strong-Heart Song of*

---

*As Josephine Waggoner would describe them, these were the "western Indians," who still
repelled all outsiders from their world, and "who would not take issues or rations from the
government."

the Lakotas, in those days "there was many a young Indian girl sold to white traders." By 1870, the furs—"buffalo robes, elk hides, beaver, mink and otter hides"—that had for so long been used by Native people as a medium of exchange, were by now an all but vanished commodity, and yet Itȟatéwiŋ's brothers and male relatives still needed to be able to buy guns and ammunition as they prepared themselves "for a defense against the invasion of their country by the whites." Traditionally, it was the women of the bands who carried out the trading, and when they saw the particular attention paid by McCarthy to their sister, they paid attention too. They consulted with her, explaining the situation carefully, and Itȟatéwiŋ had agreed to be sold. "She was decked out in her finest clothes and taken to my father.'" Her price was ten guns and several pounds of powder and bullets.

Josephine Waggoner always admired her father for the speech he made on that occasion. Most Native women were not "married" by whites in the accepted Euro-American sense, and many of these men had white wives and families still living elsewhere, to whom they would one day return. Charles McCarthy was determined to do things differently. "Father told them that he had been in the war and had traveled many places since the war; that he had never married and had no offspring, but the woman he married and who was to be the mother of his children, he intended to marry legally, the way marriage was generally performed by the white race. He told them that a marriage performed by a man of God was for life, and was sacred—it was not for a year or two, but forever."[323]

Charles McCarthy respected and honored his new wife, and their marriage seems to have been a happy one. For all this, according to her daughter, Itȟatéwiŋ was "like a bird in captivity," always "inquiring about and looking for her people who came in from the West to trade." When she met any of them, Josephine remembered, her mother would embrace them and

---

*Itȟatéwiŋ was a relatively mature woman of about thirty when she married Charles McCarthy, who was her third husband. Her first was a Hunkpapa warrior, the second a man named Ben Arnold.

cry tears of joy. By 1871, when Josephine was born, the couple had moved from Grand River to Apple Creek, North Dakota, where McCarthy had put down a claim, with "several lots in the town site." Here, in what would shortly become the new town of Bismarck, Josephine's father ran a thriving livery and feed business, as well as owning "many horses, mules, wagons, sleighs, and buggies."

It is hard to imagine what Itȟatéwiŋ thought of the coming of the railroads to those once-peaceful prairies. Soon, people of all nationalities "were camped along the railroad right-of-way; expert drivers were hired; wages were good; settlers came in covered wagons, traveling with the graders." Where there was no wood to put up houses, they built sod houses instead. And between these new emigrants "there was just as much trouble as there ever was among the wildest of tribes. There were shooting scrapes, gambling and killing going on every day." Josephine's father was appointed the first sheriff of the newly created Burleigh County.

Just a few years later, disaster struck. In December 1874, while giving chase in the middle of a blizzard to a man accused of murder, the sheriff's sleigh fell through the ice and Charles drowned in the frozen waters of the Missouri. Only his gloves and his sealskin cap, which had been left on the riverbank, were recovered. "My mother was prostrate with grief," Josephine remembered. Although Charles had been a wealthy man and a considerable landowner at the time of his death, neither his wife nor his daughter ever knew what became of his property.* Instead, Itȟatéwiŋ would return all but empty-handed to her own people. She bought a large tent and, taking only a few household belongings with her, traveled back to the Grand River agency. Now located some fifty miles north of its original position, the agency was known as Standing Rock.

Standing Rock, on the northeastern periphery of the Great Sioux Reservation, was one of a number of agencies at which the plains Tribes could

---

*Josephine Waggoner's daughter believed that Itȟatéwiŋ gave most of her money to a Catholic priest at Bismarck for safekeeping but that it was never returned.

receive their rations and other goods, according to the terms of the Fort Laramie Treaty. On issue days, the place would be "teeming with traffic, the prairie alive with horses." The dust on the trails "looked like the smoke of a prairie fire." But whereas not so long ago Native Americans had looked to these agencies as places that served their interests, they were increasingly becoming places of control. Attached to the government distributions of blankets, quilts, clothing, and food were numerous rules and regulations, even "restrictions about leaving the reservation without a permit." When these things were explained to them, through interpreters, there was a growing feeling among them that "they had no rights at all, even in their own country," and they would disperse as quickly as possible. "From a distance the procession looked like a row of ants crawling along until they disappeared into the dust." Whereas one day there would be thousands of tents, the next there would be "nothing but emptiness remaining."

The following summer, when her people were still free to roam, Itȟatéwiŋ decided to take her two daughters out West, to Powder River country.* After life at the agency, the journey to Powder River was a halcyon experience for a little girl. Itȟatéwiŋ, who had traveled back to Standing Rock with all her possessions loaded into a prairie schooner, would now take them overland the traditional way, by horse and travois. Josephine's grandmother, Waštéwiŋ ("Beautiful Woman"), was also part of that summer caravan, and she too had a packhorse and a travois. Itȟatéwiŋ loaded up her travois with cooking utensils and many pounds of beads, intending to trade them for deer and beaver skins. Waštéwiŋ rode her horse, giving Itȟatéwiŋ the chance to ride behind; the two children, Josephine and Marcella, were pulled along on the second travois. "Mother had put boughs of willow on the wickerware and put a sheet over it so we were in the shade. We could walk if we wanted to or jump on and ride."

In this way, they traveled in easy stages of about twenty miles a day. The buffalo herds were still relatively plentiful on the northern plains, and large

---

*Josephine had a half-sister, Marcella, from her mother's previous marriage.

herds of antelope, sometimes as many as a hundred strong, grazed on the hillsides. Men would go hunting, taking the travois with them to carry back the meat. Josephine's mother and grandmother had to work fast, getting the meat dried and cured so it would not be wasted. They fixed long poles over the fires "so the smoke would blow on the meat to keep insects away while it was drying."

While the small children were kept busy collecting wood from the creeks to keep the fires burning, the older boys would go to the river to water the horses in the shallows. They would keep a careful watch, lying flat on the ground and holding their horses by a lariat, "gazing into the distance for chance travelers." In the evenings, with the smell of supper cooking, Josephine enjoyed herself with the other small girls, playing and running between the tents. According to custom, "the girls were never allowed to play with the boys. They were kept separate, so much so that the male dialect was different from the female. . . . Some nights mother would make me listen to the bellowing of the buffalo; [but] the smoke of the campfire generally scared them away."

Josephine would learn many things on her journey to Powder River country. In Montana, they came to a place where pine trees grew in abundance. Everyone in the caravan went to collect the pitch gum, and for a while "nearly every boy and girl, even the men and women, were chewing gum." The yellow flowers of the pine trees were also harvested to be used as dye. When the blooms were mixed with a certain type of red berry, it made a "brilliant scarlet of every shade" with which decorations such as porcupine quills and feathers could be colored. Farther on, they came to another place where yellow ochre could be found in the rocks. Another type of dye, in the form of oxidized iron, was dug up from the ground. "The Indians knew where the best red powder was because the prairie dogs had thrown it up in digging their holes."

After many weeks of traveling, the caravan approached the Powder River valley at last. It was the custom of the Lakota to move leisurely from one river valley to another. Their huge tipi villages could be as many as a thousand lodges strong. A single Lakota tipi could be made with as many as twenty buffalo hides and was often filled with imported luxury goods: red and blue Navajo blankets, dried pumpkins and cornmeal from Mexico, silver rings from Germany, glass beads for making necklaces and earrings—as well as state-of-the-art Remingtons and Colt six-shooters and the ammunition to go with them. "It was a beautiful sight to see the countless white tents that were pitched in a circle on the green grass," Josephine wrote. "The winding river was lovely with its border of dark green trees as we approached."

Beyond the sparkling river, on either side there were impassable ranges of mountains, so densely wooded that the tracks through them were unknown to whites. About a hundred miles away was the headwater of the Little Missouri, "whose rough banks and badlands were impassable except for travois traveling," while to the east lay the headwaters of the Cheyenne River, which could be followed into the Black Hills if ever a retreat were necessary.

In 1875, the Powder River country may still have been a place of safety and plenty for the Lakota, but it was a closely guarded stronghold too. Knowing that outside their domain were not only buffalo hunters and white trappers but also soldiers and railway surveyors, none of them "on any friendly business," the Lakota kept a careful watch. Each night in the great council tent different scouts were appointed to patrol the country. "If anyone was coming, these scouts made signals from the high mountains that were watched all the time."

Even when the caravan in which Itȟatéwiŋ and her family were traveling was within sight of the Powder River camp, precautions were taken before they could approach. "The men that were ahead gave a signal from the top of the hill, where the processions stopped. A young man rode back and forth on a white horse several times. The white horse meant that all was clear. The main camp sent the flash of a looking glass, which meant come on." After this, they came quickly down from the mountains into the river valley. "The people were so glad to meet each other," Josephine Waggoner wrote.

"There was exchanging of gifts, invitations from place to place. It was a reunion of joy and pleasure."

Josephine would spend the whole summer, and much of the autumn, camped at the Powder River village, not returning to the agency until November. In contrast with life at Standing Rock, where they had been entirely dependent on government rations, and even then often had barely enough to eat, her time on the Powder River was a revelation. Although, even here, the bison herds had been depleted, it was still "the heart of the game country." That summer Josephine ate "almost every kind of wild meat there was." As well as elk, deer, buffalo, and even bear meat, they had wild eggs, duck, sage hens, and chickens. There was an abundance of fruit, and the rivers teemed with so much fish that the boys, simply by tying a string to their arrows, could draw the fish in "as fast as they were shot." These included "the speckled mountain trout, catfish three feet long sometimes, bullheads, pike and sunfish."

That summer, Itȟatéwiŋ worked hard, spending her time tanning deer skins and smoking the hides until they were golden yellow. She did the same with buffalo hides, carefully choosing those with the heaviest winter fur, although it was tiring and heavy work. Other furs, such as mink, otter, and beaver, could still be obtained here, and she knew she could sell them to the US Army officers back at Standing Rock. "Most of the officers wanted beaver collars on their buffalo-hide overcoats" and would pay her well for them. Josephine and her sister also benefited from their mother's hard work. For them she made new winter suits: "beaver-hide moccasins with the fur inside . . . buffalo calf-hide leggings, coats, and mittens and mink-hide hoods trimmed with white rabbit fur."

It was not all work. The Lakota were passionate about their horses, and racing them was a great sport in the summertime. The horses, richly caparisoned, would be led around in front of the crowds, "that the people might use their judgement of which was the best [one]." Betting could often reach fever pitch; "there would be so much excitement [that] some of the men would bet their last horse." Women would bet their most treasured beaded moccasins, and sometimes even the dresses they stood up in, "and if they lost out, they had to give up their dresses right then and there."

But this love of horses was not only about excitement and parade. There was a quality to the relationship between the Lakota and their horses, a sacred bond that Josephine was aware of, even as a little girl. "So great was the pride in owning a herd that owners just fairly lived with them," she wrote. To see to their horses was the first thing they would do in the morning and the last thing at night. She wrote, too, of "the grooming, the pampering, and even painting ornaments on their pet horses." The herds were driven down to water twice a day and taken out to fresh pastures "as though they didn't know enough" to do so on their own. "I have seen Indians talk to their horses as though they were human."

Other, more serious matters intrigued her too. She became fascinated by the great council lodge in the main camp, and by the four council men who sat cross-legged on buffalo robes by the door. Inside, the chiefs of all seven Lakota bands had their allotted places. It was here, Josephine learned from her mother, that all matters pertaining to their people could be discussed and debated, and it was here, too, that their laws were made, although at the time of her writing all those customs had been abolished, "and there are very few living who can remember how the laws and rules were made in those old tribal days."

Although women were not allowed into the council tent, everyone was aware of the most pressing issue of the day. The Northern Pacific Railroad had already reached Bismarck, and it seemed only a matter of time before it would be pushing its way still farther west. Three years previously, and in direct contravention of the 1868 Fort Laramie Treaty, surveying teams, accompanied by an escort of more than a thousand US Army soldiers, had entered the Yellowstone Valley but been forcibly repelled. The following year, a second expedition, this time escorted by an even greater military force, among them none other than George Armstrong Custer's Seventh

Cavalry, was again sent to survey the river basin.* Yet again, the Lakota succeeded in forcing them to retreat. "'Why didn't the soldiers stay off the Sioux territory?' were the arguments asked at the council lodge. The Sioux claimed the country south of the Yellowstone according to the treaty with the government, but in the constant invasion of soldiers, freighters, hunters and trappers—regardless of the provisions of the treaty—they sensed danger and were nervous."

Josephine Waggoner would later estimate that the camp she had stayed in that summer was only about fifty miles south of the Yellowstone Valley. The scouts appointed each day at the council lodge were charged with keeping a close watch on any movements in the area. "Every move that the soldiers made was watched by the signal riders, where the horses were kept at night and where they grazed through the day; every steamboat that came up the river was reported, what kind of supplies it unloaded, whether the boats were bringing more soldiers or not." The same scouts even knew when buffalo hunters or white trappers were within a fifty-mile radius of the camp; if they found them, some of the scouts would bring home scalps "to show they were not idling their time away." Even so, the future seemed clouded.

ELIZABETH AND GEORGE CUSTER had arrived in Dakota in the spring of 1873 and soon took up residence at Fort Abraham Lincoln, just to the north of the Standing Rock agency. When he found out that Josephine's

---

*The Yellowstone Expedition of 1873 amounted to a small army. It included 79 officers, 1,451 men, 353 civilian engineers, 27 Indian scouts, 275 wagons and ambulances, and more than 2,000 horses and mules. Although the Lakota were a formidable fighting force, part of the reason the expedition had retreated was because that same year the financiers of the Northern Pacific, Jay Cooke and Company, had defaulted on its loans, causing a financial crisis. "Fifty-eight railroads went bankrupt, and half of the nation's iron foundries failed . . . the Northern Pacific Railroad lay dead on the Missouri near Bismarck, its untouched, pointless rails covered in grass." See Pekka Hämäläinen, *Lakota America*.

mother was an expert hide tanner and seamstress, Custer commissioned a fringed buckskin hunting suit from her, the same one in which, before his death, he would often be photographed. In addition to cutting and sewing these suits, Ithatéwiŋ would decorate the collars and cuffs with beads. "Her beadwork was beautiful, her color combinations were perfect," Josephine wrote; "she was an artist in that line" and was often commissioned to do beadwork for the Army officers' wives, as well as the men.

In this way, Ithatéwiŋ came to know Elizabeth Custer as well as her husband. Ithatéwiŋ did other work besides sewing for her: Elizabeth would often send for her when her own cook, the formidable Eliza, was ill. "Mrs. Custer was very much pleased with the work my mother did. She took her visitors into the kitchen to show them how an Indian worked. My mother could understand English a great deal better than they thought. She heard Mrs. Custer say that when the Sioux were captured, she was going to have Indian girls for servants. In after years, my mother thought of this remark and commented how little we knew of the future."

By 1875, there had been so many white assaults on the Lakota's unceded territories that it had become clear to them that the US government was no longer to be trusted. It was not only the Northern Pacific Railroad's surveying expeditions to the Yellowstone River that were the issue. In 1874, Custer had been chosen to lead another expedition, this time into the Black Hills, the most sacred of all the Lakota's lands. Officially, the purpose of the 900-soldier-strong cavalcade was to look for a potential site for a new military fort—in itself an egregious treaty violation—but the convoy also had with it a geologist and some miners. Before long, traces of glittering yellow metal were found.

A triumphant Custer was quick to announce the discovery. As well as miners, he had taken three journalists with him on the expedition, and before long the news that gold had been found in the Black Hills had been reported, often in exaggerated terms, all over the country. In the inevitable gold rush that followed, an estimated fifteen thousand prospectors flooded west to the Black Hills.

At first, the US Army made efforts to keep the trespassers out, but the rush of miners was simply too great. For the Lakota, the invasion of the Black Hills by Custer and his troops was nothing short of a declaration of war. For the US government, too, it was clear that a breaking point had been reached. A Lakota delegation, led by Red Cloud, Spotted Tail, and Lone Horn, was invited to Washington, and some desultory talks ensued, but they did no good. Another attempt to negotiate the sale, or at least the lease, of the Black Hills for mining purposes, which took place at the Red Cloud agency in late September that year, also failed. By now it was clear that a final showdown was inevitable. Rather than declare outright war, President Grant, his "Peace Policy" in tatters, decided to "let things flow spontaneously into bloodshed."[324] In December, in a deliberate attempt to hasten this end, word was sent out that all Native people living outside the reservation boundaries were to report to an agency by the end of January 1876—an impossible proposition in the dead of winter. Those who failed to do so, such as the bands who had coalesced around Lakota chiefs Sitting Bull and Crazy Horse, were to be brought in by force.

At Standing Rock, even though it was many hundreds of miles away from Powder River country, rumors abounded. Itȟatéwiŋ was on good terms with the wives of the US Army's Indian scouts, and from them she gleaned much information. In the spring of 1876, she learned that Custer had moved out of Fort Lincoln and was headed west again. His mission was to bring in Sitting Bull and his Hunkpapa bands, among whom were many of Itȟatéwiŋ's own relatives, including her mother, who had remained behind at the Powder River camp when she returned to Standing Rock.

Although Josephine, by now a child of six, was too young to understand much of what was happening, the atmosphere at the agency was palpable. On issue days, in particular, there were whispered conversations everywhere, and it seemed, even to her, that "death and gloom hung over the heads of all." Ever inquisitive, she tried to find out the cause of all the tension: "I wanted to ask questions, but I dreaded to know what the answers would be; my mother would not permit me to ask any questions when people came to our house."

Although the women and children wanted peace, the men, daredevils who "were born to fight," were in silent agony. Every day the infantry at the nearby garrison, Fort Yates, could be heard at target practice, and the cavalry seen carrying out their drills. More ominous still, their cannons were already trained on the camps. Everyone knew that it would be madness if the men took up arms and went to help their relatives out West. To do so would mean death to all.

One day, when Josephine was out with her mother visiting friends at one of the camps on the prairie, she noticed a lone man standing way out in the foothills. At first she was too absorbed in playing games with the other children to pay him much heed. The game they were playing was called "Beaver, put out your paws." She remembered this particularly because it was the only game she ever knew in which boys would join in with the girls. "Someone covered up under a robe, the rest all danced around the robe singing, 'Beaver, put out your paws.' Every once in a while, the one under the robe would put out his hand a second and jerk it back again as someone would try to snatch it. Whoever caught the hand would have to be 'it.'"

Later, when the game was over, Josephine asked her mother what had made the lone man stand on the hill so long. Ithatéwiŋ told her that the man was called Black Bird, and he was doing a devotion to the Great Spirit, fasting and praying for three days. "He was crying to the sea of silence that his relatives out west may be safe from harm, that he may see them again this side of the life plane."

It took a strong man to do this fasting and praying devotion. On the third day, Black Bird, weakened by living only on bread and thin coffee, had fainted. "Such a devotion on a light diet was most damaging. Half a dozen went up the hill on horseback. He was given a cool drink, was rubbed to consciousness, put on a horse, and brought back down to camp, for he was too weak to walk."

One day in June, Ithatéwiŋ was out working in her garden when three riders were seen approaching. When they got closer, she recognized them as some of her relatives, among them a particularly favorite uncle of Josephine's, Nahaha, or "Walks Stealthily." Inviting them in for coffee, Itȟatéwiŋ sent the two girls out to the store—a ruse that Josephine only realized much later was to make sure they were safely out of the way. They had brought the news that every soldier under Custer's command, including Custer himself, had been killed. The soldiers had attacked a village at a place the Lakota knew as the Greasy Grass. Whites called it the Little Bighorn.

On June 25, some six thousand American Indians, of which half were Lakota, Cheyenne, and Arapaho who had left their reservations to join forces with Sitting Bull, were camped along the river, in a village that extended for almost three miles. Among them were two thousand warriors. Custer had pushed his men, already exhausted from their long march through unknown terrain, to attack at once. Outnumbered four to one, the fighting took barely an hour—"as long as it took a hungry man to eat his lunch." The Battle of the Little Bighorn, as it would become known, was not so much a battle as a rout.

Long before word reached any of the whites at the fortresses and settlements along the Missouri, who would have to wait for their messengers to arrive by boat, the news of the battle was known in every camp at Standing Rock. And yet this, the greatest Native American victory in all the Plains Wars, would also mark the end of the Lakota's free-roaming life. Determined to avenge Custer and his men, the US Army would now hunt down each remaining band, one by one.

"The Indians had struck, then retreated out toward the snowcapped, rough and reckless Bighorn Mountains, where pursuit was almost impossible." Among those who had fled were many of Josephine's relatives, including her grandmother, Waštéwiŋ, who had stayed behind on the Powder River the summer before. "My grandmother ... was all the world to me," Josephine wrote. When she asked her mother if she would ever see her again, she always received a cheerful answer; all her sons, and two other daughters, were with her, as well as many other grandchildren who would help take care of her, Itȟatéwiŋ explained. Josephine tried to take comfort from this, but it was no good. She would sit and try to imagine how it was out there in the mountains, "ghostly, white-topped, high and misty, unapproachable, repellent, and delusive—where nothing but wild animals could exist," and she knew in her heart that she would never see her grandmother again.

Of all Josephine's many relatives who followed Sitting Bull, only one of her uncles, Grasping Eagle, would live. From the Bighorn Mountains, they would follow their chief still farther north into exile in Canada, and here, like many others, they died of "privations, hardship, and famine," including her beloved grandmother.

Those who remained behind suffered too. Even the men and women at the agency, who had had nothing to do with the fighting, were ordered by the military to give up all their guns and ammunition. This was not all that would be taken from them. One stiflingly hot day in August, a great plume of dust could be seen in the distance. Together with her mother and sister, Josephine climbed to the top of a hill to see what it was. As they watched the dust clouds getting nearer, gradually it dawned on them. Vast herds of horses were being driven in the direction of the agency garrison, Fort Yates.

When Custer had raided Black Kettle's village on the Washita, he had ordered the slaughter of some nine hundred Cheyenne horses, but this was not to be the fate of the Lakota herds. Most of these horses were driven to Minnesota to be sold. The horses from the agencies at Cheyenne River, Crow Creek, Rosebud, and Oglala were taken south to Omaha, also to be sold at auction. Others, either through incompetence or corruption, found their way more locally to farmers "looking for a bargain for little or nothing," to livery stables in Bismarck, and, perhaps bitterest of all, to the railway grading camps. At the Standing Rock and nearby Cheyenne River agencies, attempts were made by the people there to hide as many of their horses as possible by taking them to distant pastures, but it did no good. The commander of the Department of Dakota, General Alfred Terry, threatened to withhold their rations if they did not comply, and they were forced to bring them in. In this way, an estimated five thousand horses belonging to the Lakota were taken away, never to be seen by them again.*

"So the horses were all gone," Josephine Waggoner wrote, and with them "the life, the hope, the pride of the Indian" were all gone too. "No one in this machine age could ever understand the love between master and horse. The love of a man toward a spirited, courageous horse was wonderful. It was like the love of a beloved child, only a man is dependent on a horse." To lose their horses was like losing both father and mother.

Along with other children from the reservation, Josephine and her sister would often climb the hill behind Fort Yates. There they could see the "wind-whipped tipis in the dust-beclouded prairies for many miles away without a horse moving around." Instead, they could only watch as men and women moved slowly to and fro, "laboriously dragging wood home, or carrying small quantities on their backs. Every tent seemed to be silent except where children were crying for food. Silence, because there was no enjoyment in talking, no enjoyment in singing, only a wailing song at times came with the wind, a song of grief and regret."[325]

---

*The Lakota would try for decades to receive compensation for their stolen horses. "Pony claims" from Standing Rock, among other agencies, lasted until 1944. See Emily Levine's notes in *Witness*.

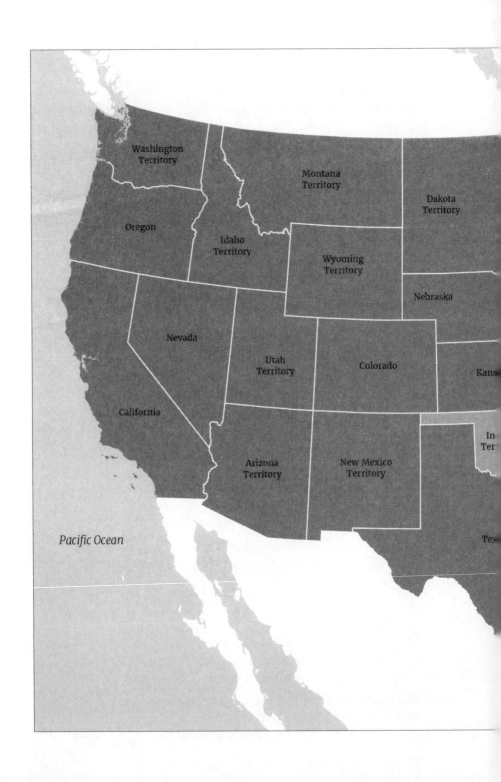

USA in 1880

CONCLUSION

———❧———

B y 1877, as the Second Great Sioux War finally came to an end, white Americans' acquisition of the West was all but complete. On the northern plains, almost all Native people had now been forced onto reservations, and any last pockets of resistance were brutally suppressed. In July 1881, Sitting Bull and his last surviving followers, exhausted and starving, gave themselves up. On the reservations, children were taken forcibly away from their parents and sent to white schools, sometimes thousands of miles away from their homes. In an egregious attempt to Christianize, and therefore "civilize," them, everything that linked them to their own culture—their belongings, their clothes, even their names—was taken from them.

Many of them survived, but in California it was a genocide. A combination of "colonization policies, abductions, diseases, homicides, executions, battles, massacres, institutionalized neglect on federal reservations, and the willful destruction of indigenous villages and their food supplies" had reduced the population of the Native people there by as much as 80 percent.[326]

In three decades from the end of the Mexican-American War in 1846, the numbers of Indigenous people in California had been reduced from perhaps a hundred and fifty thousand to thirty thousand.

For every Native American living on the plains, there were now almost forty whites. In the decade following the end of the Second Great Sioux War, an estimated four and a half million more settlers, both white and African American, went west, almost half of them pouring onto the western prairies, creating new settlements, farms, and even towns in a region that had once been thought too harsh for human habitation. After the Dawes Act of 1887, even the last remaining pocket of land—all that remained of the vast continental landmass that was once designated Indian Territory— was opened up to white and African American settlement. By 1890, no Native people in the West were living freely on their own land. In a bulletin that same year, the US Census Bureau announced that up to and including 1880 the country had a frontier. "After that, it didn't."[327]

At the very beginning of the century, when the US had first purchased the Louisiana Territory from Napoleon, the American president, Thomas Jefferson, had estimated that it would take a thousand generations for the US to people it. It had taken just five—in historical terms, no more than the blink of an eye. For some of the earliest settlers, those who had made the first tentative journeys along the Oregon Trail fewer than forty years previously, it had happened within their own lifetime. Matilda Sager had been a child of five when, together with her parents and six siblings, she had made the journey to Oregon in the emigration of 1844. One of only four survivors in her family, in later years she had returned east to visit her daughter in Maryland and was able to see firsthand the changes that had taken place. "On the vast plains, where years before my childish eyes had seen vast herds of buffalo roaming at will and where all was Indian territory from the Missouri river to the Rocky Mountains, where the immigrant's wagon had toiled slowly and painfully along, with the menace of privation and death a constant attendant, railroads had thrust their slender bands of steel; large cities had been built and prosperous farms dotted the land." It was, she wrote, as if a magician had traveled alongside her "constantly waving a magic wand before my surprised eyes."[328]

Matilda Sager would also return, just once, to her former home at Waiilatpu. On the fiftieth anniversary of the Whitman Massacre, all the survivors were invited there to see the monument that had been erected to the memory of those who had died. When the workmen were leveling the ground, they had found a number of bones, and Matilda was asked to help identify them. A woman's skull with large eye sockets she was convinced was that of Narcissa Whitman, who she remembered as having "large, light blue eyes." Another, with gold fillings in some of the back teeth, she was

sure was that of Dr. Whitman, since his nephew Perrin had once told her that he had accompanied his uncle to the dentist in Saint Louis before traveling west in 1843 and that this was the first time he had ever seen dental work done—a procedure that had impressed him greatly. Like the woman's skull, this one had been sawn in half—"an old trick of the Indians upon some victims." She asked one of her com-

Catherine, Matilda, and Elizabeth Sager

panions to hold the two halves together, "and as I went back in memory, and imagined the skull clothed in flesh, I felt it was Dr. Whitman's."

The second time Matilda returned to Oregon was perhaps still more overwhelming. In 1916, now an old woman of almost eighty, she attended the reunion of the Oregon Pioneer Society in Portland, a huge gathering of sixteen hundred people who assembled in the city auditorium. For Matilda, it was an ambivalent experience. The jamboree included a trip for the "pioneers" up the newly made Columbia Highway—not in wagons or carts, or even by train, but in automobiles. At first it had been this novelty that had most impressed itself on her mind. She had been amazed by "the beautifully finished roadway, with its wonderful curves, solid masonry, [and its] gentle grades." But soon these marvels seemed to fade from before her eyes, and instead "I saw a little party of forlorn and homeless refugees rowing down that same river in the old fashioned, flat-bottomed bateaux, thankful to be alive, but always hurrying to put more and more miles of water between them and the tragic place called Waiilatpu." Memories from the past and "the chill of those misty winter days again crept into my heart." She remembered "the childish awe that filled my soul as I noticed the girth and height of the forest trees on either side of the murky, greenish water that swept on past them with a strong current, leaving sandbar after sandbar a gleam of tawny color against their masses of dark green foliage; and I thought of a moment when we saw a little cluster of five log houses and knew that we could see [Fort Vancouver]. Then as I looked toward the magnificent city of today [Portland], with its homes, churches, schools, its parks and business places, I felt that I must be waking from a Rip Van Winkle sleep and the magic of the moment almost overcame me."[329]

There can be no doubt that these changes had been bought at enormous, perhaps unquantifiable, human cost. Emigrant women such as Matilda Sager had been part of it, but they too had paid a price. "Those wer the days that tryed mens soul and bodys too, and womens constitutions," wrote Keturah Belknap, "they worked the mussel on and it was their to stay."[330] One woman described nearly going blind, she looked so hard across the prairie for another human being. In the words of a later homesteader, theirs had been "a life and death struggle with the most primitive enemies of man, namely against hunger and drought and dust storms and grasshoppers and hail and blizzards and cold, and against failure, frustration, loneliness and despondency."*[331]

---

*In 1875, the largest swarm of grasshoppers in recorded human history, comprising an estimated three and a half trillion insects, ravaged the Great Plains. It was 110 miles wide, 1,800 miles long and a quarter to half a mile deep. In one of the most dramatic scenes in *On the Banks of Plum Creek*, Laura Ingalls Wilder describes how it ravaged her family's wheat crop.

Having no political power, and, generally speaking, no public voice, in the past women have always stood obliquely to what are generally thought of as the great moments in history—treaties, war, government and Tribal negotiations—the moments that usually make it into the history books. And yet it is precisely because of this that they are important.

The story of the American West is one of the great epics of all time, a moment in history, I would venture to say, quite unlike any other: more thrilling, more nail-biting, more heartbreaking than any movie or any children's tale could ever be. If no neat conclusions are possible, it is because the repercussions are still being felt. The questions it raises have never been more relevant than they are today. Who owns the land? Who gets to say who can come here and who cannot? And, perhaps most importantly, how do we best look after this extraordinary inheritance—this "dream landscape, full of sacred realities"—for the benefit of all?

Taken on their own, each of the stories contained in this book is fragmentary, isolated, partial; and yet at the same time, each is a tiny, jewel-like drop of human experience, a prism through which the light of history shines, refracts, and is reconfigured. Even taken together as a whole, they can never tell the full story—perhaps nothing can—but they can illuminate it in powerful ways. Even when they are in direct opposition to one another, each possesses a piece of the truth, and helps us to tell more complex stories about ourselves.

ACKNOWLEDGMENTS

It is fashionable in the literary world to complain that no one edits books anymore, but happily this is not the case with either of my publishers, Virago in London and Spiegel & Grau in New York, both of whom have been painstaking in overseeing every step of the process of publishing *Brave Hearted*.

At Virago, my particular and heartfelt thanks go as always to my editor, Lennie Goodings, who commissioned this book six years ago now; also, to Susan de Soissons in publicity, to Linda Silverman who sourced the illustrations, to Ellen Rockell for the cover design, and most especially to Nithya Rae for meticulously overseeing all the many moving parts that go into producing a book. Daniel Balado was painstaking in his copyediting and has saved me from many errors. Also in the UK, my thanks to Richard Solly and my brother, Andrew Hickman.

In the US I would like to thank Sam Nicholson, Julie Grau, and everyone at Spiegel & Grau for believing so passionately in this book. I am grateful also to Professor Stephen Greenblatt for putting me in touch with Dr. Robert Lee and Dr. Matthew Spellberg, both of whom generously answered questions from a complete stranger. My particular and very warm thanks also to Dr. Andrea McComb Sanchez at the University of Arizona for her careful and sensitive reading of the manuscript. Any errors that remain are, of course, my own.

ACKNOWLEDGMENTS

I began writing *Brave Hearted* in March 2020, at the very beginning of lockdown, and I finished the main draft of it in June 2021, as chance would have it within about a week of the lifting of the last of the British lockdown restrictions. My sole companion during almost all this time was my husband, Matthew Ruscombe-King, who not only listened patiently to every story but who lived with me through all the highs and lows of writing them down, and whose enthusiasm helped make this otherwise extremely demanding process also one of huge satisfaction.

Katie Hickman
November 2021

NOTES

1. Ken Burns, *The West*, episode 1, "The People" (PBS documentary, 1996).
2. Pekka Hämäläinen, *Lakota America: A New History of Indigenous Power* (Yale, 2019).
3. Keturah Belknap, in Cathy Luchetti and Carol Olwell (eds.), *Women of the West* (Utah, 1982).
4. Caroline Fraser, *Prairie Fires: The American Dreams of Laura Ingalls Wilder* (London, 2017).
5. Sarah Raymond Herndon, *Days on the Road: Crossing the Plains in 1865* (New York, 1902).
6. Clifford Merrill Drury, *Marcus Whitman M.D., Pioneer and Martyr* (Idaho, 1937).
7. Ibid.
8. Narcissa Whitman and Eliza Spalding (ed. Clifford Merrill Drury), *Where Wagons Could Go* (Nebraska, 1997).
9. William H. Gray, *A History of Oregon 1792–1849, Drawn from Personal Observation and Authentic Information* (Oregon, 1870).
10. Whitman and Spalding, *Where Wagons Could Go*.
11. Gray, *History of Oregon*.
12. This and all the following quotations from Narcissa Whitman's diaries, unless otherwise stated, are from Whitman and Spalding, *Where Wagons Could Go*.
13. Osborne Russell, *Journal of a Trapper; or Nine Years in the Rocky Mountains, 1834–1843* (New York, 1921).
14. Narcissa Whitman, quoted in Julie Roy Jeffrey, *Converting the West: A Biography of Narcissa Whitman* (Oklahoma, 1991).

15. Eliza Spalding, in Whitman and Spalding, *Where Wagons Could Go.*
16. Gray, *History of Oregon.*
17. Ibid.
18. Jeffrey, *Converting the West.*
19. Quoted in Whitman and Spalding, *Where Wagons Could Go.*
20. Ibid.
21. Narcissa Whitman's diary, September 3, in ibid.
22. Charles Wilkes, *Narrative of the United States' Exploring Expedition*, vol. 4 (Philadelphia, 1845).
23. Ibid.
24. Ibid.
25. This and the following quotations are from Whitman and Spalding, *Where Wagons Could Go.*
26. Narcissa Whitman's diary, November 1, in ibid.
27. Jeffrey, *Converting the West.*
28. Douglas Deur, "An Ethnohistorical Overview of Groups with Ties to Fort Vancouver," Northwest Cultural Resources Institute Report no. 15 (Washington, 2012).
29. Ibid.
30. Ibid.
31. Wilkes, *Narrative of the United States' Exploring Expedition.*
32. Elizabeth (Miller) Wilson, "Oregon Sketches," quoted in John A. Hussey, "The Women of Fort Vancouver," *Oregon Historical Quarterly* 92, no. 3 (Autumn 1991).
33. Quoted in Hussey, "The Women of Fort Vancouver."
34. Reverend Beaver to A. C. Anderson, June 17, 1837, MS 599, vol. 1, folder 1, BCA—from Nancy Marguerite Anderson, online blog, November 4, 2017.
35. Hubert Howe Bancroft, "History of Oregon," quoted in Hussey, "The Women of Fort Vancouver," 338–47.
36. Quoted in Jeffrey, *Converting the West.* See also T. C. Elliott, "Marguerite Wadin McKay McLoughlin," *Oregon Historical Quarterly* 36, no. 4 (December 1935).
37. Verne Bright, "The Folklore and History of the 'Oregon Fever,'" *Oregon Historical Quarterly* 52, no. 4 (December 1951), 241–53.
38. Ibid.
39. Ibid.
40. Ibid.
41. Quoted in ibid.
42. Lillian Schlissel, *Women's Diaries of the Westward Journey* (New York, 1982).
43. Bright, "The Folklore and History of the 'Oregon Fever.'"
44. Quoted in Schlissel, *Women's Diaries of the Westward Journey.*
45. Nancy Kelsey, "Reminiscences of 1841" (exhibit in Northeastern Nevada Museum, Elko, Nevada).
46. Exhibit in National Pioneer Museum, Independence, Missouri.

47. J. Goldsborough Bruff, July 22, 1849, National Pioneer Museum, Independence, Missouri.

48. Tabitha Brown, in Kenneth L. Holmes (ed.), *Covered Wagon Women: Diaries and Letters from the Western Trails, 1840–1849*, vol. 1 (Nebraska, 1995).

49. Catherine Haun, "A Woman's Trip Across the Plains in 1849," in Schlissel, *Women's Diaries of the Westward Journey*.

50. Elizabeth Dixon Smith, in Holmes, *Covered Wagon Women*, vol. 1.

51. Fred Lockley (ed.), "The Recollections of Benjamin Franklin Bonney," *Quarterly of the Oregon Historical Society* 24, no. 1 (March 1935), 36–55.

52. Sarah Damron Owens, "Pioneer Women of Clatsop County," in Bethenia Owens-Adair, *Some of Her Life Experiences* (Portland, 1914).

53. Dixon Smith, in Holmes, *Covered Wagon Women*, vol. 1.

54. Francis Parkman, *The California and Oregon Trail; being Sketches of Prairie and Rocky Mountain Life* (New York, 1849).

55. Lansford Warren Hastings, *The Emigrants' Guide to Oregon and California* (Cincinnati, 1845).

56. This and all the following quotations are from Keturah Belknap, in Luchetti and Olwell, *Women of the West*.

57. Sallie Hester, 1849, in Holmes, *Covered Wagon Women*, vol. 1.

58. "Circular to California Emigrants," in the *Daily Missouri Republican*, March 27, 1850, quoted in Shirley Ann Wilson Moore, *Sweet Freedom's Plains: African Americans on the Overland Trails 1841–1869* (Oklahoma, 2016).

59. Wilson Moore, *Sweet Freedom's Plains*.

60. Parkman, *The California and Oregon Trail*.

61. Wilson Moore, *Sweet Freedom's Plains*.

62. Charlie Richardson, in *Slave Narratives: A Folk History of Slavery in the United States from Interviews with Former Slaves, 1936–1938*, vol. 10, "Missouri Narratives" (Washington, 1941).

63. William Lewis Manly, quoted in Wilson Moore, *Sweet Freedom's Plains*.

64. Wilson Moore, *Sweet Freedom's Plains*.

65. Keturah Belknap, in Luchetti and Olwell, *Women of the West*.

66. Herndon, *Days on the Road*.

67. Catherine Sager in Catherine, Elizabeth, and Matilda Sager (ed. and annotated by Harry M. Majors), *The Whitman Massacre of 1847 (with additional accounts by Sager family of their journey west on the Oregon Trail in 1844)* (Washington, 1981).

68. Lockley, "The Recollections of Benjamin Franklin Bonney."

69. Quoted in Kenneth Holmes (ed.), *Best of Covered Wagon Women* (Oklahoma, 2008).

70. Ibid.

71. This and all the following quotations are from Mary Richardson Walker, in Luchetti and Olwell, *Women of the West*.

72. Ibid.

73. Keturah Belknap, in Luchetti and Olwell, *Women of the West*.
74. Quoted in Schlissel, *Women's Diaries of the Westward Journey*.
75. Catherine, Elizabeth, and Matilda Sager, *The Whitman Massacre of 1847*.
76. Ibid.
77. Whitman and Spalding, *Where Wagons Could Go*.
78. Hämäläinen, *Lakota America*.
79. Quoted in Whitman and Spalding, *Where Wagons Could Go*.
80. Narcissa Whitman, letter of October 6, 1841, in ibid.
81. Narcissa Whitman, April 19, 1846, quoted in Drury, *Marcus Whitman M.D.*
82. Mary Richardson Walker, December 4, 1838, in Luchetti and Olwell, *Women of the West*.
83. Mary Richardson Walker, in ibid.
84. Narcissa Whitman, May 2, 1840, quoted in Whitman and Spalding, *Where Wagons Could Go*.
85. Marcus Whitman, letter of May 16, 1844, quoted in Drury, *Marcus Whitman M.D.*
86. Marcus Whitman, letter of May 21, 1844, quoted in ibid.
87. Marcus Whitman, letter of April 6, 1844, quoted in ibid.
88. Sarah J. Cummins, "Autobiography and Reminiscences," quoted in Drury, *Marcus Whitman M.D.*, 362.
89. Thomas McClintock, "James Saules, Peter Burnett and the Oregon Black Exclusion Law of 1844," *Pacific Northwest Quarterly* 86, no. 3 (Summer 1995), 121–30.
90. Ibid.
91. Fred Lockley, "Some Documentary Records of Slavery in Oregon," *Quarterly of the Oregon Historical Society* 17, no. 2 (June 1916), 107–15.
92. Keturah Belknap, in Luchetti and Olwell, *Women of the West*.
93. Quoted in Drury, *Marcus Whitman M.D.*
94. Catherine Sager, in Catherine, Elizabeth, and Matilda Sager, *The Whitman Massacre of 1847*.
95. Ibid.
96. Matilda Sager, in ibid.
97. H. K. W. Perkins, quoted in Drury, *Marcus Whitman M.D.*
98. Appendix XII in Helen Hunt Jackson, *A Century of Dishonor: A Sketch of the United States Government's Dealings with Some of the North American Tribes* (London, 1881). She is quoting an anonymously written article by "a well-known army officer" that originally appeared in the *Army and Navy Journal*, November 1, 1879.
99. Hastings, *The Emigrants' Guide to Oregon and California*.
100. Ibid.
101. This and all the following quotations are from Sarah Winnemucca (ed. Mrs. Horace Mann), *Life Among the Piutes: Their Wrongs and Claims* (Boston, 1833).
102. Ibid.
103. Ibid.
104. Ibid.

105. Virginia Reed Murphy, *Across the Plains in the Donner Party: A Personal Narrative of the Overland Trip to California* (Connecticut, 1996).

106. John D. Unruh Jr., *The Plains Across: The Overland Emigrants and the Trans-Mississippi West, 1840–1860* (London, 1979).

107. Tamsen E. Donner, letter of June 16, 1846, in Holmes, *Covered Wagon Women*, vol. 1.

108. Reed Murphy, *Across the Plains in the Donner Party*.

109. Parkman, *The California and Oregon Trail*.

110. Keturah Belknap, in Luchetti and Olwell, *Women of the West*.

111. Lucy Ann Henderson Deady, 1846 (National Pioneer Museum, Independence, Missouri).

112. Lockley, "The Recollections of Benjamin Franklin Bonney."

113. Tabitha Brown, letter of August 1854, in Holmes, *Covered Wagon Women*.

114. Ethan Rarick, *Desperate Passage: The Donner Party's Perilous Journey West* (Oxford, 2008).

115. Ibid.

116. James Reed, letter of July 31, 1856, in Karen Zienert (ed.), *Across the Plains in the Donner Party, by Virginia Reed Murphy, with Letters by James Reed* (Connecticut, 1996).

117. Reed Murphy, *Across the Plains in the Donner Party*.

118. Rarick, *Desperate Passage*.

119. Ibid.

120. Virginia Reed, letter of May 16, 1847, reprinted in Holmes, *Covered Wagon Women*, vol. 1.

121. Reed Murphy, *Across the Plains in the Donner Party*.

122. Schlissel, *Women's Diaries of the Westward Journey*.

123. Burns, *The West*, episode 3, "The Speck of the Future" (PBS documentary, 1996).

124. *New York Tribune* correspondent, July 1852, quoted in Dee Brown, *The Gentle Tamers: Women of the Old Wild West* (New York, 1958).

125. Margaret A. Frink, "Adventures of a Party of Gold-Seekers," in Kenneth L. Holmes (ed.), *Covered Wagon Women: Diaries and Letters from the Western Trails, 1850*, vol. 2 (California, 1983).

126. This and all the following quotations are from Catherine Haun, "A Woman's Trip Across the Plains in 1849," in Schlissel, *Women's Diaries of the Westward Journey*.

127. Sallie Hester, "The Diary of a Pioneer Girl," in Holmes, *Covered Wagon Women*, vol. 1.

128. Herndon, *Days on the Road*.

129. Hester, "The Diary of a Pioneer Girl."

130. Diary of Mrs. Byron J. Pengra, quoted in Luchetti and Olwell, *Women of the West*.

131. Lavinia Honeyman Porter, *By Ox Team to California: A Narrative of the Crossing of the Plains in 1860* (California, 1910).

132. Luchetti and Olwell, *Women of the West*.

133. Helen Wiser Stewart, quoted in ibid.

NOTES

134. Mrs. Francis Sawyer, quoted in Schlissel, *Women's Diaries of the Westward Journey*.
135. Caroline Richardson, in ibid.
136. Cecelia McMillen Adams, in ibid.
137. Hämäläinen, *Lakota America*.
138. Josephine Waggoner, *Witness: A Hunkpapa Historian's Strong-Heart Song of the Lakotas* (Nebraska, 2013).
139. Susan Bordeaux Bettelyoun and Josephine Waggoner (ed. Emily Levine), *With My Own Eyes: A Lakota Woman Tells Her People's History* (Nebraska, 1988).
140. Ibid.
141. Herbert Asbury, *The Barbary Coast: An Informal History of the San Francisco Underworld* (New York, 2008).
142. Ibid.
143. Ibid.
144. Ibid.
145. Ibid.
146. Ibid.
147. Rodman Wilson Paul, "In Search of Dame Shirley," *Pacific Historical Review*. 3, no. 2 (May 1964).
148. Ibid.
149. Mrs. Lawrence, "Appreciation," quoted in ibid.
150. This and all the following quotations are from Louise A. K. Clappe (with introduction and notes by Carl I. Wheat), *The Shirley Letters from the California Mines 1851–1852* (New York, 1949).
151. Ibid.
152. Letter Tenth, November 25, 1851, in ibid.
153. Letter Seventh: A Trip to the Mines. From Our Log Cabin, Indian Bar, October 7, 1851, in ibid.
154. Letter Tenth, November 25, 1851, in ibid.
155. Ibid.
156. Letter Eighth: A Trip into the Mines. Indian Bar, October 20, 1851, in ibid.
157. Letter Tenth, November 25, 1851, in ibid.
158. Letter Twenty-Fourth, October 16, 1852, in ibid.
159. Luzena Stanley Wilson, *Luzena Stanley Wilson, Forty-Niner: Memories Recalled for Her Daughter, Correnah Wilson Wright* (California, 1937).
160. Frink, "Adventures of a Party of Gold Seekers," quoted in Quintard Taylor, *In Search of the Racial Frontier: African Americans in the American West, 1528–1990* (New York, 1998).
161. Letter Sixteenth, May 1, 1852, in Clappe, *The Shirley Letters*.
162. Letter Tenth, in ibid.
163. Letter Sixteenth, May 1, 1852, in ibid.
164. Gae Whitney Canfield, *Sarah Winnemucca of the Northern Piutes* (Oklahoma, 1983).
165. Winnemucca, *Life Among the Piutes*.

166. Ibid.
167. Benjamin Madley, *An American Genocide: The United States and the California Indian Catastrophe, 1846–1873* (Yale, 2016).
168. Ibid.
169. Ibid.
170. Ibid.
171. Theodore Johnson, *Sights in the Gold Region, and Scenes by the Way* (New York, 1850), quoted in Madley, *An American Genocide.*
172. Ibid.
173. Ibid.
174. Ibid.
175. Madley, *An American Genocide.*
176. Jill Cowan, "'It's Called Genocide': Newsom Apologizes to the State's Native Americans," *New York Times,* June 19, 2019.
177. Gladys Ayer Nomland, "Sinkyone Notes," *University of California Publications in American Archaeology and Ethnology* 36, no. 2 (December 31, 1935).
178. Ibid.
179. Bordeaux Bettelyoun and Waggoner, *With My Own Eyes.*
180. Ibid.
181. Ibid.
182. Hämäläinen, *Lakota America.*
183. Thomas Fitzpatrick, or "Broken Hand," quoted in ibid.
184. Jeanne Oyawin Eder, *A Dakota View of the Great Sioux War, with Stories Collected by Michael Her Many Horses,* quoted in ibid.
185. William Vaux, quoted in Emily Levine's notes to Bordeaux Bettelyoun and Waggoner, *With My Own Eyes.*
186. Waggoner, *Witness.*
187. General W. S. Harney, quoted in Hämäläinen, *Lakota America.*
188. Bordeaux Bettelyoun and Waggoner, *With My Own Eyes.*
189. Ibid.
190. This and all the following quotations are from the journal of Priscilla Merriman Evans, quoted in Luchetti and Olwell, *Women of the West.*
191. *Nauvoo Expositor,* June 7, 1844.
192. Mary Ann Hafen, *Recollections of a Handcart Pioneer of 1860: A Woman's Life on the Mormon Frontier* (Nebraska, 1983).
193. Miriam Davis Colt, *Went to Kansas; being a thrilling account of an ill-fated expedition to that fairy land, and its sad results* (Watertown, 1862).
194. Frances W. Kaye, "Little Squatter on the Osage Diminished Reserve: Laura Ingalls Wilder's Kansas Indians," *Great Plains Quarterly* (University of Nebraska Press) 20, no. 2 (Spring 2000), 123–40.
195. Davis Colt, *Went to Kansas.*
196. Ibid.

197. Kathryn Zabelle Derounian-Stodola and James Arthur Levernier, *The Indian Captivity Narrative 1550–1900* (New York, 1993).
198. Ibid.
199. Ibid.
200. Ibid.
201. "Arrival of Miss Oatman," *Los Angeles Star*, April 12, 1856.
202. A. L. Kroeber and Clifton B. Kroeber, "Olive Oatman's First Account of Her Captivity Among the Mohave," *California Historical Society Quarterly* 41 (December 1962), 309–17.
203. "Five Years Among the Indians: Story of Olive Oatman," *Daily Evening Bulletin* (San Francisco), June 24, 1856, quoted in Margot Mifflin, *The Blue Tattoo: The Life of Olive Oatman* (Nebraska, 2009).
204. *Los Angeles Star*, quoted in Mifflin, *The Blue Tattoo*.
205. A. L. Kroeber, "Olive Oatman's Return," Kroeber Anthropological Society Papers, 4 (Berkeley, 1951), 1–18.
206. Ibid.
207. "Notice," *Times and Seasons* (Nauvoo, Illinois), December 1, 1842.
208. Mifflin, *The Blue Tattoo*.
209. Quoted in ibid.
210. Ibid.
211. Royal B. Stratton, *Life Among the Indians or: The Captivity of the Oatman Girls among the Apache and Mohave Indians* (San Francisco, 1935).
212. Ibid.
213. Ibid.
214. Ibid.
215. Mifflin, *The Blue Tattoo*. She is quoting from Baldwin Mollhausen, *Diary of a Journey from the Mississippi to the Coasts of the Pacific with a United States Government Expedition* (London, 1858).
216. Kroeber and Kroeber, "Olive Oatman's First Account of Her Captivity Among the Mohave."
217. Ibid.
218. Quoted in Mifflin, *The Blue Tattoo*.
219. Ibid.; 2007 interview with the director of the Colorado River Indian Tribes Museum and Mohave scholar Michael Tsosie.
220. Ibid.
221. Anonymous diary quoted in J. F. Elliott, "The Great Western: Sarah Bowman, Mother and Mistress to the U.S. Army," *Journal of Arizona History* 30, no. 1 (Spring 1989), 1–26.
222. Elliott, "The Great Western." He is quoting from James B. O'Neil, *They Die But Once—the Story of a Tejano* (New York, 1935).
223. Elliott, "The Great Western."
224. Ibid. He is quoting from Samuel E. Chamberlain, *My Confession* (New York, 1956).

225. Frances Anne "Fannie" Boyd (Mrs. Orsemus Bronson Boyd), *Cavalry Life in Tent and Field* (New York, 1894).

226. Mifflin, *The Blue Tattoo*.

227. Ibid.

228. Elliott, "The Great Western," quoting O'Neill.

229. Ibid., quoting from the manuscript copy of Samuel Warner's "Memoir."

230. Sarah L. Larmier, *Capture and Escape: or, Life Among the Sioux* (Philadelphia, 1870).

231. Ibid.

232. Elizabeth Custer, *Following the Guidon* (Nebraska, 1994).

233. Burns, *The West*, episode 5, "The Grandest Enterprise Under God" (PBS documentary, 1996).

234. Cheyenne Railway Museum.

235. Larmier, *Capture and Escape*.

236. Anne M. Butler, *Daughters of Joy, Sisters of Misery: Prostitutes in the American West 1865–1890* (Chicago, 1985).

237. Ibid.

238. Hämäläinen, *Lakota America*.

239. Ibid.

240. Ibid.

241. George W. Kingsbury, *History of Dakota Territory*, 5 vols. (Chicago, 1915).

242. Bordeaux Bettelyoun and Waggoner, *With My Own Eyes*.

243. Hämäläinen, *Lakota America*.

244. Ibid.

245. Waggoner, *Witness*.

246. Ibid.

247. Commissioner G. P. Beauvais, quoted in Hämäläinen.

248. Hämäläinen, *Lakota America*.

249. Ibid.

250. Butler, *Daughters of Joy, Sisters of Misery*.

251. This and all the following quotations are from Boyd, *Cavalry Life in Tent and Field*.

252. Ibid.

253. Theodore Davis, "A Stage Ride to Colorado," *Harper's New Monthly Magazine* (July 1867).

254. Dick Kreck, *Hell on Wheels: Wicked Towns along the Union Pacific Railroad* (Colorado, 2013).

255. Ibid.

256. Boyd, *Cavalry Life in Tent and Field*.

257. Dan De Quille, *A History of the Comstock Silver Lode and Mines* (Virginia, 1889).

258. Custer, *Following the Guidon*.

259. Ibid.

260. Boyd, *Cavalry Life in Tent and Field*.

261. Jennifer L. Lawrence, *Soap Suds Row: The Bold Lives of Army Laundresses 1802–1876* (Wyoming, 2016).

262. Ibid.

263. Butler, *Daughters of Joy, Sisters of Misery*.

264. This and all the following quotations are from Elizabeth Custer, *Boots and Saddles; or, Life in Dakota with General Custer* (Michigan, 1975).

265. Lawrence, *Soap Suds Row*.

266. Custer, *Boots and Saddles*.

267. Butler, *Daughters of Joy, Sisters of Misery*.

268. Burns, *The West*, episode 6, "Fight No More Forever Forever" (PBS documentary, 1996).

269. Butler, *Daughters of Joy, Sisters of Misery*.

270. Boyd, *Cavalry Life in Tent and Field*.

271. Custer, *Following the Guidon*.

272. Butler, *Daughters of Joy, Sisters of Misery*.

273. Ibid.

274. Hämäläinen, *Lakota America*.

275. Ibid.

276. Bordeaux Bettelyoun and Waggoner, *With My Own Eyes*.

277. Mari Sandoz, *Cheyenne Autumn* (New York, 1953).

278. Custer, *Following the Guidon*.

279. Ibid.

280. Shirley A. Leckie, *Elizabeth Bacon Custer and the Making of a Myth* (Oklahoma, 1993).

280. Ibid.

282. Sandoz, *Cheyenne Autumn*.

283. Ibid.

284. Peter Brown, letter of 1852, quoted in Taylor, *In Search of the Racial Frontier*.

285. Dolores Hayden, "Biddy Mason's Los Angeles 1856–1891," *California History* 68, no. 3 (Fall 1989), 86–99.

286. Taylor, *In Search of the Racial Frontier*.

287. *Alta California*, April 20, 1853, quoted in Hayden, "Biddy Mason's Los Angeles."

288. Hayden, "Biddy Mason's Los Angeles."

289. Ibid.

290. "Suit For Freedom," *Los Angeles Star*, February 2, 1856, quoted in Hayden, "Biddy Mason's Los Angeles."

291. Ibid.

292. "(1856) Mason v. Smith (The Bridget "Biddy" Mason Case)," State of California, County of Los Angeles, BlackPast, January 24, 2007, https://www.blackpast.org/african-american-history/mason-v-smith-bridget-biddy-mason-case-1856/.

293. Ibid.

294. Hayden, "Biddy Mason's Los Angeles."

295. Ibid.
296. "Suit for Freedom," *Los Angeles Star.*
297. "(1856) Mason v. Smith."
298. Charles Frederick Holder, "Chinese Slavery in America," *North American Review* 165, no. 490 (September 1897), 288–94.
299. Benson Tong, *Unsubmissive Women: Chinese Prostitutes in Nineteenth-Century San Francisco* (Oklahoma, 1994).
300. Ibid.
301. Holder, "Chinese Slavery in America."
302. Ibid.
303. *Daily Morning Chronicle,* March 15, 1868, quoted in Tong, *Unsubmissive Women.*
304. *An Agreement Paper by the Person Mee Yung,* Congressional Record, 43rd Congress, 2nd Session, March 1875, quoted in Tong, *Unsubmissive Women.*
305. This and all the following quotations are from Mrs. Frank Leslie, *California: A Pleasure Trip from Gotham to the Golden Gate* (New York, 1877).
306. Leslie, *California.*
307. *Biographical Dictionary of Chinese Women: The Qing Period 1644–1911* (New York and London, 1998).
308. Ibid.
309. Tong, *Unsubmissive Women.*
310. Ruthanne Lum McCunn, "Reclaiming Polly Bemis: China's Daughter, Idaho's Legendary Pioneer," *Frontier: A Journal of Women's Studies* (University of Nebraska Press) 24, no. 1 (2003), 76–100. She is quoting from Countess Gizycha's *Diary on the Salmon River, Part II* (1922).
311. McCunn, "Reclaiming Polly Bemis."
312. Ibid. This information was provided by Huang Youfu, from Beijing University's Research Department of Northeastern and Inner Mongolian Nationalities.
313. Mrs. E. V. Robbins, quoted in Tong, *Unsubmissive Women.*
314. Congressional Globe, 42nd Congress, 3rd Session, March 3, 1873, quoted in Hämäläinen, *Lakota America.*
315. Waggoner, *Witness.*
316. Ibid.
317. Old Lady Horse, in Alice Marriott and Carol K. Rachlin (eds.), *American Indian Mythologies* (New York, 1968).
318. Custer, *Boots and Saddles.*
319. Ibid.
320. Richard Irving Dodge, quoted in Burns, *The West,* episode 5, "The Grandest Enterprise Under God" (PBS documentary, 1996).
321. Old Lady Horse, as told to Alice Marriott, in Marriott and Rachlin, *American Indian Mythologies.*
322. Sandoz, *Cheyenne Autumn.*
323. This and all the following quotations are from Waggoner, *Witness.*

324. Hämäläinen, *Lakota America.*

325. Waggoner, *Witness.*

326. Madley, *An American Genocide.*

327. Fraser, *Prairie Fires.*

328. Catherine, Elizabeth, and Matilda Sager, *The Whitman Massacre of 1847.*

329. Ibid.

330. Keturah Belknap, in Luchetti and Olwell, *Women of the West.*

331. Dr. Bessie Rehwinkel, in Marcia Meredith Hensley, *Staking Her Claim: Women Homesteading in the West* (Wyoming, 2008).

SELECT BIBLIOGRAPHY

PUBLISHED SOURCES

Anderson, Gary Clayton, and Alan R. Woolworth, eds. *Through Dakota Eyes: Narrative Accounts of the Minnesota Indian War of 1862*. Saint Paul, 1988.

Anderson, William Marshall, *see* Morgan.

Asbury, Herbert. *The Barbary Coast: An Informal History of the San Francisco Underworld*. New York, 2008.

Bagley, Will, ed. *Across the Plains, Mountains, and Deserts: A Bibliography of the Oregon and California Trails*. Salt Lake City, 2015.

Bancroft, Hubert Howe. *History of Oregon*. Vol. 2, 1848–1888. San Francisco, 1888.

Belknap, Keturah, *see* Luchetti and Olwell.

Bettelyoun, Susan Bordeaux, and Josephine Waggoner. *With My Own Eyes: A Lakota Woman Tells Her People's History*. Edited by Emily Levine. Nebraska, 1988.

Biographical Dictionary of Chinese Women: The Qing Period 1644–1911. New York and London, 1998.

Bordeaux, Susan, *see* Bettelyoun.

Boyd, Frances Anne "Fannie." *Cavalry Life in Tent and Field*. New York, 1894.

Brown, Dee. *Bury My Heart at Wounded Knee: An Indian History of the American West*. London, 1971.

Brown, Dee, *The Gentle Tamers: Women of the Old Wild West*. New York, 1958.

Brown, Tabitha, *see* Holmes.

Butler, Anne M. *Daughters of Joy, Sisters of Misery: Prostitutes in the American West 1865–1890*. Chicago, 1985.

Canfield, Gae Whitney. *Sarah Winnemucca of the Northern Paiutes*. Oklahoma, 1983.

Chardon, Francis A. *Chardon's Journal at Fort Clark 1834–1839: descriptive life on the Upper Missouri of a fur trader's experiences among the Mandans, Gros Ventres, and their neighbors, of the ravages of the small-pox of 1837*. Edited by Annie Heloise Abel. Nebraska, 1997.

Clappe, Louise A. K. *The Shirley Letters from the California Mines, 1851–1852*. New York, 1949.

Colt, Miriam Davis. *Went to Kansas; being a thrilling account of an ill-fated expedition to that fairy land, and its sad results; together with a sketch of the life of the author etc.* Watertown, 1862.

Cox, Anna-Lisa. *The Bone and Sinew of the Land: America's Forgotten Black Pioneers and the Struggle for Equality*. New York, 2018.

Custer, Elizabeth. *Boots and Saddles; or, Life in Dakota with General Custer*. Michigan, 1975.

Custer, Elizabeth. *Following the Guidon*. Nebraska, 1994.

Custer, Elizabeth. *Tenting on the Plains; or, General Custer in Kansas and Texas*. London, 1888.

De Quille, Dan. *A History of the Comstock Silver Lode and Mines*. Virginia, 1889.

Derounian-Stodola, Kathryn Zabelle, and James Arthur Levernier. *The Indian Captivity Narrative 1500–1900*. New York, 1993.

Drury, Clifford Merrill. *Marcus Whitman M.D., Pioneer and Martyr*. Idaho, 1937.

Evans, Priscilla Merriman, *see* Luchetti and Olwell.

Ferris, Warren Angus. *Life in the Rocky Mountains: A Diary of Wanderings on the Sources of the Rivers Missouri, Columbia and Colorado, 1830–1835*. Edited by LeRoy R. Hafen. Denver, 1983.

Fraser, Caroline. *Prairie Fires: The American Dreams of Laura Ingalls Wilder*. London, 2017.

Frink, Margaret, *see* Holmes.

Glasond, Bruce A., and Michael N. Searles, eds. *Black Cowboys in the American West: On the Range, On the Stage, Behind the Badge*. Oklahoma, 2016.

Gray, William H. *A History of Oregon 1792–1849, Drawn from Personal Observation and Authentic Information*. Oregon, 1870.

Greene, Candace S., and Russell Thornton, eds. *The Year the Stars Fell: Lakota Winter Counts at the Smithsonian*. Washington, 2007.

Hafen, LeRoy R., ed. *Mountain Men and Fur Traders of the Far West*. Nebraska, 1965.

Hafen, Mary Ann. *Recollections of a Handcart Pioneer of 1860: A Woman's Life on the Mormon Frontier*. Nebraska, 1983.

Hämäläinen, Pekka. *The Comanche Empire*. Yale, 2008.

Hämäläinen, Pekka. *Lakota America: A New History of Indigenous Power*. Yale, 2019.

Hastings, Lansford Warren. *The Emigrants' Guide to Oregon and California*. Cincinnati, 1845.

Haun, Catherine, *see* Schlissel.

Hayden, Dolores. *Seven American Utopias: the architecture of communitarian socialism, 1790-1975*. London, 1976.

Hensley, Marcia Meredith. *Staking Her Claim: Women Homesteading in the West*. Wyoming, 2008.

Herndon, Sarah Raymond. *Days on the Road: Crossing the Plains in 1865*. New York, 1902.

Hester, Sallie, *see* Holmes.

Hill, Pamela Smith, ed. *Laura Ingalls Wilder. Pioneer Girl: The Annotated Autobiography*. South Dakota, 2014.

Holmes, Kenneth L. *Covered Wagon Women: Diaries and Letters from the Western Trails 1840–1849*. Vols 1–11. Nebraska, 1995.

Jackson, Helen Hunt. *A Century of Dishonor: A Sketch of the United States Government's Dealings with Some of the North American Tribes*. London, 1881.

Jeffrey, Julie Roy. *Converting the West: A Biography of Narcissa Whitman*. Oklahoma, 1991.

Jeffrey, Julie Roy. *Frontier Women: The Trans-Mississippi West 1840–1860*. New York, 1979.

Jensen, Richard E., ed. *Voices of the American West*. Vol. 1, *The Indian Interviews of Eli S. Ricker 1903–1919*. Nebraska, 2005.

Jensen, Richard E., ed. *Voices of the American West*. Vol. 2, *The Settler and Soldier Interviews of Eli S. Ricker 1903–1919*. Nebraska, 2005.

Katz, William Loren. *The Black West: A Documentary and Pictorial History of the African American Role in the Westward Expansion of the United States*. New York, 1987.

Katz, William Loren. *Black Women of the Old West*. London, 1995.

Kelly, Fanny. *Narrative of My Captivity Among the Sioux, with a brief account of General Sully's Indian Expedition in 1864, bearing upon events occurring in my captivity*. Connecticut, 1873.

Kingsbury, George W. *History of Dakota Territory*. 5 vols. Chicago, 1915.

Kreck, Dick. *Hell on Wheels: Wicked Towns along the Union Pacific Railroad*. Colorado, 2013.

Larimer, Sarah L. *Capture and Escape: or, Life Among the Sioux*. Philadelphia, 1870.

Lawrence, Jennifer L. *Soap Suds Row: The Bold Lives of Army Laundresses 1802–1876*. Wyoming, 2016.

Leckie, Shirley A., *Elizabeth Custer and the Making of a Myth*. Oklahoma, 1993.

Leslie, Mrs. Frank. *California: A Pleasure Trip from Gotham to the Golden Gate*. New York, 1877.

Lockley, Fred. *Oregon Trail Blazers*. New York, 1929.

Luchetti, Cathy. *"I Do!": Courtship, Love and Marriage on the American Frontier. A Glimpse at America's Romantic Past Through Photographs, Diaries, and Journals 1715–1915*. New York, 1996.

Luchetti, Cathy, and Carol Olwell, eds. *Women of the West*. Utah, 1982.

Madley, Benjamin. *An American Genocide: The United States and the California Indian Catastrophe 1846–1873*. Yale, 2016.

Magoffin, Susan Shelby. *Down the Santa Fé Trail and Into Mexico: The Diary of Susan Shelby Magoffin 1846–1847.* Yale, 1926.

Marriott, Alice, and Carol K. Rachlin, eds. *American Indian Mythologies.* New York, 1968.

Mattes, Merrill J., *Platte River Road Narratives.* Illinois, 1988.

Mifflin, Margot. *The Blue Tattoo: The Life of Olive Oatman.* Nebraska, 2009.

Moody, Ralph. *The Old Trails West.* New York, 1963.

Moore, Shirley Ann Wilson. *Sweet Freedom's Plains: African Americans on the Overland Trails 1841–1869.* Oklahoma, 2016.

Morgan, Dale L., and Eleanor T. Harris, eds. *The Rocky Mountain Journals of William Marshall Anderson.* California, 1967.

Murphy, Virginia Reed. *Across the Plains in the Donner Party: A Personal Narrative of the Overland Trip to California.* Connecticut, 1996.

Oatman, Olive, and Lorenzo D. Oatman. *The Captivity of the Oatman Girls among the Apache and Mohave Indians.* New York, 1935.

Owens, Sarah Damron, *see* Owens-Adair.

Owens-Adair, Bethenia. *Some of Her Life Experiences.* Portland, 1914.

Parkman, Francis. *The California and Oregon Trail; being Sketches of Prairie and Rocky Mountain Life.* New York, 1849.

Plummer, Rachel. *Narrative of 21 Months Servitude as a Prisoner Among the Comanche Indians 1838.* USA, 1839.

Porter, Lavinia Honeyman. *By Ox Team to California: A Narrative of the Crossing of the Plains in 1860.* California, 1910.

Rarick, Ethan. *Desperate Passage: The Donner Party's Perilous Journey West.* Oxford, 2008.

Ravage, John W. *Black Pioneers: Images of the Black Experience on the North American Frontier.* Salt Lake City, 1997.

Reed, Virginia, *see* Murphy.

Ricker, Eli, *see* Jensen.

Riley, Glenda. *Women and Indians on the Frontier: 1825–1915.* Albuquerque, 1984.

Ross, Marvin C. *The West of Alfred Jacob Miller.* Oklahoma, 1968.

Russell, Osborne. *Journal of a Trapper; or, Nine Years in the Rocky Mountains, 1834–1843.* New York, 1921.

Sager, Catherine, Elizabeth, and Matilda. *The Whitman Massacre of 1847 (with additional accounts by Sager family of their journey west on the Oregon Trail in 1844).* Edited and annotated by Harry M. Majors. Washington, 1981.

Sandoz, Mari. *Cheyenne Autumn.* New York, 1953.

Sandoz, Mari. *Crazy Horse: Strong Man of the Oglalas.* Nebraska, 1942.

Schlissel, Lillian. *Women's Diaries of the Westward Journey.* New York, 1982.

Senier, Siobhan. *Voices of American Indian Assimilation and Resistance.* Oklahoma, 2001.

Slave Narratives: A Folk History of Slavery in the United States from Interviews with Former Slaves, 1936–1938. Vol. 10. Washington, 1941.

Smith, Elizabeth Dixon, *see* Holmes.

Spalding, Eliza, *see* Warren.

Stratton, Royal B. *Life Among the Indians or: The Captivity of the Oatman Girls among the Apache and Mohave Indians.* San Francisco, 1935.

Taylor, Quintard. *In Search of the Racial Frontier: African Americans in the American West 1528–1990.* New York, 1998.

Taylor, Quintard, and Shirley Ann Wilson Moore, eds. *African American Women Confront the West 1600–2000.* Oklahoma, 2003.

Tong, Benson. *Unsubmissive Women: Chinese Prostitutes in Nineteenth-Century San Francisco.* Oklahoma, 1994.

Unruh, John D., Jr. *The Plains Across: The Overland Emigrants and the Trans-Mississippi West, 1840–1860.* London, 1979.

Waggoner, Josephine. *Witness: A Hunkpapa Historian's Strong-Heart Song of the Lakotas.* Nebraska, 2013.

Walker, Mary Richardson, *see* Luchetti and Olwell.

Wheelwright, Julie. *Amazons and Military Maids: Women who Dressed as Men in Pursuit of Life and Liberty.* London, 1989.

White, Mrs. N. D. *Captivity Among the Sioux, August 18th–September 26th, 1862.* Minnesota, 1901.

Whitman, Narcissa, and Spalding, Eliza. *Where Wagons Could Go.* Edited by Clifford Merrill Drury. Nebraska, 1997.

Wilder, Laura Ingalls, *see* Hill.

Wilkes, Charles. *Narrative of the United States' Exploring Expedition. During the Years 1838, 1839, 1840, 1841, 1842.* Philadelphia, 1845.

Wilson, Luzena Stanley. *Luzena Stanley Wilson, Forty-Niner: Memories Recalled for Her Daughter, Correnah Wilson Wright.* California, 1937.

Winnemucca, Sarah. *Life Among the Piutes: Their Wrongs and Claims.* Edited by Mrs. Horace Mann. Boston, 1883.

Zeinert, Karen, ed. *Across the Plains in the Donner Party, by Virginia Reed Murphy, with Letters by James Reed.* Connecticut, 1996.

PERIODICALS AND JOURNALS

Bright, Verne. "The Folklore and History of the 'Oregon Fever.'" *Oregon Historical Quarterly* 52, no. 4 (December 1951).

Castaneda, Antonia. "Women of Color and the Rewriting of Western History: The Discourse, Politics and Decolonization of History." *Pacific Historical Review* 61, no. 4, Western Women's History Revisited (November 1992), 501–33.

Davis, Theodore. "A Stage Ride to Colorado." *Harper's New Monthly Magazine* (July 1867).

De Graaf, Lawrence B. "Race, Sex, and Region: Black Women in the American West 1850–1920." *Pacific Historical Review* 49, no. 2 (May 1980), 285–313.

Deur, Douglas. "An Ethnohistorical Overview of Groups with Ties to Fort Vancouver." Northwest Cultural Resources Institute Report No. 15 (Washington, 2012).

Deur, Douglas. "'She is Particularly Useful to Her Husband': Strategic Marriages Between Hudson's Bay Employees and Native Women at Fort Vancouver." Northwest Cultural Resources Institute Report No. 15 (Washington, 2012).

Elliott, J. F. "The Great Western: Sarah Bowman, Mother and Mistress to the U.S. Army." *Journal of Arizona History* 30, no. 1 (Spring 1989).

Elliott, T. C. "Marguerite Wadin McKay McLoughlin." *Oregon Historical Quarterly* 36, no. 4 (December 1935).

Hayden, Dolores. "Biddy Mason's Los Angeles 1856–1891." *California History* 68, no. 3 (Fall 1989).

Holder, Charles Frederick. "Chinese Slavery in America." *North American Review* 165, no. 490 (September 1897).

Horner, Patricia V. "Mary Richardson Walker: The Shattered Dreams of a Missionary Woman." *Magazine of Western History* 32, no. 3, 19th Century Women on the Frontier (Summer 1982).

Hussey, John A. "The Women of Fort Vancouver." *Oregon Historical Quarterly* 92, no. 3 (Autumn 1991).

Jensen, Joan M., and Darlis A. Miller. "The Gentle Tamers Revisited: New Approaches to the History of Women in the American West." *Pacific Historical Review* 49, no. 2 (May 1980), 173–213.

Jensen, Marlin K. "The Rest of the Story: Latter Day Saints Relations with Utah's Native Americans." *Mormon Historical Studies* (2010).

Kaye, Frances W. "Little Squatter on the Osage Diminished Reserve: Laura Ingalls Wilder's Kansas Indians." *Great Plains Quarterly* 20, no. 2 (Spring 2000).

Kroeber, A. L. "Olive Oatman's Return." Kroeber Anthropological Society Papers, 4 (Berkeley, 1951).

Kroeber, A. L., and Clifton B. Kroeber. "Olive Oatman's First Account of Her Captivity Among the Mohave." *California Historical Society Quarterly* 41 (December 1962).

Lockley, Fred. "The Recollections of Benjamin Franklin Bonney." *Quarterly of the Oregon Historical Society* 24, no. 1 (March 1935).

Lockley, Fred. "Some Documentary Records of Slavery in Oregon." *Quarterly of the Oregon Historical Society* 17, no. 2 (June 1916).

McClintock, Thomas. "James Saules, Peter Burnett and the Oregon Black Exclusion Law of 1844." *Pacific Northwest Quarterly* 86, no. 3 (Summer 1995).

McCunn, Ruthanne Lum. "Reclaiming Polly Bemis: China's Daughter, Idaho's Legendary Pioneer." *Frontier: A Journal of Women's Studies* (University of Nebraska Press) 24, no. 1 (2003).

Murphy, Virginia Reed. "A Personal Narrative of the Overland Trip to California." *Century Magazine* 42 (May–October 1891).

Nash, Gary B. "The Hidden History of Mestizo America." *Journal of American History* 82, no. 3 (December 1995), 941–69.

Nomland, Gladys Ayer. "Sinkyone Notes." *University of California Publications in American Archaeology and Ethnology* 36, no. 2 (December 31, 1935).

Paul, Rodman Wilson. "In Search of Dame Shirley." *Pacific Historical Review* 3, no. 2 (May 1964).

UNPUBLISHED MANUSCRIPT

Narrative of Adventures Through Alabama, Florida, New Mexico, Oregon and California etc. by Joel P. Walker, a Pioneer of Pioneers. Dictated by him to R. A. Thompson Esq. of Santa Rosa. Ms 550. Manuscript in the Collections of the Library and Archives of the Autry Museum of the American West, Los Angeles.

TELEVISION

Burns, Ken (producer). *The West.* Eight episodes. PBS documentary, 1996.

IMAGE CREDITS

Page 284: Seaver Center for Western History Research, Los Angeles County Museum of Natural History

Page 293: "A Slave Girl in Holiday Attire," 1895–1906; Arnold Genthe Photograph Collection, PC-RM-Genthe; California Historical Society

Page 313: South Dakota State Archives

Page 328–329: David Andrassy and John Gilkes

Page 333: Public domain/Wikipedia

INDEX

ABOUT THE AUTHOR

Katie Hickman is the author of nine previous books, including two international bestsellers of history. She has also written two highly acclaimed travel books and a trilogy of historical novels, which among them have been translated into twenty languages.

Born into a diplomatic family, Hickman had a peripatetic childhood, growing up in Spain, Ireland, Singapore, and South America. She lives in London on a converted barge on the River Thames.